Beyond
the
Winning
Streak

Beyond the Winning Streak

Using Conscious Creation to Consistently Win at Life

By Lynda Madden Dahl

WindSong Publishing

Beyond the Winning Streak

Copyright © 1993 by Lynda Madden Dahl
Author photo copyright © 1992 by Stan Ulkowski
Cover desigh copyright © 1993 by WindSong Publishing

First printing, December 1992
Second printing, October 1993

Library of Congress Cataloging-in-Publication Data
Dahl, Lynda Madden, 1943—
   Beyond the winning streak: using conscious creation to consistently win at life / by Lynda Madden Dahl
       p.   cm.
   Includes bibliographical references.
   ISBN 0-9634629-0-3 : $11.95
   1. Success—Psychic aspects. 2. Success—Psychological aspects. 3. Visalization. I. Title.
BF1045.S83D34 1993
131—dc20   92-39769
                                                               CIP

WindSong Publishing
PO Box 1-H • Eugene OR • 97440 • USA
(503) 683-6731

Dedication

This book is dedicated to six very special people who influenced its creation. To Stan, my dearest, the intertwining and unfolding of our lives, love and work continues—again. To Mom, Dad and Leta, your lives and deaths, and our reciprocal love, sparked my questioning. To Jane and Rob, your enormous courage and understanding helped me find a glimmer of them in myself.

Contents

Acknowledgments

A special note of appreciation to Mark Twain for supplying the world with marvelous quotes that have become a philosophy unto themselves.

My love and thanks to:

Matt and Cathy, the parts of me that make me most proud.

Donna, Pam and Bunny, we four blooms of the same flower, unique yet linked through love.

Melissa, for believing so strongly in me.

Flora, for many evenings spent in shared revelations and exciting discoveries.

The Committee, for guidance and consistency, even when my blinders were on and earplugs in.

Our friends in California, for helping me clarify and organize my thoughts by graciously becoming the audiences for our first seminars.

Prologue

Cotton candy clouds hung above the rugged Na Pali cliffs, white fluff accentuating the dazzling greens of vegetation and blues of sky and water. The day was postcard perfect on the west coast of Kauai that summer of 1989 as Stan, my partner in love and life, turned our rental car north through the verdant Hanalei Valley. Our anticipation grew as we approached our destination.

While playing tourists the day before, we had wandered into a tiny metaphysical bookstore on the northern coast of the island. A poster tacked on the bulletin board announced a trance channeling session to be held in the countryside the next day. The channeler, described as a well-known international personality who allowed a nonphysical consciousness to speak through him, was on his way to the Orient with this stopover on Kauai. It was just upbeat enough to get our attention, and offbeat enough to promise a unique ending to our vacation.

Stan turned inland on a narrow country road, passing a dairy farm and heading into the island's rolling agricultural land. The large blue and white striped canopy, our destination's landmark, was easy to spot, a startling modern contrast to the nearby traditional Hawaiian house. After greeting us warmly, our hosts guided us to shady seats under the awning.

While we waited for the crowd to settle in, my mind wandered back over the years and events that led two fully molded products of the computer age to so comfortably await the words of a trance channeler. In 1985, I was a manager with Apple Computer, Inc. By the time Stan and I visited Hawaii in 1989, I was vice president of a high-tech company, my income had more than doubled...and I held company stock worth one million dollars.

In the intervening years, I had stumbled upon my own kind of miracle. I discovered there is no cause and effect in the classical sense, but that I am the cause of the external events that happen to me. Fate, circumstance and luck became passé concepts. I learned the most freeing, the most exciting news of all times: We create our lives from the fabric of our thoughts, feelings and beliefs. What seems to happen *to* us is caused *by* us. What we think of ourselves, our world and the universe becomes the building blocks for the events and material objects that enter our lives.

If there is more fantastic news, what possibly could it be? Intrinsic to our being is the ability to create what we want to experience. We feed our beliefs inward through our thoughts, emotions and imagination. Our unquestioning, non-judgmental inner selves take that raw data and faithfully form events that reflect exactly what we expect to see.

But of course I didn't believe a word of it when I bought my first metaphysical book by mistake. The prose of the author's previous books, non-metaphysical in nature, had hooked me. I needed another fix. Had I suspected her latest offering of being "foo-foo" stuff, my interest would have ebbed faster than the ocean's tide.

But, fascinated from page one on, I decided to research several names she mentioned. Buried behind sunglasses, I slinked into a small metaphysical bookstore near Palo Alto, California. Cloying incense and pictures of bearded gurus holding spiritual court deepened my concern that I'd left the rational world behind at the shop's threshold. I knew I'd joined Alice on the far side of the looking glass when I gazed upon a painting of a disembodied chalk white hand pushing up through gray clouds while holding tightly to a lightening bolt.

As I approached the long-haired woman behind the cash register, I caught a glimpse of bare feet and ankle bells near the hem of a bleached cotton gown. The clicking of my high heels bounced off the crystals and amethysts in the display case jarring the serenity of the shop. I asked for the books I desired, bought them, and beat a hasty retreat back into my world of business plans and technology.

From that inauspicious beginning I moved quickly through dozens of books, branching out to new authors as I learned of them. I wasn't convinced that there's more to reality than the official world allows, but my position was softening considerably. My focus became tuned to finding books that could tell me how to make happen in my life what I wanted to see.

I finally settled on the ideas outlined in the Seth books by Jane Roberts[1] as the model I could accept. I am of a practical mind. I function well when I understand the basis for an assumption, but I'm completely unable to leap from the known to the unknown by faith alone. I don't need proof, just a glimpse of an underlying organization or structure that supports the claim.

When I'm told I can consciously create with my thoughts, I assume that if the statement is true, then there is a process a thought goes through in order to become part of a future event. A set of mechanics must come into play, albeit universal in scope but nonetheless systematic, that makes it happen. Seth, by clearly defining the nature of reality, gave me the understanding I needed to experiment with this pioneering concept of creating what I want to experience.

There was one problem, however. Neither Seth nor anyone else laid out a concise plan I could follow that would get me from here to there. They offered suggestions and mentioned some of the tools to use, but they gave me no checkpoints, no way to gauge the effectiveness of the process until my creation entered physical reality—or didn't, as the case might be. They didn't tell me what traps I could fall into, what steps would accelerate the process, what land mines awaited me. In essence, they just said I could do it...which is no insignificant message!

With a long career grounded in logic, I came well equipped into the realm of the foo-foo with attributes that eventually helped me start to break the code to conscious creation. My first simple successes came easily: I materialized parking places.

During the Christmas season, the San Francisco Bay area malls choke with vehicles bumper-fighting for the right to park. I selected that setting as my beta test site. I kept a form handy in my car, designed to capture certain data, such as when and where the test occurred, the condition of the parking lot, and whether I succeeded or failed at getting a place near my area of choice—which meant right up front.

As I neared the destination mall, I started visualizing myself nosing the car into a slot very close to the entrance I specified, feeling intense joy at having accomplished my little feat. After twenty-five hits and no misses, I threw the notebook away and chose my next project. No in-betweens for me. I set my goal for wealth.

Actually, I wanted freedom. Freedom to decide what to do with the rest of my life, to choose my own schedule, to be free of bosses, to do whatever pleased me with my days. Money could buy me that freedom, I reasoned, so wealth became my objective.

Oh, that it would have been as easy as creating parking places...but I'm getting ahead of myself.

Way back when, Stan was lovingly indifferent to my quest. "Oh, very interesting," was his usual polite murmur as I read aloud passages from my latest book. His return to his own reading material, exquisite in timing—not too soon to offend, but the exact nanosecond the way was clear—led me to suspect yawning boredom shared his side of the bed.

At the time, as head of a field service division for a large computer manufacturer, hundreds of people reported to him. His background is engineering, technical and financial. If I had difficulty leaving the supposed logical for the esoteric, Stan's leap had to be quantum. But eventually leap he did, if a slow crawl can be so colored by the paint brushes of retrospect.

In the beginning, his budding interest was frequently tempered by self-imposed reality checks, like the time he agreed to attend his first metaphysical seminar. As we were unpacking our suitcases, I enthusiastically told him conference attendees had completely booked the hotel. He opened the drapes with a flourish and stepped onto our second story balcony to better view the stunning high desert sunset.

After a moment he grew quiet, staring at the courtyard below. I wondered what was up as I moved to his side. There, in splendid regalia, were three women whose appearance suggested they had been time-transported from a wandering Old World Gypsy tribe. I smiled in appreciation of their creative dress and turned to him. His color had drained somewhat and his face was still. Very quietly he said, "What have you gotten me into?"

By the time we found ourselves sitting under the blue and white canopy watching the warm Hawaiian breeze ruffle its edges, we could see the light at the end of our personal tunnel. In four months I could cash in my stock and leave the computer industry. We were finally to be free after years of wild swings between depression and elation, desperation and knowing, complete faith and complete lack of it. We had maneuvered the waters of our consciousnesses, found riptides too late at times, but on time at others. In retrospect it was becoming clear how the process of conscious creation works and what pieces need to be in place in order to make the ride as smooth as possible. And the cornerstone of it all, of course, is the fact that beliefs create.

I drew my attention back from my thoughts to the words of the channeler now in a state of trance. But what was this I was hearing? That our belief systems have nothing to do with shaping the events we encounter? To allow the universe to make our decisions and have faith its choices will please us? To set aside the conscious mind for it only gets in the way?

One middle age man said he had stopped his high blood pressure medication to test the strength of his belief in the universe. Supposedly, if he was in alignment, his high blood pressure would be no more, right? Right. Well, he said, then he needed more faith, because his blood pressure had shot off the chart when he stopped his medication, and it obviously was his fault because he must be lacking in that one crucial ingredient.

Another man, young this time, asked for guidance on how to identify what career to pursue. He was told to drop his concern for it was ego-oriented, and wait for the universe to guide him into maybe not a career, but a job, which may or may not lead to a career, depending on the direction that would come from On High.

My thoughts flew into the atmosphere like tiny startled birds. Wait a minute! Sure it's important to align ourselves with the universal consciousness, to listen to our guidance and have faith in the assistance we receive. Sure! But whose life is this anyway? What happened to my own personal growth, or does it only involve listening to God tell me what's best? Perhaps there's more to learn than just how to listen and react. Maybe, just maybe, the universe doesn't want me to abdicate the responsibility for my learning. Indeed, will the structure of this reality even allow for such an occurrence?

What of my conscious mind, that wonderful extension of my

inner self used to monitor my life's handiwork; what of its right to decide upon action? What if my guidance suggests I'd really wow them as an actress and I just sit and wait for the phone to ring announcing the Big Casting Call, instead of placing five calls a day to the people who can help me? Perhaps I have beliefs in place that say I'm actually afraid to face that casting call and it's easier to hope the universe will make the telephone ring, release all my fear during the audition, help me gain talent through osmosis and make me a star in spite of my stutter. Fat chance.

Unless my beliefs are in alignment with what the universe suggests, I may get the job but I won't hold it for long because *I can't reflect what I don't feel inside.* Maybe I was given a conscious mind as a terrific vehicle for working in concert with my inner self to understand how things happen in this reality and then change what limits me. Maybe one of our greatest lessons is that we are co-creators with the universe, with a defined, active role to play in the unfolding of our lives. And big surprise, can we actually be whole beings right now, spirit, mind and body working in concert, all pieces equal while on earth, all critical to the creation process?

Stan and I excused ourselves at the first break and headed back to the beach. Channeled or not, the information was off track. We felt dismay at old religious ideas peeking from the folds of metaphysical garments, hampering our movement toward fresh, desperately needed understandings that can restructure our world. We talked of everyone wanting peace, but few realizing that unless enough of us change our beliefs in vulnerability and victimization it can't happen. Everyone wanting health, but most believing they are innocent lambs awaiting the onslaught of viruses and diseases that attack randomly. Who doesn't want a good primary relationship, but how many know their beliefs about self-worth or intimate involvement may be the stumbling block to love, not their mate's personality?

The bottom line is responsibility, responsibility for our belief system that causes an event—that causes an effect—that causes an emotion—that reinforces what we think. In other words, we're responsible for the tapestry of our lives, the worn, tired threads and the bright shining buttons. The whole cloth. It doesn't matter one whit if we agree that we create everything that happens to us; we do it just the same. The difference between choosing to be aware and not choosing to can be the difference between a fulfilling, abundant existence and one fraught with upheaval.

On the drive back home in the bright Kauai sunshine, Stan and I realized the day hadn't been a total bust. Serendipity, in fact, shimmered at its edges. We now knew the long-sought answer to our question of what to do with our lives once we left the computer industry. We decided we wanted to help ourselves and others stride into awareness of our potential. We wanted to suggest options to the worldwide belief that events are happpenstance and only God can kiss it and make it better. We wanted to tell whoever cared to listen that this is supposed to be fun, that we all have the inherent ability to soar into our dreams...just like Jonathan Livingston Seagull.[2]

1

God's New Clothing

When I undertook the challenge of conscious creation, I thought
my path clearly defined. I would simply incorporate certain techniques into my days and, voila!, a new me would emerge, rich,
skinny and joyously happy. And that would be that. What I didn't
yet grasp was our intimate involvement with the universe or our
interaction of purpose with it.

The decision to try conscious creation places us squarely outside the door to the universe. As our days unfold and questions
arise, the door cracks open to reveal a world we had but glimpsed
previously. What starts as a journey through conscious creation
becomes a trek through consciousness. It has to, I see now. As we
strive to change our lives by using principles intrinsic to our reality, we remove the veil of self-imposed ignorance and look the
universe in the eye.

Our lives are only mental, camouflaged to look physical. They are part of the mental web work of consciousness that literally constructs the universe. Conscious creation becomes a probe into deeper understandings of the intricacies of residing in a reality constructed of thought.

It also moves us closer to comprehending our source. We don't have to be spiritual to consciously create. We don't have to believe in anything, really, except our ability to be successful at it. But it's difficult to imagine anyone sustaining effort over the long haul without a belief in something beyond the physical. After all, the process itself defies Darwinian theory and goes far beyond the limited-self concept accepted by most of the world. If we believe we're creators, then we must eventually wonder what's happening behind the scenes of conscious creation. Our musings initially focus on the consciousness that cared enough to create us.

When we're in the throes of a painful crisis, it's difficult to believe there is a presence that cares. But, of course, there is. Call it what you choose, All That Is, the universe, God, whatever. It's a loving consciousness from which all else springs. From worlds to worms, everything is created by it as an extension of itself. Each person is a unique materialization of this loving presence, a portion of it manifested in physical reality. Our creative abilities arise from this, our heritage. For if we are an integral part of the consciousness of All That Is, then surely we share Its characteristics.

The Catalyst Called Death

As I finished writing the last paragraph, I thought how easy the words flowed, indicative of how far I'd come. I was raised in a fundamental Christian religion as a youngster and switched to the Methodist Church in my teens. I never seriously questioned the conventional understanding of God or my relationship to Him. The people surrounding me shared my belief system, so the cushions were in place to keep me snugly comfortable within it.

My world shattered at twenty-one when my mother and father

died months apart. Suddenly I couldn't reconcile how a loving God could let my parents live a life of quiet desperation, hopelessness and futility, and then take them so casually from our family. I did everything I could to mesh my reality into the picture the church painted, and I found no canvas that would accommodate both.

I didn't believe in that God any longer, and since there was no other official characterization I wanted to pursue, I let the subject drop. For the next sixteen years I immersed myself in family and career, giving no serious thought to whether or not a God existed. But it became shockingly apparent that the conflict was far from settled by the time November of 1980 rolled around.

I was attending a large computer conference in Las Vegas with twenty or so other managers from our company. We were staying at the MGM Grand Hotel when the infamous fire broke out, killing eighty-four people, including one of our managers, his wife and one of our distributors, and physically and psychologically damaging thousands.

I had awakened from a sound sleep a half hour before my alarm buzzed. Cursing myself for not sleeping my allotted time, I wandered around the hotel room in my nightgown, feeling disoriented. Suddenly I heard muffled yelling and running in the halls. Something crashed against my door. I ran to it and cautiously cracked it open, expecting to find a fight brewing in the corridor. The thick smoke and the panicking people reached my brain first, then, "Fire, fire!" Adrenaline hit. I grabbed a trench coat, some lacy slippers and my purse and rushed into the corridor. Which way to go, right or left? Where have all the people gone! Oh, my God, the smoke is thicker than I realized. Can I breathe for long? Must find an exit! Oh, dear God, which way to go.

I reached the stairwell on hands and knees, down where the smoke seemed less dense and I could see more clearly. I flew down the fourteen flights, frightened that the fire would break through the walls at any moment. Others were running with me, oblivious to their own scanty attire, many covered black with soot. In shock, I broke through the stairwell door into the chill of the early desert morning and stumbled toward the road. By then, those who were going to get out without the help of rescue crews were out. The rest of the people screaming from their windows and balconies were trapped, as it turned out, for several hours.

For various reasons, the fire crews were having difficulty containing the fire and smoke. The fast spreading rumor on the ground was that few in the hotel would survive. My shock deepened as I learned that only a handful from my company had made it to freedom. The final, gut-wrenching blow hit when I looked up to the twelfth floor and saw a dear friend and his wife on their balcony, smoke spewing out their sliding door.

I watched silently as my friend draped a very thin cord over the balcony, tightly securing it to the railing. When he slung his leg over the edge with the apparent intent of easing down to the balcony below, I started screaming, "No, no, oh my God, no!" I'm sure he didn't hear me in the cacophony of chaos, but he changed his mind and pulled himself back to his wife. Then a moment occurred that I will never forget because it forged a new relationship between God and me. They dropped to their knees and prayed.

I was stunned. My mind raced with questions, mostly sarcastic. Who was this God they were praying to, this God who was about to make their two young children orphans? Were they praying to be saved? Had the ones who already died in the fire prayed to the same God, with not so terrific results? If their God was omnipotent enough to save them, then why did He allow the fire to start in the first place? Was this a loving and kind God, or one to be feared and protected against?

Anger started growing toward this willy-nilly God that so many people put such trust in, even as disaster after disaster rolled through their lives, even when it was apparent they were really on their own and the only peace God deigned to bestow was death after life. But keep praying, baby, and if things work out for the good, do thank God. If they don't, well, for some obscure reason God wants it that way. Just accept and suffer in silence. But don't turn away from Him. Besides, where would you go?

My friends survived; I raged. I attended the funerals of our associates stiff with anger, cynical of the priest and ministers words, so mad that even an innocuous visit into a place of worship became psychologically off-limits afterwards. I looked upon all believers with contempt. They became fools blinded by fear, hoping against hope that someone up there really cared. They became the weak grasping at tendrils of illusion.

My best friend Leta felt like I did, peas from the same philosophical pod. We were of the new breed of women, hot on the career track, breaking ground where only men had previously tread, raising children and loving men and doing just fine. Until we learned Leta was dying.

It was cancer and it took awhile, with hope here and there but no last minute reprieve by a loving God. Her vibrancy replaced by chemicals, Leta came home to die. But her sharp intelligence refused to bow to destruction—and it tore at my heart. When you believe in annihilation at death, there's little comfort shared between the living and the cognizant dying. She was cool and strong as always, but neither of us could keep the bleakness from our eyes. I left her that final day, drained and defeated. I no longer raged at God. It took too much energy.

Science Meets Metaphysics

Leta died in the fall of 1983. It was in spring of 1984 that I made the "mistake" that changed my life when I picked up my first metaphysical book. My parents' deaths twenty years before had made no sense when I believed in God; Leta's hadn't made any more sense when I didn't. What I needed was a broader definition of All That Is, one that transformed God's stereotypical clothing into garments of reality and brought meaning to existence. My elucidation came from two sources: metaphysics and, surprisingly, science.

Although most scientists are far behind those of us who have experimented with and explored consciousness, there are voices increasingly heard that add credence to what we know to be true. Such are the scientists involved with "new" physics. They have taken on the old guard of physicists, questioning the very assumptions upon which the science stands.

Classical physics maintains that the universe consists of space, time, matter and forces. It says the observer is separate from what is being observed. Man, that is, stands apart from his exterior world, with no apparent link, interacting only through forces that travel through space and time. For centuries this idea has been touted as the given way the universe operates, and all research and theories have developed out of it.

However, now some scientists are saying this is not so. Physicist John Bell introduced Bell's Theorem into physics in 1964. It states that there is a connection between all points in the universe. Supported by experimental evidence, the idea that nothing exists separately is becoming more accepted. Everything, it appears, is synchronically joined in a multidimensional web work.

Albert Einstein said that although space and time seem to be different in our every day experience, they are actually the same: They are a continuum. University of London physicist David Bohm, a protégé of Einstein's, takes this a giant step further by saying that everything in the universe is a continuum, an unbroken whole.

The developing view of new physics is that the whole universe—space, time, matter and forces—emerges from consciousness, which is a field of light. Everything is woven out of consciousness, or light. Matter is moving, ever changing energy focused into non-solid shapes. Light, they say, is not linear and does not travel through time and space, as original theories suggest. In fact, there is no time and space because light, or consciousness, doesn't inherently have those characteristics. There is simply a continuous moment surrounded by the illusion of space, time and matter.

Also, it was originally believed there is a physical center to the universe that can be determined by calculations. Now scientists say the center of the universe is whatever point is being measured from. In other words, the center of the universe is everywhere. A star a trillion miles from earth is the center of the universe, as is your living room. And where does the universe expand, or create, from? Its center, the scientists say.

Let's extrapolate from this new definition of the universe a deeper definition of ourselves. If consciousness is all that is, *we are consciousness*. If consciousness is light, *we are light*. It there is no matter, *solidified form is illusion*. If there is no time, *we live in an on-going present moment*. If there is no space, *we are connected*. If the center of the universe is wherever it's being tested from, *we are the center of the universe*. If the universe expands and creates from its center, *we expand and create from our center*.

Said another way: *We are consciousness composed of light, woven from the whole, or All That Is. We are one. What we perceive around us is illusion that we create from our center, in the present moment.*

And, of course, therein lies the difference between most religions and traditional science, and metaphysics. The first two see man cut off, separated from his creator or origin; the other views man as an integral part of the consciousness that created him, with the same characteristics as that consciousness. Metaphysics says we emerge or surface into physicality from the energy of our greater self, which is an extension of the energy of All That Is. A continuum of the whole, with no true separation in spite of what our brain perceives—or doesn't.

Sparks from the Mind of God

When my daughter was pre-teen, she was very fond of Judy Blume's books. One, *Are You There, God? It's Me, Margaret*, was a special favorite. Not of everyone, it turned out. Some felt the title showed a supreme lack of reverence and humility toward God, and tried, unsuccessfully, to have the book banned in her school. Maybe God told them personally She was ticked off at being so defiled by young Margaret, who didn't have the courtesy to address Her with head bowed and lips quivering in supplication. Surely that's what happened, for why else would they think God doesn't rejoice in our feelings of comfortable familiarity? Why else would they insist on holding Her so high up on the Holy Pedestal that communication lines disintegrate over the vast psychological distance between us?

We do God and ourselves a tremendous disservice when we portray Him as separate from our world, out there somewhere looking down upon His fallen people, judging their actions and punishing or praising them accordingly. By refusing to redefine this old-fashioned, outmoded concept of All That Is, we can't possibly experience physical reality with the depth and scope that is our birthright. God is literally all that is; therefore, God is within our system of reality, within us.

This is great news for us because it's where our creative abilities come from. We are sparks from the mind of God, imbued with the power to create because as part of All That Is, we share Its characteristics. One of our purposes while in physical reality is to become consciously aware of our power so we can learn to use it wisely, efficiently and with joy.

We may seem to make errors, bring ill health, unhappiness and desolation upon ourselves, but by observing our creations we learn how to better use our abilities. We check on our inner progress and growth by seeing the physical materialization of our works. Whatever the manifestation looks like to our physical eye, even if it portrays tragedy or terror, it's still a creative achievement worthy of the power it took to materialize it. Seth says it best:

> Illness and suffering are not thrust upon you by God, or by All That Is, or by an outside agency. They are a by-product of the

learning process, created by you, in themselves quite neutral. On the other hand, your existence itself, the reality and nature of your planet, the whole existence in which you have these experiences, are also created by you.... Illness and suffering are the results of the misdirection of creative energy. They are a part of the creative force, however. They do not come from a different source than, say, health and vitality. Suffering is not good for the soul, unless it teaches you how to stop suffering. That is its purpose.[1]

Here finally was a concept that made sense. Our lives are the result of enormous creative energy at its most focused. We are the primary molder of the events we choose to participate in. We are responsible—not just theoretically, but practically—for our experiences, individually and as a race.

I now could look at the pain and tragedy surrounding our world and understand. But I also knew that where we see poverty, it can be changed to prosperity; where we see sickness, it can be changed to health; where we see war, it can be changed to peace—because what we create we can uncreate. I could see structure and reason within our universe, and I felt liberated.

When we redefine God, we necessarily redefine ourselves. When God slips off our archaic hook back into the sea of reality, the greatness of our own roles becomes apparent. Trumpets should sound, drums should roll with these words: We are little gods, with the power of creation at our fingertips!

Our world turns upside down and inside out with the impact of this statement. All the old rules change. We move into a new way of viewing reality, with fresh understandings and marvelous tools to reshape and rebuild our lives. For civilization a gift is offered, and, if accepted, a new dawn breaks.

2

Lower Case Gods

A new dawn breaks. The strident shrill of the alarm clock shatters our peace and sets the day's tone. Our coherence greatly reduced by the brain's semi-comatose state, we shamble downstairs for some caffeine—regrettably, the only type of stimulation we expect we'll experience on this day of our Lord.

Aw, hell, it's Monday.

Of Challenges and Blueprints

Lower case or not, our godly status doesn't seem to jibe with our daily life. After all, no card-carrying god would *choose* life on earth when harps and clouds seem infinitely more peaceful. Besides, aren't gods a finished product? Surely they're beyond this learning and growing stuff and are now picture perfect role models of the highest order. Right?

Well, no. Consciousness, in any reality, has one primary purpose: to expand through growth. In fact, it's impossible for consciousness to be stagnant. It is constantly recreating itself and experimenting as it goes along. Remember our learned scientists, the ones who say consciousness is all there is, say the universe (i.e., consciousness) endlessly evolves from its center. We are unceasingly creating and expanding, whether we acknowledge it or not. Denying our godly status doesn't change a thing. Acknowledging it can change everything.

In order to expand, consciousness must enter territory not previously explored. We are consciousness resident in a physical reality. How, then, do we enter new territory? We set challenges for ourselves that can't be solved without pushing our abilities and thinking beyond our comfort zones. Our challenges, generated by us on another level and based on our beliefs, set the stage for breakthroughs into new solutions and growth. The application of conscious creation accelerates the process because we take control of our lives and force the issue of learning.

So what are we growing into? Hopefully, whatever we set out to become in this existence. Before birth we established a blueprint, or psychic pattern, for our development this time around and then chose the immediate post-womb conditions through which to start the process. This blueprint contains all the information we need in order to reach the growth objectives woven into its structure. It is not stagnant, however, oblivious to the currents of change. It's a set of working plans, open to refinement and alteration.

Our blueprints are also not idealized images of perfection that we must strive toward, spiritual end-alls that once met release us from further growth. They are guidelines that *we* created before birth that hold the general outline of what we want to learn and the built-in assistance we'll need in order to meet our goals in physicality. We are naturally imbued with the desire to create our lives along the lines of our blueprint, choosing from the minute-by-minute probabilities decorating each day.

Because of the structure of our reality, where every probability we can possibly meet is there for the taking, we have significant leeway in our development. We have stuffed our psychic blueprint with a potpourri of desires and directions, knowing not all will be experienced, not intending them to be. Then we choose different versions of ourselves as we progress through new outlooks and experiences. We can take many alternate paths in this life and still dwell under the umbrella of our blueprint. So, did we miss the great opportunity to meet our Soul's Destiny by not moving to Cincinnati in 1979? No way. We continually ride a rich wave of probabilities with fresh directions just waiting to be noticed and implemented.

Thought and Questions: Our Power

Thought is the catalyst that will thrust us onto the path of our psychic plan—or into the brambles lining the far side. It is the creative power behind our life. When we think of power we usually think of nuclear or solar power, something apart from ourselves. However, the true power is the creative energy within us that leads to the development of all outside manifestations. According to Seth, one thought has more power than it takes to send a rocket to the moon!

We are all learning to handle this creative energy, and since learning is a process in itself, we will misdirect it. But what we create from our misdirections will always lead us back to inner questions. Our growth and understanding are dependent upon our searching for answers to those questions.

On the beach of our Columbia River home grows a weed that perks its head several inches vertically out of the sand. Pull on the weed and its roots are found to run for many feet diagonally across the beach, just under the surface. Our questions are similar to the weed above ground, a part of the exterior reality. However, the answers reside in the unseen world, and our search for them nudges us along our barely hidden root structure, persistently inching us toward the seed from which we sprang.

When we choose the path of conscious creation, we energize our psychic movement toward our source. The questions that arise force us to examine our role in this reality with a precision only casually applied previously. It behooves us to take a more penetrating look at the overall universal structure because change occurs more rapidly when we have a basic understanding of how and why it's even possible.

Pipeline to the Universe

Symbiotic relationship. I like the phrase. It's the perfect definition of what we share with consciousness in general and our greater selves in particular. Our greater selves...the energy from whence we came and will return. Our greater selves...the energy that is an extension of All That Is. Our greater selves...where the heck are you when we need you most?!

At our elbow, you say? *Part* of our elbow, you say?

While it seems we've chosen to go it alone in physical reality, that's only the overall illusion. We don't "break away" from our source at birth, re-initiating contact later through prayer, meditation or channeling. It's an impossibility to lose contact with the energy that formed us. We *are* a portion of that energy, flowing from and with it, pushing up into physicality with perception mechanisms in place that block from view the rest of our being.

But that doesn't mean it's not there, taking our experiences into its folds and expanding the totality of our energy structure because of them. What we learn in each life adds dimension and scope to our greater consciousness, just as what it learns through its many and varied experiences outside our private corner of reality is passed on to us as insights, knowledge and creativity.

Our inner self, that portion of our greater self that keeps us physically alive and spiritually nourished, becomes our direct link to the universe. It advises and guides us through the use of many vehicles, including intuition, impulses and dreams. It feeds information into our physical structure at the cellular and mental levels, and the physical "we," in turn, relays experiences back into our greater self through it. Our inner self is so integrated into our being that it actually extends part of itself into physical reality as our conscious mind.

Metaphysical heresy? No, just a continuous flow of energy from All That Is right through to our physical person and beyond into our environment. Just an extension of the whole, as the new physicists say.

The Marriage of the Inner and Outer Senses

Our conscious mind is our tool for assessing the physical universe. In conjunction with our physical senses and neurological patterning, it structures the way data is translated into physicality. With it, we make decisions about what we will and will not believe, and what actions we will or will not take based on those beliefs. However, the conscious mind can also reach far beyond our official version of reality into psychic territory of infinite information.

The conscious mind is, then, the probe that assists in exploring both the inner and outer realms of consciousness. It's the vehicle we use to question the how and why of life on earth and our place in the universe. It pushes us on to new insights as our questions draw answers, which bring new questions.

There are other senses, though, the inner ones, that are just as valid.[1] While the physical senses allow us to perceive our lives through a physical filter, the inner senses guide us across the psychic threshold, into the exploration of inner reality. As inner perceptions, characteristics of the inner self, they operate whether or not we have a physical form. By using them, we can access knowledge from the inner self about any subject we care to explore, including the nature of the universe, its structure and purpose.

When we initiate an altered state of consciousness, we change our channel of awareness and start using the inner senses. We move our consciousness off its usual path onto one with different ground rules. Now we can begin to perceive reality as it exists independently of the physical world. The use of the inner senses allows us to experience clairvoyant, telepathic and other metaphysical happenings, and with each experience we develop a deeper surety of our independence from physical matter.

As we strive to change our lives through conscious creation, we grow our inner abilities automatically. When we look into ourselves, the very effort involved thrusts us into new territory and stretches our assumed limitations. So it's the combination, the marriage, of the intellect and the intuition that leads us into our greatest potential. The conscious mind, though steeped in skepticism, must be allowed to process new data, because much of it comes from the inner self, our fountainhead of information and inspiration, as a method of breaking limiting thought boundaries.

About a year after beginning to consciously create, a friend and I attended a day long workshop on developing psychic abilities. We were seated in a circle, and after guiding us into an altered state of consciousness, the leader passed around her wedding band. Each of us was to hold the ring for as long as necessary to get impressions and then tell what we were experiencing. I watched that ring coming slowly toward me and heard the vague statements being made by each current ring holder. I thought, not me, lady. I'm not going to make a fool of myself. I'll get the ring in my hand, pretend to think about it, and then pass it on as quickly as possible with a "no comment."

The surprise was on me. When the ring landed in my palm, I jerked my head up and blurted, "Has there been a tragedy in your life in the past year?" She said yes, but offered no further information. I hurriedly passed the ring on, flustered and embarrassed. For two hours I stewed over whether or not to ask the leader what this supposed tragedy entailed. Maybe it wasn't what I'd call a tragedy. Perhaps she lost something of material value, or maybe she had relationship troubles. You know, stuff general enough not to count. But I did finally ask, only to learn her son had died in an auto accident twelve months previously.

Another time, Stan and I were enjoying a short vacation on the Central California coast. For most of the day I had been toying with the concept of manifesting. I rolled the word around my tongue to get a feel for it, and asked Stan to discuss it with me so I could form some impressions. When we went to sleep in the motel that night, I was still moving it through my mind.

Several hours later I awoke with a start. The room was inky black, not a sliver of light sneaking through the heavy drapes. My mouth was dry so I decided to get a drink of water. The place was so dark I had to find the wall and feel my way to the corner that led to the sink.

After five or six paces, I lifted my eyes from the direction of the floor to about shoulder high. There in front of me was a spark of light the size of a small apple, hanging in space. The word *manifesting* jumped into my head, and the spark disappeared. Your guess is as good as mine as to what caused it, but I feel that my intense focus on the word invited my inner self to demonstrate the skill of actualization.

While these and similar events had their own merit, their impact far exceeded their surface value. I wanted to know more about the unknown reality and how I could tap into it. I wanted to explore consciousness with an open mind and a probing focus. I wanted to understand—but I wanted to understand *yesterday*.

Faith and Lack Thereof

About a year and a half after I started consciously creating freedom through money, I became so disillusioned with my progress that I packed up my metaphysical books, threw them into a drawer and walked away for six months. Stan is a pilot, and I became a student pilot. We spent every free moment in the sky. All of the focus I had been applying to the study of consciousness

I transferred to flying.

I had jumped into metaphysics from the springboard of agnosticism. While I intellectually embraced the new ideas, I held conflicts yet unresolved. Was I acting the fool, blindly accepting esoteric nonsense that had no basis in logic? After all, the world's religions have been around for a long time, and various systems of psychology and science are widely accepted. Could they really be wrong about cause and effect, and I right? Was I so blinded by the hope inherent in the idea of being the creator of my tiny parcel of the universe that I had stepped over reality's edge? And if I was by some slim chance right, why was I not seeing the result?

If it were faith I lacked, I felt it justified. Faith, I thought, leads us to ignore logic, to profess belief in the most outrageous doctrines. Deny the body to reach spiritual transcendence; spin your chakras[2] thirty times to the right to find inner peace; truth is found in this book and no other; God kills. From these heights, some sink even further into the muck of exclusionary dogma: No blacks allowed in this church; Woman, the taint of antiquity forbids your equality with our men; Leper, keep your distance from us holy people; AIDS is a punishment by God against homosexuals.

My error was in assuming faith is what we attach to an object of our belief, whether it be a theology, science, person or concept. A distorted shadow of the construct of universal faith, a ghost of the real thing, we use it to stake out our territory, the boundaries of which we protect at all costs. Woe be it to the heretic who questions our stance, for he raises our deepest doubts and challenges our safety. Until we change our mind, that is, and put our faith in another place.

Universal faith isn't attached to anything. It's part of the psychological make-up of consciousness. It provides the security by which all action can be taken without fear, without the anticipation of impediments. It's the catalyst that converts our thoughts into manifested symbols. It is the basis of trust in our needs being met, in the natural order of a supportive universe. It's what children and animals feel, until taught otherwise.

As a youngster Stan always assumed that what he wanted would come to him, and it did. He never questioned, never doubted, never realized some people did. Somewhere along the way he lost his precious gift. He doesn't remember when, but the adult world finally infringed on his secure turf with its beliefs in uncontrollable luck and vulnerability. We adults lose faith in a safe universe and pass our loss on to our children as Truth, but that truth was birthed in the compost pile of fear.

Faith is not necessarily part of our conscious understanding, but it's always there, waiting for our nod of acceptance. Our dulled vision toward faith doesn't diminish its presence. It can no more not be present than All That Is. When we don't consciously know faith, a vacuum forms and fears enter. Without faith, growth cannot happen. With faith, our world opens up to child-like wonder, curiosity and exploration.[3]

From my own experience and the stories told to me by others, clearly many of us share a simmering uneasiness throughout our lives. At times it reaches boiling point and bubbles up as full-blown fear. But often it lies half asleep, languidly prodding us with its staff of nervousness, goading us to believe the other shoe sits on the cliff above our heads, ready to drop at a moment's notice.

For protection we're in the ring, gloves at the ready, with the rest of the world. Survival of the fittest, that's the name of the game. Competition, stress and anger become accepted operating procedure. A tooth for a tooth becomes our battle cry. We go about our lives earning our keep, feeding our families, all the while wondering if—more likely when—the bottom will fall out.

If we were granted but one wish by our fairy godmother, it would be wise to choose the gift of faith. Faith releases us from fear. With faith, the impediments to a safe, fulfilling life disappear, not because of blind acceptance of an unfounded belief, but because of a new found sense of ease, freedom and certainty. It literally creates a condition around us that is free of blockages. Optimism prevails. We are no longer afraid, therefore we stop creating fearful situations. We get on with our lives, snug in a cozy cloak of contentment.

Although faith permeates the universe, it springs alive within us when we recognize our connection with consciousness, when we understand that our presence has meaning, and guaranteed within that meaning is a safe existence.

How do we find faith, especially when we never felt it before, at least as adults? Through our insights and intuitions about the true nature of reality. The choice to consciously work with the universe to create a better life leads us into situations loaded with illumination and breakthroughs in comprehension. It also can force us to face our monumental lack of faith, a potentially lethal state for conscious creators.

I'd love to report that when I returned to the esoteric after six months of flying I embraced faith like a long lost cousin. I tried. Intellectually, I fell back in step quickly. The beauty of the ideas outlined in Jane Roberts' books awed me. I studied faith, and said, "Yes, yes! That's it. That's my ticket out of the old and into the new. Faith, combined with the clearing of limiting beliefs, is the answer."

It is, but I couldn't make the final leap into faith that easily. I worked with beliefs; I visualized; I meditated. I studied techniques developed by others for accessing unconscious information, including reincarnation material. I wrote reams of insights I received in a light altered state. I attended seminars and workshops. Somehow, though, I couldn't reach the place of freedom from fear that I longed for. I kept clearing beliefs, but new ones would arise that justified the fear.

After several years, I was worn down. Not that dramatic, exciting situations hadn't happened through my efforts, but now I wanted life to be easy for a change. I wanted to reach a goal and feel wonderful, not as if I needed to protect the fruits of my labor with constant vigilance upon risk of losing them. I wanted to stop waiting for the other shoe to drop.

This period of transition took longer than it does for most, I think. My dedicated focus had been on understanding the mechanics of conscious creation right down to the most minute detail. I expected it to be neat and tidy, with the result obviously tied to its psychic cause. When I couldn't find a reason for a delay, I lost faith. When I didn't see a result in the form I expected, I lost faith. When an unsettling event occurred, I lost faith.

After the six months of flying, I never lost faith in the metaphysical material or its possibilities again. It was myself I doubted. Had I found, and eliminated, my limiting beliefs around my goal? No, obviously not, or I'd be there. Was I hearing my inner self, or was it just me talking? It must be me, or surely it would be louder, more definite. If I don't feel joy, how can I expect to manifest it in my life? Yet, how can I manifest it if I can't feel it?

On and on the doubts flowed. I took them on one at a time, mentally shouting for help out of my latest quagmire. Remarkably enough, I'd get sudden energy or the solution to a problem. I began to take greater notice of coincidences, glimpsing an order within the invisible. I started to feel as though someone or something was pulling for me, applauding my advances, supporting my stumbles. The rift between faith and intellect started to heal, the distance between shortened and blurred. Finally, thankfully, I started feeling like a whole person, body, mind and spirit inexplicably interwoven around a center core of consciousness.

That it took me until recently to settle into my at-ease position with faith is verification of my long held, very active beliefs that we're really on our own here, that while help comes when asked, it's not continually with us, that we have to hound ourselves with supervision lest we overlook the latest belief that will trip us up. That, in essence, unless we stand vigilant, the universe will dish up a nasty situation in response to our thoughts. I wasn't giving the universe enough credit for the depth of its assistance, and, ironically, it was my own beliefs I constantly bumped into, verifying their truth. A cat chasing its tail, a web woven in circles.

Our Eternal Godly Status

Spiritual awakenings for most of us are the unfolding of understandings and changes that take place over time, not shining visions, calls to the altar, revelations of Truth. If working with the universe through conscious creation to bring ourselves out of unhappiness on the job brings us closer to comprehending our source, we have taken steps down the path of spiritual awakening.

Great illuminations and moments of spiritual transcendence are not necessary to prove our divine flowering. Nor must we follow more supposedly evolved brethren—ministers, saints, priests, holy men, avatars, New Age leaders. If they have chosen to become role models for the ones who feel the need, their singular commitment is appreciated.

However, we really don't need them if we understand and acknowledge our godly status. For we are their equals, of the same source and with the same information, insights and illuminations at our fingertips.

Each of us can probably teach them a thing or two by the time this life ends anyway, things that right now we wouldn't be so bold as to call spiritual growth. Like my niece Melissa, who, in spite of what seems to be rejection and judgment from those she cares for, knows the shift from not loved to loved starts within and has the courage to uncover her vulnerability and allow the internal mending process to begin. Like my sister Pam, who, by dint of strong desire, is breaking the chains of the past and redefining herself to new standards, developing inner strength and outer control as by-products of the process.

That we lower case gods in our personal little worlds can bring such momentous, freeing change to our consciousness is as great an accomplishment as Sathya Sai Baba of India materializing matter from air. We are truly great spiritual beings, right now and ever more.

Please, God, help us to remember it.

3

> *Consider well the proportions of things. It is better to be a young June-bug than an old bird of paradise.*
>
> – *Mark Twain*

The Winds of Change

Early earth peoples arrived at fundamental insights into the nature of the universe from an intuitive sense, their only tool. They had no books, no mass media, no organized religions to tell them what to believe. They simply knew the truth. They knew the universe is with intent and purpose, that our destiny is not to maneuver the maze of life without assistance. They saw meaning where we see nothing; they saw design where we see coincidence. They saw signs within each event that helped reveal reality's structure. We can also, if only we believe there is a different face to reality than the one we know and love.

Unusual events occur around all of us constantly. We usually work diligently at not recognizing them. They come in all guises, from telepathy to snippets of past lives thrust into today's world. But come they do, parading through our days with horns blowing and messages unfurled, shouting, "Hello! Anybody see? Anybody care?"

Accepting Psychic Phenomena

One of our souls' shared goals while on earth is to understand the universe with as much depth as possible, and that means broadening our interpretation of what we will allow reality to be. One way to open to more intense comprehension is to try conscious creation. Another is to accept the obvious manifestations of psychic phenomena.

Outrageous experiences need to be recognized for what they are when they occur, not sloughed off as quirks of nature, fantasies, or scary unexplainable phenomena. Swamped by uncertainty and skepticism we may be; open to other-world insights we can become.

An honest-to-God psychic event was dished up for me recently when some geese and a seagull pulled a vanishing act. It happened one day as I walked the huge white-tailed deer refuge near our home. I had just reached an area bordered by the Columbia River on one side and acres of field on the other, and I was walking between the two on a slim blacktop road. A group of noisy geese rose up from the large meadow and took flight, forming their instinctual vee.

I watched them approach, squawking loudly as they headed for the river at an altitude of maybe forty feet. They flew directly over my head, and as they reached the bank of the river I dropped my gaze for a few seconds, then turned to watch them continue their journey. Only they weren't there.

I scanned the river for clouds, and there were a few, but none close to the bank and none that low. I thought it was some kind of optical illusion, that perhaps there was a cloud I couldn't see due to an unusual atmospheric condition...or something. Then a lone seagull lifted off the same field and headed my way. I thought, okay, this time I'll not even blink as it flies overhead. I didn't. The seagull simply disappeared into thin air about thirty feet past the river's edge.

Once I glimpsed the continuation of the soul at the birth of my granddaughter, Courtney. I was in the hospital nursery alone with her, just minutes after she arrived. I was doing what all grandmothers do, touching her cheek, feeling her soft, silky hair, watching her eyes come half open and then involuntarily squeeze shut.

My attention was drawn to another crib when a newborn burst forth in angry protest. When I turned back to Courtney, she was wide awake, lying very still, staring at me. The intelligence and knowing in her eyes startled me. It was only moments before her baby eyes returned, but we had communicated on a level difficult to explain. She knew me and I knew her, as adults.

Stan's son Chris told us an interesting story from his childhood. When he was nine or ten, he lay in bed one night staring at the table lamp. He focused strongly on it and pictured it turning off. All of his attention riveted on making the bulb go out. It spooked him greatly when it finally did, of its "own" accord.

But all events don't seem psychically charged, they just seem odd. Once, when Stan was at his most vulnerable, we had an attack of moths in our walk-in bedroom closet. All our wool suits and sweaters hung side by side. His were eaten to shreds; mine were completely untouched, not a nibble to be found.

We consider dreams commonplace, but what a wealth of information the universe sends our way, predictive and otherwise. I dreamt my son Matt was a little boy climbing a tree just outside our kitchen window. As I watched, he moved very far out on one of the limbs, and I realized he had put himself in great danger if the limb broke. It did, and he crashed, frightened and tearful, not allowing me or anyone else close enough to comfort him.

In waking reality, that's what happened shortly thereafter, only it wasn't a tree limb, it was his job, and it was drastic enough to change the course of his life. He thrust himself far beyond reach emotionally for several years, but his fear and pain were obvious, at least to a mother.

I previously mentioned the story of Stan's introduction to his first metaphysical seminar. The seminar came to my attention in an unusual way. I lay down to take a Sunday afternoon nap one January day. Before falling asleep, I glanced through a flyer that had recently arrived in the mail listing seminars for the coming year to be held in various parts of the country. Then I fell asleep and dreamt I was holding a birthday cake with candles along the front and mountains in the back. In my dream, I said, "Oh, Arizona."

When I awoke I reached for the flyer, expecting to find a seminar offered on my birthday in February in the Southwest. None was listed. Puzzled, I let it go and put the flyer down. On impulse, I picked it up again, and there it was—a seminar on Stan's birthday in Arizona. The previous September a psychic had told me the restrictions and structures of convention supporting Stan's life would start to crumble and fall around his next birthday. That's exactly what happened, and the Arizona seminar was the start of it.

From Reincarnation to Telepathy

Since consciousness is an expanding continuum, dead set on developing infinite opportunities to explore, reincarnation is not only possible, it's necessary. Our numerous and varied lives are the result of our consciousness expressing itself in as many ways as possible, spreading the development of its infinite potential across time and space, enhancing and enriching itself in the process.

Glimpses of those past (and future) lives flash before us periodically and offer rich insights into the true structure of the universe. Besides that, they're just plain fun to think about once we snare the shimmer of one in our physical net.

Before I chose to believe in the metaphysical, I was in Rome with others from my company. Alone, late one night, I walked to the closed Colosseum and stood outside its gates. A disquieting feeling that I was hearing shouting and clapping from within overcame me. My next impression was of sitting on a cold stone bench, part of a large, boisterous crowd.

Then, years later, I was ironing upstairs in our San Clemente, California, home. I had lived in that lovely city for twenty years and knew the rolling countryside well. Lost in far away thought, I glanced out the window at the view of the hills and instantly thought, "Ah, beautiful Rome!" with deep affection and familiarity.

The most intense feeling I've experienced that suggests another lifetime happened in Japan. I was riding in a corporate motor home with executives of the company I was visiting. They had graciously offered their time and vehicle for sightseeing when my trip extended over a holiday. While sitting with two Japanese at a little table discussing their country's history, I glanced out the window.

One of the men remarked that the road we traveled was the ancient passage from the Emperor's winter palace to his summer palace. Immediately, I was immersed in a vision of hot sun, dust swirls, a colorful caravan of people laughing and joking up and down the line. And there I was, a young man, a scribe I think, following a seat carried by others. It wasn't the Emperor's chair, but one of a high official's. I felt sticky and dusty.

That my first husband was Asian, my favorite food is Asian, and my home is dotted with Asian furniture and art offers an intriguing counterpoint to my experience in Japan.

Telepathy seems to be one metaphysical happening that many people have experienced to some extent, even if it was simply knowing the identity of the caller before answering the phone. Stan has a strong natural propensity to telepathic communication and it manifests in different ways.

One evening we were playing around with a deck of twenty-five ESP cards. It consisted of five sets of five unique symbols. The point was to see how many symbols could be identified by holding each card without benefit of seeing the symbol. Stan, in fun, arranged the deck symbol side down, and took the first card off the top. In one fluid movement, he closed his eyes and flipped it up to his forehead...and called out the correct symbol.

He proceeded to go through all twenty-five cards. His hit rate: twenty-one. At my urging, he did the same thing again, and got an identical score. The instructions said chance was five, ten was rather good, and eleven to eighteen excellent. Anything over that was considered incredible.

At times his talent is somewhat frustrating. While in the Middle East, I purchased a large carved wood camel for Stan's birthday, expecting to surprise him with such an unusual gift. I had it shipped home, and it arrived after I returned. Stan answered the delivery person's doorbell and carried the heavy, wrapped box into the living room where I was reading. Jokingly, and without hesitation, he said, "Well, what have we here, a carved camel?"

And then there was the time his office decided to buy a gift for a departing member. Unbeknown to Stan, they purchased a wok. As the employee unwrapped the box, Stan put his fingers to forehead, pretending to be deep in psychic thought. "Ah ha!" he said, "I see a wok. It must be a wok!"

The Ancient Resurfaces

A belief in the metaphysical (defined by Webster as "...concerned with the fundamental nature of reality and being...a study of what is outside objective experience") is not new. For approximately 1500 years, from 1100 BC to 390 AD, the Greek city of Delphi housed seers revered and sought out by people from around the world. The oracles were all women, over fifty, who had the gift of sight and prophecy. Few world rulers of the times would proceed with serious undertakings until sending or leading an envoy to Delphi to get a feel for the bigger picture.

One doesn't have to travel to ancient Delphi to meet today's version of an oracle. My good friend Flora is one of many who has made this phenomenon virtually commonplace. She held a very strong desire for clear, direct communications with the universe. Because of her focused request, it wasn't surprising when she started doing automatic writing while in meditation. But it was a shocker when she felt the urge to try voice communication. She allowed it to happen, though, and a rich, exciting world opened before her. She was introduced to a nonphysical energy source who was, it said, there to offer assistance.

At first, she was reluctant to channel for anyone other than her daughter, Stan and me. However, the process was so fascinating and the information so exceptional she eventually loosened her concern. She is now writing a book with her unseen friend who says it will cover many different subjects, with a healthy dose of information on the transference and manipulation of energy.

Coming Out of the Metaphysical Closet

Attitudes toward the supposed unknown are opening once again, in this present time and space. Some trusted leaders and well-known personalities are coming out of the metaphysical closet; many have been out for some time. Recently I read a newspaper article about Dr. Jonas Salk, the discoverer of the polio vaccine. He maintains that the formula for the vaccine came to him from a nonphysical source while in a state of altered consciousness.

Richard Bach, author of many fine books, says that his little gem, *Jonathan Livingston Seagull*, was inspired by a "voice" and two "cinematic visions."

Edgar Mitchell, Apollo 14 astronaut and founder of the Institute of Noetic Sciences says, "There are no unnatural or supernatural phenomena, only very large gaps in our knowledge of what is natural...."

Dr. Willis Harman, emeritus professor of Engineering-Economic Systems at Stanford University, member of the University of California Board of Regents, and president of the Institute of Noetic Sciences says in his book, *Global Mind Change*, that our world is going through one of the most dramatic transitions of thought in its history. According to Dr. Harman, this fundamental shift in thinking is based on the spreading belief that mind gives rise to matter. Consciousness, he says, is not the end-product of material evolution; rather, consciousness was here first, and from it emerges all else.

It's not only the well known who are questioning the validity of the status quo. The most surprising people turned the conversation toward metaphysics while I was in the corporate world. One time, the president of our company arranged for us to meet an executive from an underwriting firm at The Ritz on the Southern California coast. The purpose of our get-together was to meet a fourth person there, a British businessman in residence in a $2,500 a day suite, whose company owned a huge chunk of our stock. So the three of us, decked in our most professional garb, entered the moneyed world of the Englishman and proceeded with our meeting.

After it concluded and we were three again, our president had to make some phone calls, so Bernie and I shared a glass of wine and an interesting conversation. It seems his wife had had a precognitive dream, and it was on his mind. That started the direction of our talk. From there, he mentioned he had heard of a psychic nearby whom he thought he might visit. He said there must be more to reality than what we see, and he was curious.

I told him I was practicing the tarot cards in order to hone my intuition. He was full of questions, and when I expressed concern about my lack of advancement, he was very supportive and encouraging. I'm sitting there, looking at this man in his pinstripe suit and wing tip shoes discussing metaphysics with me after a business meeting, and I think, "Is this incredible, or what?!"

Miracles Versus Mutable Laws

The early earth people knew we are truly splendid creatures, part of a magnificent saga unfolding over the eons of time. Why do we, their technology-saturated, scientifically blinded ancestors have such a problem with the obvious that begs acknowledgment? So far our scientists have tested and defined our physical world and its laws. However, what if those supposed laws are actually mutable? What if they evolve from the inner order, the subjective reality we refuse to validate, cloaked in the camouflage of hard fact, but in fact, not fact at all.

Sathya Sai Baba is known as a man of miracles. His phenomenal powers, apparent since childhood, are astonishing. Documented stories abound describing his abilities to manifest objects from thin air. Thousands of people have witnessed his transformations of energy into matter, including scientists from around the world. He has even duplicated some of the miracles Jesus and Krishna were said to have performed. Eventually our scientists must start asking how this can happen, and not assume miracles are twists of immutable laws, cosmically unexplainable.

The people called stigmatists, who manifest nail holes in their hands as Jesus supposedly experienced, are also well documented. Some even create not only the holes but nails in their flesh as well. However, historical data indicates that Jesus' wounds would probably have been in his wrists where nails were normally inserted in those days. Also, it seems stigmatists tend to create holes suspiciously similar to ones seen on their favorite painting or icon. Nonetheless, they exert miraculous powers of creation.

However, the miracles of Sai Baba and the stigmatists may be nothing more than normal operating behavior once we understand their genesis. If viewed as metaphysical events, what seems miraculous may simply be glimpses of our inherent power to interact with universal forces in ways we can't yet explain thoroughly. They become not a suspension of natural laws, but the result of deeper laws not yet understood in our world. Sai Baba's miracles seem to make our psychic events pale in comparison, until we remember that we're dealing with the same source of power. He just has a better handle on it at this point.

If we bestow validity on unusual happenings in our own lives, if we recognize them for what they are and allow them to become commonplace, we start to lift the glass curtain separating us from the source of our world. Then we become free to meld and mesh with the universe without restriction, miraculously, even if not at the experience level of Sai Baba.

There are openings occurring in this time and space amongst people all across the planet who are experimenting with consciously converting energy into matter via thought, altering outdated views of reality along the way. With these collective new understandings come the winds of change, whispering that we're almost free of old restraints, nudging us to take our next step in the evolution of our learning.

Their buoyancy supports us as we attempt the prodigious job of changing, and the language of their currents brushes lightly against our ears with these words: Acknowledge the unusual, validate it by your acceptance, for by so doing you can be whirled further and faster toward awesome understandings—and desperately needed change.

Wouldn't that be a welcomed miracle?

4

Stranger Than Fiction

"Captain, we've captured an alien energy form that claims it's the causal force behind all events and material items in the three-dimensional world!"

"Obviously it suffers from delusions of greatness, this energy form. Why did it allow itself to be taken prisoner if it's so powerful?"

"Uh, well, actually we didn't exactly *capture* it. It was just hanging out on the bridge and our new instrumentation that senses energy units smaller than sub-atomic particles picked it up."

"And what does this alien energy form call itself?"

"A Belief. And it says its not alien."

Consciousness: The Cosmic Legos

What is this all-powerful creative force that materializes what it wants, whether or not we consciously agree to the whole thing? It's called a belief and it's stunning in its simplicity of definition. *It is a thought in the conscious mind, reinforced by imagination, emotion and duration.* In other words, a belief is a strongly held thought. It starts life as a thought, then when we sodden it in feelings or repetition over a period of time it becomes a belief. So, its basic components are thoughts and feelings.

Defining beliefs is easy. Understanding their power is another matter. It first takes insight into the construction of the universe, beyond what our scientists have yet to perceive. It takes catching a glimpse of the inward order of events. And since everything evolves out of consciousness, that must be our starting point.

The word consciousness sparks images of a mysterious, exalted panorama of vast universes and incomprehensible power. If we're religious, we give consciousness human characteristics and call it God. If we're metaphysical, we find it in the underbelly of a rock and the far stretches of the mind. Whatever our persuasion, we revere it, awed by its implications and sweep. And rightly so. But even consciousness can be broken into more elemental parts, making the mystery somewhat less awesome—if not by much.

Since most of science is light years behind the more advanced metaphysical teachings, we turn to alternate sources for information. Seth deals directly with consciousness in his books, most notably in *Seth Speaks: The Eternal Validity of the Soul, The Nature of Personal Reality: A Seth Book* and *The "Unknown" Reality: A Seth Book*. He says, as some physicists now do, that consciousness is all there is, that it's the basic construct of the universe.

Consciousness is composed of units of consciousness that cannot be broken down further. Each unit of consciousness intrinsically has within its structure the ability to organize, expand and develop. It is "awareized" energy, literally found in all places at once, vitalized and charged with a propensity toward expression, and existing outside time and space. And, very important, each unit is endowed with unpredictability, because anything less than complete unpredictability would ultimately result in stagnation. This unpredictability leads to the evolution of infinite probabilities and patterns.

From units of consciousness all else springs. To manifest as physical, they first group together and combine into another form, called electromagnetic energy (EE) units. EE units represent the threshold point for consciousness into physical reality. They are the basic unit of energy from which all physical matter appears.

However, EE units are not simply physical energy—they are *consciousness made physical*, and they remain aware of all structures of which they are a part. They are, in essence, consciousness allowing itself to be formed into matter for its own expansion and expression. Like units of consciousness, EE units operate as waves, particles or forces. So, units of consciousness metamorphose into EE units that then create our physical lives, including our bodies and the material items found in our world.

And now the sixty-four dollar question: What starts the transformation process of consciousness into EE units? It's *thought and emotion*. Our brain is the tool that automatically converts our ideas and feelings into this electromagnetic energy. Then it acts as a transformer, unconsciously manipulating the newly formed EE units into physicality. The more intense the feeling behind the thought and the stronger the desire, the quicker and more durable the end physical materialization.

From Cosmic Legos to Real Life

When my daughter Cathleen was in ninth grade, she clipped a picture out of a teen magazine of a Scarlet O'Hara-type white prom dress. She spent hours dreamily imagining herself in it. She kept it pinned on her wall for months, and eventually it found its way into a drawer. It was buried deep in the debris and not often observed, then eventually forgotten.

When her junior prom rolled around, we went dress shopping. In the first shop we visited she found a lovely peach dress with a soft southern look. She had the clerk hold it for her, and we spent the rest of the day still searching for the perfect gown. Nothing else caught her fancy, so our tired feet eventually walked us back to the original shop, and we bought the dress.

That night after dinner Cathy came racing out of her room, waving the old magazine picture. I said no, it couldn't be. She said yes, it was. And to prove it, she put the dress on and paraded around the living room. The only difference was that her new dress was peach, Cathy's favorite color, instead of white.

As I said earlier, a belief is a strongly held thought. It has tremendous latent power because it is the catalyst that transforms units of consciousness into EE units, or physicality. Most of the time we accept our beliefs as fact and don't question them. They lose their status of belief and instead become assumptions, facts about our world and our lives.

My oldest sister Donna died at fifty-five from a heart attack. She had it in her mind that she wouldn't live longer than our parents, who both died about that age and both of heart conditions. Seven months before her death Donna was rushed to the hospital with breathing difficulties. For two weeks the highly respected cardiologist ran every imaginable test. Even though she was a heavy smoker and about one hundred pounds overweight for most of her adult life, not a heart problem showed up—except a cholesterol level of 1300.

The doctor said she was a miracle statistic, not only because of her high cholesterol count, but because there was no artery clogging or other heart disease present. Indeed, medical students were ushered into her hospital room to view such a phenomenon. Released without a solution to the breathing problem with assurances it wasn't her heart acting up, Donna was put on medication to reduce her cholesterol. The autopsy seven months later showed a severely enlarged heart and massive clogging of the arteries. The doctor said had she been on heart medication and possibly had multiple by-pass surgery, she probably could have lived.

Donna believed she was going to die at a certain age, and probably of our family's "hereditary" heart problems, and was prepared to do so. It's inconceivable, according to other doctors, that she developed her advanced diseased condition in just seven months. I believe one of two things happened: She hid her condition from the tests, or she did indeed develop the heart condition when she was ready to die. Either way, she chose her time and circumstances based on her beliefs, and no doctor was going to stop her.

Beliefs: Fiction Becoming Fact

An interesting thing about beliefs. They have a need to validate themselves in our world. They will draw to them all sorts of proof that they're real, stopping at nothing to create the illusion of truth and fact. But the dear things don't do it out of malice, they are only following orders—our orders. What we believe, we have; what we believe, we act; what we believe, we say; what we believe, we hear. What we believe, we are.

Some typical beliefs held by many in our society are:
- I am a failure.
- Illness is a fact of life.
- I am overweight.
- Luck and fate control my life.
- I was so little, and they hurt me so.
- I am poor.
- To have money is not spiritual.
- No pain, no gain.
- If only I had a degree, I could earn more money.
- It's a dog-eat-dog world.

We hypnotize ourselves with our beliefs. We consciously accept them, focus upon them, never questioning their truth because their results look so real. That's the nature of a belief—to hide within the illusion of truth and the abundance of fact. We say, "Of course I'm overweight. It's obvious to the most casual observer!" But the weight is a characteristic of the experience we created, not the reality itself. Our beliefs around self-worth, love, nutrition, a fearful world, exercise, diet or any number of other issues are the reality—and they cause our physical experience. If we don't learn to deal with our beliefs head on, they will force us to face their results, without ever knowing the freedom of choice and change.

Adelle Davis, the popular guru of modern nutrition, died in the 1970s. Her books were hailed as breakthroughs in understanding how to live healthy lives. She died of cancer. As an avid reader and practitioner of her suggestions, I credit her with bringing me closer to appreciating the earth. But now, with new insights under my belt, I can see the traps many of us fall into when we believe so strongly *against* something.

It's clear in her books she felt she was battling a great force, one intent on poisoning us at every turn with chemicals, pollutants and insecticides. It was imperative we learn to protect ourselves against these destructive forces if we wanted to be healthy. She chose to lead the fight and did so, I thought, very courageously.

The problem occurs, though, in our belief system. When we believe in good, we think we must, by definition, believe in an opposite. If we believe in an alternate force to the one we back, we give it validity and life and impact. It becomes a reckoning force, and then we say, see, there it is. I knew it. It is a fact.

However, a fact in one person's belief system doesn't necessarily make for a fact in another's. That the world agrees overwhelmingly with one belief doesn't invalidate the opposing belief's effect on its owner. Most of our world believes in sickness and disease as outside forces intent on bringing us down, the time and place of their choosing. Some don't. Some choose to ignore AIDS and cancer death statistics and continue living.

Recently I canceled my health insurance. After years of studying my thoughts, attitudes and beliefs, I've come to the conclusion that disaster won't befall me in the form of illness or accident. For reasons I'm just beginning to understand, I seem to choose battlefields other than my body to dramatize painful events. If I start to lose faith in my freedom from illness, I'll re-address my need for health insurance, but not until I exhaust all conscious means of psychically resolving my insecurities.

Fear: The Tip of the Belief Iceberg

While the beliefs of another may not be apparent to the observer, the fear generated by the beliefs is clear, if exterior events are assumed to have a deeper dynamics than what appears on the surface. I saw this on a trip to the Middle East.

It was a month after the close of the Gulf War. I was with a group focused on understanding the purported human rights violations of the Palestinians by Israel. We entered the Middle East by way of Amman, Jordan, and after several days were transported across the Jordan-Israel border to Jerusalem and eventually to the West Bank and Gaza Strip.

After talking to a wide array of people, including government officials, royalty, Palestinian refugees, PLO leaders, doctors exiled from the occupied territories, newscasters, worldwide relief groups and Christian organizations, we clearly knew Israel would not welcome us with open arms into the occupied territories. Just entering Israel after our extensive fact-finding mission in Jordan put us in jeopardy, we felt.

The fear started growing in some of our group well before we arrived at the border for our crossing from Jordan into Israel. I don't know what one of the women in our group believed or felt, but I can relate a series of events that happened to her.

The day before we were to depart for the border, she became very ill, maybe with the flu. Minutes from Israel, she vomited. She was still ill enough a day or so later that she decided to skip our trip to the West Bank to visit a refugee camp (a potentially dangerous proposition, we'd been told, due to rogue Palestinians and Israeli soldiers). Then, she walked alone out of our hotel in East Jerusalem and witnessed a car bombing. When we visited the West Bank another day, she was hit by a thrown rock, the only person to be attacked.

The final event occurred after we left Jerusalem and re-entered Jordan. She was in her room far above the street when she heard the roaring of a crowd. Outside her window she saw hundreds of Arabs filling the street and heading in the direction of the hotel. As they came closer, she grew fearful. When many of them swarmed around the hotel shouting and thrusting their arms into the air, she ran to her bathroom and locked the door.

She huddled there for twenty minutes or so, sick with fright. Finally, she came down to the dining room, her face stark white, and told us the story. What actually had happened was a soccer game at Amman's sports arena near the hotel, and the favored team had won. The Arabs were shouting with joy on the way to their cars and bus stops.

Beliefs and the Body

Former Stanford University scientist Dr. Bruce Lipton has been a frequent guest speaker at our seminars. One story he tells has great impact on the attendees because of the possibilities implicit in the conclusion. It's about a woman, diagnosed as having multiple personality disorder, who in one persona is a pathologically verified diabetic, dependent on insulin to sustain life. The very instant she changes into another personality all signs of diabetes disappear. The cells return to normal, and her body chemistry becomes balanced, instantaneously. It is Dr. Lipton's conclusion that the different belief systems held by the woman's two personalities are what create the conditions of health or diabetes. *Then what does that suggest for a person of normal mental health with an illness?*

People have been cured by the laying on of a faith healer's

hands. Witch doctors have healed with spells and brews. People throw off colds with great doses of Vitamin C. Cripples have walked from Lourdes. Cancer patients given water injections but told they received miracle drugs have had tumors disappear in a matter of hours.

It is a person's belief in or acceptance of the instrument of healing, and her desire and intent to heal, that cause the healing. She will become exposed to remedies acceptable to her belief system, if she feels the need, when she's ready to further the process. In other words, the person heals herself but gives credit to an outside source. The question is, can an outside source help heal a person, ever, unless she is ready for it? And, can the reversal of a disease continue if the person doesn't clear away the beliefs that caused the problem in the first place? Or, if the original illness is held at bay, will another develop to take its place?

Any event, and our reaction to it, is the translation of our creativity into the physical. A true understanding of the way in which an idea becomes matter, event or disease would result in a complete revamping of our civilization. It's time we consciously decide what it is we want to believe and then make it happen, for our families and ourselves, and the world.

5

The Magical Now

One night after work I shut my office door and changed from business suit to casual clothes for a personal evening appointment. That morning while dressing I had slipped on my engagement ring from my first marriage, perhaps for the second time in twenty years. When I changed clothes in my office, I took the ring off and put it inside a silk jewelry holder, dropped it into my carry-all bag and zipped it shut. I threw the bag into the car and went on my way. That night I unloaded my bag at home, opened the jewelry holder and reached for the ring—except it wasn't there. Stan and I carefully shook and searched every piece of clothing and the far corners of the carry-all bag to no avail.

I was quite upset. Even though our marriage had ended in divorce, I have an abiding affection for my first husband and nostalgia for what we shared as young people. I'm not a keeper of things normally; by nature I don't hold on to the past. But I'd promised my engagement ring to my daughter, and I strongly wanted her to have it. I slept poorly that night, saddened by its loss.

The Return of the Prodigal Ring

Before my morning meditation I thought about the fact that linear time is an illusion, that all time is simultaneous with we humans accepting the root assumptions of time and space as part of our reality. I thought about the power of the immediate moment, that all creation must take place now since it is the only time there is. I thought of my ring, lost in a supposed past moment but somehow with me right now, and I decided I didn't want to accept the assumption of its loss.

In meditation, I dwelt on the ring and my feelings for it, the symbol of my transition from child to adult. I asked for help in finding it. I saw myself manipulate time by choosing a different probability than the one it seemed was facing me. Then I visualized the ring back on my hand, in clear detail down to the one prong repaired in the distant past.

On my way out of the front door that morning, I glanced in a mirror and groaned at my inappropriate choice of necklace. I ran upstairs, took the black strand off, flung it into the top drawer of my jewelry box and replaced it with one of another color.

Full of anticipation on the drive to work that morning, I easily tolerated the thirty miles of intolerable Orange County traffic. How would my ring return? Would I find it on my office floor where it had fallen from my fingers, never having made it into the jewelry bag? I ran into my office an hour later, slammed the door and dropped to my hands and knees. No ring. I flung the pillows off the couch, searching the most minute crevices. No ring.

That night and the next morning I meditated and visualized again...and then my little miracle happened. While dressing for work, I opened my jewelry box to retrieve yet another necklace. Sitting on top of the black necklace—discarded fourteen hours after having removed the ring from my finger thirty miles away—was my ring.

What happened? I'm not sure. I don't know all the terms for psychic phenomena and I don't want to. Definitions give structure to what is defined, and once defined it must then fit within that structure. And if the concept is larger than the defined boundaries, it's either ignored or scaled down to fit.

What I *feel* happened was that my firm conviction that all events, past, present and future are active—and malleable—in the spacious present, the now, freed me to approach a life event with a radical, pioneering eye. That freedom to explore beyond the ordinary, coupled with strong desire for the return of my ring and powerful visualization, re-formed my ring in physical reality. I had to believe in my natural ability to manipulate linear time, space and energy. *I had to believe the universe was constructed differently than I'd been taught.*

Creation's Kick-Off Point

How powerful is the now? The point of power is only in the present. We create from this moment, whether the materialization appears instantly, as a parking place might, or later as a more complex event. However, all creation takes place in consecutive nows. If we understand the depth and scope of this truth, we find an inexhaustible supply of usable energy at our command.

What we put our mental and emotional energy behind becomes real. If you want something to happen, dwell on it. If you're ill and constantly replay why and how, which doctor said what, which medication does what, and thoughts like, "I'll never get well," all you do is reinforce the condition. If you're poor and want to be prosperous, you can't get from here to there until you stop focusing on the feelings and experiences of poverty.

While living in Eugene, Oregon, we owned a cabin in Washington four hours from home. Because we didn't get to spend much time there, Stan made a point of shutting off the water whenever we left. He religiously tended to this task while voicing concerns about the mess we'd have on our hands if a pipe broke. In fact, he voiced them a lot, for almost two years.

Finally, big surprise, he found a leak around a toilet one day, and, boy, it was a good thing we'd been turning the water off or who knows what might have happened. Then he grew thoughtful and said, "Guess I must have been telepathically picking up on the fact that this was going to happen." For two years? More likely, he created the leak by his concern. He transformed energy into an event, because it's what he focused on.

The Passé Past

The interesting, and for many people unsettling, thing about believing we create from the present is that we don't have to afford the past or future one bit of importance. It becomes our choice as to how we respond to either.

It's only our thoughts, attitudes and emotions held in the moment that have power. It's not what occurred to us in the past that will force us onto a path we'd rather not traverse, as though we're destined for an emotional future based on episodes from our past; it's how dearly, how tightly, we hold on to that past by reliving its trauma and drama in our present thoughts and emotions. When we constantly re-examine our past in order to discover what's wrong in the present, we reinforce the building materials that will create exactly that which we're trying to escape.

My daughter was raped at nineteen. She lived not far from UCLA in a high-security apartment building. One late afternoon she took the elevator to underground parking and was assaulted by a man who had gained entry when a security guard broke regulations by vacating his post. For several days she withdrew from the world, staying inside emotionally and physically, trying to climb back to life from the depths of her pain. Finally the dam broke and we talked all through the night.

Fortunately, Cathy had been studying my metaphysical books for a few years. From her own knowledge she knew two very important facts. First, she had come into this life with a propensity toward victimization (she had crashed into the belief more than once). And, second, if she didn't break the cycle and stop reinforcing it through her *belief* that she was a victim, another tragic event would occur.

Remembering that she had control over how she handled her now was a mighty step toward healing. The Los Angeles Police Department officers were so wonderful to her, so solicitous and kind that she finally chose not to see them anymore. She was trying to break the mold of victim, and society is very set on reinforcing it through well-meaning, well-intentioned actions.

But for Cathy, building the clarity of mind needed to loosen the hold of victimization meant she could accept empathy for her hurts, but not sympathy devoid of understanding her part in the creation of the event.

Later, Cathy was told she could sue the apartment complex for megabucks because of the breach in security that allowed the attacker inside. She chose not to for the same reason she chose not to accept sympathy: It would only have verified and intensified her role as victim. Receiving money for playing victim would prove once again that she was vulnerable to the whims of fate, that she had no part in scripting her life. She had chosen to break the cycle, and many times that means stepping outside of accepted societal beliefs.

A Probability-Driven Reality

Understanding the power of the now is immensely important to the conscious creation process. We can't create "in the future," because "in the future" never comes. We can only do it right now. The problem is that most of our nows seem so ordinary. How can this very moment be so supernaturally powerful when all we're doing is mowing the lawn?!

The answer lies in another facet of consciousness. Back in chapter 4, I said that consciousness is endowed with unpredictability, which allows for infinite probabilities and patterns. What this translates into in practical terms is that every event that can possibly occur at this moment is a probability just waiting to happen. All probable variations of our reality, down to the most minute, exist now. They flow through the present moment, which is the point of intersection between them.

With our beliefs, emotions and intents, we select from this unpredictable group of actions those we want to happen. We weave in and out these of probabilities constantly, picking and choosing as we move through life, activating some and calling them our official present, and eventually our past.

We rest on a poised platform called our present, the result of all decisions we made and make as we move across the timeline from birth to death. We are the directors that roll our lives out into the world in colorful three dimension, calling, "Lights, camera, action!" We are the sole builders of our realities, responsible for where we are today and where we will be tomorrow, for the heights of our accomplishments and the depths of our hurt. And we're responsible for the intriguing lesser events that glitter our days.

Stan and I were driving the streets of an unfamiliar city, Vancouver, Washington, looking for a specific address. As we slowly moved through the trim neighborhoods checking out the street signs, I realized with a start that this part of town had an uncanny resemblance to my childhood hometown of Trenton, Michigan. Or, more accurately, it looked just like my friend Janet's block of homes in Trenton. When I was about fifteen I had a silent crush on her cousin who lived and attended school in a town miles from Trenton.

As Stan and I cruised this small area of Vancouver, crisscrossing from street to street and back again, I became quiet, thinking about the similarities between this neighborhood and Janet's. All I need to see now, I thought, is her cousin's school, Our Lady of Lourdes, to complete my feelings about that time long ago. Stan turned at the next corner, entering new territory, and within a block we slowly passed a large school on our left. I was only mildly surprised when I read its name, Our Lady of Lourdes.

Coincidence, you say? Seth says:

> The experiences that seem to happen, the chance encounters, the unexpected events–all of these come into your experience because in one way or another you have attracted them, even though their occurrences might seem to have insurmountable odds against them. Those odds–those impediments–do not exist (in reality).[1]

Another time, my morning had been fairly hectic. I had completed two projects on my Mac that were ready for printing. I started a printing run of twenty copies of the first on the Laser-Writer, then, before selecting the second project for printing, I decided to review it first.

I never did get around to starting the print process on it. But when I pulled the twenty copies of the first job out of the printer and flipped through them to check the quality, I found one copy of the second job about six or seven sheets into the batch. If you understand the interface between computer and laser printer, this seems an impossibility. As a *probability*, though, there it was, just waiting to happen.

Anchoring to the Now

There are two fundamental approaches to dealing with the power of the now. The first has to do with returning to it when you find yourself drifting into negative, fearful or limiting thoughts, whether they be of the past or future, and then restructuring the energy around the moment. We suggest several techniques. One is to blink slowly two or three times to clear away the thoughts, then take a minute to explore your surroundings, looking at the fine detail of what you see.

As you're absorbing your environment, remind yourself that what you've been thinking has been creating, and if you don't want to continue, you'd better get grounded right now. Consciously try to release the feeling that's holding you by refusing to give it power. Tell yourself you're surrounded by probabilities and your future is your choice, and will be based in part on what you're feeling in this present moment. Try to become calm and balanced, clear in your thinking. Let the negativity go, don't worry about it at all. "I'll not reinforce the problem," you say. "Things will work out," you say. And, not so surprisingly, they usually do.

This is not to imply you should submerge the negative thoughts or feelings, burying them under cotton candy emotions generated in the moment. Not at all. It's important to acknowledge what's going on in your world by giving it the validity it deserves. Just don't muck around in it. Get on with your life.

A real powerhouse way to restructure the negative energy entering the present entails breaking the pattern of your limiting thought or feeling instantly by thinking a pre-assigned trigger word or phrase that refocuses you back into the immediate moment.

As soon as you catch yourself with any thought or feeling, no matter how small, that is in opposition to what you want to experience, think a phrase like "past-smasher," or "pattern-break." Instantly see the pattern of the emotion or thought blowing up into minuscule particles, then visualize yourself pulling in your power from the universe to fill the void. The whole process takes a second or two, but it breaks your tie to the past and allows you to bypass its potential materialization in the future.

When we're depressed or frightened, the feelings surround us like a shroud. Another way to restructure the energy surrounding the now is to sit calmly and see a column of energy come down through your head in a straight line, all the way through your toes. See that the column of energy has no starting point above or below you. It comes from, and returns to, infinity, and you are within its center. See it as the substance that creates you, clear and strong. Within this core that is the real you, see perfect balance and freedom from fear. Think of joy and laughter. Write the words a few times, see them on paper, think the thoughts.

Solid State Living

The second approach to dealing with the now is to build inner strength, a solid basis of inner strength from which creation will take place in *all* nows, without the continual need to monitor it. Stan and I learned this the hard way.

We left our careers and Southern California two days after Christmas, 1989, and moved to the Northwest. Within the next two months, we sold all of our stock. We sold it out of fear, fear that the company would take a turn for the worse and I, now an outsider, would have no knowledge of the impending doom, fear that the economy was headed into recession, fear of watching the stock drop like a stone, forcing us back into the computer industry to survive.

Anxiety drove us until we rid our lives of the last shares. Its pace accelerated when we realized a giant mistake stared us in the face—the stock took a dramatic rise within days of leaving our hands. Over a quarter of a million dollars was left sitting on the table.

"Losing" that much money turned my stomach every time I thought of it, but an even greater anxiety arose because I knew we caused our participation in that event. When you believe you're the primary creator of your reality, and you're hammered by what you've manifested, it does lead to soul searching.

Unanswered questions surrounded us. Like, why did it happen? Could a similar event happen again? We'd cleared enough space in our belief system to allow the money to enter, but did we hold conflicting beliefs that would force us now to lose it? Why were we not happy, and why did we have more fear now than ever before? What exactly was going on?!

Every day that tail end of winter we found ourselves in panic trying to hold on to the money and grow it the best ways possible. We analyzed every financial decision as though our lives depended on it. We awoke each morning concerned that we weren't equipped to handle the situation and would blow it. So when we bought tons of another stock in March and then watched the bottom fall out days later (about 30 percent worth), it shouldn't have surprised us. No one can live in that much fear and not reap its outcome.

Our financial life was crashing and burning around us. I had to get away to figure things out. I packed a dozen metaphysical books, some meditation music and visualization tapes, and headed for the Oregon coast. The weather matched my mood. Great storms rolled in the heavens, spewing diagonal rain sheets and whipping the frenzied wind. I settled into my small rented cabin after stocking up on groceries and fire wood, and stayed inside for four days except for occasional drenching walks on the wet sand.

Have you ever had an experience where you were in great need of understanding or encouragement or enlightenment, and the right book just happened to fall into your lap? Out of hundreds of missals in my metaphysical library, my hurrying hands had unerringly chosen exactly the right ones for that trip to the coast. I read none of them from cover to cover in my snug cabin, but when a need or question arose, I randomly opened whichever one my hands fell on, to the page the universe suggested.

As the days passed, I felt my meditations become more peaceful, my visualizations less strident. I felt my fears start to melt, my anxiety wane. But more important, I felt my connection to All That Is reaffirmed. I remembered that the universe really is a friendly place, and I no longer needed to prove otherwise. I was becoming balanced once more.

By the time I left the cabin and headed home, I knew one more secret to consciously creating what we want. Stan and I had reached our goal after years of focus, but we hadn't mastered living in the now in peace, balance, optimism and an understanding of universal support. What does health, wealth, job satisfaction or anything else bring to us unless happiness permeates our lives at the most basic level? In fact, can those pleasures be sustained if wracked by doubts and fears in the now? I think not. Something must give.

Dr. Lipton says our cells are influenced by our thoughts, and will select only one of two modes to mirror back: growth or protection. Once our cells have determined the appropriate state, they create chemicals that reflect this state back to the body. But they cannot simultaneously accommodate both. So if we live in fear and anxiety, our body shuts down and growth is not possible. The same applies to our mind. The key to successfully living in the now is to stay in growth mode.

The Now Power Base

Once I understood this, I could determine a structure of what needs to occur in the present to keep it a peaceful place to reside. Fig. 5 is that structure whimsically depicted. It's called the Now Power Base, and it works like this: We strive to live each moment in harmony and balance by loving ourselves without reservation, by sensing our deep psychic connection to the universe, by accepting all people as equals, and by flooding our moments with joy.

A big order? In some ways. We are human, here to learn and grow, which often translates into bumbling through experiences. But so what? It's the process of trying that leads to becoming.

The diagram suggests the most important issues of our physical lives, when solidified in our thoughts, give us an awesome foundation upon which to stand, solid, secure, unafraid. From this base of power we can create, much more easily and surely, the events we want to experience. When our present is as balanced as possible, we are creating from a position of strength, not weakness.

POWER BASE DIAGRAM

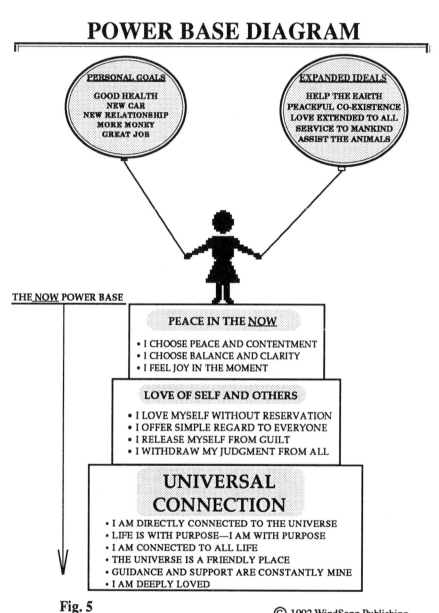

PERSONAL GOALS

GOOD HEALTH
NEW CAR
NEW RELATIONSHIP
MORE MONEY
GREAT JOB

EXPANDED IDEALS

HELP THE EARTH
PEACEFUL CO-EXISTENCE
LOVE EXTENDED TO ALL
SERVICE TO MANKIND
ASSIST THE ANIMALS

THE NOW POWER BASE

PEACE IN THE NOW

• I CHOOSE PEACE AND CONTENTMENT
• I CHOOSE BALANCE AND CLARITY
• I FEEL JOY IN THE MOMENT

LOVE OF SELF AND OTHERS

• I LOVE MYSELF WITHOUT RESERVATION
• I OFFER SIMPLE REGARD TO EVERYONE
• I RELEASE MYSELF FROM GUILT
• I WITHDRAW MY JUDGMENT FROM ALL

UNIVERSAL CONNECTION

• I AM DIRECTLY CONNECTED TO THE UNIVERSE
• LIFE IS WITH PURPOSE—I AM WITH PURPOSE
• I AM CONNECTED TO ALL LIFE
• THE UNIVERSE IS A FRIENDLY PLACE
• GUIDANCE AND SUPPORT ARE CONSTANTLY MINE
• I AM DEEPLY LOVED

Fig. 5

All of the bullet items in the Now Power Base are beliefs we can cultivate, even if they're presently frail or nonexistent in our lives. How to identify which beliefs need reinforcing and how to solidify them will be covered in chapters 6 and 7 respectively.

The Now Power Base suggests that:

• *Acceptance of a universal connection and guidance from beyond becomes mandatory if we're to accept the conscious creation process.* If we still believe that luck and fate rule our lives, and we were born flawed or sinful beings, we may never get this process to work. We must think of ourselves as God individualized, here for the purpose of expanding our consciousness, with all the assistance necessary for the asking. We should feel ourselves as one with all things of the universe, sensing kinship with all forms of consciousness in our reality and others. We need to remember that everything is contained within All That Is, including us.

Aligning our thoughts with the universe releases us from fear. When fear is present, it presupposes there is something in the future to be feared. But when we reach an understanding of our heritage and purpose, we can override anxiety and not project it forward into another fear-filled event.

• *Self-love and self-worth are synonymous. Without a basic acceptance* of our validity as a person, we will constantly create situations which mirror back an off-balance life. Self-love starts with releasing ourselves from guilt and failure, and allowing ourselves to be forgiven. When we forgive, our hearts are cleared for love. Never mind that forgiveness is a human act: All That Is doesn't forgive, because It hasn't judged the act one way or another.

Feelings of simple regard for everyone on the planet can grow once our personal guilts and judgments are released. We'll project our dislikes and uncertainties onto others until we stop chastising ourselves. When our present is filled with ease and acceptance, we'll offer it to our brethren with less hesitation.

• *Peace in the moment brings anxiety to its knees. It can't live in the* same moment as peace. It's an impossibility. One is growth, one is protection. So when we consciously focus on peace, we break the creative power of fear. Peace mellows us toward life by giving our inner self the opening it needs to interject contentment into our days.

By making joy a primary focus for our thoughts and emotions, we'll have happy events occur in our lives, because events and physical objects are solidified emotions and thoughts. Remember, what we focus on expands. Find appreciation in the last flower of spring as well as the first; laugh at the kids playing hopscotch, feel their fun and concentration; when the wind gusts against your face, tilt your head back and luxuriate in its touch. Step outside your thoughts and just be, for a change.

Real-Life Reflections of Change

I mentioned earlier that Stan and I had bought a substantial amount of stock one March only to watch its value drop 30 percent within a couple of days. The stock analysts saw no reason it should climb that high again. In fact, most had a doom and gloom attitude toward it. After the shock of the downturn wore off and we got our anxiety under control, we decided we weren't willing to let it go without a fight. A long saga of belief-work, visualization and Now Power Base-building followed. It took nine months, but finally the stock reached its magic number again and we sold.

We learned to live in the present because of that event. We had to, to keep the fear at bay while we cleaned up the mess. We also learned to listen to our inner selves and trust what we thought they were saying. Without asking and listening, we would have sold the stock at a huge loss several different times during the nine months, when it inched further downward.

Our broker even called once and said he was recommending his clients sell because the latest company analysis was quite disconcerting. As a stockholder himself, he chose to sell his personal shares at a significant loss that day. It took numerous meditations to hold on to the intuition that we were doing the right thing by waiting. This overall experience is rated as among the top three most difficult conscious creation goals we've undertaken. Yet it is also one of the most satisfying for the growth we underwent.

Living in the present in peace, without fear, leads to abundance. Abundance, like everything else in three-dimensional reality, is solidified emotion. When we master the Now Power Base, we've learned to harness the magic of the moment. Now all we have to do is keep pre-programmed beliefs from slinking into our place of power under the guise of truth and fact.

6

The Golden Key

We can't run away from our beliefs. They go where we go. They follow us from job to job, marriage to marriage, state to state, creating the same situations over and over again, maybe with a new twist but similar results. If we believe we can't hold a job, we won't, no matter how great the new opportunity. If we believe we're not good enough to be loved, a relationship won't endure no matter how deeply we care for the other person.

We can organize our lives, make the best decisions for the circumstances, move with caution when appropriate, but the basic underlying pattern won't change. Some choose to break the cycle, to seek the happiness that is our birthright. If that's our decision, and conscious creation our vehicle, we must of necessity understand beliefs and their impact.

Unlocking a Treasure Chest of Dreams

You're in Life Position A, and you want to move to Life Position B. (Read poor to affluent, lonely to involved, sick to healthy, etc.) Stan and I found two paths to the new destination. One became very familiar, until we got the message: Set a goal and go for it, with no advance preparation. In this scenario, although the goal can be reached, every belief that kept us from Life Position B is also met. How do we meet them? Usually as upsetting or stressful events.

It makes sense. Our lives, and all events in them, are symbolic reflections of our beliefs. If we have no limiting thoughts around our goal, we'd be there. If we implicitly believe we're healthy, we will be. But if today's us constantly reflects sick and our objective is health, changes must occur.

When we project a desire, the universe starts the acquisition process rolling. Down the path to our new future we stride, unfortunately, however, accompanied by our old, burdensome thought patterns. They stick like honey to our psyche, lulling us into complacency until finally they strike a blow to our progress.

But we don't have to get slapped up side the head by these contrary beliefs. Not if we know how to identify them *before* they materialize. Once they're spotted, these nasty beliefs can be magically transformed into the great golden key that opens our personal treasure chest of dreams. They'll no longer block; they'll assist. They will do us the honor of telling us why we've been stuck, and then they'll allow themselves to be shoved out of the way.

The Spotlight of Belief Scrutiny

I'm a hard core mystery reader. I love to follow the clues, analyze the situation, track the information. My sleuthing ability is developed to where, assuming the plot is adroitly drawn, I usually spot the villain before he or she is revealed. We can do that with life, too. There's such symmetry and order to what happens in the exterior world that if we follow the clues, we find the causes of our outrageous fortune.

Every day I study conscious creation in some form. I monitor my feelings and wonder what beliefs are behind them. I watch events unfold for myself and others and marvel at the intricate structure it took to pull them off. I listen to others talk and I attempt to uncover the beliefs that lead them to say what they say, do what they do.

We need to build our awareness to beliefs. We need to think about them, look for them, analyze them. We need to push them from their hiding places in our conscious mind into the spotlight of scrutiny. Notice I didn't say move them from the unconscious mind to the conscious mind. They're not hidden in some dark and murky past, flung beneath layers of psychological debris, dredged up only after countless painful experiences in a therapist's office. Beliefs are always apparent in the conscious mind if we know where to look.

While never hidden, at times they're hard to spot simply because we don't believe they're a belief. It's just the way it is, we tell ourselves, it's the way of life, the way of people. It's his character and her luck. It's my hard work and my mom's forgetfulness. He failed because he didn't prepare, she succeeded because her folks have money. But it's nothing, really, just normal, everyday life.... But we must realize that any "truth" we see is a belief. It's up to us to acknowledge it as such. Then we're where we want to be—open to change.

Of Sacred Cows and Other Misperceptions

Don't let the sacred cows of our society go unquestioned, especially the clearly defined behaviors we've been exposed to over and over again. Codependent, alcoholic, bulimic, drug-dependent, compulsive eater, etc. If we agree we fit within a box, we do. All we'll see, if we accept another's boundary, is a reflection of the word. If we believe it, we are it. By superimposing a popularized definition on top of active limiting beliefs, a whole new set of beliefs is born. As they swell, we become more firmly ensconced in a tighter band of restriction cut from sturdier cloth.

A recent newspaper article challenged the idea that the childhood experiences of "adult children of alcoholics" have left them with unique emotional patterns. It states, "New data suggests that problems reported by children of alcoholics are far from unique. Many popular assumptions are being questioned by new research, posing a challenge to the hugely popular therapy movement directed at them and other adult children of problem families."[1]

Perhaps there are no dysfunctional people easily classified into groups by exterior behaviors or similar pasts. Maybe there are only private, unique dysfunctional beliefs that manifest as self-destruction—and people choose their poison. Alcoholism may be the unconscious behavior of choice for a person low in self-love, while codependency another's.

The legacy of the "wounded inner child" has been bestowed upon this generation. The wounds stay with us, as popular theory suggests, for untold years, wreaking emotional havoc throughout our adult lives. Poet Robert Bly, an influential leader of the men's movement, gets my vote on how to deal with childhood wounds. He says you can only nurture the inner child for so long, then you have to heal the little sucker and kill it off or you'll end up pandering to it for the rest of your life. The past doesn't upset our emotional apple cart; our continual acceptance of the role of victim does.

We are not humans with such mundane issues as commonly shared psychological problems. We are consciousness with a belief system through which we interact and impact the world. When we understand more about that belief system, change becomes much simpler...and definitely faster.

A Field of Infinite Questions

Everything is an indicator of our beliefs: our bodies, memories, actions, reactions, possessions, thoughts of the future, home and work environments, guilts, internal chatter, associations, fears, loves. Indicators of their existence scatter throughout our days. Asking the right questions helps push them to the forefront of our minds.

Here's a good place to start. Ask this question continually: "Why would I (or they) _____ that?" Such as, why would I act like that? Or, why would I think like that? Why would they own that? Why would I say that? Why would they live like that? Why would I want that?

Analyze. Hash over. Delve into. Question. Why would people request an unlisted phone number, keep a month's stock of groceries, go on a diet, meditate? Everyone who goes on a diet won't have the same beliefs in play, but it really doesn't matter for this little exercise. It's our exploration of the underbelly of thoughts that's important.

So, why *might* someone go on a diet? They believe they're overweight? They believe they must diet to lose weight? They believe in the power of the calorie? They believe they must mold themselves to society's standards?

Why would a person choose to have an unlisted phone number? They believe it protects them from obscene calls? They believe it gives them privacy? They believe it's a status symbol? They believe they're vulnerable to attack by the unknown?

We're just skimming the surface of possibilities. The reasons may be more complex, but you get the idea. When you peek into your own belief system, you'll be peeling back layer upon layer of interesting thoughts, attitudes and emotions around your subject of choice, very different indeed from this simple probing.

Try some more. Why would a person say, "I am a survivor?" What might it tell you about the person's feelings of vulnerability, and the events they create to prove the feelings are justified? What would she believe, or not believe, about a safe universe? About a God that supports and protects her? About her strength under adversity? About her underlying view of life?

"I am a good parent." Sounds great, but what beliefs might lurk behind the statement? One possibility is, "I'm a good parent because I'm always there for my kids, even if it means giving up my aspirations for theirs." Or, "I am a good parent because I worry about my kids all the time." All statements should be questioned for the reality behind the exterior.

Answer true or false to these statements, then ask yourself why you chose your response: It's a dog-eat-dog world. No one wants me. There is much evil out there. I am powerless to change my life. There is no purpose to life other than to survive. My boss hates me. Illness is inescapable. People are so stupid. It wouldn't work for me. I'll always be broke.

Now, what if you were told that *no matter how you responded, it was a belief?* A belief is a belief, whether its effect on our life is positive or questionable. Supply and abundance are governed by our beliefs. Energy, money, health, time, love and friends are abundantly ours. But we have to believe it.

Do these ring true, and if not, why? Life is a joy. There is no such thing as evil. I can create conscious change. I am important to the world. I love and accept myself. I am a decision maker. I am competent and qualified, ready for advancement. My body heals rapidly. I can become exactly what I choose.

Get used to asking yourself constant questions. See the curtain rise and the play begin, your beliefs acting their parts so convincingly they deceive you with their illusion of truth. Eavesdrop on conversations, read newspapers and magazines, listen to television and radio shows with your new focus on uncovering beliefs.

Let go of logic as much as possible when reviewing an event. Don't say, "I was stopped by the cop because I was late for work and speeding." That's not the reason you were slapped with a ticket. A more accurate assessment might be found in the answer to the question, "Why did I put myself in the position of being chastised?"

How did you feel when the officer stopped you? How did you

feel afterward? What thoughts ran through your head? Were you angry at an authority that had the right to control you? Had the whole world been dumping on you lately? Did the ticket strap you financially? Had you been feeling boxed in, held back, afraid? Become an explorer, a probe, a pioneer. Figure out just what the heck is going on.

The Mirror Warped

Did you know that four out of five fourth graders in the San Francisco area are dieting? I assume they think they're overweight. Where did the beliefs come from that made them prone to fat? We look at our youngsters, out of shape at ten years old, and bemoan the lifestyle that made them that way. But it isn't the lifestyle, it's the beliefs permeating our modern ways that they're reflecting.

What if there were no rules telling them they must exercise with a certain precision each day, eat the latest definition of proper food at each meal, watch the junk food in between or God knows how horrible their bodies will look? What if there were no advertisements to convince them only the very attractive succeed...and the ranks are now closed?

What if, instead, our kids weren't judged by standards they can't possibly meet, no matter how hard they try? What if they were taught to feel safe and confident in a universe they know nurtures them; that their lives have intent and purpose? Would they automatically, naturally, choose the best food and exercise for their bodily needs? If beliefs create, the answer is yes.

It's scary what we're doing to our children because of our distorted understandings, especially in the field of health. A government panel concluded in 1991 that one in four children should get cholesterol tests. The reason, as quoted from a newspaper article that discussed the panel's conclusion: "Kids with high cholesterol are more likely to have raised levels as adults, putting them at high risk of early coronary heart disease."[2] Nothing like setting the stage for their future by firmly implanting illness beliefs right out of the chute.

Then there was the newspaper article that reported the overall rate of cancer among children is mounting steadily.[3] No kidding. What do we expect when our kids feel vulnerable to disease, frightened of the world they live in, and beaten about the shoulders with the dos and don'ts imposed on them in the name of safety. The universe *is* safe; we make it otherwise.

We can't win. Once we cut back the fat in our diets—because surely that's the way to health, as we've been told repeatedly—we read of a research report run in the *Journal of the American Medical Association* that states, "Reducing fat to 30 percent of calories would put off death for only about 2 percent of the 2.3 million Americans who die each year."[4] The "experts" can't even decide the issue, but we know the truth. It's how we *feel* about ourselves and our food that determines how healthy we will be, and how long we will live.

Personally, I like the eighty-nine year old man in Denver who has eaten twenty-five eggs a day for the past fifteen years, with no apparent ill effects. That comes to 5,300 milligrams of cholesterol a day, 5,000 more than what is recommended. Yet the man's blood cholesterol level is only 200 milligrams and he has no evidence of heart disease. Maybe he doesn't have a television to reprogram his belief system about the safety of living in this reality.

The book *The Day America Told the Truth*, by James Patterson and Peter Kim, speaks worlds of words about our anxieties, vulnerabilities and inability to create our experiences. The answer to one question on the authors' opinion survey was especially startling: Seven percent of Americans said they would commit murder for $10 million. We view the world through a mirror warped by lack and fear, and then mistake it for reality, a reality we feel holds us powerless.

From Marathon to Martyrdom

If only I'd known in 1982 what I know now. That's the year I entered the New York Marathon. I'd been seated at the finish line of the marathon for a couple of years, courtesy of the New York Road Runner's Club, its organizers. Each year my company loaned high-speed printers to the club for the creation of the bar-coded bibs worn by the runners and printed as part of the elaborate registration system.

I was usually in New York four days before the marathon and stayed at the hotel designated as its headquarters. There's a fever about the place when the runners start arriving in town. It's catching. I'd watched my friend and business associate Ron cross the finish line in 1981, and gee, it looked like swell fun. I thought I'd give it a whirl.

That I could barely complete a one mile course didn't daunt me. With Ron's help, I devised a training schedule that included five days of runs per week, with my long run on Sunday. I carefully set the amount of miles I wanted to accumulate throughout the week and the percentage of distance growth for each week's runs over the last. I had fifty-one weeks of runs planned and, by God, I was going to meet each week's goal if it killed me. I did, and it almost did.

My life revolved around my running. Stan's, out of necessity, did also. At first he ran with me, but as I progressed in miles, he took to bicycling alongside on the weekends. For a year, Saturday night lights-out happened early at our house since I ran at daybreak Sunday when peace and relatively clean air reigned.

That year my job demanded I travel heavily. The upside to being in a new city a couple of times a week was that I experienced a tremendous variety of scenery on my runs. The downside was the same thing. For a woman who likes to run at dawn, finding acceptable running territory in larger cities became an interesting challenge. One time I ran fifteen miles in the parking lot of my hotel outside Philadelphia.

It was about six months into my schedule that the toll started extracting its due. I was worn out. My days dragged with fatigue. I couldn't get enough sleep. I dreaded jet lag and stressful running conditions. My long Sunday runs loomed over my head, black clouds on the horizon. Dislike of my running schedule's incessant demand turned to hate about two months before the marathon. But I couldn't stop. I'd told the world I was going to run that damn race, and I would.

The end was finally, blessedly, near. I ran twenty-four miles one Sunday and Stan and I celebrated because now I knew I could do it. Not three days later while running a fifteen miler, I took a spill bad enough to throw my back so far out I couldn't stand upright. The next morning found me in the chiropractor's office for a week's worth of daily visits. Then, due to job pressures, I hit the road again. It was one week before the marathon. I asked my doctor if I could run it, and he said I could try.

About eight miles after the starting gun sounded on that cool November morning, and "Chariots of Fire" swelled from the overhead speakers, my right foot slipped into a small hole in the road. It was enough to jerk me sideways and throw my back out again. I walked in eighteen miles and got my medal. Well over a year passed before I would finally feel pride in what I'd accomplished, so strong was my shame at having taken over seven hours to complete the course.

When I trained for the marathon, I had no clue that what I was thinking and feeling was setting the stage for personal disaster. I wallowed in the anger and tiredness, my martyr's badge. On one hand, I believed I could finish the race; on the other, I deeply resented that I had to do it. Push, pull. I can finish, but this isn't going to be fun. I can run, but I'm going to be miserable. Somewhere—sigh—I'll find the strength to finish. However, the finish I experienced was equivalent to failure in my book.

Are there parallels to be drawn in your life? Do you martyr yourself to your family, job, art, health, money? Do you set rules and regulations around your conduct and call out success! or fail-ure! as an umpire calls the pitches? Or do you give yourself room to grow and learn without the baggage of guilt created by your own false standards? From a practical standpoint, non-judgment is infinitely more peaceful because it doesn't create events that jus-tify the presence of judgments. Think about that for awhile. The benefits soon become pleasingly apparent.

Finding Beliefs: The Root Diagram

For years after I started to consciously create, I filled note-books with my thoughts and feelings generated by my latest prob-lem. Sometimes it was a situation at work I wanted to resolve peacefully, perhaps it was a feeling of inadequacy I had at the mo-ment, or maybe a desire to create enough money to pay my tax bill.

It didn't take long to realize strong feelings were at play whenever I reached for a notebook. What I learned first hand, and Seth says repeatedly, is that behind every feeling is a belief. It fi-nally occurred to me there was a process behind what I was doing with the notebooks, and I could translate that process onto a form for easier use. It became the Root Diagram. (See Fig. 6.1. Feel free to photocopy it, if you choose.)

Here's how it works:

1. Choose a subject that has negative, limiting or fearful conno-tations for you. Select it from the past, present or future.

2. Condense it into a few words and write them in the Subject Circle. (Examples: Job, Health, Money, I have cancer, I need a friend.)

3. Think about the feelings you hold around the subject. Write each one in a Feeling Circle. You can add adjectives or descriptive words, if you choose, such as "financial anxiety," "fear of failure," "gnawing concern."

4. In the Belief Circle under your Feeling Circle, write a state-ment that summarizes your reason for the feeling. Really focus on

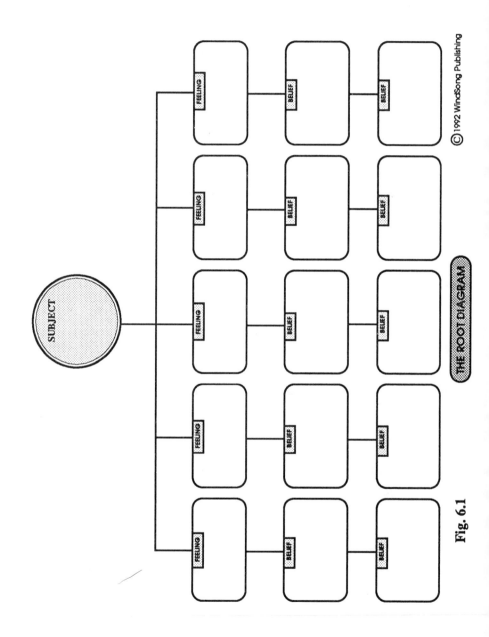

THE ROOT DIAGRAM

© 1992 WindSong Publishing

Fig. 6.1

it first, get a gut-level reaction to the feeling, and then let it lead you into your statement. If another statement seems to be hanging around your mind's periphery, write it in the second Belief Circle directly below the first. Continue until all feelings have beliefs attached to them.

What you've done is something very powerful. You've identified beliefs that are developing the events around your subject. I know, I know. They're facts, right? Well, yes they are. They're also beliefs, and therefore can be changed.

To make the Root Diagram more clear, see Fig. 6.2. This is a Root Diagram of a man named Robert. Look at the feelings he's identified around money, and the beliefs he uncovered from those feelings. This is a good first pass at delving into his financial situation. He's starting to get a handle on the dynamics that are creating his problems. He may find that one Root Diagram session isn't enough. Several passes over a period of days or weeks, possibly even months, may be necessary to get the complete picture.

The Root Diagram is one very good way of identifying beliefs. It will consistently lead to information required to change a situation. I find it especially helpful in times of crisis, when nothing seems to make sense, or I'm losing ground to fear. That's when emotions are fully exposed, and usually the beliefs are quickly spotted.

Other Belief-Identifying Techniques

For you who want an alternate procedure, try this. Get out your notebook. Select the area of your life you want to analyze and write it at the top of a blank page. Now, write what you're thinking about the subject, either in prose or bullet items. Cover as many facets as possible, such as your thoughts, some events that have occurred, and your feelings. When you're through, or even at a later time, review your writings and try to develop simple statements that summarize what you have written. Your summary will give you a good handle on your beliefs.

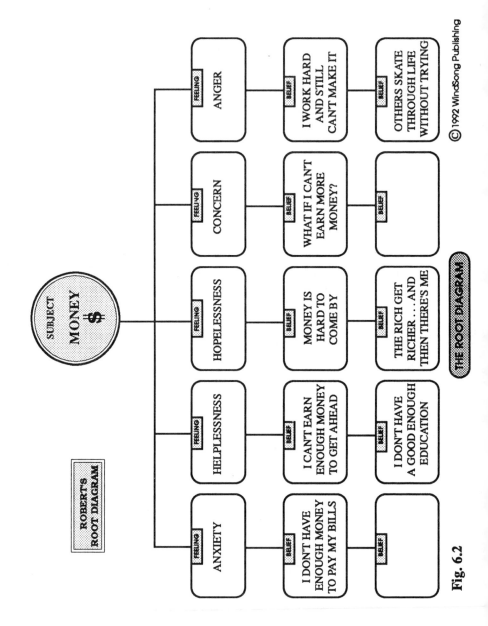

ROBERT'S ROOT DIAGRAM

SUBJECT
MONEY
$

FEELING: ANXIETY
BELIEF: I DON'T HAVE ENOUGH MONEY TO PAY MY BILLS
BELIEF:

FEELING: HELPLESSNESS
BELIEF: I CAN'T EARN ENOUGH MONEY TO GET AHEAD
BELIEF: I DON'T HAVE A GOOD ENOUGH EDUCATION

FEELING: HOPELESSNESS
BELIEF: MONEY IS HARD TO COME BY
BELIEF: THE RICH GET RICHER . . . AND THEN THERE'S ME

FEELING: CONCERN
BELIEF: WHAT IF I CAN'T EARN MORE MONEY?
BELIEF:

FEELING: ANGER
BELIEF: I WORK HARD AND STILL CAN'T MAKE IT
BELIEF: OTHERS SKATE THROUGH LIFE WITHOUT TRYING

THE ROOT DIAGRAM

© 1992 WindSong Publishing

Fig. 6.2

You'll develop your own belief-identifying techniques as you progress in your understanding of them. However, here is another one to add to your tool kit right now that, according to many people, is most helpful. Robert Williams, M.A., owner of Ki-Point Communications, Inc., in Denver, introduced it to us.

The technique, called muscle testing, is the cornerstone of Ki-Point's personal growth program. It's been used for years by various types of health practitioners to determine what their patient's mind can tell them about their body. Rob has taken it a step further by wrapping it into a system for uncovering beliefs. It's like having your own built-in personal belief detector.

Muscle biofeedback, or muscle testing, is a simple and effective way to communicate with the mind using the muscles of the body. It relies on electrical impulses sent from the brain to the body. The unconscious mind can strengthen or weaken these signals, creating a yes/no communication system. While it doesn't work for everyone, it's effective for many.

Get a partner and give it a try. Start by muscle testing your partner. Stand facing her. She will choose which arm she wants to use. Position yourself in front of that arm instead of directly in front of her body. Have your partner extend her arm shoulder high and perpendicular to her side, parallel with the floor. You then place one hand on the shoulder of her opposite arm, and three or four fingers of your other hand lightly about two or three inches above the wrist of her extended arm (see Fig. 6.3).

Now, have your partner say a true statement, such as her name (i.e., "My name is Sue."). After she makes the statement, push firmly and steadily down on her arm for three or four seconds. Your partner should try to keep her arm from moving downward. She should resist your pressure and try to maintain her arm locked into position, parallel to the floor.

If your partner's arm remains strong during the test, it is said to be switched on. If her arm goes weak and is forced to drop from its right angle toward the body, it's said to be switched off. It's not

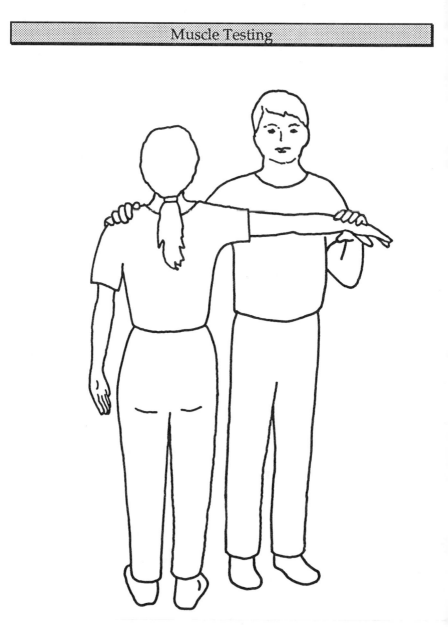

Fig. 6.3

difficult to tell when the arm goes weak, because the shoulder muscle unlocks and the arm starts dropping. If her name really is Sue, her arm should be switched on, or solidly held against your pressure.

This time have your partner say something that clearly isn't true, such as a name of the opposite sex (i.e., "My name is Roger."). Watch how her arm angles down toward her side, dropping just by inches or all the way, becoming switched off.

Now the fun starts. Listed in the Appendix are several pages of beliefs that either impact or support abundance. They're divided into categories: Money, Spiritual/Religious/Life, Self-Worth, Job/Career, Relationships and Health. Tuck yourself away with your partner for an afternoon or evening. Pick your areas of choice and muscle test each statement for a switched on or off response. Be sure to test yourselves in both the limiting beliefs and positive beliefs categories. As you determine your agreement (switched on) or disagreement (switched off) to each statement, mark the response with a notation in front of the belief.

Testing the Door of Our Beliefs

When you're through, you'll have a much deeper understanding of what you really believe about certain areas in your life. I suspect you'll be floored by some of your responses. After all, you really do believe you deserve lots of money, don't you? You're sure you're easy to love, right? You always knew you could be successful, correct? Maybe.

We have a lot of fun with muscle testing in our seminars. It brings laughter, disbelief, poignancy. Jake, an eighty-year-old friend of ours, has the body and outlook of a person decades younger. It wasn't surprising, but it was touching, when he switched on to, "I am a young man," and switched off to, "I am an old man."

Another man switched on to, "I am off balance in my life." He wanted to narrow down the statement, so he tried, "I am off balance in my physical life." He switched off (meaning, no, he was not off balance in his physical life). So he tested emotional and mental lives. He switched off to both.

We were somewhat baffled by this seeming dead end until, on impulse, I said, "How about your spiritual life?" Sure enough, he switched on. After thinking about it for a moment, he said he'd been feeling as though something was missing in his life, and it made complete sense that it was spiritual in nature.

One woman, a Christian, switched off to, "God loves and supports me." She almost shouted, "But I do believe God loves me!" So we broke the statement down to, "God loves me," and she switched on. But when tested for, "God supports me," she switched off. Her eyes glistening with tears, she told of several serious health problems she'd endured for a year, a financial crisis brewing and the possibility of losing her job. She sighed and said, "I understand God supports me. I just don't *feel* it."

Charles Hauck, award-winning Los Angeles educational television producer and worldwide lecturer on personal growth and metaphysics, tells this true story. Hundreds of people were trapped in a theater when a fire broke out. On one exit door was a sign reading, "This door is locked at all times." No one tried the door, so strong was their belief in the sign. As a result, many died who otherwise would have broken free, because the door was always unlocked.

The story is a telling metaphor for the usual way we handle our beliefs. We never test the door, so completely do we believe the belief. We don't question, we don't probe, we don't seek to uncover the reality behind the physical sign. We take other's words as truth, not trusting ourselves enough to thrust open the door and leap to freedom.

But by understanding that life has behind it a structure designed by the universe in response to our beliefs, we can then dismantle its outward construction and determine its internal building blocks. By knowing we live in a world of meaning, we can find, and change if we choose to, just what makes us tick. And what we learn along the way is worth millions...perhaps literally.

7

Training is everything. The peach was once a bitter almond; cauliflower is nothing but cabbage with a college education.

– Mark Twain

Phoenix Rising

The decision to change my life was born in a conference room in the Orient about six months after I started studying metaphysics. Part of my responsibility at Apple was to help find a company somewhere in the world that could meet price/performance specifications for a potential new printer. We needed a manufacturer that could supply us with a precisely engineered product in huge quantities at a very low price, quickly. Enter Japan.

After months of data gathering, bid requests, visits to every serious contender, we entered final negotiations with the most probable company. Because of the size of the contract about to be placed on this lucky firm's bottom line, they lavished us with perks on our visits. Our introduction to foods, inns and scenery seldom experienced by non-Japanese left me awed.

So there I am, at a conference table outside Tokyo with maybe fifteen people, some from Apple, most not. We've been in negotiations for days, hammering out detail after detail, and I'm immersed in what I'm doing. Later I told Stan, in rather nonpoetic language, it was as though time stood still while someone dumped a bucket of cold water over my head. I opened my eyes and they were clear. Questions—like in, "What the heck am I doing here?"— filled me. I felt a swell of detachment rise toward these people, American and Japanese alike. In a split second, my eyes no longer mirrored their career goals. An internal spring had sprung, catapulting me far beyond the path I was used to traveling.

The Crooked Path

The problem was the new path was a ghost image, not clearly defined. I had never actively thought of leaving the computer industry—although no such dramatic realization would have occurred unless I'd sustained a strong desire on some level of consciousness—so I had no alternate plan in mind. I just knew I had to get out, and hoped like the devil I knew what I was doing.

Of course, I was as green as an Oregon spring when it came to conscious creation. I not only carried deep misgivings about the validity of the process, I harbored doubts about my abilities to feel, hear and interface with the forces that make it possible. I knew of no one who could advise me, answer my interminable questions, soothe my uncertainty into neutrality at least, faith at best.

At first I didn't understand a thing about finding and changing beliefs, so I just started visualizing. I was already meditating, and I kept that up, asking for guidance on how to proceed. I don't remember receiving much insight, but given the state of my overall doubts, it's a wonder I heard anything at all. Real life intruded into my visualization schedule, throwing me off somewhat, but basically I tried to do it every day. I didn't know how long I should continue the moving pictures, so after a couple of months I tapered off.

As the years wore on, I constantly re-addressed visualization, pulling it from the mothballs of my mind and creating new scenarios to project. Perhaps a year after I started, I took the plunge into finding beliefs. My efforts were limited since I really didn't know what I was looking for, or if I found it. For some time I tried self-hypnosis, then subliminal programming. I did some past life regression and worked with the tarot deck, seeking answers and direction. Haphazard, at best, were my overall attempts the first couple of years.

What I started in 1984 finally manifested into reality in 1989. I have no doubt that had I known what I was doing, and what to expect, I could have cut the time frame down considerably. Things actually started moving rather quickly once I set my goal, but I didn't recognize the events as progress toward the end.

At the End of the Rainbow

After several months of visualizing, a start-up company in Irvine, California, offered me a job as vice president of sales and marketing. Part of my compensation package was to be a hefty amount of stock. I'd already been a director for two start-ups that went nose-down, and the stock I'd received could paper the bathroom wall. All in all, it seemed like a losing deal, but, since I wanted to move back to Southern California from the north, I accepted this immediate vehicle. Started on a shoestring, I figured the company had maybe a year to survive. That would give me enough time to re-initiate my Southern California contacts and circulate my resume.

While I continued to focus on freedom, I now added making the company successful to my list of visualizations. Not that I thought for one minute it was the vehicle to wealth. I just wanted to do all I could to add to its chances of modest success. We hung on through the first year and showed a significant profit the second. My income increased substantially. The president was hungry for venture capital, which we desperately needed, but no one was hungry for us. Then one day Stan brought a business associate in to meet the president, and he suggested we try to go public. Stan and he eventually introduced the president to the man who would make it happen.

Going public almost seemed like a joke. Who would possibly want to buy our stock? By now, we were moving significant amounts of product and making a name for ourselves, but by industry standards we were small potatoes indeed. Then the catalyst occurred that made it possible: We landed Microsoft as our first big-name account. The rainbow was firmly ensconced in the heavens of profitability from that announcement on. We grew, we prospered, we went public. Two years later, when my contract finally allowed me to sell my stock, I left the industry, a free woman at last.

The Universe: The Ultimate Logistics Manager

From the moment we set our goal and start the conscious creation process, the universe begins gathering the pieces to make it happen. Much of my doubting was because I couldn't see the picture developing as I assumed it would. It was three years before I realized this company could become my ticket to somewhere else.

As soon as I left Apple, Stan and I had begun focusing on buying our own business. We spent countless hours in search for and negotiations with numerous firms, never solidifying a deal. Because we assumed this was the path to the projected future, it felt like tough breaks.

That's not to say we couldn't have turned our own company into the realization of our wealth goal, but our beliefs would have had to be in alignment with that vehicle. It may have been easier for the universe to create within the structure of my career, since I felt strongly about my professional abilities.

However, it wasn't the only way for my desire to reach fruition. If I'd resigned from the company two years after joining, the universe would have shifted gears and produced other opportunities. My desire would have been fulfilled, no matter what, unless I did not change my beliefs enough to allow it.

My doubting, indicative of conflicting beliefs and not understanding the conscious creation process, made the realization of my goal drag on and on. Possibly, if I'd had more faith, I would have left the company at the end of a year or two and walked into a sweet deal worth twice the money. Or, if I hadn't changed my beliefs around my right to money, perhaps I would have left for another job, only to watch my old friends go public without me.

It's obvious we can't chart the map to our goal, but we can rest assured there is one, however hidden it seems. My advice to you who choose to try conscious creation is get your beliefs clear, visualize what you want, and keep the faith. Seth says:

> Faith in a creative, fulfilling, desired end–sustained faith–literally draws from (the universe) all of the necessary ingredients, all of the elements however staggering in number, all of the details, and then inserts into (physical life) the impulses, dreams, chance meetings, motivations, or whatever is necessary so that the desired end then falls into place as a completed pattern.[1]

The universe is well equipped to handle your wish. Get out of its way and let it.

The Conscious Creation Process

Techniques and methods reflect our belief that nature doesn't work right on its own. But until we feel comfortable just telling a belief to vaporize out of our life, and believing it will, and stating our desire to the universe once and knowing it's taken care of, it's best we build up our confidence through mechanical, practical plans and programs. Our goal, though, should be to eventually reach that place in the sun where everything happens easily, because our faith is so strong in a supportive universe and we accept the creation process with no reservations. But until then, there's work to do.

• *Setting Goals; Clarifying Desires and Choices*

Fail to plan, plan to fail. I don't know where I heard that, but it's true. If you don't set objectives and directions for your life, where do you think you'll end up going? Nowhere, most likely. The universe builds events out of our desires. However, desires have to be specified so it knows what we want. Otherwise we manifest confusion or boredom. But whatever it is we create, we feel as though life is controlling us instead of us having a hand in its development.

You've seen people muddle through life, maybe bouncing from job to job or relationship to relationship, but not progressing in thought, word or deed. They live their lives in neutral, and usually die before reaching first gear. If it's their conscious choice to do so, that's one thing. But if it's because they don't know how to set their focus, then it's a shame.

At times, life is monotonous even when we're at our most bustling. The job can be busy, but a bore. Our home can take all our extra effort, but be suffocating beyond belief. We feel we're going through life half asleep. What we need is a strong dose of possibilities. Options make life stimulating. What talents and interests do you have? What intrigues you? What would you rather be doing in your work life? What would you rather be doing *instead* of your work life?

Look into all corners of your life for dissatisfaction. How are you doing spiritually, physically, emotionally, mentally, financially? Write down what you want out of each category and see how close a fit you experience to that desire today. Where there are discrepancies, make lists of comparisons between what you have/are today, and what you'd rather have/be tomorrow. Get a clear sense of how far off base reality is from your dream.

Setting goals by definition focuses on the result desired, not the presently perceived problem or lack. Therefore, by its very nature, it's a statement in the now as to what you expect from your future. It begins the creation process. Clarify your goals as much as possible, keeping in mind that as the days progress they can change character. Don't become so structured that you refuse to allow for new considerations.

Write down what you want to accomplish, both short term and long term, and keep it handy as a reminder throughout the days and weeks. I keep four levels of goals written in a workbook and active in my mind. The first are the ones I want to accomplish within a few weeks, the second in maybe six months. The third I extend out to a year or thereabouts, and the fourth are my long range desires. This last group many times has to do with personal growth or spiritual issues I want to develop.

I keep my workbook close by so when I go into meditation, I have it handy. Then, while preliminarily quieting down, I peruse my list and choose the goal(s) I want to work on that day. The overall picture of my selectively defined future is never far from my thinking. My objective is to give it life through thought, desire and action.

Keep your goals reasonable, at least until you experience how the universe works. For instance, don't put your desire to double your salary on the quick list. Not that it couldn't happen, but you probably have some limiting belief-work to do first, and if you don't make your goal in three months, will you think the process doesn't work? Will you lose hope and start doubting? It's not worth it. You don't want to blow a whole lifetime of possibility through misperception. Make it a longer range goal and immediately start acquainting the universe with your desire.

Another slice of reasonable says if you've never played the piano and have no apparent musical talent, don't expect to become this century's version of Beethoven. Stay within reason, because it gets down to probabilities. At any point in time, we're surrounded by every probability that can happen to us. However, the ones most likely to enter physicality are the ones that match today's belief system. We have already established a body of raw material for future entries, so it would be quite improbable that we could insert a radical new line of desire into the hopper and have it develop quickly.

It's highly unlikely, for instance, that I will convert to Catholicism this year. It's never been a thought in my mind, and my belief system would have to undergo massive changes to lead me in that direction. It's quite possible, though, that I could write another book. While I have no plans to do so, I've entertained a low level thought for some time.

In your case, you may want a new job. If you desire it in your present field of endeavor or one you're educated or trained in, it may happen relatively quickly. If you want to completely remove yourself from your present work—and earn a higher income—it could take more desire and more time. Not *would*, but *could*.

• *Releasing Limiting Beliefs*

As I mentioned in chapter 6, there are two ways to approach your goal. One is to rush on in, not do any belief search or elimination in advance. The other is to clear as many limiting beliefs out of the way as possible as you start. With Way One, you'll definitely meet whatever stumbling blocks are now on your path. There's no choice. They're there, just as real and solid as natural rock. If you choose to vaporize them before you start, God in heaven will bless you with fewer mountains to climb and a pair of Bierkenstocks for your journey.

It's important not to become discouraged if you seem to lose ground as you strive toward your goal. While you'll clear away some of the beliefs causing the problem up front, chances are you won't get them all. You may end up with a set of conflicting beliefs in play. One pushes you forward into your new life; the other reminds you of whence you came, and tries to keep you there.

Take the conflict that arises as feedback. Treat it as valuable. It's giving you the opportunity to see what's hampering your way, in living color, in real-life symbols. You will now know how to get on with getting on. Try your best not to reinforce the depression that meets your slippage. It will only add new life to the old beliefs.

Theoretically, you've now found the restricting, hampering beliefs around your goal. You either used the suggestions in the last chapter or you used other methods. You made a list of these beliefs. Now it's time to release them and insert ones you'd rather experience. Although beliefs can be handled in your usual state of awareness, it's much more powerful to go into an altered state and use imagination to remove them. Seth says:

> Imagination...plays an important part in your subjective life, as it gives mobility to your beliefs. It is one of the motivating agencies that helps transform your beliefs into physical experience. It is vital therefore that you understand the interrelationship between ideas and imagination. In order to dislodge unsuitable beliefs and establish new ones, you must learn to use your imagination to move concepts in and out of your mind. The proper use of imagination can then propel ideas in the direction you desire.[2]

Here's my favorite belief-removal visualization: Picture yourself on a plateau that extends as far as the eye can see. This is your Plain of Purpose, or life's expanse. There are trees and flowers scattered about, but none are tall enough to obstruct your view of the large pillars dotting the landscape. These pillars are your limiting beliefs. You know they are your creation, solidified into stone when you wrapped emotion around a thought so strongly that it became real to you. You gave them life through your power, and now it's time to bring that power back into your energy field.

Walk up to the first pillar. See it in whatever color you choose. I use green for financial beliefs, flesh color for weight, white if nothing else fits. Ask the pillar what belief it represents. Have it repeat to you one belief from your list. Tell it you realize it was your energy that created it, and now you want your energy back. Thank it for becoming exactly what you had requested, but tell it that it no longer fits your lifestyle.

Now extend your hand toward the pillar and see a beam of light reach from your fingertips to the pillar. As you tell the pillar to vaporize, see the light glow strongly. Say, "Vaporize!" with strength and power in your imagining voice. Have the pillar instantly turn into a cloud of shimmering energy above the spot where it once stood.

Now open your solar plexus and bring the energy into your body through that opening. As it streams in, feel yourself growing larger, your energy boundaries expanding with this new addition. Sense your new power, see it as a glow in and around you. See it pulsate and, as it does, bask in the sureness of your creative abilities.

Before you take the energy in through your solar plexus, though, set a bit aside, hanging it in the air near you, formed into a small twinkling ball. (You'll use this ball at the end of your visualization.)

Look at the spot where the pillar used to stand and see a flower or tree grow. This represents a new belief that is opposite the de-energized one. Send it energy from your fingertips. Watch the colors deepen. Know it will flourish in this fertile environment. Now move on to the next pillar and repeat the process, making sure to add some energy from each vaporized column to the twinkling ball hanging near you.

When you're finished with your pillars (you may choose to work on only three or four in a session as they can become time consuming), pluck the twinkling ball from the air and hold it in your hands. Turn and face the "you" sitting or lying in your altered state. Create an edge you can lean over, and gently drop the ball on "your" head. Then the you on the Plain of Purpose should disappear.

Now, "you" see that twinkling ball of energy break into a million shining pieces and float down over your body as you sit in your altered state. It's magic, this energy. It magnifies the power within you and brings an awareness with it that you are indeed the creator of your life.

I use variations to this scenario, sometimes grouping the beliefs together and vaporizing them in one burst of energy. Other times I burn the pillars to release the energy trapped in them. I do whatever feels right at the time.

How many times do you have to do this exercise with the same beliefs until they're altered? I don't know. Sometimes it works the first time. Other times, it may have to be repeated. When I start on a new round of beliefs, I often do the visualization for five to ten days, morning and night if possible.

If you like ritual, try this. Before you do your first visualization, take a piece of clear glass, about a foot long and eight inches tall (or whatever size you have available). You'll also need a marking pen in any color you choose. I try to use a color that matches the pillars I intend to vaporize, but it's not necessary.

Go into an altered state and ask to see or feel the structure of the energy that is blocking you from your goal. Then just start drawing on the glass, slowly. When you're through, take a hammer and make a little ritual out of breaking the glass as a symbol that you're loosening the energy of the beliefs.

I take my glass out to the sandy beach in front of our house and sit on a piece of driftwood. I put a newspaper down first, then prop the glass up on another piece of wood so it's standing upright on the paper. Then I go into an altered state, feel the energy trapped on my glass—and smash it to smithereens!

After your five to ten days of belief-work are up, take another piece of glass. Ask to see any wisps of limiting energy in your belief structure that are still hanging around. Do the same thing as above, knowing you've ended your program by cutting all ties to the past's unnecessary beliefs.

Another ritual I use is to write my limiting beliefs on small scraps of paper and fold them in two. Then, back out to the beach I go and into an altered state. I take each slip of paper individually, read the belief on it, think about its implications in my life, dwell on what I really want to have instead, and then I burn it. As the smoke rises, I see it as the energy of the belief breaking free to recreate itself in a more helpful form.

Remember, energy is either materialized or not materialized. It only has two states. It's up to us to mold it into the state we choose, and we can only do the molding in consciousness.

• *Reinforcing Limitless Beliefs*

So, back into consciousness we go to insert beliefs we'd rather experience. But, of course, we *are* consciousness, so we don't have to travel very far to start our work. In fact, sometimes a belief will change automatically to its positive side once it's identified as limiting. At times it does a pirouette and turns into a lovely ballerina, light on its feet and gracious of movement, without any help from us. But if we're unsure the transformation took place, we need a fallback strategy.

Suggestion applied in either a conscious or altered state is a tool worth checking out. Remember once again that the now is the only time there is, and that thought is the selector of our probabilities. So, what we think now helps build our castle in the sky. Say over and over to yourself whatever it is you want to experience in your future, and say it as though it's in your present. Do it while in an altered state, like meditation, and in normal everyday wide-awake consciousness.

I am a clear channel for love. I am healthy and free of disease, a natural soul in a friendly universe. I am worthy of respect and friendship. I am a good money manager. I am free to be me, however I choose to define myself. I am a good public speaker, full of confidence and quick of wit. I said, at least a thousand times, "I'm wealthy and free, I'm wealthy and free, wealth is energy materialized by me."

Some people tack their desired beliefs up on the wall by their desk; some write them on the bathroom mirror. Because Stan spent an inordinate amount of time in his car when we worked in California, he stuck little colored arrows on the visors and rear-view mirror. Each colored arrow represented a belief he wished to cultivate, and his developing belief would jump into his mind when he noticed his arrows.

In my case, I wore out a few tapes of "Chariots of Fire" by running them incessantly on my way to and from work, repeating short jingles I'd crafted that flowed with the music. Whatever process you design for yourself, give it a chance to happen. Keep at your suggestions for weeks, or months, if necessary. When you really feel it inside, or you see the results in your life, you'll know you can slack off.

• *Visualizing Goals*

While the belief-work described above clears the path to our goal and fosters the growth of newly chosen beliefs, most of the building of the to-be-experienced event is done with goal-focused visualization.

Visualization cannot be underrated. It's the most powerful creating tool we have available. Seth says:

To act in an independent manner, you must begin to initiate action that you want to occur physically by creating it in your own being. This is done by combining belief, emotion and imagination, and forming them into a mental picture of the desired physical result. Of course, the wanted result is not yet physical or you would not need to create it, so it does no good to say your physical experience seems to contradict what you are trying to do.[3]

The true power is in the imagination which dares to speculate upon that which is not yet. The imagination, backed by great expectation, can bring about almost any reality within the range of probabilities.[4]

Imagination and emotions are the most concentrated forms of energy that you possess as physical creatures. Any strong emotion carries within it far more energy than, say, that required to send a rocket to the moon.[5]

Imagination is important; intensity of imagination is critical. I refer you to further Seth quotes:

> Form is the result of concentrated energy, the pattern for it caused by vividly directed emotional or psychic idea images. The intensity is all important.[6]

> The intensity of a feeling or thought or mental image is, therefore, the important element in determining its subsequent physical materialization. The intensity is the core about which the electromagnetic energy (EE) units form. In your terms, the more intense the core, the sooner the physical materialization.[7]

Just thinking about what we want doesn't create it as fast as with a healthy dash of emotion sprinkled over it. It's harder to generate great feelings of desire and joy while sitting in our bedroom with eyes focused on the familiar. However, in visualization, we can tap great veins of emotion that can then wash over our imagery. This is not to say simply thinking about our goal is nonproductive. It's a different tool, one that solidifies our desire, but doesn't fuel it.

It's your choice whether you start the goal-focused visualization before, during or after you've done your belief-work. I tend to start it as soon as I've identified my goal, prior to the belief-work phase, and continue right up to its actualization in the physical. You can't put too much energy behind your desire. The more the better. You'll find your own pace and formula with experience.

How specific should you get in your visualizations? That depends on how defined your goal is. For instance, if there's a job opening in your company and you want it, picture yourself shaking hands with whoever would tell you the good news, see yourself being congratulated by other employees, telephone your spouse or a friend with great excitement in your voice and animation in your gestures.

If your goal must be built from scratch, like meeting someone new to love, see yourself watching a sunset, heart filled with wonder at this development in your life—a new love. Visualize making dinner reservations at a cozy restaurant, and picture yourself seated at a candlelit table, reaching out to touch the hand of a loved one (a somewhat blurred outline of a person, but one obviously emanating affection back to you). Feel the joy of love, the soaring of your heart, the tears such happiness brings to your eyes.

A neighbor woman, newly retired from teaching, wanted to keep up contact with people, maybe make a little money, but she didn't want to part-time teach. She chose to visualize the feelings of good conversations, sharing stories and laughter with people in no particular setting with no particular structure, but seeing a paycheck being handed to her. She eventually got a part-time job as a small town community affairs manager.

When I was working on wealth, my visualizations changed over the years. Part of the first one had me standing on a cliff overlooking the ocean. I had an array of helium-filled balloons in each hand. One set was pink, with "Freedom!" on the balloons. The other group was green, with "Money!" written across their sides. After generating intense feelings of excitement and joy at completion of my goal, I let the balloons loose. They floated into the heavens, telling the world and the universe my desire.

Later, after our company went public, I visualized a tall ruler with money amounts painted up its sides. As in the carnival game, I saw myself swing a sledge hammer at the base of the ruler, and watch as a bright ball soared heavenward, slamming into a noisy gong, signifying I'd hit the jackpot. Then, as always in visualizations, I permeated the scene with laughter, joy, feelings of success.

But whatever moving picture you use, here are a couple of good wrap-up scenes. See your goal as one of numerous probabilities surrounding you. Then visualize it coming closer than the others, taking form and clarity. See the rest of the probabilities being pushed to the back and sides, and your goal becoming the obvious dominant image, finally sitting right in front of you, the next event on your path to the future.

Another is a wrap-up visualization showing two paths. One is what you don't want to experience any more, and the other is your desired goal. From where you stand, both are straight ahead on your future path, but one veers off slightly to the right and one to the left. Light up the scene that you don't want to meet; feel the anxiety, sadness and despair emanate from it. Then draw a huge black X through it and dim the lights. Now turn to your desire and light the stage. Generate a wide array of wonderful feelings toward the scene, let the scene become alive within you. Then see yourself walk into it, knowing that this marvelous play is your near future.

There are two basic reasons for trying to create an event: one is to get yourself into a situation you'd like to experience, the other is to get yourself out of one you'd rather pass on. The fun ones to work on are the former; the pressured ones the latter.

High on my list of happy events we've created was finding our house on the Columbia River. This event of creation was Stan's baby. He kept very clear about what we wanted, and he made it happen. We lived in Oregon and were looking for a piece of property on water in Washington. We stumbled onto the house one weekend while touring Washington for the second time in search of our dream. We saw a for-sale-by-owner sign and pulled into the driveway. Before Stan even opened the car door, he said, "This is it."

Another type of future event, already a possibility on the horizon and laden with potential unpleasantness, can be softened before it enters reality. I call it mitigating the future circumstances. For instance, one year I worked on lowering my tax bill, which I knew was going to be hefty. To my creative drawing board I went, looking at all kinds of beliefs, many reflected in my feelings toward the Internal Revenue Service. Then I did what I could to release them.

Next, I started my visualizations. I pictured myself in my tax accountant's office, sitting there while he rolled the numbers down to the bottom line. What excitement, what happiness I felt when he told me how surprised he was at the final bill! I saw myself spring up, pump his hand, leave his office and jump and shout for joy in the hallway. Next scene: I run into our house, throw myself into Stan's arms as we both laugh with pleasure.

What happened was close. About half way through the tax process, my accountant had a completely legal bright idea that gave me the break I needed. When I left his office and entered the hall, I did jump for joy—but quietly. Stan and I then went out to dinner to celebrate.

Hope springs eternal in us, and thank goodness. Without hope we would never test the waters of our creativity with conscious creation. The problem with hope, though, is that we can mistake it for strong possibility. We think that an outside, remote probability can be repainted as fact because we diligently apply all our desire and visualization know-how to it. The universe works in mysterious ways, but that doesn't usually include slam-dunking us through unrealistic hope into the land of materialized events.

Once when I had a piece of metaphysical philosophy I wanted published, I chose the publisher with care. In fact, I narrowed the field down to the only one I would consider. I chose that particular company because I had met its founder, I liked her enormously and thought we were on the same wavelength metaphysically. I felt very comfortable approaching the company, as though I was re-initiating contact with old friends. So off my work went, and I started visualizing the outcome.

As the days turned into weeks, I started getting uneasy. I was reading more of what this company publishes and the realization dawned that we actually had quite a chasm of difference between our philosophies. Would this great divide cause a conflict? No problem, I told myself. I'll handle it after my work is accepted...and on I went with my strong focus of visualization. Suffice it to say I was back out searching for a publisher several weeks later.

Visualization is powerful, mighty, potent. But it's not miraculous and it's not a cure-all. It's a tool that can bridge our desire to another's, *if both sides are amenable to the outcome.* The lesson I personally learned: Don't limit my success by forcing the universe to try to make a winner out of a loser. Stay clear on the goal—like, get the darn thing published—and forget the extraneous stuff. Because of the limits I placed on the number of probabilities I allowed the universe to deal in, the conclusion snagged. The universe could have served me better, and more quickly, had I but given it a veritable potpourri of potential publishers to work its magic on. Then up from the sea of probabilities would have come the answer to my desire, in a time frame I found more acceptable.

• *Putting Power Behind Desire*

All creativity springs from desire. To try to eliminate it is the most foolish of acts. To flow with our desire, to ride the thrust of our lives brings us in parallel with the vaster desire and power that created us. It activates us on levels we don't comprehend in conscious awareness.

Your strong desire becomes your probable future. Do everything you can to keep desire burning in your heart for whatever it is you want to accomplish, be or have. Constantly dwell on what you want out of life. Act the part. Objectify it in the outside world by doing something to say you have it. If you're broke, buy the more expensive loaf of bread. If you're ill, get dressed and comb your hair, take a walk outside if possible.

If you want to be an executive, walk into the biggest, most ostentatious office building you can find. Stroll the halls, picturing yourself arriving for work, opening the carved door at the end of the corridor, and entering your private office. If you want a beautiful home, drive to the part of town you want to live in. See yourself sitting on the lawn of your choice, sipping tea and enjoying the view.

If you feel silly with this play-acting, remember that you are consciousness, and consciousness creates from its center in the now based on what it thinks, feels and believes right at this moment. By initiating a course of action in the present, you automatically reinforce a belief that change is possible.

Action is thought in motion, physically perceived. So, seek out new methods of meditation and visualization. Rent or buy video tapes that give you suggestions of a metaphysical nature. Think up your own programs for eliminating beliefs. Find new metaphysical books to read if your beliefs in conscious creation start lagging. Focus on changing.

Read. Read everything you can get your hands on that reinforces what you're trying to make happen, or books that remind you that you can do it. If you want to travel, buy books on your country of choice. If you want to make it big in the stock market, read financial magazines, books on the market, various newsletters published by experts. Do you want to start a career as a watchmaker? Go to the library and dig in for the afternoon, studying and dreaming.

At times choose small, uncomplicated things to create, just so you can see immediate results, and thus reinforce the belief that you can indeed manifest what you want. Parking places are always good for starters. How about finding the perfect piece of jewelry to go with the new dress? Maybe a great restaurant in an unknown town? A vacant seat next to you in a semi-crowded airplane?

One time Stan and I were hurrying to catch a ferry that runs from Washington to the Oregon side of the Columbia River. We not only visualized making it on time, but we saw a space for our car once we arrived. We got to the dock just in time and were assigned the last available spot.

When we focus on an intention or goal, imagining that it is already so, the inner self gets set to achieve that goal in ways that the conscious mind can't plan or understand. Great power is brought to bear on our desire.

Don't let a day go by without thinking about what you want. Bring it into your thoughts at home, work, in the car, at the beach. Think how it will feel to have it, where you'll be when it arrives, how it will look, how you'll smile with pleasure. When you see something that reminds you of your goal, study it, wonder about it, live it.

Basically, make it as easy as possible for your inner self to fulfill your desire. Give it every break you can. Help it along by play-acting your new part so convincingly that you create more of the raw material of desire for it to work with. It will see your focus more clearly, ambiguities will disappear, the path will crystallize. You'll get exactly what you will allow to happen.

Now go back to chapter 2 and review the section on faith. You may need it.

8

Corn, Shrimp and Watermelon

Each moment rests on a rich bed of probabilities. We weave in and out of probabilities constantly, selecting this one or that one as we move through the moment into the next. We choose the ones that match our overall purposes, desires and intents, and they become the official version of our life. We have a bank of probable abilities and characteristics that we can develop; we have potential unlimited just waiting our nod of acknowledgment.

We also have failure, depression, chronic illness, hatred, victimization and other nasty things we can pull into our lives instead. We reside in an environment that offers complete freedom of creative expression. If we are prisoners, it is a prison of our own mental construction.

Replaying the Habits of Emotion

Since you've already heard a hundred times that beliefs determine the selection of which probability we'll experience, I'll skip mentioning it. But I will talk about a very powerful force in human life, powerful because it carries within it great potential for probability-selection, and because its magic usually goes unnoticed as a creative force. It's called emotion and it behooves us to understand and manage it, because it will drop us onto a new probability line faster than a blink.

Beliefs generate feelings by triggering our brain to send the emotion we associate with the belief to our body. After consistently responding the same way to a belief, the emotion that's generated becomes firmly ensconced in our neurological patterning. We react to it just as surely as would Pavlov's dogs. Feelings become habit when replayed enough times. Whether they empower or distress depends on what associations the belief generates in our mind.

Some of us are stuck in a groove of limiting beliefs. They're ingrained into our days, not even recognized because they have become habits of thought. But from habits of thought rise habits of emotion, and emotions accelerate the creation process.

Ask what started the feeling way back when and many can't tell you; the original cause has been slip covered and stored in the attic of the past. The genesis of the feeling isn't important, though. The beliefs underlying it have probably changed faces over the years, anyway, until today's version barely recognizes its ancient ancestors. But for us, the emotion persists. Worry casts its shadow throughout our days, or uncertainty swamps us at the oddest times. Perhaps a generalized fear of the future waves over us, or caution dogs our footsteps. Whatever it is, it needs to be addressed, for it has great creative power which, by default, kicks in every time the feeling rushes our psyche. I know. I speak from depressing experience.

Breaking the Bonds that Bind

Corn, shrimp and watermelon. Who would have thought those four words would finally break me free of the bindings of financial anxiety, which of course had beliefs underlying it. I had worked on financial stuff for years; it seemed to stick to me like flypaper, no matter how many beliefs I uncovered and changed. I got so sick of looking at my thoughts in that area that I just wanted to bury my head under a pillow and cry it away. That doesn't work; I had to find a different approach.

Actually, Stan found it for me. He had been studying the process of change with a critical eye for some time. My eternal battle with money worries, concerns I couldn't seem to shake no matter how well padded my bank account, particularly struck him. He took a look around at friends studying, and then applying, the conscious creation process and wondered. He wondered why the seemingly deeper seated issues within some of us are more difficult to alter. He watched people with health problems, some with relationship woes, others with destructive behaviors try to cut the restrictive bands of emotion that kept them firmly rooted under the ceiling of limitation.

One of the first things he noticed was that there seemed to be stronger, more consistently generated feelings in these areas. Next he realized that where people had already altered their lives through conscious creation, the old, negative emotions were no longer evident. Instead, there seemed to be a general sense of acceptance, like the battle was won and all was right in that little part of their world. In other words, they had changed their emotional state toward that issue.

In my case, my money anxiety budded when I was a little kid; I had years of experience at keeping it alive and flourishing. It was effectively knotted and bound to my belief that sudden loss could occur momentarily, tearing my life asunder. So ingrained was the emotion that the usual conscious creation process didn't budge it. Sure, I still created financial comfort around it, or in spite of it. But its presence in my belief system led me on a financial roller coaster ride I could do without, thank you very much.

What usually happens in conscious creation is that by setting goals, identifying and releasing beliefs, and visualizing what we'd rather experience, we alter the past limiting associations around our area of choice. Where we saw ourselves a failure, perhaps, we now believe we're success personified; where we described ourselves as illness prone, we now feel we control our body. We've changed a negative to a positive by setting a new expanded course of thinking. It seems at times, though, we must turn our power spotlight onto our emotions and hit the belief by way of a frontal attack on our feelings.

Stan discovered one way to do it by experimenting with breaking the pattern of deep emotional reactions in his own life. He started out by making a list of his limiting beliefs, the ones that caused repetitive downers. Then he made another list of beliefs, this time empowering ones he wanted fully ingrained into his brain and neurological system. Next, he made yet more lists, one detailing what would happen to his life if he *didn't* blast the ceiling off his potential, and another listing what wonderful probabilities would transpire in his life if he *did*.

Finally, he spent time reviewing his lists...and let his emotions flow. He made himself feel absolutely lousy when he thought about where he *wouldn't* go in life if he didn't address his limits, and he soared to new heights of excitement when he conjured up what his life would become, if only he changed. Finally, he took his list of great, empowering beliefs and built "future pictures" around them, scenes he wanted to walk into. He assigned a trigger phrase to each image, that, once thought or said, brought the future picture into his mind. Now he was ready to smash the old pattern when it reared its unforgiving head.

He felt he could soften the habit of the emotion first, though, by reacting in an off-the-wall manner when it arose. So, he did some silly thing, like making extraordinary faces and waving his hands when he felt the first stirrings of the negative feeling. Or he lightly smacked his cheek. Sometimes he broke into a pre-chosen song. At times he danced around the room. Then, when the old pattern was smashed immediately upon feeling it, he followed up with a one-two-punch: He thought of his trigger word and automatically pulled in his future picture, laden with pleasurable emotion.

Replacing Fear with Freedom

Stan's results pleased him, so now it was my turn. I tinkered around with various future pictures, not really comfortable with my designs, until I remembered this event: One breezy late summer evening, Stan and I had fixed a light dinner of sweet corn-on-the-cob, jumbo shrimp boiled in their shells and juicy watermelon. We ate on our deck, watching waterfowl dunk for fish in the river, listening to the quiet. At one point, our gaze was caught by a bald eagle winging our way from its nest across the water. We talked with expansiveness about our future, what we wanted out of it, where we saw ourselves next year and in five years. We counted our blessings, feeling immensely peaceful and secure. No problem or fear dared enter our sanctuary, suspended as we were in a perfect moment in time and space.

That was it. That was the snapshot of how I wanted to feel—all the time. I remembered the complete freedom from financial anxiety I experienced and the excitement about our future. I clearly knew I didn't want to take that anxiety with me into my new life; in fact, I worried that it would keep us from manifesting it. I had a bright idea. I ran to find Stan. "What does corn, shrimp and watermelon mean to you?" I blurted. "Dinner," he replied.

No help there until I reminded him of that summer evening and the feelings we'd shared. We agreed there was so much pleasure associated with that memory that it might be a useful tool for reprogramming my anxiety into another feeling, one based on freedom from fear and the excitement of a wide open future. So whenever I felt the anxiety rise into my upper chest I broke the emotion with a physical movement (I used the same one repeatedly instead of changing it each time as Stan had done), and then said to myself, "Corn, shrimp and watermelon." Instead of replaying the old tape of the past, I ran the new one of the future.

It helped immensely. What we learned is that if we break the habit of emotion and insert a pleasure-filled thought picture of our future, we have a good shot at finally ridding our life of its presence. We still need to follow the outlined conscious creation process, but now we withdraw this new tool from our bag and put it to work also.

Preselecting Our Future Platform

So far we've been talking about habits of negative emotion, the ones that bubble to the surface throughout our week, inconsistent in intervals but very consistent in appearance. However, all feelings create, not just these heavy-duty sluggers. To paraphrase Seth, form is the result of vividly directed emotion, *any* emotion. Whether its results are positive or limiting depends on the feeling.

On the downside, we may have an illness we keep refueling with our depression and phobic concentration. Or we rage around the office in disgust until we force a creative act, like spilling coffee on our new white shirt...or someone else's. But these are examples of out-of-control or unmanaged emotions. What happens when we *consciously* select our feelings throughout our day, soaking our moments in upbeat, go-for-the-gold emotions, refusing to allow ourselves the comfortable familiarity of negativity? It's obvious. We create happy events, a more fulfilling life, and an existence less cluttered with problems.

The way to override quick-to-ignite negative feelings (anger, frustration, futility, sadness, resentment, loneliness, etc.) is similar to breaking the more formal habits of emotion. Snap yourself back to the present with a pre-assigned physical movement; choose a feeling you'd rather experience (generosity, peace, excitement, happiness, love, forgiveness, etc.); flood your moment with the memory of that feeling.

It helps if you do some homework prior to opening the flood-gates of your desired emotion. Take any feeling you wish to culti-vate and clearly remember a time when it permeated your mo-ment. Think about it deeply for a few minutes, and again several times throughout the day. Store the remembrances in the vestibule of your mind so when you're caught in a bout of negativity, you have only to open the door of your inner home and there it will be, fresh and ready for use.

If you practice the process diligently for awhile, this new technique will become ingrained into your habit patterns. And don't forget to build your Now Power Base, as explained in chap-ter 5, so your strong, positive beliefs by their very nature keep negativity to a minimum.

What exactly are we doing in these little exercises? We're using the now to select our future. We're drenching the immediate moment in marvelous feelings and a clear picture of what we de-sire. We are halting the negative emotions that have been kicking in by habit—and, by default, creating exactly what we don't want to experience. We're teaching ourselves to control our power of thought by breaking the hold of the past. We're managing our emotions so they don't control us. That's all.

Self-Healing with Focused Emotion

Let's take this newly minted, controlled emotional power a step further now, and apply it directly to the conscious creation of special events. Glue emotion to visualization and watch out. You are a dream machine just waiting to produce.

For instance, one time my foot started to throb like a toothache. It became so inflamed I could barely tolerate the pres-sure of a sock, and I certainly couldn't stand on it. Since I seldom use my body to reflect negativity, I had no track record of healing myself through thought. But when I awoke the second morning at

4:00 a.m. in severe, aching discomfort, I knew it was either that or visit a doctor for the first time in many years. Between the constant pain, my desire to avoid doctors at all cost, and concerted focus on learning to alter situations through conscious creation, my motivation to self-heal was great.

Since I knew the cause of the defective foot, I didn't have to do a search and destroy mission on beliefs and attitudes. Just by knowing what had occurred freed me to progress to the next steps: 1) Flood my immediate moment with the feeling of personal creative power, and 2) alter the future foot by seeing it healed in the present.

I worked up excitement by going into meditation and sensing my power as a lower case god, knowing I hold the universe-bestowed gift of creation at my psychic fingertips. Next I visualized white light entering my foot, expanding the blood vessels and allowing blockages to break free and flow out of the affected area. I then filled my foot with amethyst light, seeing it radiate healing energy, bringing the tissue back to its normal healthy state.

Throughout it all, I kept deep emotion flowing, stretching for the feeling of direct interaction with the universe, experiencing my part in the creation process and the power I hold as a soul in physical. I closed the fifteen minute session with the amethyst light still in my foot, secure that it would continue its healing process throughout the day.

I went back to bed for a few hours, got up and did another visualization similar to the first, propping my foot on a hassock to keep the blood from rushing to the battle zone. That afternoon and evening I did it again. After the next morning's visualization, I walked for almost a mile, slow and somewhat cautious due to residual soreness. By evening, after two more visualizations, I walked six miles without a twinge.

My scant stockpile of beliefs supporting the need for medications and doctors probably expedited my self-healing. But it's true for us all that if we address the psychic cause of the hurt, focus our emotions and picture our body in its natural state of health, we can perform our own healing without outside assistance. It's not always easy, but it's possible. With diligence we can get to the bottom of any problem, health or otherwise, and reduce or eliminate its effect in our life.

Taking on Mother Nature

So emotions become a valuable tool in selecting the direction we want our lives to take. On a lesser scale, they can create a quality that may not be future altering, but still very intriguing, suggesting that their use transcends the serious.

I take long walks every day that my schedule allows. My favorite takes me down a small dirt road leading through remote forests and fields about a ten minute drive from our home. It's usually just the animals and me within a several mile radius. Winter and spring in the Northwest are notorious for rain, but while I enjoy wet weather, it's not high on my list of fun to be caught on a dirt road that's quickly turning to mud around my ankles, with three miles of it between my car and me.

About ten minutes down the path one day, the sky became overcast and ominous. As I saw it, I had three choices. I could turn around and head back home; I could continue with my walk, mentally preparing for discomfort; or I could try to consciously hold off the rain. The latter appealed to me, so I took stock of my situation. First, it hadn't yet started raining. That was good psychological news, because for a budding conscious creator it seemed a far more difficult task to stop the rain than hold it in abeyance.

Next, I realized I was in virgin energy territory, so to speak, since no humans were within miles of my epicenter. Therefore, I wouldn't be in conflict with other's thoughts, attitudes or beliefs about whether or not it was going to rain. And finally, I remembered I had my "Chariots of Fire" tape with me, my old standby that could always generate powerful uplifting emotions within me in a matter of seconds. So, I made the decision to take on Mother Nature. I plunked the music tape into my cassette player and walked briskly into the darkening field.

I had no idea of where to start the creation process, so I asked my inner self for guidance. Then I just went with the flow of the music. First I built up my emotions to an unstoppable pitch of joy, awed by my creation ability and the cooperation that flows between the universe, nature and me. Then I felt great energy building over the field, huge and powerful. I took part of that energy and formed it into four giant legs that I stuck into the ground, forming a square with me in its center.

The rest of that massive energy was then molded into an enormous clear glass disc, spinning over the field, honing itself into a solid ceiling that would keep me dry. Finally, I let the glass disc drop onto the four legs, saw the heavens open and dump rain, wetting the countryside everywhere but under the protective covering—which, of course, is where I stood. I played my tape three or four times, going through the same scenario.

It didn't rain on me that day, although it did pour at our house. It didn't rain on me any of the dozen or more times I did it throughout the season, either. Once, it started to lightly sprinkle about an hour after I had erected my glass ceiling, but after another conscious creation session, it stopped.

I believe two important factors were in play that allowed me to interact with nature on such a personal, conscious level. One was the fact that I didn't have to deal with the beliefs of other people in the vicinity. The group events we participate in are the results of the combination of energies flowing from the ideas, thoughts and focus of the whole. The whole was me in this event. Thus, I had more immediate control of the situation and could manifest my desire more quickly and accurately. However, another factor just as important, maybe more so, was the intense emotion I generated and focused toward my goal.

Emotions create, and if given a clean, positive slate upon

which to work their magic, they create fun and happiness. They create pleasant days free of major hassles, excitement on the job, love in our relationships, health in our bodies. But they must be monitored, and altered if necessary, if we're to experience the ultimate from life. We can learn to consciously select and implement emotions of choice; indeed, we should if we hope to grow beyond the limitation of negative emotional responses...and break the code to conscious creation.

9

For all the talk you hear about knowledge being such a wonderful thing, instinct is worth forty of it for real unerringness.

– Mark Twain

The Celestial Nudge

Two friends of ours, unknown to each other, quit their jobs, saying the universe would guide them into what it wanted them to do with their lives. Six months later both were still without work and hurting financially, emotionally and spiritually. They sincerely thought the mysterious workings of the universe included taking responsibility for decisions and action out of their hands.

Metaphysical undertakings are relatively new to the majority of us. We're learning as we pioneer new concepts. We don't have much practical application under our belts that tells us how to relate to All That Is, what our responsibilities are to make things happen and what All That Is will pitch in and do. Our relationship seems unclear at times. And when we get information like Stan and I did in Hawaii from the trance channeler who said to give it all up to the universe to handle, it muddies the metaphysical waters further.

We are not simple, meek souls needing the All Powerful to lead us into a better life, or one with purpose. All That Is assists, It doesn't direct. It's our responsibility to question our direction, then ask and listen for information that will assist us in making decisions. The ball's definitely in our court. We're on a journey in physicality, one we chose to participate in for our own reasons, and one we hope will lead to more understanding of our role in the universe and the nature of consciousness. From time to time our inner self will remind us of what we had hoped to accomplish this time around, but it comes as a gentle nudging, a soft whisper, a comforting word of encouragement.

The Cosmic Answer Generator

Now, we can go this journey alone, believing our ego can call our best shots, or we can finally start requesting help. Don't drag your psychic feet before asking for universal guidance on which days to schedule your vacation, or which computer to buy, or how to become a clearer channel for love. Then stay open to a response, maybe not in the form you might expect. The heavens won't thunder open and a celestial note drop to your feet telling you whether your baby will be a boy or a girl, but an answer will come.

I've found it fascinating to watch the creativity of the universe in getting answers into my hands. Sometimes it picks the line of a song that keeps running through my mind, until I realize, there it is! My answer. Other times I happen to run into an old friend, and our conversation eventually offers up the answer I need. Once, I found one on a billboard. Often I get them from randomly opened books, especially metaphysical ones.

As I get better at this, I find myself simply settling more quickly and confidently into a decision or conclusion, feeling that the universe is behind me on it. But at other times the answer can be rather apparent, rather quickly.

Several years ago Stan and I needed a name for a company we were forming. We wanted a word or two that would express mankind's connection, its literal oneness, with All That Is and each other. Over dinner one night at a little Greek restaurant, we hashed over a list of possibilities. None was quite right, so when we returned home I went into meditation and asked for the best possible name for our company based on our criteria.

The word *nexus* floated through my mind. Since I had no idea what it meant I tried to disregard it. It was persistent enough, though, to force me out of meditation and into our computer room where Stan was working. I asked him what the definition of *nexus* was, and he said, "I don't know exactly, but I think it has something to do with devil worship." Terrific. Obviously I had experienced a miscommunication. Back to meditation.

Nexus again popped up, so we got out the dictionary. The definition of nexus is "connection, link, to bind, a connected group." The perfect word.

Following the Humdrum Into Life's Purpose

A frequently asked question in our seminars is how to uncover our life's purpose. While we've chosen definite directions to explore in the physical, individually and en masse, and while there's an overall growth objective built into our psychic blueprint, it may at times be broader than our selves in linear time can comprehend. That's not to say, however, that it's completely hidden from us or we can't take concrete, conscious steps in its direction. Indeed, we should question our inner selves, our personal advisers, on the subject and choose to follow the advice given. But our purpose may be so broad or varied as to necessitate revelation by a mosaic of hints spread across our lifetime, instead of one definite, obvious path.

One of the vehicles of communication our inner selves use to head us in the direction of our blueprint is called an impulse. Jane Roberts, in *Psychic Politics*, suggests that impulses rise from our deepest sources, suited to our specific needs and desires. She says they are:

> ...self-knowing, in that they're geared to release and activate the most fitting, most fortunate and fulfilling abilities under the circumstances at hand, and in line with present life conditions. They are pattern-activators, stimulating action in certain directions at specific times, with a view to the larger heroic pattern of our lives that is unknown at the usual level of the personality.... Part of the learning process involves the acceptance of these heroic impulses after they're recognized.[1]

Pattern-activators is a key phrase when discussing impulses. The impulse to call an old friend, to walk a different neighborhood path, to buy a certain product, to change a schedule all seem mundane and not particularly cosmically directed. But if it's the intent of our inner self to get information into our hands, fulfill a desire we've requested, or open our minds to new possibilities, our daily lives are the most reasonable vehicle to use. We don't live in moments of momentous proportions; our lives have a basic fabric woven of daily habits and schedules. But the following of our impulses in the humdrum is necessary to allow for the manifestation of our material wishes and to glimpse our soul's direction.

Stan's an amateur photographer. One day he spotted a traveling camera show and dropped in to view the wares. He found a unique telephoto lens he'd been interested in for a long time. While holding it, he noticed the serial number was 131313, unusual in itself but with added significance to him because it's similar to the pin number he selects for all banking cards and computer access codes. He decided not to purchase the lens that day, but asked the merchant where and when the next show was to be held. Several weeks later, he drove 160 miles to the show only to find the lens had been sold.

While on the Oregon coast shooting pictures three weeks later, Stan stumbled onto the traveling camera show in residence in a seaside village for the weekend. His first thought was to ignore the show and continue with his photography, but on nagging impulse he entered and went directly to the table of the same merchant. As he was perusing the man's wares, up walked a man carrying a telephoto lens like the one Stan wanted. He told the merchant he'd bought it from him five weeks previously, and he wanted to sell it back. It seems he was in financial difficulty and had driven 200 miles in hopes of recovering his investment. Stan asked to see it, and, sure enough, it was serial number 131313.

Good for Stan. He got what he wanted. But what's so cosmically compelling about finding an object he coveted? First of all, he manifested what he wanted, and that's an accomplishment worthy of note. However, the event might also be viewed as an attempt by his inner self to raise his curiosity about coincidence and luck and chance—to make him question the supposed chaotic order of life when he sees such symmetry. And if he comprehends the connection between his desire for the lens and the fulfillment of that desire, it's assumed he would question who or what had directed the action behind the scenes. That small breakthrough might be the vehicle that carries him into a new level of universal awareness, another tiny piece of mosaic in the big picture of his spiritual growth.

The Impatient Vote for Patience

If Stan hadn't questioned the creation of the circumstances, as we assume his inner self might hope, what then? His inner self would try again, extending its gift of insight over and over until he caught on, if not in this life, maybe another. Patience, a characteristic of our inner self.

Patience, an anathema to me for most of my life. Impatience was the fuel that propelled me beyond what I "should" have been into a glimmer of what I could be. My flight from borderline poverty and social unacceptability as a child was launched by impatience. The battles waged in pursuit of professional equality were fanned by the flames of impatience. My strength, impatience. When I entered the world of metaphysics, I heard the echo of my religious upbringing: Patience is a virtue, said my church; patience is necessary, said the esoteric. Impatiently, I flew over the subject of patience, treating it as I do *meek* . . . with disdain.

This was one of my slower learning experiences, and the primary cause of the slings and arrows littering my life. My error was in assuming there is no value to patience, that only impatience crystallizes events. I used impatience as a talisman against fear, fear that nothing would happen unless I interceded and forced the issue.

By its very nature, impatience is limiting because we've defined our egos as the creator of events. They're the gods that control what happens to us. They're the sole builders of our destiny. When pressed artificially by time, we don't stop to listen to the creator within, and therein lies the flaw in impatience.

Whether we're metaphysical or not, our inner self tries to lead us along the best path for our growth, and to create our desires as defined by our beliefs and intent. Impatience forms a towering black column of denseness around us, frustrating the persistent attempts of our inner self for communication and keeping us within the range of the spark that ignites anger.

Our inner self says, "Turn right and you'll meet a dear friend who will tell you how to treat your sore knee." We turn left in a rage over our treatment by the sales clerk, limping painfully toward the door. It says, "Think peaceful thoughts at the staff meeting to mellow the problem." Instead, we light the tinder with our angry dissent.

Impatience eliminates our internal quietness, the well-spring of inner direction, thereby forcing us to face life by our wits alone. While it can open doors and whisk us through unscathed, it sometimes forgets the door is closed and smacks us into solid-feeling barriers.

Patience has to do with time unfolding itself, and our not getting in the way. Patience has to do with giving the universe room to maneuver, space to insert experiences into our lives that take us where we want to go without hassle and hurt.

After dwelling on the idea of patience for a day, I had an interesting dream. I held in my hand a luminescent globe the size of a cantaloupe. Once I knew I had released all doubt and fear, and that the power of manifestation was mine, I laid the globe down on my life line and watched it roll a couple of feet. During the roll, it peeled back its outward shell, revealing an event I wanted to experience. It was obvious the event was now ready to enter my life. But it was also imperative that my thoughts stay clear of impediments, including impatience. At one point in the dream, I was close to forcing the globe to reveal its secret, but the image I got, translated into words, was, "Don't force the issue. The event will unfold itself on time, in time."

According to Stan, the universe's idea of patience and mine are still at odds at times. But, my goodness, I can't just sit around and wait forever, I mean it's so slow in happening, like I really need to see something *now*.... Know what I mean?

The Ouija Board: From Storage Into Action

The universe supplies us with information on any subject and through any number of vehicles, some pretty creative—and highly suspect, by our rigid standards of allowable communication—like our entry into the Ouija board world.

Stan and I had been seeking vehicles to build our money easily and quickly. One we chose was stock mutual funds. For months after we entered several of them in the early fall of 1991, our return on investment was incredible. But predictions had been flying through the print and air waves for weeks that the market was ready to crash, heavily, like a stone falling through paper. We chose to stay in, though. Then, on November 12, Stan had a definite feeling he should buy several puts, which in layman's terms are bets that the market will tumble instead of climb. He didn't follow his impulse. On November 15, the Dow Jones Industrial Average plummeted 120 points, a heart-thumping drop.

Our mutual funds' paper profits dropped steadily over the next three weeks, but we had no fears, not even a glimmer of concern. Then one morning I awoke with a small slice of unease resting on my breastbone. I spent the day Christmas shopping, and the feeling grew. By the time I arrived home that evening, I was in a foul financial mood.

As is my habit when I need counseling, I spontaneously woke up at 4:00 a.m. and went downstairs to the living room. I lit a stick of incense and a fire in the wood stove, propped up my back with two throw pillows on the couch, and closed my eyes. I went into my usual altered state of consciousness, felt the presence of something more than me, asked to be guided to a resolution of my simple request: Please help me understand this simmering dread. Nothing happened. No earth shattering proclamations, no psyche-shaking informational data flow. So I went to sleep.

I awoke with the faded December morning sun languidly pushing its reflection off the river and into the fog, entering our windows as white haze. My first feeling was of lingering unease, the second was to get out the Ouija board. Stan and I had dug it out of storage a week previously, blown the dust off and, as the song goes, proceeded to blow our minds. With each question we'd asked, it had whizzed around the board giving in-depth answers and lightly joking with us. We'd had a couple more sessions since that first time, and now I cajoled Stan into another go-round with his first cup of morning tea.

We learned several important items from the energy behind the moving pointer that morning. The first was that Stan's inner self had prompted him about the eminent fall of the Dow in November. He had ignored his impulse to buy the puts and missed a nice financial opportunity.

We also learned that my unease was another prompt, but a prompt to what or where? We couldn't get a clear direction out of the Ouija, as in was the market going to take another dive, as predicted by the bears, and should we take our few remaining dollars of profit and tear rubber to the nearest money market fund until the economy heaved itself out of recession? Or should we stay put, siding with the bulls who maintained that the Dow was in a temporary lull? It seems our nonphysical friends wouldn't advise us of what to do; that was the job of our inner selves, our intuition, they said. But they did say that if our beliefs were strong enough, we'd be just fine.

Beliefs, it always comes back to beliefs. On the one hand, we felt somewhat confident in our financial beliefs; on the other, we suspected more clearing needed to take place. We asked the energy behind the Ouija, which Stan jokingly started calling The Committee, if we still had conflicting financial beliefs in play. Yes, they said, you sure do. Well, Stan and I are slow at times, but not stupid. If we have conflicting beliefs around money, and if we're in a very volatile market, do you think we're going to take the time to work out the conflicts before or after getting out of the market?

I immediately called each of our mutual funds to redeem our shares, cringing with every number dialed, expecting to hear that all the profits, and maybe some of our capital investment, had evaporated with the latest drop of the Dow. But the incredible had happened. Our funds were almost up to their all-time high reached before the November crash. In other words, our profits, which had dematerialized with the fall, were shining on the bottom line again. We sold everything and temporarily moved into a money market.

Trusting the Universe's Choice of Communications

Here's how Stan and I summarize the learning that was inherent in the situation: 1) We both need to listen to our impulses constantly and with faith in their correctness. Stan's lapse of faith held him back from a money coup with the puts; mine, to pick up the Ouija board, led us to information that made us question the security of our mutual funds. 2) Our inner selves will give us a nudge, like a feeling of unease, to get our attention so we will start to analyze our situation. But the key is feeling or hearing it so action can be determined and a change of tack initiated, if we choose.

No, maybe that's not really the key. Perhaps it's trusting ourselves and our inner selves enough to *allow* the nudges or requested information to rise into our consciousness and be noticed.

But that trusting doesn't always come easy. In my case, I would ask for an answer or solution to my latest question or dilemma in meditation, hear or feel what I thought it was, and then muddle around in uncertainty as to who was doing the talking, my inner self or me. One day while Stan and I were conversing with The Committee, I had the bright idea to verify the answers I'd received in meditation that morning. They agreed to do it, and their responses matched what I thought I'd heard. I was elated. Now I could check on all my answers before acting on them!

Not a chance. After a few days of verifications, The Committee told me it was time I started trusting my inner self and myself. They said they weren't a replacement for checking in with my inner guidance, and, besides, it was inconvenient to pull the Ouija board out each time I wanted confirmation.

Oh, give me a break, the Ouija board, some say with rolling eyes. Why not the Ouija board? we say. Why not tarot cards? Why not channeling? Why not automatic writing? Why not tea leaves mixed in cow dung, if we choose? What's the point in limiting the vehicles we'll allow the universe to transmit to, and us receive from, just because of society's contemptuous attitudes?

The most important issue is to open to our guidance. If we build trust and faith in our communication with our inner self, some might call that a major breakthrough in our soul's development. Because it's unconventional makes it all the more interesting. After all, the conventional hasn't done such a magnificent job of leading us out of illness and war, sadness and poverty. Maybe that says something of its value.

The Myth of Separation

Over a period of time Stan and I finally learned how easy it is to communicate with our inner selves. In fact, it's done naturally, instant by instant, as long as we're alive, through intuition, impulses, inner voice and dreams. For a more pro-active approach, and as a focused, conscious way of attaining information, a light to medium altered state usually works.

But this ease of interaction in an altered state came slowly for us. For years we thought it was very difficult, that we had to be in deep meditation, unable to feel our bodies, lost in our consciousnesses. Many leaders of the time said so, and we listened.

We practiced guided and self-hypnosis to move us into that precious place of quietness. We used sound contraptions that dropped us into the deepest state possible, just this side of sleep. We used video tapes of swirling, throbbing colors and graphics to make our conscious minds go numb.

We used metronomes to focus our attention beyond thought. And heaven forbid we should be so presumptuous as to think we could contact our inner selves without opening our chakras first, without reciting a spiritual prayer, without filling our bodies with white light, without the repetition of a mantra thrown in for good measure.

We clearly bought into the supposed experts' beliefs that it's difficult to prepare the body and clear the mind to the presence of our inner self. But it turned out only to be a belief—theirs. It's not true. In fact, it's as easy as breathing. Our inner self *is* us, but since we believe so strongly in separation from any part of All That Is, we automatically assume there's an order of difficulty in communication.

The Fluidity of Our Greater Selves

When we set a goal to understand the universe with as much clarity as possible, it's amazing the insights we become privy to...because what we ask for with focus and force, we get. One of the most startling discoveries for Stan and I was that the energy of our greater selves—that energy from which we emerge into physicality—is much more fluid than we humans understand. And we learned it in varying ways.

As our experience on the Ouija board built, and as we worked more with our inner selves, we slowly came to the realization that the energy behind both is of the same parent source—our greater selves. Part of the energy of our greater selves got our attention through the Ouija board because we would accept it. The reason they wouldn't, as The Committee, validate the information we received in an altered state was to force us to practice our skill of inner listening, as it is part of the learning we all sign up for when we decide to become physical.

That revelation started our unending questions regarding the fluidity of our greater selves. It really got interesting when we started piecing together hints flowing from The Committee over a period of months. They had cautioned us, again and again, to remember that physical reality was (and is) designed and constructed by the participants in it, and functions under our pre-set rules. The main governing rule in this reality is that beliefs create. The rules don't change, *not even when interacting with energy sources outside our time and space.* We will only accept certain data into our mind's processing center, and that information we mold, or manipulate, to fit what we will allow it to be.

Coloration of a Greater Construct

So, what's the point? Well, try this. Many metaphysical people, including us until recently, believe nonphysical guides, teachers, etc., are stand-alone entities, separate and apart from our own energy source. It seems, though, that nonphysical beings are extensions of our whole, or greater, energy...but usually awash in our coloration. In other words, they are a direct part of us, personified and once-removed by us because it's easier to believe in something outside ourselves as wise and knowledgeable. We unconsciously give them personalities and characteristics that they then conform to, and they in turn offer us information and insights that we mold to fit within the boundaries of our accepted structure of thought.

Some of us in the Western world will design a Higher Self as just this side of God, the Christian God, that is, quick to choose words right out of the Bible for its discussions. Others of us will make our teacher full of laughter and a quirky sense of humor. Some will assign their channeled entity to a planet, and have it visit this world with insights from afar. Indian guides may be somewhat passé now, but they were hot items maybe ten, fifteen years ago. An angel or two get conjured up now and then by some folks, especially if they're of a spiritually uplifting frame of mind. I called my guides Lexon and Ruth, and had Lexon specialize in wisdom and guidance, Ruth in nurturing and comfort.

Our greater selves play many roles depending on what we believe, desire and will accept, all in the name of illumination. The Committee, in fact, seems quite amused at our need to exteriorize and personify our own energy source. But isn't that what religions have done throughout recorded history, personified their intuitive understandings of a greater construct into gods? And doesn't it now start to make sense as to *why* they did it, as that's what the people of the time would accept?

However, the bolder questions we face are more modern. Are we still limiting our understandings, our depth and breath of knowledge, by forcing our most awesome connection—which is an extension of ourselves—into caricatures of itself because we haven't progressed enough to let the old structure go and start afresh? Is it time to get a firmer grasp on the basic construct of consciousness, how it forms various realities...and why?

The Fallacy of a Dangerous Unknown

It's interesting, sometimes amazing, how people respond to the universe from a position of anxiety or fear when they view it through the colored glasses of past models. Much of the new is still couched in terms of the old. As we grow more sophisticated in our understandings, the devil goes up in flames, but fear of the unknown may linger. Some people think they can be hurt or negatively affected by unseen forces or entities that have the power to manipulate or control them. Some object to the Ouija board because they believe spirits might come through and attach themselves to the people in the room.

And it doesn't help when metaphysical teachers perpetrate the fallacy of vulnerability with their own misunderstandings. We heard one producer of metaphysical seminars say he surrounds his house with "protective" white light during each night's meditation because he believes people who attend his seminars may try to project their consciousnesses into his home to snoop around. We also had the dubious pleasure of listening to a highly-educated woman address a large group at a local college. As absurd as it sounds, she insisted not just one crazy nonphysical entity but dozens can possess us, all at one time, and that it happens regularly.

The fact that we are the causal force in the creation of our life *never* gets suspended. There is no way anyone or anything can hurt us unless we walk in fear. Fear, in fact, creates negative forces. They don't exist unless we give them life through our creative power. But with the gut-level realization that we're the ones that manifested the event, it will definitely halt, if we so desire, because that's how our reality works. We get what we are willing to believe and focus on.

Reincarnation Rethought

Hey, wait a minute! What about reincarnation and karma? Don't they affect me no matter what I believe in this life? Answer me that will you!

I'd rather not. It's a touchy issue with metaphysical types, a metaphorical cauldron of conflicting ideas and sensitivities.

But, what the heck....

Back to the basics. Everything happens in one continuous moment. Linear time is a characteristic of this reality, honed by the mechanisms of perception found in our physical bodies, but not real. It doesn't exist as a universal construct. All our lives are being lived in the spacious present, each shaped by the probabilities we activate through beliefs, focus and intent. Our past and future selves are part of the fluidity of our greater selves, sent out, if you will, to experience. Through dreams and other interesting events we contact past and future selves often, learning from them and sharing perceptions.

Reincarnation, said another way, is the multitudinous, multidimensional self following probabilities through numerous historical time contexts, all existing at once.

So, where does that leave karma? Nonexistent, if by karma we mean being born into this life in consecutively spaced order from our past, replete with a bag of mistakes flung across our shoulder, headed for our date with destiny.

While our past and future lives influence us somewhat, the effect is small: They have little power and sway over us. We do come in to each life with a proclivity toward certain tendencies, characteristics and dispositions. They are our choice, for our reasons, and meant to plant our feet onto a generalized path of learning this time around. If they are similar to ones held in other lives, so be it, but the similarities don't magnify the issue.

The problems these tendencies may produce in other lives are different from today's, and the learning that takes place does so within the parameters of our belief system at that time, and with whatever symbols we select. It may be appropriate for the us of 1302 to express our belief in powerlessness by being thrust into slavery. Today's reflection of powerlessness may manifest as being two hundred pounds overweight.

The propensity toward a belief in powerlessness may enter the twentieth century with us, but it's not hidden in the far corners of our subconscious. By probing the outwardly manifested symbols surrounding us, it becomes obvious.

So, does remembering our life as a slave bring new insights to our conscious mind that the usual method of belief-identification can't uncover? No. It can make us *feel* that we've uncovered new material, though, thereby possibly bringing a new urgency to handling it, or a different slant of insight through which to address it.

Or it can get a headlock on our psyche and throw us to the mat. For, after all, it's been with us through the centuries, which makes it extremely tenacious and difficult to remove . . . doesn't it? It's not just a little bitty belief in powerlessness that we can overcome easily this time around, it's really deep and wide, solid as stone, almost...well, overpowering...you know?

If it helps us to look at past lives, it's our right. At times, we'll even imaginatively create a past life that will accurately depict today's problem outfitted in yesteryear's clothing. However, since the answers to today's dilemma are easily found in the conscious mind as thoughts, feelings and attitudes, we don't need past life work to break today's cycle. The paths to change surround us constantly. They're called probabilities. We need to alter this life's thoughts if we desire a different future.

But the fun of delving into other lives can't be overlooked. When kept in perspective, they become exciting whirlwind adventures into consciousness.

A Fresh Look at Spirituality

Many people unconsciously ride the fence between old religious views recast in modern metaphysical language and the true nature of reality. The good news is that as we open our thinking, we'll be able to slide off the fence into the land of freedom, with a new definition of spirituality that accelerates our learning and compounds our growth.

But we can start bouncing today's definition of choice off the knowledge we have accumulated about the structure of the universe so far and see if it sticks. Like, as a *literal* part of All That Is, do we need to grow into our spirituality? How about, since the consciousness of All That Is is all that is, and no angels have fallen from grace lately, is there anything to fear but fear in our universe? Like, consciousness has the implicit desire to expand and experience; so, doesn't that cover a lot more territory than just spiritual-type strivings? And since all our lives happen simultaneously and each moment within each life is immersed in probabilities awaiting activation, does karma or the evolution of the soul in a linear fashion make any sense?

Et cetera, et cetera, et cetera, until we come up with a definition of spirituality that fits the true reality of what the universe is all about, minus restricting dogma that squeezes the life out of that truth and leaves it a husk of its actual self.

10

From Chaos to Clarity

With eyes wide open and brimming inexperience, Stan and I stepped into a hidden swirl of chaos when we decided to try conscious creation. Issues that are so clear now, so simple, were obscured by the veil of the unknown. We faced hundreds of questions over the years, some we figured out, many still dwell under a pile of question marks.

Someday we'll all get together from around the globe, we twentieth century pioneers of conscious creation, and swap stories of these early years, laughing at our mistakes and misperceptions, shaking heads at our naiveté, glad we did it but thinking how much easier it could have been had we only known what we know now. I suspect "what we know now" is but a micro-cosmic speck of paint on the creative canvas, but at least it's a start.

Stan's and my learning came from many different sources. Certainly our own experiences led the list of teachers, with enormous assistance coming from our inner guidance and The Committee. The participants of our seminars taught us much, and watching friends and family, whether they followed the same philosophy or not, offered vignettes to draw from. And always Jane Roberts' and Seth's books kept us holding on, as at times did other authors.

Here, in individual nutshells, are some snippets from our personal library of insights. A few I've mentioned previously, but they're worth repeating.

Catching on to Basics

• We learned that conscious creation is not passive. We must participate in its development by working things through in the physical. This is a do-it-yourself reality with assistance when requested. All That Is expects us to lay the groundwork for our desired manifestations by participating in life, not by sitting on a remote mountain top striving to reach new heights of noninvolvement.

My nephew Tommy tells the story of a man who, upon reaching the pearly gates, complained bitterly to God. "All I ever wanted was to win the lottery," he said. "That's all I ever asked of you. But no! You wouldn't even grant me that one wish." And God; with great compassion in Her voice replied, "But Henry, first you had to buy a lottery ticket."

• We learned that as we expand our understandings through conscious creation, we attract a greater scope of information. The same information would have fallen on barren ground earlier because our psyche hadn't requested it, couldn't correlate it and therefore wouldn't consider it.

Information, all information, is already alive in the universe, patiently awaiting our magnetization. However, it isn't sitting in some heavenly data bank, filed by type and summoned by a stroke of the cosmic keyboard. And it doesn't reside in a universal records library. It's connected to the consciousness of all who seek, use, develop and understand it. It desires our attention and wishes to meet with us as much as we seek it.

• We learned that we are consciousness funneling its learning into the greater whole. Our experiences are absorbed into the universal consciousness for others to use and build upon. As the greater consciousness expands with our new insights, it alters the thinking of others. So when we change, the world changes. When we drop the role of victim by refusing to sue for perceived hurts, and instead figure out how to internally change so we are automatically, naturally protected; when we use our focused consciousness to heal our bodies instead of visiting the doctor at first twinge, rocketing health care costs to the moon; when we stop asking the government to subsidize our lives for inordinate periods of time and instead learn how to reclaim our inherent power to create what we want to experience, then we lay the first bricks of a new civilization.

• We learned we don't have to learn through adversity. There's not a reason this side of eternity why we need to suffer in any way. As Seth said in an earlier quote, suffering is not good for the soul; the only reason to suffer is to figure out how not to do it. Emotional and physical pain are not learning experiences dished up by the universe for our growth. They are caused by our thoughts and attitudes. If our beliefs were different, we wouldn't have experienced the mashed hand or Alcoholics Anonymous.

• We learned that the universe is open to helping us with any assistance we think we need. I talk blithely about calling on my inner self for financial advice, treating it as the most natural thing in the world. But that's after several years of absolute, unequivocal refusal to raise such issues with the powers that be. I could ask for guidance in any other area of my life, but Lord help me if I deigned to request money advice. It simply wasn't spiritual.

Break the boundaries between your acceptable areas of request, borderline ones and downright improper ones. The sooner you allow the universe freedom to assist you, the sooner you'll learn to feel contentment. Remember, it's all illusion anyway, and the universe doesn't rate our illusion on a scale of one to ten before deciding what level of assistance to offer.

• We learned that asking the universe for help in finding the perfect couch doesn't necessarily mean we should buy it when it materializes. The universe responded to our specific request; we didn't ask it to validate our purchase decision. As I mentioned previously, the name for one of our companies came through inner guidance. However, we were supplied with what we asked for, a name, not a sign from heaven that we were destined to form the company.

Some people look on any response from the universe as Divine Guidance, the voice of our Higher Self leading us to our Destiny. But that smacks of old religious thoughts transferred to metaphysics. The new definition of the universe says it's here to help in practical as well as spiritual ways, and its advice flows through our days with a rhythm that we should assume is natural, normal and constant.

Stretching for Understanding

• We learned that some metaphysical people will ask the universe for an event, like release from a particularly onerous health or marital situation, and then ask others to add energy to their request to help make it happen. There is no way in the universe to bypass our belief system. If we change, it's because we desire it and our beliefs support it. The universe won't alter our beliefs for us; that's our job. Another's energy may help in temporarily relieving the symptoms, but eventually back we go to the problem, possibly now cloaked in new garments but nonetheless still active...until we change our limiting beliefs.

• We learned that, while it's supposed to be simple to transform energy into what we want, it seems so extraordinary, so powerful, that a belief grows that it must be difficult. Our leaders at times give us complex processes to use, fueling our budding belief that we're undertaking an incredible task when we choose to consciously create. Try to remember that we create everything in our lives anyway, unconsciously. Consciously doing it can be just as simple.

• We learned there's no way to tell how long it will take our goal to reach actualization. At times, things we think difficult to create show up quickly. At other times, the wait for the smallest of desires seems interminable. Some of the timing has to do with the number and force of limiting beliefs in the way, but other pieces must be in place also. For instance, if you're in a situation where a number of people and/or events must be aligned, it might stretch the waiting period. Or, if the item you request is rare, like an ancient book, it could take longer.

• We learned it's not only *our* beliefs that determine the outcome of a group event. In the case of the start-up, the company wouldn't have succeeded with just my visualizations and focus. While most of the other employees weren't metaphysical, and thus not into conscious creation, they still expended desire for its success. I assume that since I was trying to program freedom, if my co-workers hadn't been attuned to the company's growth, I would have left for different pastures, even if I didn't consciously know what I was doing.

• We learned that we don't always create what we put effort into. For instance, one time we were offering a seminar in Oregon. I wanted it to be a huge success, with everyone getting what they wanted out of it and the room completely filled with attendees, so I did some work in consciousness. The seminar succeeded in that we had a good time, but the room was only half full. I don't know what happened. We were so busy the days following the seminar I never searched for answers.

Logically, our beliefs and strength of desire hold the key—but which beliefs, how much desire? Beliefs are drawn to an event from directions one would never expect, and the oddest of them can water down the final result, especially if our desire is also waning. Maybe I really would rather have been vacationing the week previous to the seminar, instead of expending effort on its logistics, and that created a lesser affair. Possibly I felt we'd held too many seminars in that city, and my focus was wavering. Maybe I had my thoughts on creating new material for a future workshop, and it distanced me from this one.

But whatever the cause, it's apparent we don't possess full freedom to create exactly what we want all the time. It seems that less faithful versions of our imagined ones may appear, and at other times our visualization will entirely be blocked due to hidden thought patterns.

• We learned that the beginnings of success can be spotted through peripheral events. While we may not see our goal on the immediate horizon, there can be indications it's on its way. Had I seen the doubling of my salary within two years of leaving Apple as an indicator that I was headed in the right direction, I may have loosened my concerns more quickly.

While that amount of money doesn't signify wealth, it made a strong statement that my limiting beliefs around money were easing. Also, when my ring reappeared in my jewelry box, it should have raised a flag that I was doing something right in my interactions with the universe and, therefore, was on the right track with conscious creation.

• We learned that when we cross the line from desire to desperation, we blow it, desire being the state where anything seems possible, desperation saying we've lost faith and we must, just must, figure out how to make our goal happen. Desperation reinforces old beliefs instead of enhancing new ones. We start focusing too much on our perceived problem instead of our wish. The solution: remember how the universe works, that our thoughts and feelings hold creative power. Get back into the peaceful now as quickly as possible. And keep in the forefront of your mind the understanding that you will get what you desire if you stay clear and balanced.

Moving Slowly, but Still Moving

• We learned that, even though we project success with great desire, we can block its final manifestation out of fear. Fear of what? Fear of success, usually. My daughter Cathy has wanted to be an actress since childhood. After high school she entered college, but her heart wasn't in academia per se. Finally, she dropped out of school and set her sights on an acting career. She visualized, meditated and did belief-change work. Then she auditioned for summer repertory theater and won good parts for three of the four summer productions. She was getting a lot of interest from the directors and many leads for future acting roles. She even made it on to the Oprah Winfrey Show, although not because of her acting ability.

But then in fall everything came to an abrupt halt, no phone calls, no parts, no one who cared showed up on her doorstep. She went back to searching her belief system for the cause of the blockage and discovered she was facing fear that she just might succeed and not be good enough. She started visualizing and meditating again, worked at releasing old limiting beliefs, tried to live in the now.

By late winter things were moving again. She was getting daily work as an extra in numerous TV programs and films. Her contacts were growing at a fast pace, and she was getting exposed to directors and producers.

• We learned that this belief search stuff can be an ongoing process, at times necessary to prod us closer to our goal. Certainly Cathy found it to be true. She's aware that becoming a full-fledged actress may take more rounds of belief exploration and change, but the important thing is that she has a tool identified that can assist, if used.

• We learned that unless we change our beliefs, we can force the issue through focused intent and get what we want, but we may not be able to keep it. A woman in one of our seminars told this story: She and her husband really wanted to experience the lap of luxury. They wanted to live in a magnificent home and have servants at the call. While their beliefs about their ability to manifest the amount of necessary money were weak, they nonetheless created an interesting situation.

A very wealthy family was planning to spend several years in Europe and was looking for a reliable couple to mansion-sit. The couple would have all the home's conveniences at their disposal, including a cook and servants. Our seminar participant and her husband joyously accepted the job.

In less than a year they resigned. They felt incredibly guilty living in the lap of luxury while their friends and family had so much less. Their relationship became much too strained and the solution seemed to be to return to their previous life. They now know what beliefs caused the problem and are directing their efforts to opening themselves to permanent abundance.

Why does anyone fall from power, love, health, happiness? They had it in the bag; why couldn't they keep it?

I had an accountant friend who became co-founder of a tiny high-tech company in the South. We traveled together often, since our companies sold compatible equipment and we marketed our products jointly. He was intensely focused on making his company successful, and he and his partner did just that in a few short years. Once they went public, my friend became a millionaire many times over. But shortly thereafter he was forced to resign for lack of performance. From an armchair observer's perspective, I think he outgrew his belief in his ability to handle the job. He was in waters he'd never before tread, and the current was moving so swiftly he lost faith in his native intelligence and couldn't keep afloat. He certainly had the wherewithal to continue running his portion of the company, but he lacked the beliefs.

• We learned that once we change our beliefs, we can't make the same mistakes as in the past. Suppose we owned a company that went belly-up several years ago, and now we want to start another. Concern holds us back: What if it happens again? If we've eliminated the beliefs that caused our defeat, there's no way we can experience the loss as it was structured then. We still could lose our company, but it won't be due to old causes.

• We learned that an event is not over until it's over. In other words, what seems to be an ending may still harbor opportunities for alteration. For instance, once I lost my wallet. Immediately I decided I wanted it back. As I walked around the store where the loss occurred, I projected thoughts of its return. I felt its presence and visualized my delighted reaction when I found it. As I entered each successive aisle, I expected the wallet to appear. It didn't, so I returned home and continued visualizing, building on the assumption that it would return.

It finally showed up. The man who found it drove fifty miles to the old address still on my driver's license and had the new owner telephone me with the good news. The Committee later said another man was primed to pick it up, but when I instantly decided to challenge the event, the energy of the moment altered and allowed another person with different intent to enter the picture.

A Continuation of Insights

• We learned that we live in a probability-driven reality; therefore, no event can be predicted with one-hundred percent reliability. No psychic can absolutely tell what the future holds, not even the famous mystics of the past, because there is no predestined future. They can only sense the most likely outcome based on the event's probability factor at the moment of the reading. Our world is driven by the current beliefs of the souls residing in it, individually and en masse. Thus, it's impossible to call an event as predestined, because as people change, so do probable outcomes.

Using my wallet as an example, a psychic may have told me I was going to lose it, never to see it again, as that was the strongest probability. Hearing it from such an authority, I might have assumed it to be the only truth, when, in fact, other truths surrounded the event also, just waiting for me to activate them through desire and intent. The same ground rules apply to national and world events, also.

The lesson is if you don't like what you hear, don't unequivocally accept it. Understand that it may be the most prominent probability at the moment, but that you have a great shot at changing it. If, on the other hand, the forecast is good news, pump more excitement and desire into it to solidify the probability of its entry into your life or our world.

• We learned that we need to apply discretion and discernment to information received from psychics, channelers, the Ouija board, the tarot cards, etc. Information is not intrinsically valid just because it arrives at our door on the wings of the foo-foo. It can be colored by the belief system through which it plays, be it another person's, ours or both. While our greater selves will try like crazy to get clear information into our hands, they still have to contend with our belief systems. The error in misinformation is not on the side of the universe.

• We learned that we can mistake worries for precognitive information, and by assuming the information is an accurate description of the future, materialize it as such. Once I had a dream where I picked up a bundle of clothes and under it was a letter from the Better Business Bureau regarding a company that was doing some renovation work for us. Upon awakening, I assumed the worst, that trouble was just waiting to happen.

I gnawed around the edges of the dream for a day, steeling myself for its materialized result. Fortunately, I consulted The Committee the next day. They said the content of the dream was not precognitive, but the result of worry. A prior incident of sloppy workmanship with this company had raised my concern. The Committee suggested I drop it because there was no problem on the horizon...but my deepening uneasiness could create one.

Another time, I read of a woman who insisted she had cancer. She visited a succession of doctors, none of whom could find any disease. Finally, after several months, a doctor did indeed find the dreaded cancer. He considered his colleagues incompetent for not having made the discovery sooner. When we asked The Committee what had happened, they said the woman had manifested it by her concern, but it had taken awhile to solidify. It simply was not present when the earlier doctors had tested her.

• We learned that too much concentration on old beliefs we want to change causes them to swell with life. By excessively focusing on them, we give them energy and, therefore, they stay active. Stan and I beat finances to death and kept the beliefs alive longer than necessary. Find your limiting beliefs, change them, let them go. Don't hover around, peeking from your hiding place, checking to see if they've disappeared. Have faith that you're quite capable of removing them, and know that indeed you already have.

• We learned not to give any conscious negative consideration to events that we didn't want to happen. Any such concentration, to whatever degree, ties us in with those probabilities. Remember, events occur based on focus, whether the focus is positive or negative. It's counterproductive to negatively dwell on possible future events that make us mad, fearful or hurt.

As against nature as it seems, this advice applies to immediate problems as well. The best thing we can do is drop the negative emotion as much as is humanly possible. If we focus on it, it grows . . . literally. If we let it go, its impact is lessened substantially. In fact, the problem may dissipate into nothingness, removing itself naturally.

• We learned that future events fraught with possible unpleasantness can be diluted in the now before their introduction into this reality. What you do is send calming energy into the upcoming event, lacing the scene with feelings of happiness, friendliness, love. Go into an altered state of consciousness, see the scene, the players and the subject of the event. Then feel everyone mellow out, look at ease with each other, if not friends, at least not enemies.

Remembering that we are consciousness, that all events are our creations, and that there is no time or space makes this seem more rationally possible. If you're headed into court over a traffic ticket, try mitigating the outcome; if you have to attend a dreaded meeting, set the stage in advance; if you're to be reprimanded, soften the blow. This is a quick fix to the problem you're about to face; it may not alter the outcome completely. It can, but it also may just soften the negativity enough so reasonableness prevails.

The Never Ending Lessons

• We learned that there are patterns between actions, and they can lead us to great insights, and point to necessary belief changes. For instance, if a person is overly concerned with home and car security, is cautious in dating and constantly worries about proper nutrition, he or she could have a core belief of personal vulnerability. By nature it will limit the person's enjoyment of life and freedom of experience. So, by looking at our lives as a whole, we may find a mega-belief squatting right smack on our forward path.

• We learned that old patterns, if deeply rooted, can re-assert themselves after we think they've been eliminated. My battle with the bulge is a case in point. So strong were my negative beliefs around the calorie and my body that no matter how thoroughly I cleansed my belief system, I'd catch myself on the same treadmill of weight gain–count calories. I'd waved good bye to "normal" weight at ten years old, and every day for the next thirty-eight years reinforced my belief that I was too fat, no matter what I weighed. None of my visualizations and belief-work ended the cycle until recently. I learned from The Committee that had I trusted my impulses and intuition, I could have changed the outcome years ago.

A note about the body. According to Seth, our cells "precognate." In other words, the condition of our body is not so much the result of our past as it is of our future, which is created in the present. So, when we look in a mirror we see the result of what we projected into our future. Our new body starts being structured, then, from this moment on.

• We learned that new beliefs enter and leave our psychic structure constantly, automatically, when we accept new data that replaces the old. If you think your doctor is simply wonderful and then learn she has been molesting little boys, there goes the old belief out the window. And if your president says, "Read my lips," and later...well, you know the outcome of that one.

Let's say we feel our performance on the job is lackluster, but our boss encourages us to try a new tack, explore deeper possibilities. And what if we do, only to find we really can handle the job with ease? Does that change our beliefs around self-esteem? You bet.

So, our lives change character constantly, with or without conscious belief-work. Our application of the conscious creation process only gives us a leg up on choosing our life's course now, instead of waiting for happenstance to kick in.

• We learned that a critical or dramatic situation in our life can signal great momentum toward change. Our lives can reflect a cauldron of many beliefs in conflict, beliefs that cover both sides of the issue. For instance, our friend Cecil desperately wanted out of his job. He knew he had greater potential, and he wanted the chance to prove he could handle more responsibility. On the other hand, it's a tough, competitive world out there, he believed, and there must be tons of people more qualified. He also was afraid to leave his company because he felt safe. Finally it came to a head when he was laid off. He was forced to face his new desires, and carve a better life out of chaos.

• We learned we can share an environment with someone and reap different results. Not everyone prospered with our start-up company's success. One manager, quite knowledgeable in stocks and finances, hired on after the initial stock offering. He refused to buy any stock, because, based on his experience (i.e., beliefs), it couldn't possibly rise any further. He was astonished as the movement upward continued, but he still refused to buy in.

My sister, on the other hand, who knew nothing of stock but had a strong belief in me, bought in and made a nice profit. Another employee held a good chunk of the stock, watched it sky-rocket, and then was forced to sell to hold his family together during extremely trying times, losing what was to be the down payment on a house.

• We learned to acknowledge coincidences for what they are. When I was interviewing for the start-up job, I felt it was a waste of my time. But the trip to Orange County for the second interview gave me the opportunity to visit family in the area, so I agreed to it. While waiting to board the plane in San Jose, I ran into an old friend also headed into Orange County. We changed our seating to be together and shared a conversation that was pivotal in my accepting the job.

Unbeknown to me, my friend Clark was one of the original founders of the company I was on my way to visit. He knew the president and vice president of engineering, both founders, very well. He was delighted at their interest in me because he thought our personalities would mesh and that we would complement each other's working styles. He also told me he felt the company could prosper with the right management. I listened closely, and since I trusted Clark's judgment, I added his words to my decision-making process.

Still Delving Into New Ideas

• We learned we can reprogram the past, thereby changing the probabilities of our future. According to Seth, since there is only the spacious present, the past is very much alive and all probabilities we could have drawn from then are still possible. When we, through visualization and belief-work, delve into our pasts and recast them, we move across the line from one past probability into another, and it becomes our dominant past. Probabilities then appear in our future that were not possible before.

For instance, if we were hurt emotionally as a child, we can revisit the scene, change the script, alter the feelings that were generated. Then, our future compensates for the changes and adds new pathways not previously optional. Seth says this isn't theoretical, but a very concrete way of helping the future self.

• We learned that our thoughts, positive or negative, heavily influence other people. We use a technique in our seminars taught to us by Rob Williams, of Ki-Point Communications, that demonstrates the immediate impact of our energy on another. What happened to Tami, a seminar participant, dramatically drove the point home.

During our workshops we select a volunteer who has never seen the energy demonstration. We ask them to think of a very pleasant memory, and then we do a muscle test. Their arm invariably stays in the upright, locked position (switched on). We then have the volunteer leave the room, and while out we ask the other participants to close their eyes and think of an extremely negative event. After a minute or so, the volunteer returns to the room. Now we ask the volunteer to remember the pleasant memory and build up the original feeling. Then we muscle test again. Their arm flops to their side, signifying a radically different energy response than before.

When volunteer Tami rejoined the room, she said she felt apprehension start to grow the moment she came through the door. It built to a crescendo during the muscle testing, until she felt she'd been hit in the solar plexus. When her arm dropped to her side, she burst into tears. We did a procedure to change her energy back to positive, but her response lingered in our minds. The power of our thoughts had been so graphically demonstrated that it took us aback. Think how we must impact our families, partners, peers, employers—indeed, everyone we come in contact with—every day of our lives.

There's an interesting footnote to the story. Tami called her husband, hundreds of miles away, after the seminar and reviewed the odd episode. Before she told him what time it occurred, he said around 2:00 that afternoon (the approximate time of the energy experiment), his left wrist and thumb became very painful, just like when he'd broken his right hand. All he could think of was, "What's wrong with Tami? Something's happened to her!"

• We learned that thoughts of peace have great power. They literally settle down the negativity of the earth, according to The Committee. We now send soothing thoughts of peace around the globe during meditation, and while we obviously can't judge the impact, we're told it does much to bring individuals a settling in of hope and calmness, if they're desiring it. The bumper sticker, Visualize World Peace, has its genesis in truth, it seems.

• We learned that while an altered state is preferable for visualizing, there are auxiliary methods that also hold power. For years I drove the California freeways for long, exasperating hours. That wasted time and the hours I spent walking or running seemed ripe for manifestation work, if only I had a tool to keep me focused. The solution was so simple, and so effective. I recorded about a three-minute, powerful generic visualization on an audio cassette and carried it wherever I went. I still play it almost daily on my Walkman while out exercising, or in my car for trips over fifteen minutes, rewinding it endlessly.

The tape is structured to start generating deep feelings almost immediately around my desire of the moment. First it tells me to think of what I want. Then it has me feel the desire deep within, building to a pitch. I'm told to see my goal materialize and then feel imagination and expectancy sparkling around it. Allow it to work, I'm told. Choose to have it.

The purpose of the tape to this point has been to build emotions and belief in my ability to make the goal happen. Now it moves me to visualize, see the scene, feel the feelings more deeply. It ends with me knowing my goal's been accomplished.

I've spent thousands of hours listening to copies of my tape, using it for dozens of goals. It's been invaluable in my creation process.

Perpetual Growing

• We learned to let go of guilt about what we have, are or want. I heard a woman say that having more than others made her feel so guilty she couldn't paint her kitchen or buy a new refrigerator. This sounds extreme, but on another level many of us react the same way based on our beliefs; it just may not be as apparent as in this example. Guilt is destructive. It won't help you, and it certainly won't help the person or situation you feel guilty about. How to get rid of it? It's caused by beliefs, like any feeling. Get to the root of the problem by uncovering what your beliefs are that make you feel guilty.

Wanting money raises the serpent head of guilt in much of the population, especially for those who equate money with greed or non-spirituality. But money is energy made manifest just as a love sonnet is energy made manifest. The universe doesn't place judgment on our desires. We do, through our beliefs. The root of all evil is in our belief in evil, since what we believe in, we create.

• We learned that someone else's belief system is theirs, and not particularly a reflection of the truth. Their truth, certainly, but not truth of universal proportions. Like the man who believes beliefs are held in chakras and they just need to be "cleaned" to change the beliefs. It works for him because he sees it as truth. If we do, it will work for us also. However, if we lose faith, it all falls apart because there's no intrinsic validity beyond the illusory belief.

• We learned we can't alter another's belief for them. Have you ever been able to change a friends' or relatives' beliefs about their financial condition, no matter how much money you loaned or gave them? Did their reality change, or did they just run out of money again? The deeper question on the table is, does giving money help or does it actually hinder? We're reinforcing their limiting beliefs by agreeing that money is continually scarce, and the solution is to get it from an outside source instead of creating it from within. Would we do them a greater service by giving them a copy of Jane Roberts' *The Nature of Personal Reality?*

• We learned it's not wise to advise others on what's best for them. We don't *know* what's best for someone with a completely different belief system than ours. We think we do, at times, especially if the person is a family member. But any advice we give must come through the filter of our beliefs. Thus, while what we suggest may work for us, it may not for someone else.

Another reason we can't advise others with a modicum of confidence in our suggestions is that we don't know the direction their inner self hopes they will take, which can be quite a different path than what we'd like to see.

I worked with a man years ago who always seemed so melancholy. He was a successful computer salesman in his mid-forties, but it was apparent he moved through life with little anticipation. One day over lunch, I heard his story. Until his early twenties, his life had been dedicated to art. Since a small child, painting had been his all-consuming love. But his parents thought he needed to get a "real" job, and prodded him constantly to do so. When he married, his wife added her voice to his parents', and Pete finally put his paints away. Years later, his sadness still clung to him like transparent skin. He was a shell of his deeper potential because he hadn't followed his dream.

On life's lesser scale, it's still not wise to push our choices on another. A friend of mine became very concerned about her son. He had dropped out of college for a year immersed in a gut-wrenching depression he couldn't shake. After months of avoiding decisions, he finally accepted the offer to visit a good friend in Hawaii. His mother was beside herself. She logically weighed the pro's and con's as she saw them, and felt it wasn't a good idea. He went ahead with his plan, thankfully. He became involved with helping disturbed children, and the effort it took moved him out of himself and back to the land of the living.

Moving Through Odds and Ends

• We learned the importance of getting away alone for two or three days every couple of months. When you set a program of conscious creation, you need time to think. You'll want to analyze your goals, reset priorities, devise new techniques, and converse uninterrupted with your inner self. You'll also want time to read your latest metaphysical book, listen to the audio tape you never find time for, and build the feeling of joy without stressing out over the unwashed dishes. Time away is a precious gift that will return you to the outside world with faith high and visions sparkling.

• We learned the slow, crippling rate of a somnambulistic life will pick up dramatically if we don't sidestep decisions. In fact, indecision is usually the cause of our crawling days. Decisions expand the probability count by opening paths not previously available. New possibilities open up once decisions are made, no matter what their initial outcome.

• We learned that not everyone gets the same level of response from the Ouija board that we do. If you decide to try the board and don't have success with one partner, try another. The new combination of beliefs, desire and intent may do the trick. Also, The Committee suggested you picture a layer of light energy about eight inches above the board. Then see the energy press down on your hands, connecting you with the process.

• We learned that death changes character when we believe in the continuation of consciousness. Life and death become but two faces of the same existence, both natural phenomena. The integrity of the self, we come to understand, cannot be annihilated.

When my mother and father died, I was beyond consolation. Years later at the funeral of my sister I was able to stand relatively composed in front of the mourners in the chapel and talk of

Donna's transition in consciousness. On the one hand, I grieved. On the other, the adventure opening before her was exciting to contemplate. Knowing she had made the choice to die, as we all do, helped me honor the rightness of her choice, and wish her Godspeed until we meet again.

• We learned that we need to know what joy feels like in order to consciously create the experience of it. I dwelled on this dilemma for days, trying to figure out how I could bring a joyful event into my life in order to capture its essence. Then one night an incredible sunset blazed over the Pacific Ocean. Stan and I walked to the cliffs overlooking the sea, and I thought, "The sunset must feel joy at its awesome beauty. If I were part of the sunset, I'd feel joy, too." So I went into a light altered state standing on the cliff, and saw my molecules disperse throughout the sky and into the sunset. I felt pure joy for the first time, and could then build on that joy in future altered states.

• We learned that feelings of joy bring a quick response in the now. After a recent joy meditation, I left to do the grocery shopping. I rounded an aisle with my cart, deep in concentration. I looked up as an elderly man turned from the shelves toward me. He flashed a big smile and said hello with such verve I thought I must know him. I smiled back, wracking my brain for a name, but he just walked on by. Not five minutes later the same thing happened again with another man. Then, as I was straining to reach deep into the almost empty milk case, I heard a woman's voice behind me suggesting she get the milk as she was much taller. I finally connected my joy meditation with this shopping experience. I then proceeded to walk the store with an idiotic grin on my face.

• We learned the influence of television on people's beliefs. I stopped watching TV in 1969, and probably haven't seen a hundred hours since. Stan has a similar track record. But seminar participants tell us of the difficulty of trying to hold on to their new beliefs while saturated in the victimization scripts believed by the world and portrayed in living color every night in their homes. Health alerts, crime reports, stories of trickery and manipulation, "accidental" death, and fear, great fear, permeating it all. So, stop watching television. If that's too radical, watch it with a cynical eye adept at uncovering the false beliefs being portrayed as reality.

• We learned to focus on the good happenings in our lives, to appreciate our abilities and talents, be thankful for our families and our environment. Feelings and attitudes create, so dwelling on the feeling of good produces good.

• We learned that not everyone is thrilled with the idea that there are no victims. One woman walked angrily out of one of our seminars when we discussed the victimless event of rape. Another became furious while stating she certainly was a victim when her house burned to the ground. And always the question of the six million Jews killed in the Holocaust arises. The idea that we create our participation in all events in our lives is so foreign, so against what seems reality, that it becomes a mountainous impasse for some.

• We learned we can't justify our new understandings and philosophies to those who challenge them. So don't try. You've got one person to worry about—you. It's not important that anyone else believes in what you're doing. Just work on your own stuff. Then the amazing happens: People start entering your life with similar views who are just as excited as you to have found someone to talk to. And as you bring change into your life, others will want to know what you've done to make it happen. Some you'll be able to share your ideas with, some not. But eventually you'll have a circle of friends and acquaintances who think conscious creation is the most natural thing in the world.

Which, of course, it is.

11

The Brass Ring

Our civilization is at the beginning of a quantum leap in consciousness. Around the world we are opening intuitive channels long ago closed with the mass decision to solely develop the intellect. The understanding that we are multidimensional energy straddling realities breaks us free from many old, useless concepts of who we are and what we can become. As we learn more of our abilities and the vastness of their implications, we will begin acting like dignified members of our species, with respect for ourselves and the rest of the world.

So what are the new rules to follow, since our old ones are

being unmasked as fallacious pretenders? There aren't any. The validity of our greater selves, our kinship to all consciousness, the workings of the universe and our interaction with it gives us a structure of understanding from which to conduct our lives. It's the bed-rock from which all else can then grow, safely and with inherent good intent. Individually, we create from this solid ground, we play with the universal ideas in whatever ways we choose, following no dogma that is supposedly correct for all people, but seeking the experiences that best lead us on our personal journey through life.

Jane Roberts' "Psychic Manifesto"

A few months ago I visited friends and relatives in Southern California. Of the five people I met with individually over a cup of tea, one was facing divorce and the impact of learning her daughter had been molested by her husband for ten years; one, nearing retirement, had lost a significant amount of money in an investment, his fourth such loss in recent years; another had a new boss who was just as much a tyrant as her last three; one is a hypochondriac; another, facing late middle age, said life was without purpose, and there was no reason to continue.

What's wrong in our world when life is one hit after another, when circumstances seem to spin out of our control, when meaning and purpose ring hollow? Is that what life's all about? Chin up, old fella. There are people in this world much worse off than you. Tomorrow is a new day. This too shall pass. Be strong. All the old bromides that tell us to persevere because it's all we can do.

Is it?

Not unless we choose to live this life based on ludicrous ideas and limiting theories that we had no say in creating, and, by God, we don't have to accept them. In *The God of Jane*, Jane Roberts expresses through the first verse of a poem, "A Psychic Manifesto,"[1] exactly what many of us feel:

My life is its own definition.
So is yours.
Let us leave the priests
to their hells and heavens,
and confine
the scientists
to their dying universe
and accidentally created stars.
Let us each dare
to open our dream's door,
and explore
the unofficial thresholds,
where we begin.

The Seeds of Change

Present culture reflects a hostile reality, one it seems we must constantly protect ourselves against. Drugs, crime, war, anxiety, debilitating and fatal diseases, extensive protective measures in place both personally and by country are outward signs of the fear that shrouds our world. If it grows unchecked, it will lead to a world that can't continue. It will pull down the curtain of doom as a reflection of the despair. Despair feels as though nothing matters and no meaning exists. Religions can't alleviate the despair, because none addresses the truth and depths of our origin. And only that can prove to us our worthiness and our sacredness . . . and reveal the opportunity to change our lives and our world. We must be led beyond what we are today, into our potential.

Far too often we persuade ourselves to accept the way things are. We feel guilty expecting more. We should be expressing gratitude, we say to ourselves. It's wrong to want things to be better, we think, when most of the world has less. We shut up. We settle.

However, a great disservice is handed humankind when we individually allow guilt to override growth. There is a new world waiting to be born, and its genesis is in our changing. The seeds of evolution are not in our bodies, but in our minds. The collective consciousness expands and experiences as we do; in fact, that's the only way for it to change. So as each of us tries to understand the structure of reality, as each of us applies fresh knowledge to our own lives, we aid in the birth of a new civilization.

Stan and I share the same emerging vision held by many others in this time and place. We see a world at peace, our earth so healthy and abundant that a new level of joy is shared between it and its inhabitants. We see illness recognized for the illusion that it is and, therefore, rejected as a possibility. We see people gathering with good intent, holding each other in simple regard. We see new civilizations being forged, based on emerging disciplines of thought and understanding as to our true connection with the universe. And we see the power of thought being harnessed into productive energy that can literally move mountains.

Since we the people are co-creators of the planet along with all living things, and since beliefs are the building blocks of our reality, we must start our outward journey through time and space at the only starting point there can be—an inward journey through our individual consciousnesses. We must identify what it is we think about the world and our participation in it, what we believe about ourselves and others. Then we must start to change. For only when private change occurs will the world stand a chance of surviving.

Inward is the only journey of validity. Every time one of us experiments with his or her beliefs and tries to understand how they create and why, and when we apply that knowledge to making ourselves more loving and at peace, our world lights up with hope.

We on the planet today who attempt to understand the secrets of consciousness are the pioneers of the emerging vision. We stand at the beginning of the unknown, placing one foot cautiously in front of the other, moving through new ideas at times with relish, at other times with skepticism, but still moving. Our spirit of adventure, born of need, will eventually lead to the truths

that will ultimately transform our world.
  It's called grabbing the brass ring.

> *Against the assault of laughter, nothing can stand.*
> — *Mark Twain*

Epilogue

Black, thunderous clouds roll in over the Plain of Purpose. Winds whip at my gown, pressing the light material to my body. Lightening slashes across the roiling heavens, outlining the mysterious Gothic pillars rising like monoliths from the barren landscape.

I hesitantly approach the largest pillar, fear tingling my spine. I reach out to touch the cold white marble and gads! a neon sign bursts from the edifice, flashing a message of warning...Do Not Touch!

As I watch, stunned, Day-glo green words spew from the face of the stone. "I am the Leader of the Pillars of Disgusting Beliefs. What I decree becomes law on this Plain of Purpose; and my decree is that you will be fat, fat, fat—ever more!"

I cower at its heavy words, whimpering into my flowing

sleeve. Oh, no! Oh, no! Anything but that!

I throw pride to the wind and plead with the Disgusting Leader, I mean Leader of the Pillars of Disgusting Beliefs. "Please, please," I cry. "Let me be free from your spell! I am but a skinny girl just trying to get through life the best way she knows how, and all this flab gets in my way! Please, please, let me be free!"

The green neon flashes and curls with glee. It's laughing! I look around. They're all laughing!

I fall to my knees, a crumpled heap of humanity, defenseless in the face of such power!

Ah, but then I feel a light touch to my shoulder, and hear a gentle voice. "Get up dear. You'll muss your dress."

I stagger to my feet, suspicious of the glowing light figure twinkling beside me. Too much damn glow around here, I muse. The figure looks familiar somehow, and as I strain forward to scan its lily white face, I know. I know deep down in my being who it is! The cavalry has arrived.

"I am your Inner Self, dear, here, once again, to assist you with your desires. This flab thing is just too, too old to keep carrying about. I've told you this before but," Inner Self tilts its nose and (I swear) sniffs, "you just don't listen at times."

"I'll do anything, anything to break the spell of these Disgusting Beliefs! Please help me, please help me," I plead, as I grasp the robe of IS.

"Dignity, dear, dignity. Now, you have much to remember before you can return the Plain of Purpose to its natural, pillar-free state. First, you must remember that you are the creator of everything that occurs here."

I look at IS, startled. In a wavering voice I say, "You mean I created these bozos?"

"Yes, dear, you did. That's the bad news. The good news is you can uncreate them just as easily."

By now, IS has my full attention. I hear the Leader of the Pillars of Disgusting Beliefs starting to babble incoherently in the background. I coldly ignore it. "Just tell me what to do, IS. I'm up for anything," I say, squaring my chubby shoulders.

"Good girl. Here's the deal. Each pillar was formed by energy you wrapped around a thought, turning it into a dastardly belief. The energy was generated by your feelings as you wallowed in self-pity—not listening to me," another sniff, "tell you it was all illusion. A sickly picture, dear, but true. Now, what you have to do first is ask each pillar to expose itself."

"Expose itself?" I say weakly. "I mean, like *expose* itself?"

"Yes, dear. You must ask each pillar what belief it hides within its cold column."

"Oh! Expose itself!"

"Well, yes, dear. You start with Leader. Boldly stride up close to it and demand to know its secret. By universal law, it must tell you."

I haven't boldly strode up close to any pillars lately, but I'm game, sort of. I head out, turning only once or twice to make sure IS is okay, I mean not in any trouble or scared or anything. As I draw near, it looks to me like Leader has regained its composure, which is bad luck, I think, because this could turn into a real battle of wills.

"No, dear. Stop that thinking immediately. You're in control here. Never forget it." I guess it doesn't matter that the voice is in my head, but it sure sounds like IS.

"It is me, dear. Now pay attention to what you're doing."

I stop abruptly, face the sneering slash of neon mouth, and choose my words carefully. "Just what the hell do you think you're doing on my Plain of Purpose, scumbag?" No response except for a deepening of Day-glo creases around the lips.

"Dear..."

"Tell me, O Fearless Leader, just what secret belief of mine you hold deep within your being." I smirk a little, and turn to IS. IS must be kind of tired, yawning like that.

My attention is quickly riveted back onto Leader when lightening flashes overhead and thunderclap words spew from its mouth, crashing against my ears, revealing my horrible secret belief: "I am overweight!"

Stunned, I turn to IS. "But...but I don't understand! It tells the truth! I AM overweight! Oh, my God, Leader has created me in its image! Look! A round, shapeless white pillar, that's what I am! That's what I'll always be! Ohhhhhh......"

"Calm down, dear. Get a grip on yourself. This is basically the problem you always have. You so strongly believe your belief that you keep manifesting it. The trick is to dissolve the belief so the cycle breaks...and that means Leader and his band of slimy God imitators must go."

I dry my eyes, I tighten my lips. After all, IS didn't reach this position by giving out bum advice. "Okay, what do I do?"

"Pretend this is an altered state of consciousness you're in, here on the Plain of Purpose. Calmly walk up to Leader. Ask it again what it stands for. Once you hear its answer, tell it you no longer need it in your life. Tell it you're withdrawing your creative energy from it, and order it to vaporize into thin air. Then see its released energy flowing back into you, making you more powerful, more solid, more balanced. Where Leader used to stand, see a flower grow. This is a new belief, one that says you're thin. Believe it. Water it. Feel joy at its presence. Then move on to the next pillar and do the same."

Later ...

I come out of my altered state of consciousness, warm and fuzzy inside. IS has retreated into my shadowy inner regions, leaving me calm and free. A slight scent of roses wafts by my nose. I smile, remembering.

What a night we had. We moved across the Plain of Purpose, me vaporizing all my old, limiting beliefs and IS encouraging me onward. Such a team we made, a light being and me. Funny thing, though. IS materialized a camera and snapped a Polaroid of us clowning around. Sounds kinda odd, but I swear I looked like a light being, too. Must have been an illusion.

Appendix

Beliefs That Affect Abundance
(As referenced in Chapter 6)

Money

Limiting beliefs:

_____I must work hard for the money I earn.

_____I must work hard for any money that comes into my life.

_____I need more money than I can generate.

_____It will take a long time to finally get ahead.

_____I feel helpless in changing my financial picture.

_____I don't earn enough money.

_____If I had a better education, I could earn more money.

_____If I were (older, younger, male, white, etc.) I could earn more money.

_____If I were (married, single) I would have more money.

_____In the future, I can earn more money.

_____Fate and luck control my financial life.

_____Money slips through my fingers.

_____I feel guilty having money.

_____I feel guilty having more money than some people.

_____I feel guilty because I don't make enough money.

_____I feel guilty because I earn too much money for the work I do.

_____People won't like me as much if I'm better off than them.

_____All I see for the future is more money going out than coming in.

_____I can't earn enough money to support my desired lifestyle.

_____It's wrong to focus on making money.

_____I don't want to seem too well off to people.

_____To want more money is greedy.

_____Rich people are greedy.

_____Rich people look down on me.

_____I must work hard to find my beliefs around money.

_____I must work hard to eliminate my beliefs around money.

_____It takes money to make money.

Positive beliefs:

_____Money is a natural manifestation of the universe.

_____The ability to manifest money is my birthright.

_____I have a strong belief in my ability to manifest money.

_____Money is no longer my chosen battlefield.

_____My thoughts are clear and balanced around my ability to change my financial picture for the better.

_____I am open to changing my beliefs around money.

_____I have released all fear and desperation around money.

_____It's OK for me to earn lots of money.

_____It's OK for me to spend lots of money on myself and others.

_____I am a superb money manager.

_____I deserve lots of money.

_____I carry no guilt for having more money than others.

_____It's fun and easy to make lots of money.

_____I am filled with confidence in my financial abilities.

_____My financial selections are sound and valuable.

_____It's OK to be rich.

_____Rich people are nice folks.

_____I release all guilt around being rich.

_____I can create everything I want in life, including money.

_____Money is energy that I materialize into my life.

_____I always have financial security because I generate what I want from the universe.

_____My thoughts are always filled with the abundance of the universe.

_____I don't have to work hard for my money.

_____I create money quickly and easily.

_____I am open to great financial abundance.

_____The creation of money is my forte. I am good at it.

_____My financial success is assured.

_____I am destined for great wealth.

_____I am a master wealth builder.

_____I create money as easily as I breathe.

_____Creating money is as natural and right as creating love.

_____I am not afraid of the IRS; it is not out to get me.

_____The IRS only reflects what I impose upon it.

_____My thoughts are clear and balanced around my taxes.

_____I'm wealthy, I'm free. I'm wealthy, I'm free. Wealth is energy materialized by me.

Spiritual/Religious/Life

Limiting beliefs:

_____Wanting money slows my spiritual growth.

_____It's wrong to focus on making money.

_____To have money is not spiritual.

_____Money is the root of all evil.

_____To struggle is why we're here.

_____Suffering is good for the soul.

_____My "self" is flawed from birth.

_____I must work to overcome my sinful self.

_____Life is to be feared.

_____Life is to be protected against.

_____I am vulnerable to life and fate.

_____I am powerless.

_____It's a dog-eat-dog world.

_____There's a lot of evil out there.

_____There will never be peace on earth.

_____I will never have peace in my life.

_____Life is to be controlled.

_____I'm on my own in this life, with no support from anyone or anything.

_____Living wears me down.

_____Suffering is to be expected.

_____Luck and fate rule my life.

_____There is no God that cares.

_____The universe supports me in spiritual matters, but not in making money.

Positive beliefs:

_____The universe and my life are with purpose and meaning.

_____The universe is a friendly place; I no longer need to prove otherwise.

_____Money and spirituality are not in conflict.

_____The universe is with meaning.

_____Happiness starts now, in this very moment.

_____I create everything I want from life with the full support of the universe.

_____I am here to learn energy manipulation, and that includes money manifestation.

_____My inner self gives me constant and clear guidance.

_____I am never alone.

_____Life just keeps getting better and better.

_____I can have everything I want.

_____Life is a joy!

_____It's fun to be alive!

_____I am created perfect.

_____I am one with the universe.

_____Peace is within me.

_____I am filled with the power of creation.

_____I trust the universe completely.

_____The world is a safe and sane place to live.

_____I have the power of the universe at my fingertips.

_____God loves me.

_____Nothing is to be feared, for fear is an illusion.

_____As a child of the universe, I am love.

Self-Worth

Limiting beliefs:

_____I'm not smart enough to figure out how to change my life.

_____Indecision is a normal state of mind for me.

_____Only aggressive people make it in life, and I'm such a wimp.

_____Everybody always judges me a failure.

_____I am a failure.

_____I can't make things happen.

_____I'm a victim of circumstances.

_____I'm always burdened with problems.

_____I'm so guilty over my past mistakes.

_____I don't usually make good decisions.

_____I have nothing to offer the world.

_____I don't deserve a better life.

_____I'm not easy to love.

_____I am a victim of fate.

_____I'm (fat, ugly, skinny, plain, etc.).

_____My body is disgusting, and I hate it.

_____I'm not attractive to the opposite sex.

_____People look right through me.

_____I am insignificant to the world.

_____Everyone shuns me.

_____It's all my parents' fault.

_____I can never forgive them.

_____I was so little, and they hurt me so.

Positive beliefs:

_____I am fully capable of taking complete control of my life.

_____I am a unique person with special contributions to my world.

_____I believe in myself totally and completely.

_____I am OK. I am fully acceptable to me.

_____My self-worth is strong and growing daily.

_____I love and accept myself.

_____My attractiveness shines through to the world!

_____I'm at ease with my body and my looks.

_____People respect my conversation inputs.

_____I am liked and respected.

_____I am easy to love.

_____I am a success at whatever I choose to do.

_____I know my self-worth, and it is great.

_____I enjoy the process of change.

_____I treat others with simple regard.

_____I love who I am.

_____I am proud of me!

Job/Career

Limiting beliefs:
_____I only get dead-end jobs.

_____No one appreciates me.

_____I'll never be really successful.

_____Everyone expects too much of me.

_____The jobs I'm qualified for will never bring me the money I want.

_____I'm not aggressive enough to advance in my field.

_____There are many people who can do the job better than me.

_____Almost everyone is more qualified than me.

_____My skills are lacking in critical areas.

_____My co-workers don't like me.

_____I always draw abusive bosses.

_____My job offers no creativity.

_____I hate working.

_____I'll never be able to do this job as it should be done.

_____Everyone else gets promoted, but not me.

Positive beliefs:
_____I have the ability to go far beyond the position I now hold.

_____I am a successful, complete person, open to new ideas.

_____I see depth and possibilities on my job I never saw before.

_____I am competent, qualified and ready for advancement.

_____I am a dynamic contributor, well-liked and confident in my abilities.

_____I deserve acknowledgment and thanks for my performance.

_____I am well worth more money to my company.

_____I get great satisfaction from watching myself grow on the job.

_____I am comfortable with myself and my performance.

_____I am at peace with myself.

_____My inner strength grows daily.

_____I can handle whatever comes my way.

_____I am a decision maker.

_____I am open to change and new experiences.

_____My opinions are valued.

Relationships

Limiting beliefs:

_____No one wants me.

_____I always get ____(hurt, dumped, used, fill in the blank).

_____I must protect myself from vulnerability.

_____I refuse to give up my freedom.

_____I lose control in a relationship.

_____Relationships are one compromise after another.

_____Only a person "below" me would be interested in me.

_____I can't be really open and honest with my mate.

_____I'm too old to attract a mate.

_____All the good ones are taken.

_____Sex isn't safe any more.

_____There's not a person out there who can meet my

_____requirements.

_____Love never lasts.

_____Love scares me.

_____I have to do everything (his, her) way.

_____Men don't like independent women.

_____I won't have a marriage like my parents.

_____I can't be myself or I won't be loved.

_____I don't know how to love.

_____God doesn't want me to be sexual.

_____I am ashamed of my sensuality.

_____I'm not good enough for my mate (or to find a mate).

_____Jealousy shows how much I love someone.

_____I hate rejection.

_____Only weak people forgive.

Positive beliefs:

_____I am worthy of love.

_____Relationships are fun and exciting!

_____I create good, strong relationships.

_____I trust myself and others.

_____I am capable of feeling safe and loved.

_____I am patient and forgiving.

_____I enjoy touching and being touched.

_____I feel completely at ease in new experiences.

_____I release all guilt surrounding past relationships.

_____I openly receive and accept love, support and respect.

_____I cherish my individuality and allow others the same
right.

_____I can be myself and still be with a mate.

_____I no longer expect perfection from a relationship.

_____It is safe for me to be open.

_____I move beyond limitations and express myself freely.

_____I am open and receptive to all points of view.

_____It is safe for me to be in love.

_____Loving myself and others gets easier every day.

_____There is no right or wrong.

_____It is strong to forgive and let go.

_____I take responsibility for my own life.

Health

Limiting beliefs:

_____Illness is inescapable.

_____Viruses attack randomly.

_____If someone gets a cold, it's a sure thing I will.

_____Sick people are victims of fate.

_____Vitamins protect me from ill health.

_____I am helpless to heal myself.

_____Cancer is caused by smoking.

_____My energy level is always low.

_____I heal slowly.

_____Going through the change is going to be tough.

_____As I grow older, I will be prone to osteoporosis.

_____I am prone to heart disease because it runs in my family.

_____I can only feel better with outside help.

_____The only way to lose weight is to diet.

_____Losing weight is the biggest battle of my life.

Positive beliefs:

_____I am not a victim to my body's whims.

_____I control my health through my beliefs.

_____I am filled with energy and enthusiasm.

_____My mind is at peace and all is well.

_____I am willing to move forward with ease. I welcome change.

_____I love and appreciate all of myself.

_____The world is a safe place to live.

_____I am healthy and whole.

_____Good health is within me always.

_____My body heals rapidly.

_____There is no condition that I cannot heal.

_____I draw energy from the universe for healing.

_____I love my body as it is.

_____I can become exactly what I choose.

_____My mind shapes my body, and my mind says I'm beautiful!

_____Everything I eat blesses my body.

_____Food is a most wondrous gift to give my body.

_____I will die peacefully and comfortably at the right time.

_____I move with ease, joy and comfort.

Notes

Prologue

1. Seth, as he defines himself, is an energy personality essence no longer focused in physical reality. For over twenty years, until her death in 1984, Jane Roberts received information from Seth on the true nature of reality. With the assistance of Robert (Rob) F. Butts, her husband, Jane and Seth wrote eight books together. She published another fourteen that evolved from Rob's and her work with Seth; and there is unpublished material for at least ten more books. Seth's information was gathered during more than 4,000 trance sessions. Much of it is now archived at Yale University.

2. From Richard Bach's book, *Jonathan Livingston Seagull: A Story* (New York: Avon Books, 1970)

Chapter 1

1. Jane Roberts, *Seth Speaks: The Eternal Validity of the Soul* (New York: Prentice Hall Press, 1972), Session 580, p. 358-9.

Chapter 2

1. Jane Roberts, *The Seth Material* (New York: Prentice Hall Press, 1970), Chapter 16, p. 216.

2. Some people believe there are seven major energy centers associated with the body. They are sometimes called chakras.

3. The subject of faith is covered in-depth in Jane Roberts' *The Afterdeath Journal of an American Philosopher: The World View of William James* (New York: Prentice Hall Press, 1978).

Chapter 5

1. Jane Roberts, Notes by Robert F. Butts, *The Individual and the Nature of Mass Events* (New York: Prentice Hall Press, 1981), Session 825, p. 127.

Chapter 6

1. "Popular theories on alcoholism face challenges," *The Oregonian*, 27 February 1992.

2. "How to get kids on the low-cholesterol track," *USA Today*, 9 April 1991.

3. "Cancer rate for children rises," *The Register-Guard*, Eugene, Oreg., 26 June 1991.

4. "Research report casts some doubt on low-fat diets," *The Register-Guard*, Eugene, Oreg., 26 June 1991.

Chapter 7

1. Jane Roberts, *The God of Jane: A Psychic Manifesto* (Englewood Cliffs, N.J.: Prentice-Hall, Inc., 1981), Chapter 2, p. 13.

2. Jane Roberts, *The Nature of Personal Reality* (New York: Prentice Hall Press, 1974), Session 619, p. 64-5.

3. Jane Roberts, *The Nature of Personal Reality* (New York: Prentice Hall Press, 1974), Session 627, p. 121.

4. Jane Roberts, Introductory Essays and Notes by Robert F. Butts, *Dreams, "Evolution," and Value Fulfillment, vol. 1* (New York: Prentice Hall Press, 1986), Session 891, p. 183.

5. Jane Roberts, *The Nature of Personal Reality* (New York: Prentice Hall Press, 1974), Session 625, p. 112.

6. Jane Roberts, *Seth Speaks: The Eternal Validity of the Soul*

(New York: Prentice Hall Press, 1972), Session 530, p. 102.

7. Jane Roberts, *Seth Speaks: The Eternal Validity of the Soul* (New York: Prentice Hall Press, 1972), Session 525, p. 79.

Chapter 9

1. Jane Roberts, *Psychic Politics: An Aspect Psychology Book* (Englewood Cliffs, N.J.: Prentice-Hall, Inc., 1976), Chapter 26, p. 349.

Chapter 11

1. Jane Roberts, *The God of Jane: A Psychic Manifesto* (Englewood Cliffs, N.J.: Prentice-Hall, Inc., 1981), Chapter 15, p. 152.

Suggested Reading

Books by Jane Roberts, Dictated by Seth

Roberts, Jane. *Seth Speaks: The Eternal Validity of the Soul*. New York: Prentice Hall Press, 1972.

___. *The Nature of Personal Reality: A Seth Book*. New York: Prentice Hall Press, 1974.

___. *The "Unknown" Reality: A Seth Book, vol. 1*. Notes and Introduction by Robert F. Butts. Englewood Cliffs, N.J.: Prentice-Hall, Inc., 1977.

___. *The "Unknown" Reality: A Seth Book, vol. 2*. Notes and Introduction by Robert F. Butts. Englewood Cliffs, N.J.: Prentice-Hall, Inc., 1979.

___. *The Nature of the Psyche: Its Human Expression*. New York: Prentice Hall Press, 1979.

___. *The Individual and the Nature of Mass Events*. Notes by Robert F. Butts. New York: Prentice Hall Press, 1981.

___. *Dreams, "Evolution," and Value Fulfillment, vol. I*. Introductory Essays and Notes by Robert F. Butts. New York: Prentice Hall Press, 1986.

___. *Dreams, "Evolution," and Value Fulfillment, vol. 2*. Introductory Essays and Notes by Robert F. Butts. New York: Prentice Hall Press, 1986.

Books by Jane Roberts, Related to Her Work With Seth

Roberts, Jane. *How to Develop Your ESP Power*. New York: Pocket Books, 1966.

___. *The Seth Material*. New York: Prentice Hall Press, 1970.

___. *The Education of Oversoul Seven*. New York: Prentice Hall Press, 1973.

___. *Adventures in Consciousness: An Introduction to Aspect Psychology*. New York: Bantam Books, 1975.

___. *Dialogues of the Soul and Mortal Self in Time*. Englewood Cliffs, N.J.: Prentice-Hall, Inc., 1975.

___. *Psychic Politics: An Aspect Psychology Book*. Englewood Cliffs, N.J.: Prentice-Hall, Inc., 1976.

___. *The World View of Paul Cezanne*. Englewood Cliffs, N.J.: Prentice-Hall, Inc., 1977.

___. *The Afterdeath Journal of an American Philosopher: The World View of William James*. New York: Prentice Hall Press, 1978.

___. *Emir's Education in the Proper Use of Magical Powers*. New York: Delacorte Press, 1979.

___. *The Further Education of Oversoul Seven*. New York: Prentice Hall Press, 1979.

___. *The God of Jane: A Psychic Manifesto*. Englewood Cliffs, N.J.: Prentice-Hall, Inc., 1981.

___. *If We Live Again: Or, Public Magic and Private Love*. New York: Prentice Hall Press, 1982.

___. *Oversoul Seven and the Museum of Time*. New York: Prentice Hall Press, 1984.

___. *Seth, Dreams and Projections of Consciousness*. Walpole, N.H.: Stillpoint Publishing, 1986.

Additional Authors

Ashley, Nancy. *Create Your Own Reality: A Seth Workbook*. New York: Prentice Hall Press, 1984.

___. *Create Your Own Happiness: A Seth Workbook*. New York:

Prentice Hall Press, 1988.

___. *Create Your Own Dreams: A Seth Workbook*. New York: Prentice Hall Press, 1990.

Bach, Richard. *The Bridge Across Forever: A Love Story*. New York: William Morrow & Co. Inc., 1984.

___. *Illusions: The Adventures of a Reluctant Messiah*. New York: Dell Publishing Co., Inc., 1977.

___. *Jonathan Livingston Seagull: A Story*. New York: Avon Books, 1970.

___. *One: A Novel*. New York: William Morrow & Co., Inc., 1988.

Bohm, David. *Wholeness and the Implicate Order*. London: Ark Paperbacks, 1980.

Chopra, Deepak. *Quantum Healing: Exploring the Frontiers of Mind/Body Medicine*. New York: Bantam Books, 1989.

Gawain, Shakti. *Creative Visualization*. Mill Valley, Calif.: Whatever Publishing, 1978.

Harman, Willis. *Global Mind Change: The Promise of the Last Years of the Twentieth Century*. Indianapolis, Indiana: Knowledge Systems, Inc., 1988.

Murphet, Howard. *Sai Baba: Man of Miracles*. York Beach, Main: Samuel Weiser, Inc., 1973.

Siegel, Bernie. *Love, Medicine and Miracles: Lessons Learned About Self-Healing From a Surgeon's Experience with Exceptional Patients*. New York: Harper & Row Publishers, 1986.

Stack, Rick. *Out-of-Body Adventures: 30 Days to the Most Exciting Experience of Your Life*. Chicago: Contemporary Books, Inc., 1988.

Talbot, Michael. *Beyond the Quantum*. New York: Macmillan Publishing Co., 1986.

___. *The Holographic Universe*. New York: HarperPerennial, 1991.

Watkins, Susan M. *Conversations with Seth, vol. 1*. New York: Prentice Hall Press, 1980.

___. *Conversations with Seth, vol. 2*. New York: Prentice Hall Press, 1981.

___. *Dreaming Myself, Dreaming a Town.* New York: Kendall Enterprises, Inc., 1989.

About the Author

Lynda Dahl lives in Washington on an island in the Columbia River. She moved there *after* she learned how to consciously create her experiences. In her prior life, she was one of the first wave of women to hit the management ranks and executive offices of America, including a stint with Apple Computer, Inc. as a marketing manager. She ended her computer industry career in 1989 as vice president of sales and marketing. At present, Lynda is president and chair of the board of directors of Seth Network International, and vice president of WindSong Publishing. She was recently selected for inclusion in *Who's Who Registry of Global Business Leaders*.

For those interested in inviting Lynda and Stan
to speak to their group or organization,
please send your inquiries to:

 WindSong Publishing

PO Box 1-H • Eugene OR • 97440 • USA
(503) 683-6731

• • •

For information on SNI, a nonprofit
organization dedicated to exploring
the Seth/Jane Roberts material,
please write to:

 SETH NETWORK
INTERNATIONAL

P.O. Box 1620
Eugene, OR 97440 USA
(503) 683-0803 FAX (503) 683-1084

The Wizards of Conscious Creation

Who are the wizards of conscious creation? All of us…once we decide it's possible, set our goals, alter our beliefs enough to allow change, and stay focused. One of our next projects at WindSong Publishing is to compile a book about people from around the globe who have become the pioneers of this new frontier. If you, dear reader, have created a special something in your life or have changed your circumstances in a significant way through focused conscious intent, we'd love to hear from you!

If you're interested in sharing your story with the rest of the world, please drop us a typed or printed note with your name, address, telephone number and a page or so describing your situation. Stories come in all sizes. Some will take a paragraph in the book, others will cover pages. No matter how short or long, we'll pay you for your story. After acceptance we will contact you, possibly for a telephone or personal interview. You can elect to have us use your given name in the book or request an alias.

For those of you just starting down the path of conscious creation, keep us posted on your progress. There are other projects planned for the future you may want to participate in.

We look forward to hearing your stories, ye lower case gods!

Lynda Dahl and Stan Ulkowski

WindSong Publishing

PO Box 1-H • Eugene OR • 97440 • USA
(503) 683-6731

The Wise Child

By the same author:

JESSICA STIRLING
The Wise Child

St. Martin's Press
New York

Library of Congress Cataloging-in-Publication Data

Stirling, Jessica.
    The wise child / Jessica Stirling.
        p.   cm.
    ISBN 0-312-05182-4
    I. Title.
PR6069.T497W5   1990
823'.914—dc20   90-37307
                                                                 CIP

First published in Great Britain by Hodder and Stoughton.

Contents

One

The Leaning Tower

Eight families occupied the close at No. 154 Canada Road. The breadwinners were all employees of Greenfield Burgh Council; a fireman, an inspector of weights and measures, and six policemen. In addition there were a score and a half of that class of citizen disparagingly recorded as 'dependent relatives', by which was meant children and wives.

On the ground floor lived the Boyles, Free Church adherents, who had scrimped and saved to buy their only child, Graham, the benefits of a private education. They were quiet and stand-offish in contrast to the McAlpines. Constable Andy McAlpine was a rowdy devil given to heavy drinking and, when the mood took him, to punching his wife, Joyce. On the top floor resided the Pipers, a large family devoted to Gaelic culture who were forever skirling on bagpipes or practising strathspeys to the detriment of the Swanstons' ceiling below.

The empress of the close occupied the middle landing. Jess Walker's husband was a sergeant which gave her status as well as an extra six bob a week in the pay packet. In addition she already had one son in constable's uniform and three more shined and polished to follow in father's footsteps. For all her airs and graces Jess Walker was a kindly soul and often looked after Kirsty Nicholson's child when no other minder could be found.

The Nicholsons were something of a mystery to the other occupants of the close. The husband was tall, handsome and as dour as sin. He had come into the Police Force by the back door and was known to be supercilious and ambitious. Kirsty was as different from her husband as chalk is from cheese. She was fresh and obliging, always ready to make the best of things. She'd had a lot to put up with this past twelve months for the year of 1898 had not been kind to her. She'd had her husband's family to contend with, then she had lost a baby three months

1

into term and finally, just as the New Year began, her old friend Nessie Frew had died, though Kirsty, it was said, had come in for a bit of money in the will.

It did not bother Jess Walker that Kirsty was late returning from an errand to St Anne's church that February afternoon. What did bother her was a distressing rumour that had reached her through Mrs Swanston who'd had it off John Boyle who had just come off day-shift at Ottawa Street station.

Jess took everything that Eunice Swanston said with a pinch of salt. Nonetheless she was disturbed by the story which did not, for once, seem exaggerated. What made her uncomfortable was that she had charge of Kirsty's child, Bobby. Inevitably she would be the first to confront the young woman when she returned from her outing. She was uncertain what to do, what to say, and Jess Walker was not used to indecision.

She had made a batch of scones and had rolled out an extra length of dough to keep her youngest, Georgie, and Bobby Nicholson amused. Georgie was almost ten now but you never really lost the urge to play with soft dough and Bobby's visit provided a grand excuse for childish high jinks and maternal indulgence.

As the afternoon wore into evening Jess became more and more apprehensive. Both her husband and eldest son were on back-shift and would not be home until after ten so that she could not check with them the validity of Mrs Swanston's tale. If only Madge Nicholson, Kirsty's mother-in-law, had still been lodging in Canada Road, Jess might have put the problem into her hands. But Madge had lately married Albert 'Breezy' Adair and, with her younger son and daughter, had moved up in the world. That too had been a source of much gossip in the close and had caused a serious rift in the Nicholson family for, in Craig's opinion, Breezy Adair was more crook than businessman.

Kirsty Nicholson's connection with St Anne's and the posh folk of Walbrook Street was not held against her by the other police wives. The fact that she could hobnob with her betters and not seem out of place was a bit of a triumph for a lass who'd been raised in an Ayrshire orphanage and had drudged on a remote hill-farm until Craig Nicholson had run off with her and brought her to Glasgow several years ago.

Jess Walker was more astute than her neighbours, however. She had sensed in Kirsty's unhappiness a lack of fulfilment that

2

stemmed from her man's anger and resentment, from the fact that he seemed to despise her for the very qualities that other folk found admirable and appealing.

Jess was waiting on the landing when at last Kirsty climbed the stairs. She had Bobby by the hand. He was dusted with flour and had pressed a moustache made of dough to his upper lip. Georgie Walker was similarly adorned but was more selfconscious about it.

"See, see, Mammy," Bobby cried as soon as his mother appeared.

Kirsty crouched to study her son's disguise.

"My, my! What a fine 'tash you've grown."

"Better'n Daddy's?"

"Oh, far better."

Kirsty glanced up at Jess who, oddly, did not seem to be engaged with the game but looked distant, almost perplexed.

Jess was a small, sturdy woman, heavy-bosomed. Her light-brown hair was flecked with grey. She wore it in a tight roll fastened with three jet combs. Now that the family had two wages coming in she indulged her taste for floral taffeta dresses and wore one even about the house.

Not to be outdone, Georgie said, "How 'bout mine, Mrs Nicholson?"

"Aye, it's a cracker too."

At that moment the moustache became detached from Georgie's lip and fell with a plop to the stone floor. The boys stared at it, dismayed, then Bobby disengaged his hand from Jess Walker's and patted his pal consolingly.

"Ne'r mind, Georgie. I not got one neither." Bobby peeled the dough from his face and flung it to the floor in a gesture of solidarity. "See, my 'tash gone too."

Kirsty felt a wave of affection for her son. But with it came the first pang of guilt at what she had done that afternoon. She had made love with David Lockhart, an act as distant from Bobby's innocent world as China was from Greenfield, yet one, she now realised, that might ruin his little life if ever Craig found out.

"Georgie," Jess Walker snapped. "Pick up that stuff this minute. I'm not wantin' my clean landin' soiled."

Schooled in obedience Georgie did as bidden. He knelt and scraped the dough strips from the stone and crumpled them into his fist.

"What's wrong, Jess?" Kirsty lifted her son into her arms. "Has Bobby been a nuisance?"

"No, no. He's been as good as gold."

Guilt grew in Kirsty, making her breathless.

"I'm – I'm sorry I'm so late. I was – detained."

"No matter."

Jess sounded unusually tart. Could Jess have found out what had happened that afternoon in the servant's room in No. 19 Walbrook Street? Could news have reached Greenfield in less time than it had taken Kirsty to walk home?

Until that moment Kirsty had felt no regret for what she had done, only a strange sense of relief that David and she had finally been together. It would have been different, of course, if he had not been leaving for the North China mission field tomorrow morning, if there had not been the hurt of final parting to contend with and the knowledge that, in all probability, they would never meet again.

"Somethin' is wrong, Jess," said Kirsty, anxiously. "Won't you tell me?"

Jess shook her head. "It's nothin' really. Mrs Swanston's been gettin' on my nerves again, that's all."

"What's she been sayin' this time?"

"Och, just some daft story."

"About – about me, was it?"

"Some nonsense from the station," Jess said. "You know how Eunice makes mountains out o' molehills. I expect Craig might be late home tonight, though."

"Another street fight?"

"Somebody didn't turn out for muster," Jess said. "Sergeant Drummond'll be readin' them all the riot act, I imagine."

Kirsty understood only too well how minor disruption to Ottawa Street's routines could affect not only a husband's mood but could also throw out of kilter the harmony of the home.

"Who was it?" Kirsty asked.

"I really couldn't say," Jess Walker told her. "Georgie, go inside an' take the wee pan off the stove. Be careful not to spill it."

"Aye, Mam."

"I'll not keep you," said Kirsty, taking the hint. "I'll just thank you again for lookin' after Bobby."

To Kirsty's surprise Jess nodded, stepped back into the house and abruptly closed the door.

Kirsty hesitated. She was filled with doubt and apprehension, not about the trivial gossip from the station but in respect of what had taken place at Walbrook Street. It had seemed so natural, so safe. Tomorrow David would be gone from her life and she'd supposed that she would have no lingering regret about their love-making, only the pain of being without him. Now she was not so sure.

She shrugged Bobby close against her shoulder and carried him upstairs. He had become long-bodied and heavy of late. He would probably be as tall as his father when his growth was full gained.

"Did you have a nice time, son?"

"Uh-huh."

She was anxious to be indoors, safely alone in her own kitchen. She was relieved that Craig was on shift and selfish enough to hope that he might be kept late at the station. Tonight of all nights she did not want him to come to her bed.

In fact it had been weeks since Craig had shown a sexual interest in her. He had been distant and indrawn for most of February, not simmering with rage and frustration, though, as he had been at New Year, smarting over his mother's marriage to Breezy Adair and the 'desertion' of his sister Lorna and brother Gordon. Wounded pride had hurled him into those black moods but what had given rise to his recent withdrawn state Kirsty had no idea. She was, however, certain that Craig had not guessed that she had been in love with David Lockhart.

In spite of all that had happened she was still grateful to Craig for having rescued her from servitude on Hawkhead farm. And yet she had fallen in love with David. Now David was gone, summoned by duty to his family in the China mission, by his calling as a minister.

Once more she was isolated in the tenement suburb with her child and husband. Nothing had really changed because of what she had done that afternoon. She realised now that by her foolishness she had only compounded the predicament of her common-law marriage.

She unlocked the front door and pushed into the narrow hallway. It was dark in the kitchen, no flicker of fire in the black iron grate. Craig must have left the house early, long before he was due to report for shift.

5

Kirsty's disquiet increased. She set Bobby down and groped across the kitchen to the gas jet by the side of the hearth. Bobby remained by the kitchen door, waiting for light to make the kitchen friendly again.

"It's all right, son," Kirsty assured him.

But it was not all right.

Even with the gas lighted the kitchen did not seem like a haven.

She put down the brown paper parcel that David had given her. It contained an old album of photographs of China that had once belonged to Nessie Frew. She took off her coat and flung it across the bed in the recess. She still reeked of Lily-of-the-Valley. She still wore her best petticoat, her blue garters and the silver pendant that Nessie had given her in happier times. She must take them off, must hide them away, together with the album. She must wash the scent of perfume from her body before Craig got home. What had happened that day must remain her secret.

She had other secrets too, secrets from the neighbours and secrets from Craig. She had told him that she had received only fifty pounds from Nessie's estate. In fact it had been two hundred pounds. She had deposited the balance in an account in a Glasgow bank in her own name; money enough to leave him if it should ever come to that, money enough to pretend that she could escape.

"Mammy?"

Bobby was standing by the table. He had stuck a strip of the old dough that Georgie had slipped to him across his upper lip.

"Gotta new 'tash, see."

"My, so you have! That's amazin'!"

On impulse she picked the child up and seated herself on one of the kitchen chairs, settled him on her knee.

"Like Daddy?" Bobby asked.

"Yes, just like Daddy."

She hugged him to her breast, rocking gently.

She must not cry, not for the loss of David, not for herself. There was nothing to be done but get on with the life that she had chosen in the hope that it might change for the better.

She sighed, sniffed and kissed Bobby on the brow.

"Tea time," she said. "Are you a hungry policeman, Constable Nicholson?"

And Bobby proudly answered, "*Yes*."

*   *   *

Dusk had settled into the lane that backed Ottawa Street police station. The February day had been clear and mild. Now a prickling white frost rimed the bars and worn stone coping of the basement window. Head in hands, Craig could hear the familiar sounds of the station clearly but paid them no attention. He remained slumped on the three-legged stool in the bare basement room, motionless, his back to the door.

Change shift had taken place. Constables gone clumping off into the cold streets. Others had gone hurrying home to supper. Those who were lucky enough to be unmarried would be sitting down to a piping hot meal in the police barracks around the corner in Edward Road.

Craig waited.

The door of the sergeants' room slapped open and shut. A desk lid thumped. Voices were raised in laughter and immediately silenced by Sergeant Drummond's gruff reprimand. From the lane came the clack of horses' hoofs. Ordinary sounds, part and parcel of everyday routine. Tonight, however, they seemed edged and menacing, turned inward and downward and pointed against him.

He had been alone in the holding-cell for what seemed like hours, waiting for something to happen, for somebody to take action. His muscles were tense, his mind fogged, not with alcohol but with the shock of rejection. Worst of all, he no longer gave a damn what they did to him, even if they booted him off the Force. He wanted them to arrive. He was desperate to get it over with, to be discarded, punished, dismissed.

He tried not to think of Greta. He tried not to think of her laughter, her derision.

He had offered everything, the sacrifice of his marriage, such as it was, and a fresh start in another part of Scotland. He had shown her the forty pounds that he had signed out of the shared account. He had assured her that he would be true to her, would cherish her and her child, would never desert or abandon her.

And she had laughed in his face.

She'd asked him if he'd gone loony.

He'd told her he thought she loved him.

She'd laughed again.

He'd taken the banknotes from his pocket and had shaken them in her face and she'd shouted at him not to be so bloody daft, that she'd never run off with another woman's husband.

The kitchen had been dappled with afternoon sunlight.

The bairn, Jen, had been seated at the table, eating bread pudding, thick, yellow and studded with raisins. Her cheeks had been smeared with the stuff. She'd been wearing a blue frock with a lace bib and she'd watched him warily, as if she could see right through him, as if her innocence made her perceptive and wise. He could never bring himself to hate the wee girl but at that moment he'd come mighty close to it. He'd pulled Greta round to face him.

He'd shouted, "What the hell's wrong with me?"

"You want too damned much, Craig Nicholson."

He'd tried to be calm, to explain what was on his mind, the new life, the new beginning.

"I don't fancy a new life, not with you, Craig, not with nobody," Greta had told him. "It's not me that's runnin'. It's you."

"What about Jen? Doesn't she need a father?"

"The last thing she needs is a father like you."

Again he'd shouted, "What's wrong with me?"

"If you're willin' to do it once, you might do it again. As soon as you got tired of us, you'd be off."

"It's different wi' you, Greta. Last time was a mistake. Anyway, Kirsty doesn't need me."

"An' we do?"

"I've – I've taken the money."

"Put it back."

"Is that it?" he'd shouted. "Is it because you think I'm married?"

"God, you've a right cheek on you, Craig, to assume I'd give up everythin' for you, married or not."

"You gave me plenty in that bed."

"It's what you wanted from me."

"You *liked* it."

"I'm not denyin' it. But that's no reason to give up my house, my work, my freedom – "

"Greta, don't you understand: I love you."

"I doubt it."

"What can I say, what can I do to convince you?"

"Nothin' will convince me, Craig."

Jen had giggled then. He'd found her femininity, her archness infuriating. Her dark eyes had seemed coy and full of something instinctive, not learned. He'd been torn between a desire to pick her up and hug her protectively and a fleeting urge to smash her head against the table.

Sensing danger, Greta had said, "Stop it, Jen."

He'd taken a deep, deep, deep breath.

"I'll never ask again, Greta," he'd told her.

"You should never have asked in the first place."

They had been lovers for almost a year. He had met her in the streets, had been drawn to her gradually. She was all the things that Kirsty was not, or so it seemed. She was perfect for him, a perfect mistress, shameless, independent, available. But he hadn't imagined himself to be in love with her until recently.

"More money, would that do it?" he'd asked.

"Not all the bloody money in the world."

"Is it the job then? Don't fret about that. I wouldn't be a copper any longer."

"It's the best thing you can be," she'd told him. "It's the best thing you'll ever be."

The child had gone back to her pudding. She'd supped it with a large, long-handled spoon, gripped not in her fingers but in her little fist. Her back had been to him and she'd swung her legs, rapped her heels on the spar of the chair, blotting him out of her existence and humming contentedly as she did so. That innocent rejection had hurt him more than anything.

No, he mustn't think of them. He must try to put Greta Taylor and her child out of his mind.

Polished black boots with metal-capped toes tapped on the stone steps; Sergeant Drummond. It hadn't been Drummond who'd been on the desk when he'd staggered into the station earlier that afternoon but Sergeant Stevens, a lean, dry man from Islay, who had smelled the whisky on his breath and had yanked him out of the muster and bundled him unceremoniously down into the basement.

Archie Flynn and Peter Stewart, his pals, had tried to prevent him turning out, had scuffled with him. He'd even had the whisky bottle on him, a conspicuous bulge in his notebook pocket. He'd told his pals to bugger off and had reeled into the muster room as bold as brass.

"On your feet, Constable Nicholson."

For a split second he resisted the command. He could make sure of it right this very minute. He could stand up, swing and punch old Drummond right in the mouth. That would do it. By God, it would. That would free him from the job, and from all obligations.

"Do you not hear me?" Drummond demanded. "Are you still so intoxicated that you cannot find your pins?"

Thirty years in Glasgow had not roughened Sergeant Hector Drummond's lilting Highland accent. He was over fifty now, clean-shaven, crop-haired, portly. He had served all his days in Greenfield Burgh Police and had witnessed the rise of many a constable and the downfall of many more. He was old now, or nearly so, stoical, efficient and caring. Craig could not bring himself to strike old Drummond. If it had been Sergeant Stevens things might have been different. But not Drummond.

Craig got to his feet.

"I am not intoxicated, Sergeant."

"Not now, since you have had time to sober yourself."

From behind his back Drummond produced a half-pint bottle, labelless and nearly empty.

"Can you deny that this bottle was removed from your person by Sergeant Stevens after you had presented yourself for duty at approximately ten minutes to three o'clock this afternoon?" Drummond said.

"I can't deny it, Sergeant."

"Can you deny that you had been imbibing from said bottle an alcoholic beverage and that you entered the station for duty in a condition that was less than sober?"

"Slightly less than sober," Craig said.

Drummond nodded. "Where did you purchase the whisky?"

It was an offence under the Burgh Police Act of 1892 to supply drink to a constable in uniform and carried a penalty of five pounds. Craig realised that he was more recovered than he had thought himself to be. He answered without hesitation. "I bought the bottle last night, Sergeant, when I was in mufti."

"Where?"

"I can't remember."

"Och, don't lie to me, son. I know shebeen whisky when I see it. You bought this from an illicit source."

"No, Sergeant."

"Who filled the bottle for you? Was it Jackie Neville, by any chance?"

"No, Sergeant."

"Was it her?"

"Who?"

"The woman in Benedict Street with whom you've been keepin' company?" Drummond said. "Did she give you the drink?"

"What woman in Benedict Street?"

"Aye, I should have nipped that relationship in the bud a long time ago," the sergeant said.

"There was nothin' to nip, Sergeant Drummond."

"Were you with her this afternoon?"

Craig said nothing.

"I have to know the truth," Drummond said, "or I can't help you."

"Yes, I was with her," Craig said. "But not in the way you mean. I've never been *with* her in that sense."

"I have a bit of trouble believin' that, son."

"It's the truth, Sergeant." With a strange sense of separation Craig heard himself say, "In case you've forgotten, I've a lovin' wife at home."

"Tell me what happened. Tell me why it happened," Drummond said. "And, most important of all, tell me it will not happen again."

God, Craig thought, Drummond's buying the lie. He was going to get away with it after all. He had not had to admit anything, not even that he had bought the whisky from the back window of Jackie Neville's house, where the odour of illicit distillation was strong enough to kill rats. He had not had to bow and scrape, swear on his father's grave that he had done nothing awfully wrong. All he'd had to do was invoke his loving wife, to conjure up Kirsty as a goddess of humdrum respectability and let sentimentality do the rest.

"Is it not recorded?" Craig asked.

"Aye, of course it's recorded," Drummond answered. "Sergeant Stevens is very meticulous, as well you know. He was not well pleased at your truculence."

"I – I only had a taste."

"How is it then that the bottle is near empty?"

He thought of Greta and how she had spurned him. He thought of her sprawled on the bed, near-naked, and imagined that she had lured him into the affair just to humiliate him, to take revenge on all that he represented, decency, security, a disciplined society.

"I took it from her, from the woman in Benedict Street," Craig said. "You're right. It is shebeen whisky. She drinks a lot of it."

"You should have reported – "

"It's not my beat," Craig said. "In any case, Greta Taylor's not the sort you sweep up off the street."

"What sort is she?"

Craig shrugged. "She has a hard life, Sergeant. The drink's her only consolation. I worry about the child, though, her child. She's a holy terror for wanderin' off, that bairn."

"And you took it upon yourself – "

"To keep an eye on her, yes," Craig said.

It was easy, so easy to fly on the back of lies.

"And to share her bottle?" Drummond raised one grey eyebrow.

"It was a warm day," Craig said. "I only had one suck. I never realised that it would be so potent."

"Pot whisky has floored better men than you, son," Drummond said. "How do you feel now?"

"I've a bloody thick head, Sergeant, I can tell you."

"So you would have now."

Craig said, "Have you ever – you know?"

"Once," Drummond said. "By accident."

"I suppose you could say it was an accident, Sergeant," Craig went on. "Not that that's an excuse. I know I have t' take my medicine."

"You won't be dismissed," Drummond assured him. "Not for a first offence."

"You have my word that it'll never happen again."

"And the woman in Benedict Street?"

"That's over," Craig snapped.

"Over?"

"She'll just have to look out for her own welfare from now on."

"John Boyle'll keep an eye on the child."

"Good," Craig said. "What happens now, Sergeant Drummond?"

"You go home."

"I should be on back-shift."

"Not tonight. You go home now and polish your buttons, son. Tomorrow at nine o'clock you report to Lieutenant Strang at Percy Street."

The sergeant reached behind him and opened the gate. Two pairs of boots vanished from the top of the stairs at the gate's oily clang. Craig wondered who had been listening to his reprimand and to his lies. Friends or enemies?

"You're not due in court tomorrow, are you?" Drummond asked.

"No, Sergeant, not tomorrow."

"Nine o'clock, Percy Street," Sergeant Drummond said, and, standing to one side, let the chastened young constable precede him upstairs.

*　　　*　　　*

Craig's sudden appearance caught Kirsty off guard. She had not expected him before half-past eleven at the earliest. She jumped from her chair at the table with such a start that Bobby, who had been feeding himself with two spoons, was frightened and began to wail. Craig had his helmet off and tunic unbuttoned before he entered the kitchen and one glance at his face filled Kirsty with fear.

The album of photographs that David had given her was still on the bed, together with her garters and frilly petticoat. To Kirsty the air seemed redolent of Lily-of-the-Valley. But Craig paid no attention to any of these things. He flung his tunic on to the bed, went at once to the sink and twisted the brass tap. He stooped and drank from the flowing jet, swirled water in his mouth and spat it out into the sink. Bobby continued to wail.

Kirsty said, "Craig, what is it?"

She was utterly confused and close to weeping. She went to him and put her hand on his back, felt the muscles under his shirt go tense. He flinched and he shook her off but did not otherwise acknowledge her presence. He was, she noticed, trembling.

"Craig, Craig, what is it? Have you been hurt? Are you sick?"

He did not turn around but offered her his shirt collar as if that were an answer. Automatically she took it from him and stared down at it. Craig washed, laving his face and neck with soap,

13

splashing water everywhere. Bobby climbed down from the chair and, still keening, clung to the back of Kirsty's skirt.

"Can you not shut him up?" Craig snapped.

"Why are you home so early?"

She handed him a towel as he rose, dripping, from the sink.

"Ach, you'll hear soon enough, I suppose," he said. "I got sent down for bein' in drink."

"Oh!"

She was enormously relieved at the information. She swung away from him to hide it. Craig buried his face in the towel and dried himself vigorously. Kirsty lifted Bobby and walked with him towards the bed. She lifted the tunic, folded it one-handed and dropped it on the brown paper parcel, drew the curtain over the recess. She turned just in time to catch the towel that Craig threw to her.

"Is *that* all you can say about it?"

"Was it true? Were you in drink?" Kirsty said.

"I had a touch, a taste, that's all."

"Did Drummond smell it on you?"

"Stevens. He hauled me out the muster."

"You haven't – I mean, you haven't been dismissed?"

"Christ, no. One shift, that's all."

"They'll dock you a week's pay, though, won't they?"

Craig peeled his shirt over his head. "How do you know so bloody much about it?"

Bobby had quieted. He studied his father now with an expression of belligerent curiosity that was pure Nicholson.

"Joyce McAlpine told me. It's happened to Andy more than once. He's on final warnin'." Holding Bobby firmly against her hip Kirsty stretched out and shifted the kettle on to the hot plate. "It could have been worse, I suppose."

"Fifteen bob an' a black mark on my record," Craig said. "I'll draw cash out the bank account tomorrow so we'll not go short. Right?"

It was on the tip of Kirsty's tongue to remind him that the money in the shared account had been intended as protection against the proverbial rainy day, not to pay for his indulgences. She kept silent, though, sensing the blackness of his mood.

Craig's father had been a drunkard, quiet and undemonstrative but hardly ever sober. She had always believed that it was Madge who had driven Bob Nicholson to drink, that the solace of whisky had become his only escape from her nagging dissatisfaction with the life he had given her. Craig, though, had nothing to escape from, unless it was marriage itself, marriage and its responsibilities.

"I'll make your supper," Kirsty said.

"No need. I'm goin' out."

Again she felt relief and, tonight, no sense of exclusion.

Something else had happened at the station, of that she was sure, something that Craig had not revealed. She would find out tomorrow. Eunice Swanston, or one of the other wives, would tell her. There were precious few secrets that did not seep from Ottawa Street into Canada Road.

"Da . . . Daddy?"

"What is it?"

"I . . . I got a 'tash."

"What's he bletherin' about?"

"Oh, he's made a moustache out o' dough," Kirsty explained. "He wants you to see it."

"Well, he'll just have to wait," Craig said. "I've no time for his nonsense right now."

Without another word to either his wife or son, Craig left the kitchen for the bedroom and, within minutes, was gone from the house once more.

Two

Dinner with Dolphus

Gordon Nicholson would have been better pleased if he had been the only guest invited to dine with James Randolph Adair and his family. Even his rudimentary knowledge of social niceties, however, told him that such favours were not on. As it was he was flattered to be asked to visit the home of 'the other Adairs' without his mother and stepfather tagging along and managed to convince himself that it was Amanda, Randolph's eldest daughter, who had put her old man up to offering the hand of friendship to the latest addition to the clan.

Hobnobbing with the well-to-do was still a novelty for Gordon. He felt quite comfortable when Breezy was in the company but the prospect of sitting at Dolphus's board, under the man's scrutiny, shook even Gordon's confidence somewhat. He could not quite trust his boyish charm to see him through the ordeal. He was afraid that he would make some dreadful gaffe that would confirm Dolphus's opinion that he was nothing but a bumpkin and an upstart and that would have Johnnie Whiteside and Eric hooting with laughter for weeks thereafter.

"Dinner with Dolphus, eh!" Breezy said when Gordon showed him the formally worded letter of invitation. "My, but you are honoured."

"Johnnie and Eric will be there too."

Whiteside and Eric Adair were the managers of Breezy's large warehouse in Partick East and Breezy seemed to trust and depend upon them. Gordon had worked under the pair for the best part of a year now but he hadn't quite fathomed where he stood in the pecking order or what the cousins really thought of him.

"The younger generation, yes," said Breezy.

"Why does he call himself Dolphus?"

" 'Cause he's a snob," said Breezy. "Bein' just plain Jimmy wasn't good enough for my dear brother. We all called him

Randy for a while, until he threatened us with violence. Dolphus it became."

"What do I call him?"

"You call him *Sir*," said Breezy.

"I can't think," said Gordon, "why he'd bother to ask me to dinner."

"Oh, stop fishin', son," said Breezy. "It'll be that pretty wee daughter that's keen to see more of you."

"Amanda?" Gordon tried to sound surprised.

"She's just come on the market for a man."

"What?"

"A husband's what I mean," said Breezy. "An' what Amanda wants, Amanda gets. Besides, old Dolphus has four of the bloody things on his hands."

"What bloody things?"

"Daughters," said Breezy. "He's given them enough by way of education, now he wants them married an' settled down, startin' with Amanda."

"Wait a wee minute," Gordon said. "You don't mean that I'm – well, in the runnin' as a – well, husband?"

"Why shouldn't you be?"

"I mean, well, surely she can have her pick."

"Meanin'?"

"She's rich. I'm not."

"Amanda's not worth a penny in her own right," Breezy said. "In fact, between you an' me, son, Dolphus hardly has two brass farthin's to rub together. He didn't make his money. He married it."

"He married Olive Carruth, didn't he?" said Gordon.

"Indeed he did," said Breezy. "An' you know what that means."

"I'm not sure I do."

"Then you haven't been readin' your *Glasgow Herald*," Breezy said. "Beer money. Brewery money, that's what it means. Last year Carruth's turned over one hundred and fifty *thousand* pounds."

"Dear God!"

"Olive's father was the brains behind it all. He was shrewd enough to purchase prime barley land in Lothian and Angus and he was one of the first of the Scottish brewers to expand the market south. Tied houses, managed houses, Carruth was fast off the mark

to seize all the advantages of progress. Dolphus was brought in as
a salesman after he'd wooed an' won Olive. Give my brother his
due, when it comes to raw commerce he's not as big a fool as he
looks."

"An' I thought you were King Midas in this family," Gordon
said.

Breezy grinned. "I gave the beggar his start. I helped him
earn his first half-crown. In fact it was through me that he met
Olive Carruth in the first place. He doesn't like to be reminded
of those early days, by the way. I wouldn't start a conversation
about muckin' out byres, if I were you."

"What should I talk about?"

"Thoroughbreds."

"Hell!" said Gordon. "You know I can't talk about horses."

"Direct your conversation to Olive, if you can."

"The wife?"

"Aye, she's human," said Breezy. He added, with a wink,
"Well, nearly."

*   *   *

'The Knowe', James Randolph Adair's estate, lay six miles north
of the city, an inconvenient base for anyone who did not possess
a stable of horses and umpteen carriages with which to cart the
family to and from the railway station at Milngavie.

Set in four verdant acres the house was a huge double villa
designed and built in the 1850s by the famous architect 'Greek'
Thomson. The knoll that had given the place its name had been
dug away to form a protective horseshoe against the winds that
whistled over the Moss. The grounds were planted with gigantic
evergreens to protect the glazed colonnades and Romanesque
windows from excessive weathering and when you came rattling
up from the station all you could see of The Knowe was a corner
of the deep-eaved roof and the glint of a window or two through
the dense dark mass of the trees.

Dinner with Dolphus was not exactly the sort of event that you
anticipated with unalloyed pleasure, Gordon discovered. Seated
in a big bow-fronted Sovereign with the coachman cracking his
whip over your head and the tree-buried house looming closer,
you could not help but feel your palms sweat a little and your
mouth go dry.

Even those worldly-wise men, Johnnie and Eric, puffed with

forced nonchalance on their small cigars and fussed with their dickie-bow ties and stand-up collars. They too were nervous, though for what reason Gordon could not deduce. After all they were true-blue nephews of Uncle Dolphus and had been brought up in the privileged circle. Not only that, they were five or six years older than Gordon, and displayed, as a rule, a cynical arrogance that he could never match.

Gordon had glimpsed James Randolph Adair only once, on the occasion of Madge's wedding to Breezy. He had been impressed by Dolphus's height and straight bearing, by the daring razor-cut side-whiskers that he'd sported in defiance of fashion. In the confusion of relatives, however, he had not identified Olive Carruth Adair. Later, at New Year, he had been so mesmerised by Amanda that he would not have noticed if she'd been accompanied by the band of the Grenadier Guards.

By the time the Sovereign halted in front of a portico lit by two glass footballs clutched in wrought-iron claws Gordon was in a funk of anxiety. Down came the master to greet his guests. Rehearsed phrases fled from Gordon's memory. He left Johnnie and Eric to do the honours and only managed a grunt when the lordly Dolphus shook his hand and led them all into the library off the hall.

"The bride's boy, hah," Dolphus said. "My daughter wanted you here. Can't for the life of me think why. Sherry?"

"Yes," Gordon whispered. "Please."

He was given the glass. It contained only a dribble of sour liquid. He sipped at it, coughed.

Johnnie and Eric glowered at him and Dolphus Adair, positioned before the fireplace's one smoking log, chuckled.

"Not used to gentleman's liquor, hah." His voice was tortured by unnatural inflexions. "Rather have ginger pop, would you? Hah?"

"No . . . thank you, sir. Sherry is . . . fine."

In fact the sherry was dreadful, the sort of stuff that only desperate alcoholics could down without a grimace. Breezy would not have cleaned drains with it.

"Not used to it, you see," Dolphus told his bona fide nephews, sure of their support in ragging the upstart.

The room was lined with tawdry volumes that had probably been purchased by the yard from some cheapjack dealer. The rug was not genuine Persian but an imitation that had been washed too many times. The beautiful stone fireplace held but one green log, and the chairs were tattered and the tantalus from which an aged servant had poured the wine could have been purchased from Adair's warehouse for a couple of shillings. The contrast between Dolphus's reputation as a man of substance and the trappings of the big house set Gordon on his guard and prepared him for worse to come.

"Drink up, my boys," said Dolphus. "And we'll join the ladies in the drawin'-room, hah."

Dolphus plucked the glass from Gordon's fingers and put it on the tin-plated tray that the servant held out, then he spread out his arms and gathered unto him Johnnie and Eric and led them towards the door, leaving Gordon to follow humbly in their wake.

*   *   *

Dining with Dolphus was like being in the cast of one of those complicated dramas that got booed off the stage of the *Queen's*. It was not the warmth of the welcome that melted Gordon's self-consciousness and restored some of his cockiness but the various layers of unpleasantness that were uncovered as the evening progressed.

Mother, for instance, was as sweet as pie to her guests, indifferent to her daughter, patronising to the servants and viperish in addressing her husband. She wore a gown that was laced so tight that her breasts seemed to swell out between the flounces and she fawned over Gordon and fanned his cheek with her eyelashes as if she, not Amanda, were in the market for a beau. Dolphus showed no sign of being piqued by such behaviour. Perhaps he was used to his wife's outrageousness. He responded by paying an excessive amount of attention to Amanda, nuzzling her cheek with his razor-cut whiskers, squeezing her tiny waist with his arm. Amanda, in turn, played up to her father and batted her eyelids and pursed her rosebud lips in a performance that Gordon found almost sickening. Between Amanda and her mother, though, Gordon detected not rivalry but complicity.

In all this shuttling of emotions between the Adairs the darkest thread was that of Dolphus's attitude towards his wife. It was one of such subtle, unexpressed hatred that you could uncover it only if you were sharp enough to intercept a glance or catch the faint sneering inflexion in an apparently innocent remark.

So intent were the Adairs on scratching at each other that there were spells throughout dinner when not only Gordon but Eric and Johnnie too were ignored and had no alternative but to concentrate on supping puddly soup or chewing stringy mutton.

Amanda, however, almost made up for it. She looked breathtakingly beautiful by candlelight, gowned like a woman, not an adolescent. Her bare arms, though, showed gooseflesh for the dining-room was as cold as a tomb and the food, in its old silver dishes, was no better than lukewarm.

"Not cold, darling, are you, hah?"

Amanda gave her father a smile that would have melted an icecap. "Warm as toast, thank you, Daddy."

Dolphus glowered at his guests. "And you, hah?"

"No, sir."

"Fine, sir."

"Very . . . very comfortable, sir."

"Oh, males are always hot-blooded at their age." Olive leaned over the Eve's pudding and brushed a finger against Gordon's frozen cheek. "He's quite on fire, in fact."

It could not be the wine that had loosed Olive Adair's inhibitions; the wine was weaker than tap water.

"What do you have to say to that, Nicholson, hah?"

"Nothing, sir."

"Not old enough to have opinions?"

"Not . . . not about body temperatures, sir."

"Don't you realise that my spouse was paying you a compliment?"

"I hadn't . . . Yes, of course." Gordon dredged up one of his professionally boyish smiles, so cherubic that Dolphus could not possibly take offence. "Thank you very much, Mrs Adair. I am just pleasantly warm, that's all."

Olive emitted a gentle sigh and, to Gordon's vast relief, leaned away from him at last, as if she had been defused by his rustic naivety.

Eventually the family seemed to grow bored with skirmishing and the talk turned to horse racing and the breeding of winners. Naturally Johnnie and Eric were well versed in the subject and once more Gordon found himself excluded from the conversation. He crumbled a small piece of cheese on his plate and dabbed up the fragments with his fingertip. So far Amanda had paid him no special attention. He could not imagine why he had been summoned to appear before the Adairs. He began to wonder if the whole thing was some sort of plot to test his initiative and aplomb under pressure.

Dinner was disposed of in less than an hour. Dolphus escorted his wife and daughter off 'to do their little duties' – a phrase that made Gordon squirm – while the boys repaired to the library for coffee and brandy.

From a humidor on an Indian table Johnnie removed a cigar that was as dry as tinder and the colour of birch bark. He wrinkled his nose and put the object back into store. "He's gettin' worse, I fancy."

"And the Olive Branch?" said Eric. "What about her?"

"What the Olive Branch needs is another encounter with a sturdy young buck," said Johnnie.

"Any volunteers?" said Eric, nudging Gordon.

"What?"

"'Quite on fire'! That's rich!" said Eric. "God, I wouldn't take mine out in this house if my very life depended on it."

"Frostbite would have it," said Johnnie, "if nothing else."

"I thought some of the other fillies might be trotted out for inspection," said Eric.

"What?"

"Daughters."

"The second in line is just comin' into bloom."

"What age is she?"

"Fourteen, fifteen," said Eric.

Gordon took a tiny cup and saucer from the tin-plated tray, poured coffee from the pot. "Is she as stunnin' as Amanda?"

"It's all in the eye of the beholder, ain't it?" said Johnnie.

"Listen," Gordon said, "I don't quite understand what Dolphus expects from me."

"Gratitude, humility and respect," said Eric.

"What?"

"Do stop sayin' that, old chum."

"Sorry," Gordon said. "It's just that I can't understand why you chaps aren't in the runnin'."

"He who gets Amanda also gets the pelf," Johnnie said. "And old Dolphus knows us both too well to trust us to keep a bargain."

"What bargain?"

Neither of the cousins answered.

Eric said, "Come to think of it, the second might be more your type, Gordon."

"What's her name?"

"Phoebe," said Eric. "Feeble Phoebe, as she's known in the trade. Yes, she might be just the ticket for you."

"Aye, an' a punch on the ear might be just the ticket for you, Eric," Gordon said. "Anyway, I haven't given up hope of throwin' my hat in the ring for Amanda."

"Oh hoh! Vaultin' ambition here, I see."

"I like her. She's gorgeous."

"Highly desirable," John Whiteside said. "But would you have her under any conditions?"

"I might," said Gordon. "If she'd have me."

"It's all a bit beyond you, Gordon, ain't it?"

"I can't deny I'm puzzled," said Gordon. "It's some damned family, that's all I can say."

"Damned is the word," said Johnnie.

*   *   *

Dolphus seated himself on a scuffed leather greatchair by the hearth. He crossed his legs and thoughtfully swirled a film of brandy about the base of his bowl. He had returned without the women and had offered no explanation for his prolonged absence. He puffed on one of the pale, dry cigars, sipped from the glass and said, "Now, young fellow, tell me about this famous brother of yours."

Gordon was taken aback. "What?"

"There he goes again," said Eric.

"The brother who comes stridin' out of a hayfield and immediately starts catchin' dangerous criminals," said Dolphus. "That one."

"Craig's a policeman with Greenfield Burgh," said Gordon. "Catchin' criminals is his job."

"Perhaps so," said Dolphus. "I hear that he does not much approve of us."

"I don't think he knows you, sir."

"He was exceedingly stiff with my cousin Sinclair."

Sinclair Smith was a bookmaker, one of several connected with the Adair family. No doubt it would be to Sinclair's advantage to have a copper in his pocket so that he or his runners would not be harassed while plying their unlawful trade on the streets. But

23

Sinclair Smith, so Gordon believed, represented the low end of the Adair hierarchy and it was hard to credit that the chairman of the board of Carruth's could possibly be interested in what went on in the back streets of the Greenfield.

"Craig doesn't much care for bookies," Gordon said.

"He's a handsome lad, though," Dolphus said. "My wife remarked upon it at the recent nuptials."

"Craig's married an' has a child." Gordon lapsed deliberately into a broad Ayrshire dialect. "Merrit tae a bonnie wee lassie frae the Carrick grazin's."

Gordon assumed that Dolphus was still trawling for husbands for his daughters. Why he did not search among eligible bachelors from his own social class Gordon could not imagine. He wondered where the three daughters were hidden. Phoebe and her sisters were probably upstairs, locked in some arctic dormitory with Nanny on guard at the door. Did they approve of Father bartering away their lives for some nefarious purpose of his own? Amanda didn't seem to mind.

Gratitude, humility and respect: was that all that Dolphus would demand from a son-in-law? Something sinister was going on and Gordon felt his curiosity quicken and the last wisp of self-consciousness vanish with the challenge. Breezy had been right to warn him not to underestimate James Randolph Adair.

"Can't my dear brother find a place for your dear brother?" Dolphus asked. "Hah?"

"I don't think Craig's interested in commerce, sir."

"I could find a place for him, I'm sure."

Gordon said, "My brother's a policeman, an' that's all there is to it."

"In this family," said Dolphus, "we look after our own. I would prefer it if your brother was in rather than out. Could he manage one of my public houses, do you think?"

"I doubt if he'd want to. Being a copper suits him perfectly."

"What about you, hah?" said Dolphus. "What would suit you?"

"I'm a salesman. I work for Breezy."

Gordon rose and helped himself to another cup of coffee from the pot on the tray. He did not return to his seat on the sofa but remained on his feet, the saucer balanced on the palm of his hand.

The cousins lay back in their chairs, legs stretched, watching

24

him. Apparently Dolphus did indeed wish to snare a Nicholson. Gordon could see a point to his own entrapment as a suitor for Amanda, assuming he passed the test. But why was Dolphus so interested in Craig? From far down in his consciousness Gordon fished up the image of Greta Taylor, the woman from Benedict Street. Johnnie and Eric knew her, knew her rather too intimately for comfort. Could there be a connection with Dolphus too, something that James Randolph Adair was anxious to cover up?

Gordon opened his mouth to put a question then prudently changed his mind.

"Something to say, hah?"

"Yes, sir," Gordon told him. "Where's the lavatory?"

*   *   *

He came out from the closet under the dark oak stair and found himself alone in the spooky hallway. The library door had been closed behind him and he could imagine the three Adairs behind it, their heads together as they murmured and schemed. There was no sign of servants and the only sound was the gush of water in the cast-iron cistern and a faint groaning in the pipes.

"Gordon?"

He almost jumped out of his skin. He swung round.

"What?"

"Here. I'm here."

She beckoned to him from the doorway of a darkened room. She looked as ethereal as a phantom, slight and pale and insubstantial. He hesitated.

"Come to me, Gordon," she whispered.

He went on tiptoe.

Her hand was icy cold when she touched his fingers and drew him into the great vaulted drawing-room.

"Where's your mama?" Gordon hissed.

"Retired."

"Already? What time is it?"

"Oh, it's been awful for you, Gordon," Amanda said. "Hold me in your arms."

"What?"

"Please, hold me."

He could not be sure but he thought that she had been weeping, that her cheeks were not only cold but were damp with tears. He put an arm awkwardly about her waist and left the rest of the embrace to her. He was gratified to discover that she was smaller than he was and her daintiness made him feel both tall and strong.

The drawing-room door was ajar. They stood just inside it. A wan slit of gaslight fell upon her face when she tilted it up towards him. He could not help but kiss her and, yes, her cheeks were wet. She gave a tiny sobbing sigh and clung tightly to him. He was aware of her breasts pressed against his chest and her stomach against his waistcoat, and the softness of her. But his feelings were tender not lustful and the kiss was light and not prolonged.

"I must see you again, Gordon. Soon."

"How?" he said. "I mean, where?"

"Johnnie will arrange it."

"Johnnie?"

"Yes," she whispered. "Kiss me again, my darling."

She clung to him for several seconds then abruptly tore herself away, slipped past the door and across the hallway. Gordon watched her ascend the staircase. His heart was pounding and he felt that he could hardly catch his breath. She paused on the first landing, leaned over the balcony and blew him a parting kiss.

A quarter of an hour later it was all over and he was back in the Sovereign with Eric and Johnnie, heading down the avenue of trees towards the Milngavie road.

Squinting at his pocket watch, Eric Adair said, "Dinner with Dolphus in two hours dead. Not bad, eh!"

"He has it down to a fine art, the old boy," said Johnnie. "He'd be frightened that we'd smoke his other cigar if we stayed longer."

"Is it always like that?" Gordon asked.

"Usually it's worse," said Eric.

"Why does he bother?"

"Feels it incumbent upon him to be hospitable from time to time," said Eric. "The annual garden party is the giddy limit, though. Avoid it at all costs."

"Join the army," said Johnnie, "or run away to sea."

"Tonight had a special purpose, of course," said Eric. "Dolphus was so keen to meet you."

"Be glad he did," said Johnnie.

"Why the hell should I be glad?" Gordon said.

"Because he liked you. He approves."

"Does he?" said Gordon. "He's got a bloody funny way of showin' it."

26

"Dolphus likes you. Olive likes you," John Whiteside said. "In fact, Gordon, we all just think you're grand."

"Oh, aye!" said Gordon sceptically, and for the rest of the journey to the station kept his mouth shut and his suspicions all to himself.

Three

Second Best

For almost twenty-four hours Kirsty saw nothing of Craig. She had been in bed in the kitchen recess before he had returned on Wednesday night. She had heard him stumble into the hall and on into the front bedroom and could tell by the racket that he was the worse for drink.

In their first year of living together Kirsty would have dragged herself out of bed to go to his assistance. She would have made sure that he got out of his clothes and into his nightshirt. She would even have held a basin for him if he'd been inclined to be sick. But no longer. She'd listened to him blundering about the bedroom and then, when he'd fallen quiet, she had simply turned on to her side and had soon dropped down into a deep, deep sleep.

On Thursday morning she was roused by the guttural cry of a coalman as he made his deliveries. She had taken Bobby into bed with her and he slept on, snuggled against her flank. She listened to the rumble of a coal load as it was discharged into the Swanstons' bunker, the clatter of the man's clogs as he went downstairs again. Next she heard the throb of a factory hammer and, soon after, the jangle of a handbell from the Forrester Primary School in the street adjacent to Canada Road. She sat up abruptly.

The handbell told her that it was approaching nine o'clock. Obviously she'd forgotten to set the American alarm and had overslept. If it hadn't been for Bobby she would have leapt guiltily from the bed. But he was so peaceful that she disentangled herself carefully from the bedclothes and left him to his rest. She must pull up the blinds at once, though, to let the world know that she was up and about. God knows what the neighbours must think of her lying abed until this late hour of the morning, and her not even ill.

It was chilly in the kitchen but sunshine had already melted the frost from the window-panes and the tenement walls were slashed with brilliant light. Down in the backcourt Mrs Swanston was pegging a family wash to the drying-line and the wash-house chimney sent up gritty black smoke that rose straight as a fakir's rope into the china-blue sky.

Kirsty peered at the clock on the mantelshelf: five past nine. She snatched her clothes from the chair by the fire, struggled into her vest and drawers, rolled on her stockings, hopping on one leg. Still dazed by her long sleep it was several minutes before she realised that she'd heard no sound at all from the bedroom. She knubbled her eyes with her knuckle and tried to recall why today had special importance.

"Oh, God!" she groaned.

Half-clad she rushed through the hall to waken Craig who had told her that he was due to appear before the Chief Constable that morning.

The bed was empty. His uniform was gone from its heavy wooden hanger. The drawers of the tallboy had been yanked open, his clean shirts rumpled, a tie hanging out like a strangled tongue. He had left without breakfast, without a word of farewell. She felt annoyance and guilt in equal parts. She tried to appease the feelings by tidying up the bedroom, without success. Perhaps, she told herself, he was too ashamed to face her first thing. Not much consoled by the excuse she had wished upon him, she returned, frowning, to the kitchen.

"Mammy, see."

Bobby popped his tousled head through a gap in the curtains.

"Lie still for a bit, dearest," she told him. "Keep yourself warm until I light the fire."

"Right-he-ho," said Bobby, and promptly vanished.

Where did he learn such expressions? What other unsavoury phrases would her son pick up now that he was old enough to associate with the rapscallions in the close and to emulate their cheeky patter?

She buttoned her blouse and tied on her apron, opened the vent under the grate and raked the embers noisily with a poker.

"*Eee-righteee-hoooh*," Bobby chanted for his own amusement. "*Walla-walla-walla-wooo.*"

"Bobby, be quiet."

Out came the head, bright as a new thrupenny piece.

"Daddy still sleepin'?"

"Yes," Kirsty fibbed.

"*Oooooo-aaah!*"

"I'll *oh-ah* you, m'lad, if you're not quiet."

Though he had only recently crossed the bridge from babyhood into boyhood, Bobby had already learned respect for the bread-winner. He dived instantly behind the curtain and bounced about on the mattress, unseen but not unheard. Kirsty was too absorbed in her own thoughts to take pleasure in her son's exuberance this morning.

By now David would be on the train to Inverness to take leave of his uncle. On Saturday he would travel to London on the overnight express and, in a week or so, he would embark for China. He had promised to write to her but Kirsty was not at all sure that she could bear to receive letters from him. True feelings could not be put down on paper. Besides, her news would surely seem trivial in reply. David's kindness, his tenderness would not seem the same when conveyed in stilted handwritten sentences. Letters, perhaps, would only serve to increase the distance between them. Deep within her Kirsty knew that she had never been right for David Lockhart. She could never have been his wife even if she had not been bound by common law and twisted loyalties to Craig Nicholson.

She would miss David but, oddly, she would miss Nessie Frew even more and the two hundred pounds that Nessie had left her was no compensation for being deprived of a good and trusted friend.

If the day had not got off on the wrong foot, Kirsty might have found a moment to indulge in tears. As it was, though, she was all behind and would have to scurry to catch up, particularly as she did not know when to expect Craig or what he would require by way of a meal.

She ran her hand along the mantel in the faint hope that he might have left her a note. It was not in Craig's nature to communicate, however. It seemed that he, like a lot of men, expected not just service but second sight from a wife.

"Bobby, get back into that bed," she snapped. "Set one foot on the floor before I've got the fire lit an' I'll spank."

Bobby sank through the curtain, arms akimbo, in a perfect pantomime of passive obedience.

"Stay there. Don't move," Kirsty warned. "I'll only be a minute."

"Aye, Mammy."

Kirsty left the house door open and hurried downstairs to the water closet on the half-landing. She had not washed her face or combed her hair yet and must look a right ticket. The other wives in the close would have been up and at it for a couple of hours or more and she had probably lost her share of the drying-line and would have to negotiate with Mrs Swanston for an extra rope.

The shafts of sunlight that soared through the stair window seemed to taunt Kirsty for her laziness as she went on downstairs to the ground-floor level.

Constable John Boyle had just entered the close. As a rule he would have bidden Kirsty a polite good morning. But today he seemed startled to encounter her. He was a sandy-haired, sharp-featured chap in his late thirties but his Christian seriousness made him seem older.

Kirsty nodded. "Mornin', Mr Boyle."

He deliberately turned away. He studied the ceiling of the close as intently as if it had just been repainted by Michelangelo. He was, Kirsty realised, pointedly ignoring her. Before she could challenge him, put any sort of question, however, the door of the Boyles' apartment whisked open and Mrs Boyle rescued her husband from further embarrassment.

"Come in here this minute, John," the woman barked, without a trace of civility.

John Boyle slunk past Kirsty and into the house and Florrie Boyle slammed the door shut. Kirsty felt as if she had been slapped. What had she done to offend them?

Guilt took possession of Kirsty again and she hesitated before going on down the three shallow stone steps to the little close that led into the backcourt. The usual washday puddle stained the flagstones at the door of the brick house and water gurgled rudely in the drain. Mrs Swanston's pail and empty basket stood by the open door.

As Kirsty approached she could not help but hear the women's voices amplified by the building's hollow shell. They were talking about her.

Kirsty blinked in the brilliant sunshine. The air, however, was cold and held the sooty taste of cheap wash-house coals and the sharp odour of soap with which Mrs Swanston had made suds. She loitered just out of sight by the side wall and, in spite of herself, listened.

31

"It's no surprise t'me that Craig Nicholson was discharged from muster," Mrs Swanston was saying. "I wouldn't shed a tear for him if he was discharged from the Force."

"It's her I'm sorry for," said Mrs Piper.

"The wife's always the last t' know, so they say."

"I wonder if she does know," said Mrs Piper.

"I doubt it," said Mrs Swanston. "I mean she's got the patience o' Job puttin' up wi' that beggar at the best o' times. But when a man starts t' wander then I say it's time t' walk out."

"Who is this other woman?" asked Mrs Piper.

"Just a common tart."

"Never!"

"It's the truth; a street woman wi' a bastard bairn."

Marie Piper was a large, soft-bodied woman, cheerful and not, as a rule, malicious. It was only the quality of Eunice Swanston's gossip that intrigued her.

"How could y'not have heard, Mrs Piper?" said Eunice Swanston. "Did your man no' drop a hint?"

"He said not a cheep."

"Aye, they can be as thick as treacle when it suits them, men."

Marie Piper cleared her throat before asking the big, indelicate question. "Is the bairn – eh – is it his?"

"It's the first thing that crossed my mind too," said Eunice Swanston. "But, naw, it can't be his. It's three or four years old, so I'm told, and Craig Nicholson hasn't known her for more'n a year at the most."

"How do you know all this is true?" asked Mrs Piper.

Experienced gossips would never have challenged the authenticity of Mrs Swanston's information or enquired as to its source. Marie Piper, however, was quite new to the game and could be forgiven her gaffe.

Mrs Swanston sniffed. "Well, y'see, the bunty bides on John Boyle's beat an' he's been observin' the comin's an' goin's since it all started."

"So Mrs Boyle told you?"

"Aye, but Holy Jock would be mad if he knew she was spreadin' stories."

Kirsty leaned her shoulder on the brickwork. She could not believe that Craig had been unfaithful to her and had taken a mistress somewhere in the Greenfield.

"Where does he – eh – do it?" asked Marie Piper.

"Benedict Street. The bunty has a house there."

"My! That's terrible!" said Mrs Piper, with a note of genuine sympathy in her voice. "I wonder if his mother knows, an' her married t' that nice Mr Adair."

"Nice Mr Adair!" said Eunice Swanston scornfully. "Oh, I could tell you some tales about him, believe me." She sniffed again. "But I'm not one for idle gossip."

"No," said Mrs Piper. "No, you're not."

"Listen, Marie, just for curiosity's sake I'd like t' find out what happens at this mornin's discipline meetin'. The sergeants are bound t' know. I'd ask Jess Walker but you know what she's like; tight as a cat's tail when it comes t' neighbourly conversation."

"He'll be warned an' fined, I expect."

"Aye, aye," said Mrs Swanston. "The thing is, though, will they black mark him just for the drink or will they read the high-an'-mighty Craig Nicholson the moral clause an' all?"

"I doubt if Calum would tell me."

"Ask him," said Eunice Swanston.

"I suppose I could," said Mrs Piper, doubtfully.

"Well, I've blethered long enough, Mrs Piper. I'd better get back t' the tub before the weather changes."

Kirsty slipped away from the wash-house and into the close, appalled at what she had heard, at the irony of the situation that had closed about her. Her guilt and Craig's guilt, her sin and his, had become tangled like dirty washing in a tub.

She took the stairs two at a time. Shaking, she threw herself into the hallway and closed and bolted the door behind her as if truth could be locked out like a wicked intruder.

Bobby was chanting happily to himself in the kitchen. From the street behind Canada Road rose the coalman's ritual cry. Kirsty hardly heard the sounds now. She was blinded by tears, filled with outrage and anger, with fear of what would happen when Craig at last came home.

*   *   *

Kirsty waited all the long morning and into the afternoon for the sound of Craig's footsteps on the stairs, the rattle of his key in the lock. The first moment of their meeting would be crucial, that instant when she looked into his sullen eyes and saw there – what? Shame, lasciviousness, defiance?

She realised how badly she had misjudged the tenor of Craig's moods. He had not been smarting at the insult to his pride at all. He had been involved in an affair, had been sullen because he was afraid she would find out. She saw the taking of a bunty as a revenge against her, payment for her inability to give him what he wanted, the unquestioning admiration that he demanded as his right.

By noon she had calmed down, outwardly at least.

She cleaned the grate, polished the range, lit the fire with the fuel that was in the bunker in the hall. She did not dare put her nose out of doors, however, in case she encountered Mrs Piper or one of the other neighbours. She could not face their inquisitiveness or their sympathy right now.

By two o'clock or half-past she had turned and shaped the thing in her mind so obsessively that, if she had not settled on a strategy, she would have gone mad with it.

She must proceed circumspectly. It would be insane to confront Craig directly and in a temper. The events of the past few days had distorted her perspectives too. She did not trust herself to behave rationally and must give him no excuse, at this time, to desert her. Nor must she run the risk of blurting out that she had been loved by David Lockhart. Whatever happened, that must remain her secret, one that she must carry to her grave. In men like Craig Nicholson there was no grain of compromise, no atom of forgiveness.

While she fed Bobby his dinner Kirsty contemplated the prospect of life without Craig. She did not find it wholly displeasing. After all, she had salted away one hundred and fifty pounds of Nessie Frew's legacy to set against a day when *she* might leave *him*. Somehow, though, that was different. To be forced back on her own resources carried a certain challenge. To be abandoned in favour of a street woman, however, would bring nothing but shame and humiliation.

Whatever had happened in the office of the Chief Constable it seemed improbable that Craig would be sacked. Andy McAlpine had been carpeted several times for his drinking and had not been dismissed. Police authority might be strict but high-rankers weren't daft enough to throw trained constables on to the rubbish heap without serious cause. If the Chief Constable had heard of Craig's affair with the woman in Benedict Street, though, the consequences could be very different.

Whatever happened, Craig would be smarting.

She was scrubbing his shirts in the big zinc bath on its rubberised sheet on the kitchen floor when the thought came to her: what if he had gone to the woman's house to seek comfort and reassurance?

She sat back on her heels.

She had made Bobby a tiny boat out of an empty matchbox. He was guddling happily in the little lakes that formed on the rubber sheet and, when Kirsty sanctioned it, would lower the boat into the bath and fan it to its doom on reefs of flannel and cotton. When she sat back, her hands red and hair straggling, he seemed to sense her need of affection and paused in his play to rub himself against her like a kitten.

"Mammy?"

"Aye, son?"

"Daddy comin' home?"

"Not yet, Bobby."

"Soon?"

"Quite soon."

How could she tell her son that his father might not come home at all that day, that he had found another woman – and another child – to pay him attention.

She got up and lifted the bath, staggered to the sink with it.

Outside, the sun had dipped behind the tenements just to remind everybody that it wasn't spring after all. Eunice Swanston was taking down her washing from the lines and Joyce McAlpine, far too late as usual, was pegging hers up.

Kirsty tumbled the dirty water into the sink, mopped the sheet with a cloth and hung it to dry on two chairs. Bobby crawled beneath it, changing gear on his imagination, becoming a gypsy in a tent instead of a ship's captain.

Kirsty did not have the heart to reprimand him, though the rubber sheet was still unpleasantly damp. She was leaning on the rim of the empty bath, looking disconsolately down into the backcourt when the doorbell rang.

"Daddy!" Bobby shouted optimistically.

Fear cramped Kirsty's stomach and her mouth became dry.

The bell rang again. It could not be Craig. Craig never forgot his latchkey.

She hurried into the hall and opened the door.

Her brother-in-law, Gordon, stood sheepishly on the doorstep.

35

"Hope you don't mind, Kirst," Gordon said with a grin that made him look like a truant schoolboy not a man-about-town. "I was just passin' so I thought I'd pop in."

"Gordon. Oh, Gordon."

"Come at a bad time, have I?"

"Anything but," said Kirsty.

*   *   *

Sergeant Drummond's handwritten report had been on Lieutenant Strang's desk in the airy office on the second floor of Police Headquarters in Percy Street, and Strang had consulted it several times during the course of the interview and interrogation. No mention was made of Constable Nicholson's imprudent association with Greta Taylor of Benedict Street and the proceeding was all very cut-and-dried: a wigging, the imposition of a fine of fifteen shillings and a warning that he would not be treated so leniently if it ever happened again.

Craig left Percy Street in a peculiar state of disappointment. He felt that he'd been dealt with much less rigorously than he deserved.

For a fleeting instant he had been tempted to tell Strang straight to his face that he could stuff his bloody job. But common sense had swiftly prevailed and he had taken his punishment with due murmurs of contrition.

Disgruntled at his own cowardice, he stalked down the steps of Police Headquarters and headed at once for the bank.

It was all so damned easy, patching up the mess. It took only five minutes to re-deposit the forty pounds he had lifted from his shared account with Kirsty, no questions asked. Only Greta knew what he had planned to do. He doubted if Greta would tell anyone, though he still could not understand why she had turned him down.

Suddenly he realised that he was very tired. He had spent Wednesday evening in a dusty pub, consuming several pints of beer. He had not been drunk, not even merry, when he'd walked home through the still, hazy-cold streets, though he'd banged and bashed about a bit to give Kirsty the impression that he was half-seas-over.

He could not have faced her last night. There was something too wholesome in Kirsty's wide-eyed expression, a candour that he had once found attractive but that now irritated him intensely.

Kirsty had never understood what made him tick, never would. He wished he could be more like other men, content with security, with pattern, with squeezing out a wee bit of respect now and then. But he hungered for more than that. He wanted something that he could not define. In Greta he thought he'd found it. How wrong he'd been.

It was only ten past ten o'clock. He had the best part of five hours to kill before he showed up for back shift. He did not want to go home. Truth was, he hardly ever wanted to go home these days. He needed something to eat, though, and a place to rest his weary bones. Benito's Café would do just fine.

The café was on the extreme edge of Greenfield, not a regular haunt of police constables. At that time on a weekday morning it was deserted and Craig took a seat in one of the cubicles behind a chest-high partition. He leaned his elbows on the mock-marble table-top and stared at his thumbs, wondering if he could possibly keep going until eleven that night.

Tying on his long striped apron Benito waddled out of the gloom of the backshop, took Craig's order for a fried breakfast and a pot of coffee and returned with the plates within ten minutes.

Craig sprinkled vinegar on the sausages, punctured the heart of the fried egg, and, uninterestedly at first, began to eat.

Benito was a portly Glasgow-born Italian with buffalo-horn moustaches and knowing brown eyes.

"You wanna paper?" he asked. "Noosepaper?"

"Nah," said Craig. "Thanks all the same."

"You gonna pay the bill?"

"Sure, I'm goin' t' pay the bill."

"You notta friend o' his?"

"Huh!" Craig said. "I'm not a friend o' anybody's. An' I'm a copper who pays his way. Right?"

"You wanna more coffee, then?"

"I could do wi' another sausage if you've got one handy."

"Nae borrah," said Benito.

His appetite, it seemed, had returned. The café owner brought him two sausages on a wire fork, dripping fat and piping hot, and slid them on to his plate. Craig nodded his thanks.

If he had not been so bound up in brooding about Greta he might have asked Benito which particular copper scrounged free meals here. He chose not to pick up the hint, however, and ate with gusto now, clearing his plate quickly. He poured a second cup of black coffee and lit a cigarette. He felt better, more awake.

"Well, well," said a familiar voice, "if it isn't the black sheep of Ottawa Street."

He blinked and looked up at Constable Ronnie Norbert.

"Smokin' in uniform too," Ronnie said. "Tut-tut! I got to report this, y'know. It's my duty. I'll just make a note in my wee black book, shall I?"

"Ach, shut your face, Ronnie."

Constable Norbert removed his helmet and seated himself in the cubicle opposite Craig. He had a long chin, smug, slate-coloured eyes and a swaggering manner. He had served as a Probationer under Craig and had never quite forgiven Craig for shortening his high opinion of himself. He had no blemish against his name as a made-up constable, however, though he was lazy in matters of procedure and bent regulations to suit himself.

"So this is where you come t' lick your wounds," Ronnie said. "What did they dock you?"

"Fifteen bob," Craig said.

"Could've been worse," Ronnie said. "Benito, my usual black coffee."

"Are you on duty, y'lazy bugger?" Craig said.

"I won't tell if you won't tell."

"An' I'll bet you're the copper who never pays."

"Old Bennie peach on me, did he?" Ronnie Norbert said.

"Old Bennie didn't have to," Craig said.

"I'm the copper who keeps the wild boys from wreckin' the furniture when the school gets out," said Ronnie. "An' I'm the copper who squares up to Billy King when Billy tries to put the bite on our Italian. I reckon I earn the odd *café noir*. You don't grudge me a little refreshment, do you, Bennie?"

"No' me," said Benito, putting down the china cup.

"If you ever get caught . . ." Craig said.

"I won't," said Ronnie. "Anyway, it's only coffee. Drummond won't smell it on *my* breath."

Craig stubbed out his cigarette in the tin ashtray and made to rise. "I'll leave you to it, Ronnie."

"Wait," Ronnie said. "Don't gallop off, man. You're not on duty for hours yet. Sit down an' give me your patter."

"I don't have any patter."

"All right," Ronnie said. "I'll give you my patter."

Craig sighed and settled into his seat again. He lit another cigarette and watched Ronnie sip from the china cup. There was something faintly fishy about Norbert's manner, more so than usual.

Ronnie hesitated.

He said, "Who did you see this mornin'? Mr Organ?"

"Lieutenant Strang."

Ronnie said, "Did he happen t' mention your wee bunty, the lady from Benedict Street?"

"Christ, Ronnie!"

"Come on, Craig. Everybody knows about you an' Greta Taylor."

"Aye, well, everybody's jumpin' to the wrong bloody conclusion."

Ronnie pursed his lips, made a small puttering sound.

Ronnie said, "I heard somethin' about the lady in question just last week."

Craig said, "What, for instance?"

Ronnie said, "What's that you're smokin'? Gold Flake, is it?"

Craig glanced behind him. Benito had gone back into his kitchen. Craig took the packet of Gold Flake from his pocket, opened it, shook out one cigarette and placed it gently between Ronnie Norbert's waiting fingers.

"I hear a lot o' things, you know," Ronnie said. "I make it my business to keep my ear t' the ground. I can say, wi'out fear o' contradiction, that I know more about what goes on in this neck o' the woods than any ten coppers put together."

"What about Greta?"

"What do *you* know about her?" Ronnie said.

Craig said, "She sells clothes in the Irish market."

"The bairn; what about the bairn?"

"A bastard," Craig said. "Nothin' strange about that."

"The father?"

"A sailor; dead now. Drowned."

"Not true," said Ronnie.

Craig said, "How do you know?"

"I told you. I keep my ear to the ground."

"You mean Jen's father's still alive?"

"Aye, an' he ain't no sailor. Never was."

"You know who he is?"

"Nope."

"Listen, Ronnie . . ."

"I could perhaps find out," Ronnie said smugly. "If you're interested."

"I might be," Craig said.

"How interested?"

"What d'you mean?"

"I mean, what would you pay to find out?"

"Christ, you're a hard-nosed bastard, Ronnie."

"I do this sort o' thing in my spare time, you know," Ronnie said. "Information's valuable to some folks."

"How much?"

"Depends."

"On what?"

"How long it takes, an' how many palms I have t' cross with silver on the way."

"Can you really find out?" Craig said. "I don't mean guesses an' rumours. I mean hard fact, the truth."

"Put it this way," Ronnie said, "I can give it a damned good try."

"Where do you get this information?"

Ronnie laughed. "I might be green, Craig, but I ain't that much of a cabbage. No, no. If you want it, you'll have to pay for it. An' I can't give no guarantees."

Craig contemplated the end of his cigarette, did not meet Ronnie's eager eye.

Craig said, "Tell me one thing, Ronnie; have you ever heard of John Whiteside?"

"Sure thing." Ronnie shrugged. "He manages the warehouse in Partick East. He's Breezy Adair's right-hand man."

"And?"

"He used to be her lover."

"Greta Taylor's lover?"

"So I heard."

"Evidence?"

"Nope, no evidence," said Ronnie. "Evidence costs money."

"How much?" said Craig again.

"Fifty bob should get me started," Ronnie said. "You interested in a deal?"

"I'm interested," Craig said.

"No guarantees, though," Ronnie said. "You understand that?"

"I understand," said Craig.

*   *   *

Gordon was, as usual, accompanied by a large suitcase crammed with carpet samples. Kirsty's house and the apartments of many of her neighbours were floored with Adair's carpeting, sold by Gordon at tempting discounts. He was every inch a salesman, though he did not dress too flashily for his excursions into the Greenfield now, not since he had been set upon by Billy King and had his takings stolen.

He flipped off his snap-brimmed hat, plonked it on his nephew's head, lifted the little boy, took him on to his knee and asked him amiably, "An' what mischief have you been up to, old chum?"

Bobby peered out from under the hat and reached for the heavy chain of imitation gold that draped his uncle's waistcoat. He was forbidden to touch his father's steel-cased watch and, in consequence, was fascinated by timepieces. He loved to listen to 'the beetle' that marched inside Uncle Gordon's watch. With Gordon's permission he unhooked it and climbed down to lie on his tummy on the rug and study the mechanical masterpiece, the hat still balanced comically on his ears.

"Will you have some dinner?" Kirsty said.

"Well, since it's about that time of day," Gordon said, "why not?"

Kirsty set about making him a rarebit, glad to have him there and to have something with which to occupy herself. It had been all she could do not to burst into tears as soon as she saw her brother-in-law. Gordon had always been her friend, the only one she had left now.

"Where's the lad?" said Gordon. "On duty?"

"Back-shift," Kirsty told him. "Did you want to see him?"

"God, no," said Gordon. "I'd rather have you all to myself, thanks."

"That's enough of that," Kirsty said, managing a smile. "How's Lorna?"

"Fine."

"An' Madge?"

"Fine."

"An' how are you?"

Gordon did not answer and, when she turned from the range with the plate in her hands, she saw that he was blushing.

"Believe it or not," Gordon said, "it seems I've just become a runner in the marriage stakes."

"You!"

"You don't have to sound quite so surprised, Kirsty."

"Who is she?"

"Amanda Adair. She's Dolphus Adair's daughter. An' it seems she fancies me."

"Lucky you."

"I'm not so sure," Gordon said. "She's rotten rich, you know."

"All the better."

"I don't know that I could cope," Gordon said. "The other thing is that I'd have to change my occupation, go into the beer business."

"But why?"

"Because Daddy would demand it. That's what the family does: brewing."

"You don't sound like a man in love to me, Gordon," Kirsty said.

"If it was just Amanda . . ." Gordon said. "It's all this other stuff. Honest t' God, I feel like I've been put on the block in the marriage market."

"I thought you were ambitious?"

"I am."

"Well?"

"Money's all very well," Gordon said, "but I'd rather make my own fortune. I don't really want to be handed it on a plate."

"But you do like her?"

"'Course I like her." Gordon began to eat, forking the rarebit quickly into his mouth. "I just don't think I want to get tangled up with Dolphus Adair."

"He sounds the fishy sort."

"Oh, they're all a bit fishy, one way and another," Gordon said. "Even Breezy has more to him than meets the eye. Dolphus Adair has four daughters to get off his hands and the chap who marries the eldest will, I gather, have the runnin' of the business some day."

"Are there no sons?"

"Nope, not a one," Gordon said. "Old Papa Carruth only had daughters. Olive's the eldest. Dolphus was hand-picked to run the brewery. Now he's lookin' for somebody to groom in turn."

"An' it's you?"

"Might be," said Gordon.

"What'll you do?"

"Tread cautiously," Gordon said. "Now if only you were rich as well as gorgeous, Kirsty . . ."

"Enough," Kirsty warned. "Anyway, I wouldn't have you."

"Why the hell not?"

"You're far too young for an old woman like me. Besides, you've no prospects."

"I could remedy that," said Gordon. "I could join the police. I could lie about my height."

Kirsty laughed. She had been aware of Gordon's affection for her for some time. He had a lightness to him, a sense of fun that Craig lacked. His pride was of a different order, too. Gordon would never deceive her. The misery of her situation overwhelmed her again and she could keep it to the back of her mind no longer. Her laughter suddenly changed to tears and she pretended to busy herself at the sink to hide them.

Frowning, Bobby pointed. "Mammy cryin'."

Gordon was on his feet immediately, his arm about her.

"Here now, Kirst, what's all this? I was only kiddin', honestly."

"It's . . . it's Craig."

"What's he been up to now?"

"He's . . . he's got another woman."

She could not help herself. She turned and clung to her brother-in-law, sobbing.

Gordon patted her consolingly, awkwardly.

He was aware of Bobby, standing now, watching with huge, troubled eyes.

"It's all right, son," Gordon said. "Mammy's fine. Don't you worry about Mammy."

"Mammy got a sore tummy?"

"That's right," Gordon said. "Only a sore tummy."

"You make it better."

"Aye, I'll make it better," Gordon said.

Gordon doubted his ability to make it better. He had known of Craig's affair for some time. He had not been naive enough to swallow whole Craig's assurance that the relationship with

Greta Taylor had been platonic. He had caught them together, once, in Greta's house. He recalled how easy Craig had been there, how comfortable, how entrenched, with Greta's wee girl on his knee.

He said nothing, however, and held Kirsty to him until her sobbing diminished and she found her voice again.

"Did you know about it, Gordon?"

"I didn't think he'd do anythin' like that," Gordon answered, evasively. "How did you find out?"

"I heard the neighbours talk."

"Hell's bells, is that all!" Gordon said. "Stairhead gossip, that's all that is."

"Why didn't you tell me what was goin' on?"

"I didn't know. I wasn't sure."

"It's the truth, though, isn't it?"

Bobby watched, more curious than distressed.

Gordon did not attempt to placate his sister-in-law or to offer excuses for Craig's conduct. He had never approved of his brother's attitude to marriage, to Kirsty.

He took a spotted silk handkerchief from his breast pocket and dabbed her cheeks with it.

"Look, you've had a real rotten shock, Kirsty. Wash your face, I'll make us some fresh tea, an' we'll talk about it. It may not be as bad as you think it is."

"You know who she is, don't you?"

Gordon let out his breath, nodded.

"Tell me who she is," Kirsty said.

"Her name's Greta Taylor. She lives down in Benedict Street."

"Have you met her?"

Gordon nodded again, guiltily.

"Did he take you to meet her?"

"God, no," Gordon said. He came up with the lie without difficulty. "I sold her a carpet once."

"How did you know that Craig and she were . . .?"

"John Whiteside told me."

"Him! How did he know about it?"

"Whiteside seems to know an awful lot about folk in the Greenfield," Gordon said. "I think he had . . . had dealin's with her a while ago."

"Is she a tart, a whore?"

"I don't know what she is," said Gordon. "Look, I doubt if it was serious. You know what I mean, Kirsty? I think that if it happened at all it was just a sort of fling."

"An' that makes it all right, does it?"

"I didn't say that."

She was angry now. He couldn't blame her. She needed his comforting arm no longer. What she needed was his collusion.

"I want you to tell me everythin' about her, Gordon. Absolutely everythin'."

"What good will it do?"

"A lot of good. It'll do *me* a lot of good."

He experienced a sudden selfish longing to protect her, a reflection of the tenderness and pity that he'd felt when she'd clung to him. He owed Craig nothing, certainly not blind loyalty.

Gordon leaned on the chair-back and studied her.

He said, "Am I right in thinkin' you're goin' to put up a fight?"

"By God, I am," she said.

* * *

The motion of the shaving-brush over his cheek was soothing. The creamy lather had a scent that was sweet but not cloying, a masculine odour that did not remind him of Greta or Kirsty, or of the wealthy little bitches who'd made up to him on the night of the wedding celebration.

In the barber's chair he felt himself relax, his confidence return. He had to face the fact that his fling with Greta was all over. It should never have started in the first place, of course. He'd been daft to imagine that she was in love with him. It was of no consequence now. He had other plans for Greta Taylor.

"Try not to smile, sir," the barber said.

The razor had such a fine edge to it that he hardly felt it against his skin.

The establishment was not on street level but had windows that jutted out over Byres Road. Gordon had told him about it, extolling the pleasures of a really expensive shave. Gordon, for once, had been right. The chairs were all scarlet leather and polished brass, fitted to a floor of tiled linoleum on which hardly a hair could be seen. Everything was spotless; glass shelves with bottles and jars of pomade and astringents, porcelain basins, the jug in which the boy whipped up lather. Even the boy was spotless in striped shirt and linen apron, fair hair laid down from his crown in even layers by one of the barbers.

The shave would cost three shillings. It was worth every penny. He had returned to the bank and drawn five pounds from the account. He needed two pounds and ten shillings with which to pay Ronnie. The rest he intended to blow on himself; to hell with waiting for a rainy day.

"Not from Partick station, are you, sir?" the barber asked, conversationally.

He was a small man and the chair had been lowered to suit his stature.

Hardly daring to move his lips, Craig answered, "Greenfield."

"We don't have many clients from there." The barber had changed razors and was expertly scraping away stubble where Craig's moustache had been. "Perhaps you're acquainted with Mr Affleck, though?"

"Old Hughie," Craig said. "Yes, Hughie an' I are old acquaintances. Does he have his trims done here?"

"He does, indeed," said the barber.

Casually Craig said, "Happen to know Mr Adair?"

"Which Mr Adair would that be?"

"Breezy Adair."

"Why, yes. We have the pleasure of attendin' to Mr Albert's moustache."

"He's my stepfather."

The razor's cutting edge departed from his cheekbone and alighted on the long muscle that ran from his ear to his unhooked collar.

"Well," said the barber, after a moment's pause, "it is a small world, sir."

"Didn't you know that Breezy had a relative on the Force?"

"I don't believe he ever mentioned it, no."

"Well, he has," Craig said. "Me."

"Very nice for you, sir," said the barber and judiciously raised the towel to cover the constable's mouth.

Craig had never used Breezy Adair's name in that manner before, to gain respect. He was entitled to change his tune, however, if he felt like it, and if there was any advantage to be gained.

Scissors snipped lightly at his hair and he struggled under the sheet, sat up. "I didn't ask for . . ."

"It's just part of the service, sir."

"At no extra cost?"

"Certainly not, sir."

"That's all right then," Craig said. "Carry on."

*　　*　　*

It was after three o'clock before Gordon hoisted his case under his arm and dashed off with even more alacrity than usual. He had stayed much longer than he had intended and Kirsty was grateful to him. His visit had steadied her and she felt better now that she had shared her fears with somebody she could trust.

Bobby did not resist when she put him down for an afternoon nap. She sat with him on the bed and brushed his hair gently with her fingertips, something that he found soothing. He was soon asleep.

She had learned a great deal from Gordon about the woman from Benedict Street and the tarnished lives of other street people too. She could not help but recall that her mother had also lived on the knuckle and had probably had no scruples about encouraging husbands to deceive their wives.

She had no image, no memory of her mother, only of the long bleak rooms of the Baird Home for Orphans, of shaven heads and pinched, unloved little faces, the starched aprons of the matrons and their broad brown-leather belts. When she tried to imagine what Greta Taylor looked like the face that came to mind was that of a poor orphan, Jeannie Gow, who had been her friend for two or three years until she'd died of scarlet fever.

Bobby did not waken until after four and it was dusk before Kirsty left the house to buy groceries.

She slunk out of the close like a sneak-thief, wrapped in a worn shawl, her son clinging to her hand, and headed for the shops on Dumbarton Road where she would be less likely to encounter one of the neighbours.

Twilight defined the tenements along Dumbarton Road and the new railway bridge seemed to float on the afterglow like a black log. The trains that passed over it were black too, silhouettes attached to cords of smoke that thinned to cinnamon and gold as they drifted away over the chimneytops.

Kirsty was in no mood to appreciate the beauty of the twilight hour. She scurried along the pavement with her head down, making for the fish-shop to buy haddock.

She would not have noticed him at all if Bobby had not dragged on her hand and cried out, "Daddy."

Shopping expeditions were frequently interrupted by false alarms; every blue uniform contained his father to Bobby's childish mind. This time, however, her son was right.

"See, Daddy, it's me."

In his excitement Bobby would have darted headlong into the traffic if Kirsty had not grabbed him and swung him into her arms.

Apprehension made her catch her breath. She would have hurried on, pretending that she had not recognised Craig if he had not already spotted them. He was already crossing the road, tall and agile, dodging horses, handcarts and tramcars. She was surprised, and dismayed, to find him out of the Greenfield, more surprised that he did not simply wave and move on. On or off duty, Craig was never very keen to be seen talking to his wife and child in public.

Bobby was yelling his head off, however, and that, coupled perhaps with a nervous sense of guilt, brought her husband to her.

"Daddy?" Bobby's tone changed to one of uncertainty.

"It's me all right, son," Craig said.

Without the full dark moustache Craig appeared younger, less authoritative. He glanced at Kirsty, awaiting judgement.

"What did you do that for?" she asked.

"Do what?"

"Shave it off."

"I felt like a change, that's all."

"Are you not on duty?"

"Of course I am."

"What are you doin' in Partick then?"

"Deliverin' a message for Drummond," Craig said.

She did not believe him. If he had told her that it was Thursday, she would have doubted it, suspected him of some glib lie.

"What happened at Percy Street this mornin'?"

"Oh, that!" Craig shrugged to indicate indifference to punishment. "Fifteen bob an' my knuckles rapped."

"You weren't suspended then?"

"Don't be bloody daft," he said. "Look, I've drawn a few quid out of the bank account so we'll not go short this week. All right?"

Kirsty nodded curtly.

He would have been less off-hand about the loss of fifteen shillings in earnings if they'd been scratching by on it. Her money protected them and she felt resentment well up again. Craig seemed to be his old self, swaggering and so arrogant that she could have choked him on the spot.

Bobby craned forward in her arms and touched the smooth skin where Craig's moustache had been as if he could not believe that it had vanished.

Craig drew back. "I'm on duty, son."

He was obviously anxious to be on his way.

Kirsty said, "Will you be home tonight?"

"Aye, at the usual time."

He nodded, and made to turn away.

Kirsty said, "I mean, home to Canada Road."

"What?"

"Canada Road, Craig, not Benedict Street."

For an instant his eyes widened then his expression became surly, almost brutish, his eyelids lowered and his mouth compressed into a tight, undemonstrative line.

"What the hell're you bletherin' about, Kirsty?" he said. "By God, you do get some funny ideas."

Shaking his head, he swung round and walked away, striding towards the head of Kingdom Road where his territory officially began.

Drained by the encounter, Kirsty lowered Bobby to the pavement.

She hadn't intended to blurt out the remark, to give Craig the least hint that she knew about Benedict Street or anyone who lived there. Now he would have an opportunity to brood on her comment, make what he could of it during his shift, devise more plausible lies.

Behind and above them a train thundered over the bridge. Bobby groped for her skirts and pressed himself against her.

"It's only an engine, darlin'," she told him. "Nothin' to be scared of."

"No' scared," said Bobby stoutly.

Nonetheless he did not resist when she lifted him again into her arms and carried him away from the bridge's looming shadow.

*   *   *

Cynics might have said that you'd have to be short of the whole shilling to make a friend let alone a hero out of Constable

49

Craig Nicholson but, where the daft and the deprived were concerned, there were few on the Force of a mind to be critical. Most constables in Ottawa Street knew Sammy Reynolds and took turns in minding out for his welfare. They even indulged the lad's fond belief that one day he would become a copper too.

Thanks to Craig Nicholson, orphan Sam had been found work in the halls of the People's Mission and a billet in a model lodging house in Scutter Street. It was part of the station's ritual that Sam would be escorted from the halls to the lodging each and every night and Craig, as the lad's guardian angel, often did the honours just before or after shift.

Sam was no longer a child and it was comical to see this broad-shouldered whiskery young man hanging on to a policeman's hand; yet nobody laughed and nobody jeered and none of the ignorant urchins of the streets dared bait Sam for his want of wits or moon-faced vacancy unless they fancied a run-in with the law.

The kirk halls were open seven days in the week. Sam spent all his time there, making no division between work and recreation. Mr Dugdale, the caretaker, had shown him how to perform a variety of tasks, and he was fed there and, to some extent, pampered by the ladies of the groups and unions that used the accommodations. He joined in the less-disciplined activities of Sunday School and Boys' Brigade and sat in on Bible Class meetings too.

There were times when Craig envied Sammy his simple, well-regulated existence and the man would often unburden himself to the boy as they strolled to the Claremont lodging house in the late evening hour. Sammy, of course, could offer no words of advice or comfort, though he did seem generally sympathetic when Constable Nicholson was in a melancholy or complaining mood.

Anxiety and uncertainty had almost floored Craig. He'd stumbled through his duty in a kind of daze. It had been, thank God, a quiet night in Greenfield. He had found not one broken pane of glass or forced padlock, no stray dog or dithering old boozer who had lost his way home. He'd had lots of time to trudge and brood on Greta's rejection, on Kirsty's disturbing remark and what it might imply.

Peter Stewart, the constable to whom Craig handed over the

beat, had entered the Force in the same recruitment as Craig and the two young men had become friends.

"God, but you look done in," Peter said.

"I am," Craig admitted.

He had taken a roasting from his colleagues before the shift began, had been the target for unfunny jokes and much sarcasm after his name had been read out by Sergeant Drummond. Peter, however, was a gentle soul and just gave him a sympathetic pat on the back.

"Has anyone gone for Sammy?" Craig asked.

"I'll step round that way, if y'like," Peter offered.

"Nah, I'll get him before I sign off."

It was not far out of his way, an extra half-mile. He could manage that without collapsing.

Sammy was seated on the steps outside the locked door of the Mission halls. Mr Dugdale had stayed with him in case one of the constables didn't manage to collect the lad, as happened now and then. So unswerving was Sammy's faith in the Force that he would have sat on the cold step all night long.

"So it's yourself tonight, Constable Nicholson," said Mr Dugdale when Craig arrived.

"Sorry I kept you," Craig said.

"No bother. No bother at all."

After bidding Craig and Sammy good night, the caretaker turned up his coat collar and set off for home, a step around the corner. Craig and Sammy Reynolds set off in turn for the Claremont model lodging house.

Sammy wore a long melton jacket and patched tweed trousers. A hand-knitted scarf was wound about his neck, a gift from old Miss Carbury, a pillar of the Ladies' Union.

"Do y'want to take my hand, Sammy?"

"Eh – aye."

"Here, take it then."

"Eh – I'm gettin' too big."

"Who says?"

"Mrs Lumsden telt me so."

"Never mind what Mrs Lumsden says. Here, take it."

The young man's hand closed on his; chapped, dry winter skin, callouses from the coal shovel, stubby fingers with bitten nails. It made Craig feel better.

Sammy gave a skip of pleasure. He had not wanted to take heed

51

of Mrs Lumsden's repeated attempts to make him see reason and sense. It was a sore thing to be informed that you were too big to be given a hand.

Sammy had been brought up in a filthy cellar in the Madagascar, a notorious slum. His father had been drunk most of the time, and God knew who the mother had been. Sammy had run foul of the law; innocent theft. He had been birched for the petty offence and, when his old man finally drank himself to death, would have been destined for the workhouse asylum if Craig had not rescued him. When you boiled it all down it was about the one good thing to come out of his years of service.

The Claremont was kept open late for Sammy's benefit. Superintendent Black, pipe in mouth and hands clasped behind his back, was waiting on the steps. Mr Black had been a soldier in his youth and still had the straight spine and squared shoulders of a guardsman.

Gruffly, but affectionately, he chased Sammy indoors and away up to his cubicle on the first floor.

"I'll bid you good night then, Mr Black," Craig said.

"One moment, Constable Nicholson."

Mr Black held out an envelope.

"What's this?" said Craig.

"Delivered here for you."

"Delivered? Who'd send me a letter here?"

"Mrs Taylor is her name, I believe."

Trying to appear unruffled, Craig accepted the envelope from the man's hand. "When was it handed in?"

"Couple of hours since," Mr Black said.

"Sorry you've been troubled," Craig said.

"No trouble."

He walked away from the shrewd, speculative gaze of the superintendent with the thin brown envelope tucked into his breast pocket as if it had no importance whatsoever. He rounded the corner into Hudson Road, a short, bald, cobbled nothing of a street that cut between warehouse walls, hurried to the road's only lamp, pulled out the envelope and tore it open.

The handwriting surprised him by its maturity; narrow, upright letters penned in violet ink. Her spelling was better than his own. He had never suspected Greta of having had an education.

My Dearest Craig,

I am sorry you came to see me yesterday. I am sorry you ask me to go away with you. I cannot. It is nothing to do with you. Jen and me will always remember you fondly. But I do not think you should come to see us any more. You will not want to, I think. I hope you might still think you are our friend. It is for the best. Jen sends her love and I also do the same.

Greta.

His hand trembled as he held the sheet of paper up to the light. He could envisage its methodical composition, see her at the kitchen table, her hair unfastened, hanging soft and dark over one cheek and that toss of the head she would give to shake it from her eyes.

The letter made him feel worse, not better. He imagined that there was calculation in it, slyness, a lie. Greta was just taking precautions in case she ever needed him again. Perhaps she had reported to Johnnie Whiteside and Whiteside had advised her to write, to placate the idiot copper, soften the blow.

Craig crumpled the letter and envelope into a small ball and, hunkering down, pushed it through the ribs of a gutter drain, prodding it until it fell into dank space.

He remained crouched for a moment, staring at the grating and then, as slowly and stiffly as an old, old man, he pushed himself to his feet. He glanced up and down the street, furtively lit a Gold Flake and, with the cigarette cupped in his hand, turned his steps wearily towards Canada Road.

It was over, definitely over. He would never hold Greta in his arms again, though he might have the satisfaction of revenge upon her if Ronnie Norbert managed to come through with the goods. Meanwhile he would have to settle for second best, for Kirsty and a humdrum life at home.

Four

Flirting with Danger

March saw an end to the cold dry spell. Warm south-west winds brought rain billowing over the river and, later in the week, gales rattled Greenfield's rooftops and moaned like saxophones in chimneypots and flues.

Kirsty found it stimulating to have a shake from the weather, to have to skip round puddles and battle the strong current of air that poured through the close, though she felt sorry for old folk to whom the winds meant breathlessness, rough handling and occasional spills. She, however, was young enough to take pleasure in the first blast of spring and to let it snap her out of apathy and self-pity.

She had waited for weeks for Craig to offer an explanation or apology. She had not goaded him again, though, had not promoted a crisis. Part of her longed for a confrontation, a clearing of the air, but another part of her was timid and cautious and afraid of how Craig might react.

Craig was much as he had been before his affair with the woman from Benedict Street had been uncovered. The fine was paid, the incident put behind him. If he had more than an inkling that Kirsty knew about his infidelity then he apparently didn't care. Suspicion, in consequence, clouded Kirsty's days for a while. She questioned every extra shift, every half-hour that he could not account for, and every casual excuse for being late home or leaving early seemed like a lie, even when logic told her that he spoke the truth.

She had bragged to Gordon that she was going to fight to keep her husband. But she did not know how. Perhaps it was weak of her not to challenge him, demand a promise that he would not do it again. But she was in no position to demand anything from him. Few wives were. Any power that they had over their husbands was acquired by stealth and by mastery of the fine art of servitude, by making themselves indispensable. Craig no longer seemed to want her, though she did not object to that. The pleasure of the bed for Kirsty was being alone in it, snuggled down while the wind raged and roared about the tenement.

Perversely it took brusque March winds and dark grey rains to cheer her up and blow away the cobwebs, though she was not yet willing to take Gordon's word for it that Craig had finally broken off his relationship with the street woman, that the affair was over and done with for good.

In fact Gordon had not clapped eyes on Craig since Christmas and the gulf between the family and its elder son seemed to grow wider as the weeks lengthened into months. This too fed Kirsty's depression, until that week of wild and woolly weather when, with Craig on night-shift, she had the house to herself.

It was during that week that she experienced a quickening in her, a desire to be occupied not with frivolous diversions but with shoring up her marriage and, at the same time, in making Craig pay for the wrongs he had done her and his neglect of her feelings.

On Saturday forenoon she wrapped Bobby in his warmest clothes and, before Craig had wakened from his daylight sleep, set off for the Irish Market and a glimpse of her rival in the flesh.

Black clouds soared over cranes and mastheads, tangled in the rigging of cargo ships and absorbed the smoke from the bum boats, dredgers and puffers that plied business on the Clyde. No rain fell, however, and clear sky showed behind the scurrying fronts. Just being out and about on the glossy pavements, heading down to the waterside, increased Kirsty's determination, made flirting with danger seem like a daring adventure.

Bobby was chirruping like a budgerigar as he hung on to Mammy's hand. He did not, of course, understand the reason for this promising excursion into strange territory. To Bobby it was an experience pure and simple, the wonder of an expanded horizon, and his senses were greedy for all the new sights and smells and sounds that the market offered up.

He wore a suit of knitted jersey that Madge, rather prematurely, had bought for him. His first pair of laced shoes were on his feet and his first Tam o' Shanter on his head. Kirsty wore her 'church social' outfit, a dress of patterned wool, a sober half-length overcoat and her one and only fancy hat, an ornamental straw held on with a chiffon scarf, a style she had copied, not wisely, from a drawing in *Lady's World* magazine.

The Irish Market was well known in Glasgow's west end. It sprawled over several acres of the disused Belfast cattle dock at the bottom of Thomas Street where horse-trams did a turnabout. From its barrows and tented stalls all sorts of second-hand bric-a-brac could be purchased, together with clothing, food, timber and old tools. By Saturday mid-afternoon it would be a scene of incredible confusion and noise with tinkers and spielers crying their wares and the bargain-hunting public out in force.

Kirsty had come rather too early, though, and not all the trestles were in place yet. From donkey-carts and hand-barrows shoddy and tin-plate goods and masses of much-used clothing were still being unloaded. Canvas awnings roped to stout poles were knotted tight today against the swirling wind. Many of the booths were manned already, of course. Brassy young women and slump-backed old women and women as blunt as hobnails cried out to Kirsty and lured Bobby to their stalls with smiles and beckoning gestures and the promise of sweets held up in their dirty fingernails. Bobby clung to his mother's hand, however, and stared back at the cajoling women with masculine implacability.

What Bobby wanted to do was to pat a donkey. He was just biding his time until he could draw Kirsty close enough to a cart to brush his hand against one of the rough-coated creatures with its comical muzzle and long ears. To Bobby, donkeys looked like toys made real and he turned and gazed at each animal as Kirsty dragged him past in her search for Greta Taylor.

Kirsty had only Gordon's description of the woman to guide her, and the knowledge that Greta leased a small stall from which she sold good quality clothing and domestic linens, stuff that had been decently washed and repaired and that would do some poor but respectable soul a turn or two before shredding.

"Mammy, look't the donkey."

"Aye, son."

"Mammy, see."

"In a minute, Bobby."

Then he caught sight of the girl child. She had a carrot. She stood right beneath the donkey's muzzle and did not flinch from the sneck of the big brown teeth that chopped the titbit delicately from her fingers.

Mightily impressed, Bobby dug in his heels.

He watched the shaggy head come down, the pale tongue and hairy lips snuffle at the tiny palm and lift the carrot top away as neat as ninepence. He could tell by the wee girl's giggle and the shiver of her shoulders under her red-cloth cape that it had tickled deliciously.

He wanted to do it too. He wanted to feed the donkey.

"Mammy, go."

He tugged free of Kirsty, who was occupied in scanning the stalls that were ranked beneath the weeping walls of the cattle sheds.

Arms stretched out, he cried, "*Me, Me, Me,*" as if tuning up for an aria, and ran full pelt towards the animal. Startled, the little girl tried to intercept him but slipped, tripped and sat down, plop on the cobbles, while the donkey, not startled at all, just dunted the stranger with its nose to fend him off.

Bobby spun and sat down too, smack on his bottom on the hard wet stones, and wailed.

It was all over before Kirsty could prevent it. Her hand flew to her mouth as her son, caught off balance, was knocked to the ground. She ran towards him in panic.

The little girl got there first, however. Fists planted on hips, she nagged him for his stupidity. "Bad boy. Bad, *bad* boy. Fright'nin' poor Neddy."

Bobby wailed louder. Tears coursed down his cheeks.

Kirsty picked him up and soothed him. His bottom and legs were wet but he appeared to be otherwise undamaged. She wiped his hands and face with a handkerchief and hugged him until he stopped crying.

"He frighten Neddy," the wee girl declared.

"He didn't mean it," said Kirsty. "He just wanted to pet Neddy, that's all."

"Ye need a carrot t' pet Neddy."

"That's enough, Jen."

Kirsty glanced round.

The woman said, "Is he hurt?"

She was small, dark-haired. A sedate black skirt and tight unmatching jacket showed off her full figure. Her concern for Bobby's welfare seemed genuine.

Instantly, and with utter certainty, Kirsty knew that this was Greta Taylor. Strangely she felt no hatred, not even dislike.

"Bring him over to my stall. I've a towel there. You can dry him

57

off with it," the woman said. "It's a lovely wee suit he's wearin'. Be a sin to see it spoiled."

Kirsty hesitated. Her first inclination was to turn on her heel and carry Bobby away. She had confronted her enemy, and had found no enemy at all.

"Sit him on the table," Greta Taylor said. "I'll just pay off Rab. He brings the stuff down for me."

Rab was as old as the Trongate tower. He had obviously done his bit for his shilling and would do no more. He sat hunched under a canvas sack on the board of his cart and accepted Greta's coin without a civil word of thanks. He flicked his cane-and-bootlace whip at his cuddy's rump and rumbled the cart away up the ramp towards Thomas Street.

"Rab's no' got a nice donkey," Jen informed Bobby. "Neddy's better. Neddy likes carrots."

Bobby had stopped crying. He had assumed that stern frown now and, apart from a bit of wriggling when he was put on to the table, he gave no sign that his ordeal had put him out.

"An' totties," Jen added.

Greta returned to the stall with a large basket of clothes braced against her side. She heaved it on to the table, grunting.

"What are you bletherin' about, Jen?" she said. "Don't you go botherin' the lady now."

"She's not botherin' me at all," said Kirsty.

"She's a real chatterbox."

"It's natural at that age," Kirsty said. "What age is she?"

"Nearly four." Greta went around the table and produced a clean but threadbare towel. "Now, young man, if you'll just stand up an' hold on to Mammy's shoulders we'll soon have y'dried off. Will I do the needful?"

"It's very kind of you, Miss . . .?"

"Greta's my name."

"I thought it might be."

The towel in hand, Greta paused. "Have we met before?"

"Not exactly," Kirsty said.

"How do you know who I am?"

"I'm Kirsty Nicholson."

"Oh, dear God!" Greta murmured. "He told you."

"No, he didn't tell me. He told me nothing," Kirsty said.

"Look, I hope you're not goin' to cause trouble."

"Would you blame me if I did?"

"God, no," said Greta. "I wouldn't blame you one bit. But . . . but, you see, I daren't lose the trade."

"I won't make a scene, I promise," Kirsty said. "An' I won't keep you long. I'd just like you to answer a few questions."

"What sort o' questions?"

"About Craig."

"I think . . . I mean, that wouldn't be right, would it?"

"It's not him that's been wronged."

Bobby swayed. Kirsty steadied him with both hands about his waist while Greta abstractedly dabbed at the seat of the jersey suit.

"Did Craig . . . I mean, did he say anythin' at all about me?"

"Never a word," Kirsty answered. "It was easy for him, I suppose, since he was out of the house at all hours."

"It's easy enough for any of them; men, I mean," Greta said. "I never intended to steal him from you, Mrs Nicholson."

"But you didn't deny him what he wanted?"

"No, I couldn't."

"Surely he didn't . . . force you?"

"No, but I . . . I liked him," Greta said.

"Did he give you things?"

Greta bridled. "If you mean money . . . No, I'm not a whore, Mrs Nicholson, if that's what you think."

"You'd hardly be here sellin' second-hand clothes if you were," Kirsty said. "It might be easier for me to cope with if you were one o' those women."

"What do you want with me?" Greta said.

"I had to see you. I had to make sure that I hadn't lost him to you," Kirsty said.

"He was never mine," Greta said. "Anyway, I wouldn't thieve another woman's man."

"Didn't you want him for yourself?"

"I thought I did, at first," Greta said. "But when the chance arose . . . No, I couldn't do it." She gave Bobby's seat a final rub with the towel. "Is that better? All right now, young man?"

"Uh-huh."

Bobby slung himself forward into Kirsty's arms and was duly transferred to the ground, where Jen Taylor had been patiently waiting for her new-found friend to join her.

"Neddy?" Bobby said.

But Neddy had been led away. He would return with the other

carts much later that evening when the lanterns had been lighted and all the unsold goods had been knocked down in a last attempt to wring an extra bob or two for the week ahead. The horse-trams had brought an influx of customers from Glasgow and others had sauntered down from Partick and Whiteinch. Some of the stall-holders had made their first sales and there was already a small queue outside the tent of Madam Rose, the fortune-teller.

"I think I'll just take him t' see Mr Barry's shop, Mammy, eh?" Jen said, innocently.

"We'll see, we'll see." Greta, for once, was not wholly engaged with her daughter.

Kirsty said, "What does Mr Barry sell in his shop?"

"Ginger," Jen answered promptly.

Opening her purse, Kirsty gave Jen a threepenny piece.

"Just one glass each now," she said. "Bobby, you hold on to Jen an' don't get lost. You hear me?"

"Uh-huh."

Greta did not protest and together the women watched as the children, hand-in-hand, stepped carefully between the puddles and headed towards the stall diagonally across the aisle. Jen giggled coquettishly and drew Bobby closer to her into a daring conspiracy of independence.

Kirsty turned. "What chance?"

"I don't . . ."

"What chance?" Kirsty said again. "Did he ask you to go away with him, is that it?"

Greta hung her head. "I shouldn't . . ."

"*Did he?*"

"Yes."

"And what happened?"

"I turned him down," said Greta.

*   *   *

Saturday, as a rule, was just another working day for Gordon Nicholson. That weekend, however, he had abandoned his usual routine and had taken the train to Balfron, beyond the city's western outskirts. There he was met by one of Breezy's cousins, Sinclair Smith, who picked him up in a jaunting-car and drove him out towards the moors and hills and the wide, wet paddocks of Bree Lodge where Sinclair's brother Russell trained racehorses.

Gordon was not averse to gambling, far from it, but he had

little or no interest in the Turf. It was Breezy who had per-
suaded him to accept the Smiths' invitation to spend a day at
the stables and to learn a few of the tricks of the trade from the
experts.

Gordon had met Sinclair several times at dinners and suppers at
Great Western Terrace. He liked the man, a quiet-spoken, amiable
sort of chap with a stomach of such well-defined amplitude that
you were tempted to pat it for luck the way you would a saintly
stone. Sinclair encouraged the habit and would wink and rub his
waistcoat himself from time to time, as if it were something quite
separate from the rest of him.

Russell, Gordon had been told, was a different kettle of fish
altogether. He was dry, lightweight, retiring. He had not even
turned out for Breezy's wedding, though Breezy did not hold it
against him as he'd been off with a horse to a race-meet in the
south and, after all, business was business. Russell Smith was
a famous trainer. His name often appeared in the pages of the
sporting press and horse-set journals for he trained amateur and
professional jockeys as well as their mounts.

Rain hung on the snouts of the Campsie Fells and cloud cut
off the high peaks that ringed Loch Lomond but no rain fell on
Sinclair Smith or his passenger on the road from the station to
the Lodge.

Bree was a fine tall house of white-painted stone. Breast-high
hedges were just beginning to bud and fences enclosed well-tended
gardens and orchards. The stables were below the house, purpose-
built, well-drained and convenient. Gallops, sprints and hurdles
lay on fine flat grasslands towards the loch and, with just a dusting
of sunlight on them, they looked rich and beautiful and smug to
Gordon's attentive eye.

Forgetful of the fact that horse-talk was all Greek to Gordon,
Uncle Sinclair had gone prattling on and on about sires and dams
and owners: "Trained a few for His Grace back in the earlies, the
famous Sea Fever among others. Picked him up for a song at a seller
in Hamilton as a three-year-old and sold him straight to the Duke
who had a good natural eye for a winner. Subsequently went on
to win the Cumberland Plate an' the Silver Bell at Lanark, givin'
weight in the latter. Went to stud like a champion, an' brought
Facility out o' Marguerite Mayflower. Now there was a mare for
you . . ."

Sinclair was still at it when he reined up at Bree Lodge and within seconds of Gordon's being introduced to brother Russell the steady trickle of facts and figures had become a flood.

Initially Gordon was quite flattered when Russell shook his hand and simultaneously guessed his weight correct to the ounce.

"Resembles Mick O'Reilly," Sinclair said, "don't you think?"

"Aye, to a T," said Russell. "Remember Mick's father, though?"

"Do I not, but," said Sinclair. "Never put on a pound in thirty years' racin'. Came off the Fallons, of course, an' they were all whippets."

"Trained with Rourke at Crabtree in Donegal."

"Rode Williamsburgh in the Chester carryin' thirty pounds, no less."

"Thirty-one," said Russell.

"Whatever happen t' yon cousin o' his?"

"Michael Fallon, you mean?"

"Am I right in thinkin' he went t' ride in Australia?"

"Rode," said Russell, with hardly a pause for breath, "his best in Tasmania in his year wi' Tom Asprey, at Hobart. Came in for three hundred guineas on Blood Orange. Same again on Secundus out o' Queen o' the Meadow."

Sinclair snapped his thick fingers. "New Zealand Derby in 'eighty-three. Marzipan Fool from Juno."

"On the nose," said Russell.

Gordon cleared his throat as loudly as he dared. Both men blinked as if he had sprung out of the gravel like a fountain.

"Well, that's who you look like, son," said Sinclair. "Mick O'Reilly."

"So you'd better come an' see the horses," said Russell with the enthusiasm of a chap who hadn't clapped eyes on a thoroughbred for at least twenty minutes.

Russell was a small, compact man, a year or two younger than his brother. He wore expensive, hand-tailored tweeds, leggings and brogues, a cravat and a brown Derby hat. His tiny hands were protected by long cuffs which he pushed back before he touched the horses in the stalls and boxes that lined the stable yard.

There were sixty-four animals in training, Gordon was informed, and others at stud. The morning canters had gone well, apparently, and a filly named Camberwell Beauty, out of Megan's Wish by Partan Lad, had shown no signs of sore shins after a strong run over heavy ground.

"She'll be ready for Newcastle at the month's end," Russell said.

"Aye, but will his highness let her run?"

"His highness?" said Gordon.

"Our cousin," said Sinclair, "Dolphus."

"It's Dolphus's horse?"

"Aye, for the time bein'," said Russell.

"No patience, no patience at all," said Sinclair. "Worst kind o' owner, really."

"Does my stepfather have horses here?" Gordon asked.

"Seven at present," said Russell. "Breezy leaves it all to me, though. Never sets foot in my territory."

"All patience, all patience," said Sinclair. "That's what an owner should be."

"Dolphus will want t' be rid o' Camberwell Beauty," Russell said. "She's not shown yet an' he won't trust me to bring her up for the season's end."

"It's the shins. He's worried about the shins," said Sinclair.

"Is she a good prospect?" said Gordon.

"Aye, she's a fine wee filly wi' a future," said Russell. "I've brought her along real nice."

"Make him an offer an' she could be yours, son," Sinclair suggested, with a wink. "Dolphus never turns down money. Aye, why don't you make him an offer for her this very day?"

"Dolphus is comin' here?" said Gordon.

"For dinner, aye," said Sinclair.

"Tonight?" said Gordon.

"Naw, naw," said Sinclair. "Dinner's at dinner time. You're not consortin' wi' toffs now, son."

"Does . . . does Dolphus know I'll be here?" Gordon asked.

"I expect he does," said Sinclair. "In fact, I know he does. I told him as much m'self."

"Mr Cochrane examined Camberwell on Monday," Russell put in. "Tendons are fine. He thinks it was a passing rheumatick."

"If he orders us t' sell an' she wins subsequently, there will be hell t' pay," said Sinclair.

"Remember what happened wi' Lincoln Green?"

"God, aye. But I'll swear he was ringed at Prestwick."

Gordon drifted away from the prattling brothers. Everything about Bree Lodge was neat, well-organised and economical; everything except the conversations.

He looked down the line of stalls to the rolling, dun-coloured fields and the mountains above Loch Lomond. A boy in an enormous chequered cap, and riding-boots that seemed to stretch up to his ears came past leading a bay stallion three times his height. In the paddock beyond the trees two men were unloading hurdles from a cart.

Dolphus was coming and an instinct told Gordon that Amanda would be with him. He understood how the Adairs conducted themselves and would not have been surprised to learn that Sinclair Smith had been wheedled by Amanda into inviting him to Bree that Saturday.

As if just thinking of her had conjured her up, Gordon saw the carriage at that very moment, and the rider on the road behind it.

Guilt and excitement twined within him. He had neglected her suggestion that he arrange a meeting with her in Glasgow. He had no inclination to be furtive, however, nor did he wish to involve Johnnie Whiteside in his courtship ritual. When the rider broke from the unfenced path and came at a fast trot across the field below, Gordon recognised her at once and realised that however leery he might be of commitment, as far as Amanda Adair was concerned indifference was no longer an option.

He ran down to the fence, took off his hat and waved it, calling out, "Amanda, Amanda! What a wonderful surprise."

She *had* known that he would be here; no doubt of it. Everything had been chosen to make an impact, the lithe chestnut hunter, the formal black dress, even the feather in the hat. She was a perfect advertisement for her class, a picture of spirited, self-assured femininity.

Dolphus watched from the window of the carriage as his darlin' daughter rode pell-mell towards the high fence and the young man she believed she loved.

"Amanda."

She rode side-saddle, wore a double-breasted jacket and wrap-over skirt. Her hair was pinned up and a little nosegay of spring flowers was tucked into the top of her waistcoat, into the folds of her silk scarf. The chestnut was a skittish lightweight of less than thirteen hands but that was more than enough to place Amanda above Gordon when she reined the animal into line with the fence.

She let him slaver and cool slowly, walking him up and down on a guarded rein, round and down and back to the fence. Gordon, grinning, tried to keep abreast of her.

"I didn't realise you'd be here too."

She adopted a haughty pose, head high. "Expect you wouldn't have come if you'd known."

" 'Course I'd have come. 'Course I would."

"If I'd been informed that you . . ." The horse walked on ten yards and was swung back tightly, Amanda braced and balanced against the sway, ". . . I most certainly would not have accompanied Daddy."

"I'm glad you did. Damned glad."

"Oh, you're not. You're only . . ." Another walk, another tight turn, another graceful motion of the upper body, ". . . to be polite. You don't have to bother, Mr Nicholson. I have taken the hint. I shan't trouble you further."

Her poise, the constant movement of the mount, her height from the ground all served to emphasise Gordon's lack of inches and of standing in her eyes. She'd probably forgotten, or hadn't even realised, that he'd been raised with horses, not fine-boned hunters maybe, but big stubborn plough-horses. He vaulted the fence when her back was to him and was waiting when she swung about.

Gordon let the hunter see him clearly and then went forward and gripped the snaffle with that little down drag that wouldn't pain the beast but would let it know who was boss now. The horse stopped, head down, and would not go forward no matter how strenuously Amanda urged it.

The ride had brought colour to her cheeks, had polished her nose. Up close, she seemed slightly less perfect, more human, more attainable.

Gordon grinned.

"Oh, aren't you the hero," Amanda said sardonically. "What a masterful little man!"

"It's time for lunch," said Gordon.

"Dinner," Amanda corrected. "It's dinner at this hour for us country folk."

"I'll help you down, shall I?"

"How gallant!" she said, and slid easily from the saddle into his arms.

*　　　*　　　*

Dinner was a hearty, informal feast served at the big table in the kitchen of the Lodge. Nobody had to go through the palaver of changing clothes, not even Amanda. Knowing this, she had brought no servant with her from The Knowe.

Dolphus was already at table when Gordon and Amanda arrived in the kitchen. He looked somewhat out of place in a city gent's black coat and stiff collar. He greeted Gordon with a hearty bray, too jovial to be sincere.

"Up from the town, hah?" he shouted. "Splendid, splendid. Come by train, did you, hah?"

"Yes, sir."

"Good, jolly good."

Seated on the broad-backed wooden chairs were Russell and Sinclair Smith and a not-so-young man in a short tweed blouse and corduroys. He, it transpired, was the famous amateur jockey Captain Tom Wells. He had bright blue eyes and a weather-tanned complexion and was not in the least stand-offish. Unfortunately, however, he was also obsessed by horse flesh and after greeting Gordon and Amanda pleasantly enough returned to an inevitable rigmarole of weights and odds and lineages. Amanda, Gordon was relieved to notice, was soon bored by it. He'd feared that she might suffer from horse fever too.

Broth was followed by an Irish stew and a treacle pudding so large that it might have been steamed in a manger. Jugs of beer and bottles of whisky were on the table and Cookie herself, assisted by a young maid, did the serving. The wind gusted against the upright house and from the window Gordon could watch clouds whisk across the moor as he ate.

No lesson in the manners of the Turf would come his way that day. The brothers were intent as philosophers on their own problems. Gordon cared not. Amanda was seated close to him. She had loosed her hair and taken off her jacket but he could still catch from her, as you can from the fur of a cat, the scent of outdoors.

At first he hardly heard what the men were saying to each other. He might never have tuned in to the conversation at all if it had not become both furtive and argumentative and if he had not noticed that Amanda had begun to listen to it too.

"I want her sold," Dolphus was saying. "She's no good at all."

"Ask Tom," said Russell Smith. "He rode her just this mornin'."

"Fit as a flea," said the Captain. "Eager to work too. She'd have run all mornin' if I'd let her."

"Mr Cochrane – " Sinclair began.

Dolphus cut him short. "Cochrane! What does he know!"

"He's the best veterinarian in the county," said Russell.

"Rheumaticks," said Dolphus. "It's always rheumaticks until the beast goes lame. Then Cochrane will support your claim that she was nobbled."

"Are you still on about Lincoln Green, Dolphus?" said Sinclair. "That horse *was* nobbled."

"Hah!"

Captain Wells intervened. "She's entered for the Spring Plate at Newcastle in three weeks' time. I'll give her the ride, if you like."

"There's an offer for you," Sinclair said.

Dolphus said, "The Spring Plate's a sellers' race, isn't it?"

"Aye," said Russell.

"Run her by all means," said Dolphus. "And when she wins, sell her."

"What if she loses?" said Sinclair.

"I don't want her to lose," said Dolphus.

Russell shrugged his bony shoulders. He had left most of his stew, Gordon noticed, and nursed a glass of whisky in both his hands, turning the glass round and round and round with his fingers, looking at it and not at his cousin.

"Lap of the gods, Randolph, old chap," said Tom Wells. "Can't go makin' rash promises. Tinker's Pride's in the field, I hear, and she has strength and experience."

"Favourite, for sure," said Sinclair.

"I want Camberwell Beauty to win," said Dolphus.

"I won't risk it," said Russell.

"I want her to win an' then to be sold to the highest bidder straight after."

"It's his licence, an' his reputation if he's caught," said Sinclair.

"Don't you owe me for Prestwick?" said Dolphus.

"Certainly not," said Russell Smith.

"You know *what* to do, don't you?" said Dolphus.

"What if I do?"

"And you've done it before, hah?"

"Seldom," said Russell, "an' not for years."

"Did it for Breezy, didn't you, back in the Ayr Cup in 'eighty-six, when he was down on his luck?"

"We'd had a bad season too," said Sinclair. "The 'flu near wiped . . ."

Dolphus had no interest in the Smiths' explanations or tales of past woes. He watched Russell drink the whisky that he'd been swirling in the glass.

"Nobody will question it," said Dolphus. "Not you, Russell. You've got the reputation; use it."

"Too dangerous," said Russell.

"I'll sell her myself then," Dolphus said.

"Hardly ethical, old chap," said Tom Wells. "After Russell bought her for you, and trained her."

"Ethics don't enter into it," said Dolphus. "In any case, I doubt if there's much ethical behaviour in this house. No, nor morality either."

"Not fair, Dolphus," Sinclair Smith growled. "That wasn't Russell's fault."

"Why do you want her sold?" said Russell.

"I don't like the mare. I've never liked the mare. I don't trust her or her damned shins. I won't get stung again, Russell."

"Put her into the Lothian auctions, then."

"Buggered if I will," said Dolphus. "Thirty guineas, if I'm lucky; after the fees I've paid to you. She's dropped more in damned manure than that."

"If it's just money . . ." said Sinclair.

"I won't be a loser again," said Dolphus.

They stopped talking as if at a sign and all four looked along the table, first at Amanda and then at Gordon.

"Good pud, what?" said Captain Tom, attempting to be friendly.

"Very good," said Gordon.

"Have some more?"

"Couldn't, thanks," said Gordon.

"Glass of beer?"

Gordon shook his head. He watched Dolphus push himself away from the table and wordlessly beckon to Russell Smith to follow him outside. He noticed the glance that the brothers exchanged and Tom Wells' discomfort as Russell pushed himself from the table too and, with astonishing meekness, followed James Randolph Adair from the kitchen.

There was silence for a moment.

Sinclair Smith filled and lit a pipe.

"I won't take the ride if she's suspect, Sinclair," Tom Wells said. "I owe him no favour. Make that clear."

"I will, Tom, I will."

The Captain gave Amanda a little bow and even managed a smile before he hustled away, his boot heels clicking on the flagstones. Sinclair continued to puff on his pipe, brooding in silence.

"We'll be leaving soon, Gordon," Amanda said. "Come, I'll show you the rest of our horses first. All right, Uncle Sinclair?"

"Aye, fine, fine."

She led him through the house and out by the front door, out into the wind that came unopposed from the lochside hills and bullied the hedges and apple trees and flung her hair across her face.

She slipped into her jacket and buttoned it, then took his arm and conducted him along a pebble path that divided the orchards from the pastures.

"I thought we were goin' to see the horses?"

"I think you've had enough of horses for one day."

"Aye, that's true," Gordon said.

She leaned against him, wisps of hair whipping across her face, her cheeks glowing. "Do you know what all that was about?"

"I've a fair idea. Will your father get his way?"

"I expect so. He usually does," Amanda said. "How much money do you have, Gordon?"

"I'm not rich, not even well off," said Gordon. "I mean, I couldn't support . . ."

She pulled him closer, pursed her lips, shook her head. "If Camberwell Beauty goes in the Spring Plate at Newcastle at the end of the month," she told him, "put your shirt on her."

"Especially if Captain Wells isn't in the saddle?"

"Tom Wells won't ride her now at any price," Amanda said. "It'll be one of the professional jockeys, a top class performer. Perry McCrae, perhaps."

"What about odds?"

"Tremendous odds," said Amanda. "But listen to me, Gordon; you must tell nobody about this. Nobody. Not Johnnie or Eric, Breezy or anyone at all. And don't put the bet on with Sinclair. He won't accept it."

"Is this a sure thing?"

"As sure as anything can be," Amanda said. "Now, kiss me and say thank you. I must go."

Her lips were firm and cold, and she did not cling to him or draw him against her. She was content, here at the orchard fence, to accept his tentative peck, and turned away as soon as it was over.

"Thank you, Amanda," Gordon said.

She waved to him over her shoulder and, ten minutes later, he watched the carriage rumble off down the long swooping track, the girl on the chestnut gelding riding meek and sedate behind it, looking from this distance as if butter wouldn't melt in her mouth.

*   *   *

It was all too easy for her to imagine Craig in Greta Taylor's arms. Now that she had met the woman she could understand the attraction. She could not offer him such singularity because she was, nominally at least, Craig's wife and it was marriage that made things complicated, marriage that brought the burdens of care and responsibility. It was not the fact that Craig had spent time in Greta Taylor's bed that angered Kirsty but the fact that he had planned to leave her, that he had been willing to sacrifice everything for an illusion. Did the fool not realise that a few stolen hours of comfort and indulgence in a stranger's house were not the same as a relationship?

Greta Taylor had understood, had seen the danger and in an odd way had saved both herself and Kirsty from Craig's headstrong impetuosity. Greta Taylor had assured her that the affair was over. Kirsty was inclined to take the street woman's word for it. She was not bitter towards the woman. Perhaps they had too much in common, apart from Craig, to be enemies. Her resentment found its focus on Craig and on Craig alone.

Kirsty did not take herself to bed early that Saturday night. Bobby was exhausted by his day in the fresh air and quite worn out by the energy of his new-found friend, Jen Taylor. He nodded off over supper and made not one whimper of protest when Kirsty undressed him and popped him into bed in the small front room. She had already decided to wait up for Craig. She could not sit still, however. As she busied herself with a multitude of household chores, she felt upon her a desire, a need to test him; not to challenge him with the truth, though, for that would be flirting with danger and she was not yet sufficiently sure of herself.

When the house was spotless and supper in the oven, Kirsty

stripped herself and, standing on a towel at the sink, washed her body with a baby sponge. All sorts of feelings meshed within her, languor, self-absorption, and the faint disturbing tension of desire. She laved her breasts, her belly and thighs with the soapy sponge and listened to the clock tick sluggishly. She dried herself with a soft towel before the fire and put on her best nightgown and her dressing-gown, then combed her hair and arranged it in two bunches tied with ribbon and not pinned. Then she made herself a pot of tea and a slice of toast and seated herself by the bright fire to await Craig's return.

He came in about half-past eleven. He nodded a greeting. He made no comment about the shining kitchen or the cooked supper. He took off his tunic and collar and seated himself at the table and began to eat, elbows on the table, eyes cast down.

Kirsty poured his tea. She was conscious of the fullness of her breasts pressing against the material of the gown. Craig glanced up at her, seemed about to say something and then looked down again. He broke pie-crust with the edge of his fork. As soon as he'd finished supper he rose, stretched, kissed her perfunctorily on the brow and went through to his bed, leaving Kirsty to clear the dishes and wash up.

Some time later, without any sense of daring or of desire now, Kirsty crossed the hall and gingerly pushed open the front-room door.

He was naked. Seated on the side of the bed, he faced the curtained window, his back to her. His shoulders were slumped and one hand covered his eyes. If he had been a different kind of man, a man like David, say, she might have supposed that he was praying. But Craig had no belief in God, no conviction.

She could see the long, strong muscles of his back in the faint light, his spine bent by dejection. For an instant she experienced a pang of longing, an urge to put her arms about him, but she did not dare. She knew that he would spurn her, would see her soft gesture as a threat and not a comfort. Suddenly he twisted round.

"Hmmm?" he murmured, his voice thick, as if he'd been crying. "Oh, it's you, is it?"

Kirsty said, "Do you want me to wake you tomorrow?"

"Naw, let me sleep," he answered and turned from her again, showing her his back.

71

She closed the door carefully and returned to the kitchen. She slipped into the hole-in-the-wall bed and lay down to sleep.

Sleep, however, would not come to her. She lay wide awake for an hour or more, thinking what she must do, what she must do to hold him and, at the same time, make him pay for his lies and broken promises.

Five

The Sure Thing

On Sundays Madge Adair's pleasure in a long lie was lessened by the assumption that half the women in Glasgow were enjoying one too.

Madge was very fond of bed in all its aspects and connotations. She liked the dark night hours when traffic had quietened and the servants were buried in blankets in the basement and Breezy turned out the light and lay against her, touching her with his hands. She liked the whisperings and chuckles that followed intimacy and the long slide down into sleep afterwards, Breezy's lean body clasped in her arms and his bristling little moustache, which never seemed to sleep, tickling her breasts.

She also enjoyed an afternoon nap, a winter indulgence; the luxury of going to your bedroom and putting on a house-dress and just lying there at ease while poor working folk struggled through the wind and rain, and servants, out of sight below, peeled the totties and basted the beef.

The real pleasure, the height of luxury, though, was having your breakfast in bed every morning in life with never a grouse from your lord and master and no penance to pay afterwards.

Madge would sit up in the broad soft bed with a bolster behind her shoulders and lace-edged pillows plumped, and Jean, the maid, would put the breakfast tray across her knees set with everything she could wish for, including a napkin in a silver ring and a posy of fresh spring flowers.

Slim though he was for his years, Breezy had developed the inevitable middle-aged dumpling below his ribs and could not be comfortable in a semi-prone position. He would rise, wash, shave and put on his silk-lined dressing-gown and red morocco slippers and partake of sausage, egg and coffee at a side-table while his lovely wife, in a Paris pink, accordion-pleated, one hundred shilling cambric tea-jacket hungrily did justice to a couple of soft-boiled eggs. And Madge would think how clever she'd been to marry a man who could coin a decent income without having to gallop off at crack of dawn like most stuffy city gents.

Sunday mornings were not quite the same. They seemed lacking in weekday shine. If Albert had had a spot too much brandy on Saturday night he would not live up to his nickname, would be somewhat less than Breezy, a shade less than bright. Now and then, for the sake of appearances, he would rise early enough to trot off to morning service at Kirklee, a duty that Madge was not inclined to share. She had no Christian conscience. She loved her body too much to be put out by consideration for an invisible soul and trusted, vaguely, to some Albert-like God to look after her ethereal essence in the life hereafter.

Albert was a wee bit worse for wear that Sabbath morning and had decided to forgo a bracer of fire and brimstone. Jean had opened the curtains and the gelid light that filtered into the bedroom made Albert look quite bleak. Prudently Madge waited until he had downed a third cup of black coffee before she raised a subject that had been on her mind of late.

"Did you see Gordon last night, dear?" she asked.

"Nope, chookie, I did not."

"Did he come home at all?"

"Would you like me to pop along to his room and make sure?"

"I'm worried about him," Madge said.

"Gordon's fine," Breezy assured her. "He's young, that's all. In any case, he was visitin' my cousins in the country yesterday an' they'd see to it that he came to no harm."

"Here," Madge said, "take my tray away, please."

Obediently Breezy removed the breakfast tray from his wife's knees and placed it on a stool by the dressing-table. He stretched, yawned and then, with Madge's sanction, lit up a small cigar.

Madge waited until he had cleared his tubes with a series of rasping coughs, then said, "Albert, what's goin' on?"

"Don't know what you mean, dearest."

"Somethin's in the wind with our Gordon, an' I think you know what it is."

"What does it matter if he stayed out all night?" said Breezy. "He was with relatives."

"That gang!"

"Hoy, hoy, steady on, love," said Breezy. "My relatives, on the whole, are a respectable lot. What's got into you this mornin'?"

"Would she be there?"

"Would who be where?"

"That girl."

Breezy blew out a stream of smoke and squinted at Madge through it. She was no longer as soft and cuddly as she'd been a minute ago, not with her arms folded and a frown on her brow. The polished headboard reflected the window in cold grey rectangles and, Breezy thought, you just couldn't keep a Scottish Sabbath out, no matter how you tried.

He said, "Gordon went to look at horses, not girls."

"He saw enough horses when he was workin' at Dalnavert," Madge said.

"Ah, but not like these," said Breezy.

"I do not want my Gordon associatin' with touts an' bookies, Albert. He's far too impressionable," Madge said. "An' I want to know more about this girl."

"You've been talkin' to my sister Polly, ain't you?"

"What if I have?" said Madge.

"Much as I like Polly," Breezy said, "she can be a bit of a prig now an' then."

"I like Polly."

"Och, we all like Polly," Breezy said. "It's that husband of hers, Charlie Beadle. He thinks he's too good for us now, just because he deals in exports. God, I remember when Charlie Beadle was like the rest o' us an' hadn't two ha'pennies to rub together."

"I suppose you made him what he is today?" said Madge.

"Between you, me an' the gatepost, Madge, I made them all what they are today."

"An' it's your plan to do the same for my Gordon?"

"For God's sake, Madge, he's as close to a son as I'll ever have," Breezy protested. "Of course I want him to succeed in life."

"Sometimes I think it was a son you wanted an' not a wife at all."

"Bloody hell, Madge. You *know* I love you."

Madge recanted immediately. "Aye, dear. I know you do. I'm sorry. It's just that I worry so."

"You shouldn't worry about Gordon, or Lorna for that matter," Breezy said. "The boy's cut from the right cloth, believe me. He's a smart, intelligent – "

Madge interrupted, "Aye, but he has a lot to learn."

"I'll see him right, never fear," Breezy said, placatingly.

He cursed sister Polly's interference.

Perhaps Polly'd forgotten those skin-scalding winter mornings in the byre at Garscadden Farm when they'd have sold their souls to have a fire to warm their hands and hot beef to fill their bellies. Polly, Heather, Donnie, Walter, Edward and Dolphus; they all seemed to have forgotten where they came from, to pretend that Mammy and Daddy weren't still out there at Garscadden, still sanctimoniously preserving their dignity, their working-class integrity, on the pension that *his* money provided.

He wondered if Madge was falling into the same deadly trap as his sisters and brothers, if she too was about to become sentimental about peasant honesty and the moral value of grinding toil. He hoped not. He might have mellowed but he had not changed his principles. He would never be so old that he would lose his faith in money and the comforts that money could buy.

"It's *how* you'll see him right that worries me," Madge said.

"Is it somethin' Polly said that's got you upset?"

On the way up there had been lots of little lies, deceptions, petty larcenies, less than scrupulous deals. He'd thought nothing of them at the time. Lately, however, he'd begun to realise that there had been a price to pay after all, that expediency had curdled into corruption and that his strength then had become the family's weakness now.

Polly did not know enough to be dangerous but, a year or two back, hints of scandal had drifted through the family circle like smoke from a smouldering bonfire and Polly had no doubt caught wind of them and jumped to the wrong conclusions.

"Polly says – if you must know – that you're jealous of Dolphus an' would do anythin' to get your hands on some of his wealth," Madge said.

"The bitch!" said Breezy. "I'm not jealous of Dolphus. I'm not jealous of anybody. This is just women's talk, damned silly chatter. Besides, what does it have to do with Gordon?"

"Polly says you'd like to see him married to Dolphus's daughter."

"An' what good's that goin' to do me?"

Madge sniffed and lifted her shoulders, had no answer.

Breezy said, "I took on Donnie's boy when he came an' asked me. I took on Heather's son, too. They've done all right for themselves, believe me, but I've never quite been forgiven for my generosity."

Madge said, "Are they your heirs?"

"That's puttin' it a bit strong, Madge," Breezy answered. "Let's just say I feel a certain obligation to Johnnie an' Eric. Their fathers wanted them to read for a profession, an' I took them into commerce instead."

Madge said, "Isn't there enough to go round?"

"More than enough," said Breezy. "But I wouldn't discourage Gordon from a marriage to Amanda Adair, if that's the way the wind blows."

"Marryin' you, Albert, has cost me one son already," Madge said. "Och, no, I don't blame you for Craig's foolish behaviour but I don't want Gordon lost to me too."

"What if Gordon's in love with this girl?"

"He's too young to marry."

"Would you stand in his way if that's what he wanted to do; marry Amanda Adair, I mean?"

"It's all too fast, too sudden for my likin'," Madge said. "I can't help feelin' there's something behind it that I don't know about."

"Do you think that Dolphus's daughter's too good for Gordon, is that it?" said Breezy.

"Nobody's too good for my son."

"It's not the marriage that's got you worried," said Breezy, "it's what it entails, right?"

"He's only a boy, Albert," said Madge.

"I own a share of seven public houses, Madge," said Breezy. "I'm not tied to any one brewer either. My landlords buy their beer where they like. But that situation will change soon. Competition's increasin' year by year."

"What does this have to do with . . .?"

"As soon as Gordon shows willin' to marry Amanda then Dolphus will take him into Carruth's. He'll teach him the business from the ground up," Breezy explained. "There are no male heirs. Amanda's the eldest daughter of an eldest daughter. In ten years' time, Gordon would be in charge of a company worth hundreds of thousands of pounds."

"An' your pubs?"

"On the day of the marriage I sell out to Carruth's."

"God, it's like a market; a marriage market."

"Dolphus gets seven prime pubs an' Gordon gets the girl he loves."

77

"If he loves her?"

"Aye, well, we'll let him reach his own decision on that, Madge. Won't we?" Breezy said and, when his wife did not reply, said again, "Won't we, chookie?"

"Albert, I . . ."

"Do not interfere, Madge. Please."

"Does . . . does Gordon know about all this?"

"Of course not, an' I don't want you tellin' him either. Let him make up his own mind," Breezy said. "Now, if you'd kindly ring the bell behind you, Madge, I think I'll go to kirk after all."

"You've left it too late," Madge said.

"It's never too late, love," said Breezy, with a grin that, under the circumstances, Madge found more disagreeable than appealing.

*   *   *

If rain had not returned then Kirsty would have escaped from the kitchen of No. 154 Canada Road during the morning of that long dreary Sabbath. But there was nowhere to go except church and the solemn dunning of bells, warped and flattened by the blustery wind, put her off the notion of joining a communal worship.

Besides, Craig was fast asleep and she had nobody with whom she could leave Bobby for an hour or two. The Walkers had gone to Rutherglen to visit in-laws. The Boyles would spend the day attending one service after another and the Pipers, after journeying to kirk *en masse*, would disperse to make music in various halls, an act not considered sacrilegious in their circles. Once Andy had wakened from his drunken stupor, even the McAlpines would roll away on the tramcar to call on his old mother in Dennistoun.

Kirsty had no relatives, here or elsewhere, except the Nicholsons, and Craig had expressly forbidden her to call upon them.

On Sunday, more than any other day, Kirsty missed David and Nessie Frew. However, she tried not to feel sorry for herself in the grey, lonely kitchen but to nurse the determination that had come into her of late, tinged as it was with anger.

She worked the blacklead brush that wee bit harder, jerked the pulley rope that wee bit tighter and chopped the vegetables that wee bit smaller than she would normally have done, aware of Craig's slumbering presence in the bed in the grey front room.

She found herself resenting the fact that he would shape the day to duty, would make of Sunday nothing but a preparation for the shift that would bring it to an end.

She wondered vaguely how a street woman, like Greta Taylor, passed a long rainy Sabbath. Who would she visit? Who would drop in to visit her, now that she had rejected Craig Nicholson once and for all?

Come half-past two o'clock Kirsty could stand it no longer. She dressed Bobby and took him down to the Forrester Park to feed the ducks, leaving Craig asleep. But the park's pathways were puddled, the trees demented, the oval pond where the ducks lived whipped into a frenzy of wavelets and brown froth. Bobby did not like such bullying weather. Bread was scattered on the waters in great haste and Kirsty soon lifted her son and struggled back into the shelter of the tenements.

Tousled, weary and wet, mother and son arrived home with nothing but a sodden bag of bread rolls and a damp newspaper to show for their pains.

Craig was up and about at last. He had put on his oldest trousers, braces dangling over his nightshirt, and old rubber pumps instead of socks and shoes. He looked unrefreshed by sleep and slouched at the stove, a cigarette stuck in his mouth, as he fried bacon and bread in a pan of grease.

"Thought you'd gone t' church," he said.

"How could I be at church when I'd Bobby with me?"

"Could've gone to the Mission."

"Now what would I want at the Mission?"

"Not fancy enough for you, I suppose." Craig shook the pan to make the fat sizzle. "They've a *crek* there, right enough."

"A what?"

"For bairns, young bairns; a *crek*."

"Never heard of such a thing," said Kirsty.

"They get looked after while Mammy's inside sayin' her prayers. They get milk an' a biscuit. It's a new idea from the Reverend Augustus."

"Is this one o' Sammy Reynolds' stories?"

"Nah, it's the truth. Mr Dugdale told me about it."

Seated, Kirsty drew Bobby between her knees, mopped his face with a towel and, both hands working in unison, simultaneously unbuttoned his coat.

Craig swung the pan from the stove, plucked three rashers and a slice of bread from it and dropped them, dripping grease, on to a plate. He slid the pan noisily on to the hob and brushed ash from his nightshirt with his fingers.

"Never saw Jen," said Bobby.

Craig stiffened.

It was all Kirsty could do to stop herself clapping a hand over Bobby's mouth. She pretended that nothing was wrong, however, smothered his head with a towel and rubbed away briskly as if she could erase what her son had said.

Bobby groused, towel-muffled, and punched at his mother's arms until she took the cloth away.

"Saw ducks," he said. "Never saw Jen."

Craig removed the cigarette from his lips, licked his fingertips and extinguished the coal, put the butt behind his ear. He seated himself at table, placed his forearms on each side of the plate and stared down at his breakfast.

"Jen?" he said. "Is she a new pal then, son?"

"Aye."

Having got his father's attention, Bobby raced around the table and positioned himself at Craig's side. Kirsty folded the towel carefully, carefully folded the little overcoat.

"Where did you meet this new pal, son?"

"Never saw her the day."

"Was it yesterday you met her, hm?"

Craig broke off a fragment of bacon and held it out, let Bobby reach up for it like a pup.

"Was it?" Craig said.

" 'Nother bit, Daddy."

A second crumb of bacon followed the first.

Craig put a hand on his son's shoulder and leaned down. "Where did you meet her, Bobby? Tell Daddy the truth now."

"Had ginger," Bobby said. "Saw Neddy. Neddy bited me but it never hurted."

"Where?"

"Leave him alone, Craig," Kirsty said.

Craig looked up. "You took him to the Irish Market, didn't you?"

"What if I did?"

Bobby said, " 'Nother bit."

Craig swept the plate from the table and set it down on the floor where his son fell on it as if he were starved.

"I don't want you goin' there ever again," Craig said.

"It's too late," Kirsty said.

"What the hell d'you mean?"

"I met her yesterday."

"Met . . .?"

"Your bunty," Kirsty said. "She seemed very nice. Too good for you, in fact."

He leapt to his feet, the chair crashing to the floor. Startled, Bobby crawled to safety beneath the table, a strip of bacon pinched in his teeth.

"You bitch! You bloody interferin' bitch!" Craig shouted. "What right had you . . .?"

"Every bloody right," Kirsty said. "I'm your wife, in case you'd forgotten. I'm the one you were goin' to abandon, desert, when you ran away with . . ."

"She told you." He tossed his arms up, palms spread. "Jesus, she told you."

"She only told me what I'd already guessed."

"Aye, an' what was that, Kirsty? What had you 'already guessed'?"

"That you don't give a tinker's damn about us."

Bobby cowered under the table. He had a child's fear of raised voices and, though he had heard his father shout often enough, never before had he heard such piercing anger from his mother. He chewed the bacon doggedly as if that were the cause of the quarrel overhead.

"I'm here, am I not?" Craig shouted. "I'm still bloody-well here."

"Only because she wouldn't take you on."

"You're one to talk, Kirsty. Christ, you won't even marry me, bairn an' all."

"I don't want to marry you."

"Naw, naw, but you'll sponge off me just as long as I'm willin' to carry the can."

"Sponge?" She could hardly find breath to form the word. "Sponge, is it? I carried your child, an' I'd have carried another if . . ."

"Aye, you couldn't even do that right."

"Oh, God help me! I lost it. I lost it an' you didn't even *care*."

He slapped both hands flat on to the table and leaned into them.

"I didn't even *know*, Kirsty. Think about that. I didn't even *know* you were pregnant again."

Bobby began to cry.

He kept it to himself, sobbing silently under the protection of the table. He could see his father's legs braced wide, his mother's wrinkled stockings, the hem of her skirt, wet shoes. He rolled towards them and lay on his side, thumb in his mouth, whimpering.

Suddenly it was quiet, nobody shouting, no big voices, and then he heard his mother say, "What are we goin' to do, Craig?"

And his daddy say, "I don't know. Honest to God, I don't know."

"Do you want me to leave?"

"Do what you like, Kirsty. No."

"Doesn't it matter to you now?"

"Not much."

Bobby saw his mammy's hands below the oilcloth's serrated edge, clasping and picking at her skirt.

Mammy said, "Where are you goin'?"

Daddy said, "I think I'll go out for a while."

"It's still rainin'."

"It doesn't matter."

"Are you goin' to see her?"

"How can I?"

"Do you really not care about us, Craig?"

"I want you to be here to take care of him, that's all."

"I'll always do that."

"Aye, I suppose you will."

Bobby put his head down into his mother's lap and felt her hand upon his hair, stroking.

Daddy said, "Where is he?"

"I've got him."

"Is he all right?"

"He's fine."

The kitchen door opened; and closed again.

Bobby clung to Mammy's skirt until she bent down, brought him out and seated him upon her knee. She held him against her body with both arms and when he saw that she was not crying, he did not cry either.

"There, Bobby, there, there," his mammy said and rocked him so gently that he forgot to be afraid.

"Daddy gone?" he asked.

"Aye," Mammy told him. "But he'll be back."

"Soon?"

"Quite soon," she said, and sighed.

*   *   *

March was not the best month for salesmen, unless you were trotting summer modes; and Adair's warehouse wasn't into fashion since competition was cut-throat in that line of business and Breezy did not believe in sweated labour, not even in these boom times.

As well as carpeting, Gordon was hawking a good line in institutional china and cutlery at prices 'considerably descendent' on market value, and he couldn't understand why the buggers wouldn't buy. His commissions were down for the month and he would have been very concerned about it if he'd had his feet on the ground. He was still floating on pink clouds, however, after Saturday's meeting with Amanda, and he extended goodwill towards all men, even hoteliers and boarding-house keepers who slammed the door in his face.

"Thank you, sir. Perhaps another time," he would cry, as he skipped down the steps with his case thumping against his shins. "Adair's is always at your service."

It wasn't all rejection and rebuff, though, and he justified his morning's slog by shifting two fifty-six-piece dinner-sets and three hundred and twelve feet of corridor carpet to the owner of the new Park Garden Hotel. When the bill was paid and percentage calculated that would bring him a bob or two to jingle in his pocket or, of more immediate concern, to wager on the nose of Dolphus's little filly.

Being smitten by Cupid's dart had not blinded Gordon to the fact that he had been offered a golden opportunity, the sort of inside, horse's-mouth type information that any punter would give his eye-teeth to possess. Trouble was, he hadn't enough cash on hand to capitalise on the hot tip as it deserved. He couldn't pass it up, though, couldn't let Amanda down. He could have borrowed twenty from Breezy, no questions asked, of course, but he was leery of his stepfather's contacts and acumen, and didn't want to betray confidences, to risk letting the cat out of the bag. Yet he had to share his news with someone, his good fortune too, and it had to be someone he could trust.

When the hotels began to warm up for the lunch trade, Gordon left his sample case in the basement of the Park Garden, whistled up a hackney and had himself driven to No. 154 Canada Road.

Kirsty greeted him with a finger to her lips.

"Is Craig sleepin' off the night shift?" Gordon whispered.

Kirsty nodded, ushered him into the kitchen and closed both doors quietly.

Bobby was delighted to see his uncle, who just happened to have a tablet of almond toffee in his pocket. The wee boy was soon seated on Gordon's knee, sucking on the sweet and humming happily to himself while Kirsty made tea and a couple of ham sandwiches and exchanged general, restrained gossip with her brother-in-law.

Seeing Kirsty like this, in a patched skirt and apron, her auburn hair straggling a bit, Gordon felt somewhat guilty for he had come to talk about a girl to a woman he admired and had once desired. Kirsty would never be for him, however. She'd made that quite clear and, no matter how he strayed, Craig would never let her go in the end.

"Did you kiss her then?" Kirsty asked.

"Sure, I did."

"An' did you like it?"

"Loved it."

"An' you didn't run away, wee laddie?"

Gordon grinned. "Not me, not any more."

"My, but you're travellin' with a fast set now, Gordon. I'm surprised you can be bothered comin' back to the Greenfield at all."

"I thought you might be interested in makin' a few shillings, Kirsty," he said.

"How soon is this horse race?" Kirsty asked after he'd explained.

"First week of the flat-racing season," Gordon said. "First Thursday in April, I think."

"And is it – what do they call it – a sure thing?"

"Like I told you, it's *almost* a cert," Gordon said. "I can't go blabbin' about it to every Tom, Dick and Harry, 'cause that'll shorten the odds. But it's too good to keep to myself. If you're in the mood for a gamble, Kirst, a little adventure on the track, then this is the one for you, take my word on it."

"How will Russell Smith make sure the horse doesn't lose?"

"No idea," said Gordon. "I've heard a lot o' talk about horse dopin' but I don't know how it's done. At the very last minute, I should imagine. Somethin' in the water that stimulates the poor beast. If it's done too obviously and she comes canterin' in by fifteen lengths, then I suppose the stewards will hold an enquiry. But I suspect Russell Smith's far too clever to get caught."

"He's doped horses before, you say?"

"So I gather."

"It's not very honest, is it?"

"It's Dolphus Adair that wants it done," said Gordon. "You're right, though; it isn't quite straight, I suppose. I shouldn't have suggested it. Sorry."

"How much are you puttin' on?"

"Not as much as I should," said Gordon. "I'm a tiny bit strapped for the readies right now. I've been buyin' clothes an' stuff with my hard-earned."

"Well, I haven't," said Kirsty.

Gordon eased his nephew gently to the floor and frowned at his sister-in-law. "I . . . I wouldn't want you to risk your savin's, Kirsty. I mean, no bet in the wide world is absolutely safe."

"I can afford it," Kirsty said. "What's more, I could use the extra money."

"You could?"

"I told Craig that Nessie Frew only left me fifty pounds," Kirsty said, in a low voice. "In fact, it was two hundred. I've one hundred an' fifty pounds sittin' safe in a bank account in Glasgow."

"Jeeze!" said Gordon.

"But I could do with more."

"What?"

"Aren't you goin' to ask me why I need all this money?"

Embarrassed, Gordon shrugged. "I assume it's in case my brother ever . . . well, ever sort of walked on you, if you know what I mean."

"Or I decide to walk on him."

Gordon made a little popping noise with pursed lips.

"Eh . . . Is this departure on the cards, Kirsty?"

"No."

"Has this all to do with her, the woman in Benedict Street?" Gordon asked.

Kirsty did not answer him directly.

She said, "I've had an idea, Gordon, an' I need money to carry it out."

"An idea?" said Gordon, warily.

"I'm thinkin' of goin' into business."

"*What!*"

"Hush, you'll waken Craig."

"Sorry, sorry, but this is all rather startlin'," Gordon said. "What sort of business?"

"A shop, probably."

"Craig will never allow it."

"He doesn't care," said Kirsty.

"Who says?"

"He's told me as much."

"Wait a minute," said Gordon. "Is the wife of a burgh police officer allowed to go into trade?"

"It's frowned on but not illegal," said Kirsty. "In any case, I'd take on a partner. The business would be registered in the partner's name."

"I see you've been givin' this a lot of thought," said Gordon. "Who would the partner be?"

"You."

"Uh-huh," said Gordon. "I reckoned that was it."

"Now you arrive with a heaven-sent opportunity to win myself enough capital to do it properly."

"Kirsty, Kirsty! I think you're bitin' off more than you can chew," said Gordon. "I mean, you've a house to keep clean, a man to feed, a bairn to . . ."

"I want it all cut an' dried, set up so that Craig can't ruin it," Kirsty said. "Will you help me?"

"I smell revenge in all of this," said Gordon. "I don't think I should be involved."

"Who else am I goin' to turn to?"

"I can see the sense in comin' to me, right enough," Gordon admitted. "Breezy could help you find suitable premises, an' he'll give you a credit line. Hell, I could arrange that myself, come to it."

"See, you are taken with the idea."

"Nah, nah, Kirst. You don't catch me that way," said Gordon hastily.

Nonetheless he was impressed with her idea. Patched skirt and apron might suggest that Kirsty Nicholson was just an ordinary wifie but she was far from that. He knew what had gone wrong with her marriage, of Craig's infidelity, but now he thought of it he realised that he too had been furious at his brother long before that.

Shopkeeping might be just the ticket for Kirsty. He could imagine a shop packed with gleaming household objects, the ornaments and trinkets to which even the poorest of women were attracted like magpies. Adair's warehouse was a repository of such odds-and-ends of domestic ware, stuff that could only be shifted through a small retailer.

"You *do* like the idea," Kirsty said.

"Aye, it has a certain attraction, I'll admit," said Gordon. "But I only came here today to see if you fancied makin' a few quid on the side, not to plunge into somethin' as complicated as this."

"You thrive on complications, Gordon."

"I suppose I do," said Gordon, flattered.

"Wouldn't you like to be a partner in a retail enterprise?" said Kirsty. "Think of all the wealthy men that have started out that way."

"All right, missus, you've convinced me," he said. "Now how much do you want to wager on this bloody horse?"

"What would ten pounds win for me?"

Gordon said, "She'll go at twenty-to-one, probably. Perhaps a little less."

"Ten pounds would win me two hundred?"

"Yep."

"Thirty pounds, then. I'll give you thirty pounds to put on for me."

"Thirty quid! Jeeze, that's a lot of money, Kirsty. I thought you might want a flutter for five bob or so. But thirty quid is serious stuff."

"What are you bettin'?"

"Ten," Gordon said.

"I could lend you another ten or twenty, you know."

"Whoa, whoa, whoa," said Gordon. "Don't get carried away. Somethin' could go wrong down there in Newcastle. It's a gamble, not a charity hand-out. Get it into your head, Kirsty, that we could lose the lot."

"Nothing ventured, nothing gained."

"Are you that keen on havin' money?"

"Yes," Kirsty said.

"It's the root of all evil, y'know."

"No, it's not," said Kirsty gravely.

"What is then?"

"I hope, Gordon, you never have occasion to find out," she said. "Do we have an agreement?"

"On a partnership?" said Gordon. "Well, I suppose so. If the horse wins, that is."

"Tell me the horse's name," Kirsty said.

"Camberwell Beauty."

"Good luck to her, then," said Kirsty, raising her teacup.

"Good luck to us, an' all," said Gordon.

On the following Tuesday at noon he met his sister-in-law by arrangement in the hall of the Bank of Scotland in Glasgow's St Vincent Street and discreetly received from her six five-pound notes, to which Gordon added three of his own; a sum of money that found its way, over the next week or so, into the satchels of a dozen unsuspecting bookmakers throughout Glasgow and, in due course, on to the nose of a sweet little filly named Camberwell Beauty to carry with her to Newcastle.

*   *   *

Imagination was never a strong point in young men who joined the Greenfield Burgh constabulary. Their desires were limited by lack of worldly experience, their ambitions by a surfeit of common sense. Now and then they might surrender to fantasy and imagine themselves leading Glasgow Rangers on to the field at Ibrox Park while the crowd roared their name in adulation. But this dream was collective, part of a mass disorder shared by small boys, kirk elders, clerks, councillors, deputy chief constables and every Clydeside riveter who ever was. More than money, more than sex, more than scaling the ladder of civic responsibility, lads old and young mooned about Association Football and the glory denied them by cruel gods and circumstance.

Constable Ronald Norbert was an exception to the rule. He was far too sensible to hanker after a bubble reputation and had discovered by the age of twelve that his toes did not twinkle and that his head and a leather bladder were definitely incompatible.

Ronnie Norbert's heroes did not wear daft knee-length shorts and reek of liniment and dubbin. They wore vicuna overcoats with silk collars, flowered dressing-gowns, quilted smoking-jackets, top hats, spats and monocles; carried swordsticks, tweezers, false beards and revolvers, and possessed an intimate knowledge of microscopes, bloodstains, toxicology and Bradshaw's Railway Guide.

Back among the seed bins of his father's store in Annan, young Ronnie had risked his eyesight by devouring the bleary print in every yellowback and lurid magazine he could lay hands on. He pored over accounts of Bow Street runners and big-city detectives like Inspector Caminada, consumed articles on Quackery, Long Firm Frauds and How Thieves are Made, as well as bloody murder. By the time he was sixteen he could not separate fiction from fact and didn't particularly want to. All Ronnie wanted to be was a master criminal or, failing that, a copper.

Becoming a recruit in Greenfield Burgh Police Force was a sad let down for Ronnie. He was too arrogant, too impatient for his own good. Besides, there wasn't an anarchist or incendiary or daring jewel-thief recorded in the sergeants' logs and bloody Craig Nicholson had already scooped the pool by nailing hard-man Danny Malone, not once but twice. Every time he chased a stray pooch, lifted a householder for letting a lum catch on fire or for dotting a nagging wife in the eye, Ronnie felt cheated. He was young, however, lived in hope of better days to come, and sharpened his skills by observing the burgh's low life and consorting, cautiously, with Glasgow's less salubrious citizens.

It wasn't the promise of fifty bob that switched Ronnie on to 'investigating' Greta Taylor. He both admired and detested Craig Nicholson who had so often made him squirm when he was a green probationer. Now he had a chance to show off and, in the same stroke, get a little of his own back.

Ronnie had no right to undertake detective work on Craig's own account or to use the uniform to gain entry into the domiciles of law-abiding folk. But the sharpers, narks and shifty sydneys that he bullied couldn't squeal loud enough to be heard back in Ottawa Street let alone by Chief Constable Organ. So Ronnie, at his own pace, pressed on unperturbed by scruple or conscience or by the fact that Craig Nicholson seemed to have lost interest in what he was doing on his, Craig's, behalf.

It was several weeks before the investigation started to show results. Even then Ronnie could hardly claim credit – though he did – for what was after all just a stroke of luck. He'd considered tackling Greta Taylor's best pal and neighbour, Isa Thomas, browbeating her into giving him a lead. But Craig had warned him against alerting Greta as to what was going on and Ronnie was wary of stretching female loyalty too far. Besides, Isa Thomas's husband was a docker and dockers, as a breed, were notoriously touchy.

Instead Ronnie struck up a drinking friendship with another occupant of Greta's close, a small, fierce widower who had been abandoned, and no wonder, by his children about ten minutes after his wife had died and had added bitterness to native intolerance and a lethal addiction to banana rum.

The widower's name was Clement Moscrop, known to all and sundry as Hog. For some years prior to his deterioration he had worked in the Benson Street pig butchery and the name had come from there. Now, however, he was nothing but a casual dock labourer, picking up a shift when he ran out of money for booze or rent. He was, Ronnie reckoned, about fifty, though it was hard to tell under the grime. At one time he had been a pal of Isa Thomas's husband but Moscrop had strained friendship too far, apparently, by trying to drag Isa into bed one November evening, in front of all the children at that, and had been deterred only by a frying-pan angrily administered to the side of his head.

Hog Moscrop drank now in the lowest public house in Greenfield, a den down in the sump of the burgh, not far from the Madagascar. He knew that Ronnie was a copper in mufti but he didn't give a damn so long as the young man was paying for the snorts of banana rum that provided Hog with his main source of nourishment.

Hog would weep in praise of his deceased wife, Aileen, call curses on the heads of his three sons and three daughters who'd gone off and left him alone and unloved. He would mutter lascivious threats against Isa and several other wives in the close and breathe promises as to what he would do to Greta Taylor one of these fine days now that she had shaken loose from her protectors.

"What protectors, Hog?" Ronnie would say.

"Bloody copper, him."

"Sure, I know about the copper."

"Aye, aye, ye would. Lad like you could tak' his place an' gi'e me ma share."

"Before the copper, though," Ronnie would say. "Did she have another protector?"

Hog would drain his glass, wipe his ragged moustache with his fingers and nod. Ronnie would shell out for another tot and repeat his question. And Hog Moscrop, who knew a golden goose when he saw one, would mumble names that meant nothing, five, six, seven names, all different, all changing night by night.

It took Ronnie a week to establish that these were butchers dead, gone or lost in the mists of the city and that none of them had ever known Greta at all.

At length even Ronnie's patience wore thin.

"Listen, Hog," he would say, "I've had just about enough of this. Do you or do you not know anythin' about Greta Taylor before she had the bairn?"

"I thought ye liked me?"

"I do, Hog. I do, believe me. But I've got good reason for askin'," Ronnie would say. "It's somethin' I need to know, see. I've scratched your back long enough. It's time you gave me somethin' in return."

Nothing but blethers would come from Hog Moscrop, however, more meaningless names, tangled with deviant longings and whimpering regrets. All Ronnie really learned from the little drunkard was that Greta Taylor had first appeared in Benedict Street with the babe-in-arms some three and a half years ago and that she had known Isa Thomas before they became neighbours.

It was now, just as he reached the end of his tether, that Ronnie had his stroke of luck.

He asked, not for the first time, "Did she come alone?" and Moscrop put him off yet again, answering, "Aye, aye, all on her own, wi' the bairn, just the bairn."

And a voice said, "Naw, she never. She cam' wi' Lizzie Straun."

Ronnie turned from the bar, found himself staring into the eyes of another shabby man, older than Hog by several years and, unlike Hog, neither fierce nor fretful.

"Who're you?"

"Ne'er mind who I am, son. Ye've been askin' him about the Taylor woman long enough."

"Shut yer fat gob, McLintock," Moscrop said.

"He never saw them. I saw them, but. She cam' wi' Lizzie Straun."

Ronnie thrust out an arm to prevent Hog Moscrop attacking the volunteer, though the volunteer was twice Hog's size and quite sober enough to take care of himself.

"Why are you tellin' me this?"

"Bitches, all o' them," said the stranger.

"Who are you?"

91

"His bloody name's bloody McLintock," Hog said. "He disnae even live in our close."

"Maybe not," McLintock admitted. "But I saw them that first night. An' it was Lizzie Straun."

"You're just wantin' your own back on Lizzie," Hog shouted.

"Is that true?" said Ronnie.

"Aye, it's true. But it's none o' your business, that side o' it," McLintock said. "It's him you've been plyin' wi' free drink, no' me. Anyhow, they're a' bitches in that trade."

Still restraining Moscrop, Ronnie said, "Where does she live, this Lizzie?"

"Last I heard she was livin' in Partick, in the Ferry Road, last I heard."

"An' she knew Greta – before?"

"She brought her here," McLintock said. "That's all I can tell ye, all I will tell ye."

"It's lies. It's blethers," Moscrop protested.

"Have a drink, Mr McLintock," Ronnie said. "Rum?"

"That muck! Gi'e me a whisky."

"It's rum for me, sonny," Hog Moscrop said.

"Like hell it is," said Ronnie.

*   *   *

It took more than a fast two-year-old from the stables of Russell Smith to surprise the racing fraternity, particularly as she'd been carrying no great weight and had been ridden by Perry McCrae who was known, even as far south as Newcastle, to have the smartest hands in the game.

Camberwell Beauty came first past the post all right but followed so close by the favourite, Tinker's Pride, that nobody could possibly guess that Perry had been holding her back from five furlongs out lest she take wing and fly to the line. Half a length was enough to satisfy Perry, Russell, the stewards and punters, and to run the Beauty's price up to four hundred and thirty guineas in the selling-ring before the sweat had dried on her muzzle and the fourteen ounces of best French brandy that Russell had fed her before the race had quite passed out of her system.

Telephone and telegraph wire had extended the empire of the tout and gambler as well as the bookmaker and had made the racing game less a colourful adventure than an exercise in greed. Sinclair Smith was glad of the marvels of modern science that day, however, and received the glad tidings a mere ten minutes after the filly came home. He mopped his honest face with a handkerchief, not just in relief that he had won several hundred pounds in laid off bets but because his brother had not been nabbed, exposed as a cheat and ruined.

Gordon got the news almost instantly, thanks to a wire run into a smelly apartment above a fishmonger's shop in Finnieston, courtesy of 'Charley Haddock' one of the Smiths' agents. There and then he collected a percentage of his total winnings from a grumbling Charley, ran downstairs and on to Dumbarton Road and found a hack to carry him to Canada Road.

He took the stairs two at a time and when Kirsty opened the door to his frantic knocking, said, "Day-shift?"

"Yes," said Kirsty.

"She won," said Gordon. "Camberwell Beauty won."

They danced a jig on the landing, arm in arm, and skipped away into the kitchen like lambs in spring.

"Have you got the money?"

"God, no, Kirst. Only a small part of it."

"Why haven't you got the money? The bookies, they haven't absconded, have they?"

"I doubt it," said Gordon. "I'll collect as soon as the papers print the final result."

"Tonight," said Kirsty. "Can't you get it tonight?"

"Easy, easy," said Gordon. "It's only money, missus. Nothin' to get het up about."

"How much?"

"For me," said Gordon, "three hundred and fifteen pounds."

"An' me?"

"Six hundred an' thirty."

"Oh, my God!" She sat down hard on a wooden chair, a hand to her mouth. "We . . . we did it!"

"We certainly did," said Gordon. "How much is that you have, all in?"

"Seven hundred an' fifty pounds."

"Congratulations. You are now officially rich."

"Did they manage to sell the horse?" Kirsty asked.

"Oh, they're bound to," said Gordon. "And she'll fetch a tidy sum now, believe me."

"That should please them."

"To hell with them." Gordon grinned, reached out and took

her hand. She did not resist. "Now, if only you hadn't married that brother o' mine, I'd propose to you right here an' now. I've always had a soft spot for wealthy women."

"Don't talk rot," said Kirsty. "In any case, I could never marry a gambler. I've seen what it can do to a man."

"Never fear, Kirst. I've had my fling with horses; that's it."

He had seated himself on a chair beside her and still held her hands in his. He looked so immature in the wing-collar coat with its fashionable window-pane checks and horn buttons.

"I . . . I don't suppose you'd . . . you'd like to give me a kiss, would you?" he said.

"I'll leave that to Amanda."

"Right now, I'd rather have you."

Kirsty detached herself at once and got to her feet. She wasn't offended at his temerity, however. It was only the mood of a moment, result of the rapport that winning so much money had established between them.

"Take off your coat," she said.

"What?"

"We've work to do."

"God, just for a minute . . ."

"Don't be daft, Gordon," she told him. "Bobby's sleepin' in the front room, so we won't be disturbed for half an hour or so."

With an exaggerated sigh Gordon said, "Spurned again," then removed his overcoat and draped it on the back of the chair. "What sort of work?"

"Our partnership, remember?" Kirsty said.

"As if I could ever forget," said Gordon.

*   *   *

The April day was soft, with puffballs of cloud against a blue sky and a warmish breeze from the east. On days like this it was easy for Craig to forget that he was miserable. The shift had passed at a canter. He had made his calls cheerfully. He had eaten his half-past-eleven meal in the back shop of the café and chatted to Peter Stewart for ten minutes before setting off towards St John's Road, the long loop of his beat that straddled the railway and the riverside.

It was peaceful down there. If he was early he would find the shipwrights lolling on the rank grass of the embankment, puffing pipes and reading newspapers and watching the energetic young apprentices kick a ball about in the cul-de-sac. The workers were gone before he got there that day, however. Only the seagulls remained, perched without fear on the sleeper fence.

Ronnie was waiting by the tunnel that led under the lines and back up to the Kingdom Road. He was not on duty, not in uniform.

Craig was not best pleased to see Constable Norbert. He had been trying to put Greta out of mind of late and the blue April day was not in tune with the wintry mood of resentment and malice that had spurred him to enlist Ronnie's aid in the first place.

Ronnie, however, had on his smug, fatuous expression and, in spite of himself, Craig felt a tweak of curiosity.

"What's in the wind, Ronnie?" said Craig.

"Somethin' interestin', I think."

They moved under the railway arch.

The tunnel dipped to a lake of sticky brown mud set with four or five large stepping-stones. Sometimes Craig would hide here to nip from the metal flask of whisky that he carried. Unless the duty sergeant came up the Clyde in a rowing-boat you could not be seen from any vantage point.

"I bet," said Ronnie, "you thought I'd forgotten all about it?"

"It never crossed my mind," said Craig.

"Detective work takes time."

"Detective work! Christ, Ronnie, I only asked you to keep an ear to the ground. Anyway, what's up? You look like the cat that ate the canary."

"Ever heard of Lizzie Straun?"

"Nope."

"Ever heard the name McNish?"

"Can't say I have. Who are they?"

"Lizzie Straun an' Sylvie McNish used to run an adoption agency."

"What the hell's that?"

"Tut-tut," said Ronnie. "An' you call yourself a copper."

"Get on with it."

"Babies," said Ronnie. "For sale."

"Naw," Craig heard himself say. "Naw, naw."

"'Fraid so, chum," Ronnie said. "Sylvie was the boss. Lizzie did most o' the dirty work."

"What does this have to do with Greta?"

"Don't know yet," said Ronnie. "But, by God, you can begin t' draw your own conclusions, can't you?"

"I'm not drawin' any conclusions until you give me proof of a connection, Ronnie."

"You want a lot for fifty bob, don't you?" Ronnie Norbert said.

"Have you spoken wi' these women, Straun and McNish?"

"Haven't tracked them down yet."

"Glasgow?"

"God knows," said Ronnie. "Lizzie Straun's supposed to be livin' in Ferry Road, Partick, but I'm damned if I can locate her there."

"How can you be sure they were baby farmers?"

"From a bloke I asked in a shop in Partick."

"What bloke?"

"Do you want me to push on wi' all this?" said Ronnie, evasively. "I can tell you this, Lizzie Straun turned up with Greta Taylor an' the newborn infant in Benedict Street three an' a half years ago. She'll know where Greta came from."

"An' will she know who fathered the child?"

"If she doesn't, Sylvie McNish is bound to."

"Tell you what, Ronnie," Craig said, "you find one or both of these women for me, an' you'll be in for another fifty bob."

"That's generous," said Ronnie, "considerin' what it's cost me in drink already. What d'you mean, find them?"

"Just that," Craig said. "You find them; I'll do the rest."

"Huh, you want me to stop?"

"Not yet, Ronnie," Craig said. "Not just yet."

*   *   *

It had been a strange week's end, marked by the feeling that spring was properly in the air at last. For Kirsty, however, there was also a sense of being suspended in an emotional limbo. She had not told Craig about her good fortune or how she intended to invest her capital; yet the acquisition of so much money cast a glow over her days.

There was more to it, though. Craig's behaviour increased her uncertainty, made her wonder if he'd somehow found out that she had become rich. She could not accept that, for once, he was just being pleasant.

On Saturday Craig accompanied his family to the Forrester

park. He played with Bobby on the grass and was generally affable, if not garrulous. Bobby was, naturally, delighted to have his father's attention and scampered about in pursuit of the soft rubber ball that Craig had bought for him at the wee corner shop with such fervour that he fell asleep in Craig's arms and had to be carried home.

Craig showed no sign of wishing to go out again that evening. After supper he lounged by the fire, feet on the fender, a newspaper in his lap and a haze of cigarette smoke about his head.

Kirsty sensed that he wanted her. He did not leave the kitchen when she washed and made ready for bed. He watched her take off her skirt and blouse and she was prepared for the moment when he would come to her, bring her to him, kiss and fondle her and had already decided that she would not rebuff him, would let him take her to bed. She had not been prepared for his courtesy, though, the change in the manner of his wooing. It caught her off guard, made her more willing, more ready than she would otherwise have been.

Afterwards Craig lay with her in the hole-in-the-wall bed, smoking. She waited for his questions, expecting strife, convinced still that he had discovered her secret and that love-making was his method of persuading her to confess. To her surprise, Craig fell asleep. He drifted off as if it were the most natural thing in the world for them to share a bed.

After a while she removed the cigarette from between his fingers and slipped from the recess and put the stub into the grate. Clad only in her rumpled nightgown, and sated, she sat by the fire and enjoyed the novel experience of feeling wicked. Craig's tenderness had not touched her, had not altered her determination, yet she had enjoyed their intimacy and, for once, had felt his equal. She had no guilt about it, or about what she intended to do with the six hundred and thirty pounds of hard cash that was hidden beneath the boards of the pot cupboard; nine years' livings, sealed into a crisp manila envelope.

In due course Kirsty got back into bed. She arranged the covers over her husband and herself and lay by him, not touching, until she fell asleep.

*   *   *

"A horse, Mrs Nicholson!" Mr Marlowe exclaimed. "You backed a winning horse!"

It was Monday morning and she had taken Bobby into town on the tramcar. First she had deposited the cash into her account with the Bank of Scotland in St Vincent Street and then she had gone to the chambers of the legal firm of Marlowe & Kearney to make an appointment with the elderly Mr Marlowe who, gratifyingly, had been able to see her there and then.

Mr Marlowe had greeted her with a handshake and had ruffled Bobby's hair with the sort of nervous cauttion with which he would have patted a smaall, fierce terrier. Bobby had not growled, however, but had accepted the gesture with stoicism and had stationed himself by his mother's side, a hand on her arm as if to add his support to her decisions.

"It's a long story how it came about, Mr Marlowe," Kirsty said.

"No doubt. What, if I may ask, was the name of the winning animal?"

"Camberwell Beauty."

"Ah-huh," said Mr Marlowe and made a seemingly casual note of the information on a memo pad on his desk. "May I ask how much you won?"

"Six hundred pounds."

"Good God! Pardon me, I didn't mean to . . ."

"It's in my bank account now," Kirsty said.

Mr Marlowe nodded. "I assume that you have it in mind to invest a portion of the money and that is why you've come to seek my advice?"

"Yes," Kirsty said. "I want to open a shop."

"A shop, indeed. And the nature of the trade?"

"Domestic wares and fancy goods."

"Do you have experience of shopkeeping, Mrs Nicholson?"

"None at all."

"Was your husband, perhaps, a shop assistant before he joined the constabulary?"

"My husband has no interest in this venture, Mr Marlowe. In fact, I'll require the trading licences to be put in a partner's name, not my own."

"Articles of partnership, yes," Mr Marlowe said, writing again. "And who will your partner be, if I may ask?"

"My brother-in-law, Gordon Nicholson."

"A meeting will have to be arranged with Gordon Nicholson, of course."

"Whenever it's convenient," Kirsty agreed.

"Premises found."

"Yes."

"Stock acquired, staff hired."

"Yes."

"It's not your intention to sell excisable goods, is it?" Mr Marlowe said. "Tobacco, spirits, gunpowder?"

Kirsty laughed. "Certainly not."

"Just items of decorative hardware, soft goods, that sort of thing?"

"Yes."

"You will need a supplier, one who'll render you a certain amount of credit," Mr Marlowe said.

"Adair's warehouse."

"Ah, yes. You've a family connection with the Adairs. I'd forgotten that."

"Gordon Nicholson is stepson to Albert Adair, and in the trade."

"Have you discussed your scheme with Albert Adair?"

"Not yet."

"But you will?"

"In due course, perhaps," said Kirsty.

"Now, Mrs Nicholson." The lawyer put down his pencil and folded his hands together on the desk, fixed her with his most professional stare. "Let me ask you; is it profit that you're after?"

"Aye, of course it is."

"In which case, if I might be so bold, would it not be more expedient to put your money into stocks and shares?"

"I prefer to earn my profits, Mr Marlowe."

"Shopkeeping demands a great deal of time and energy."

"I *have* a great deal of time and energy, Mr Marlowe."

"I see, yes."

"For the moment, Mr Marlowe, I don't wish my husband to know anythin' of this plan of mine."

"It won't be possible to keep it secret for long, Mrs Nicholson."

"I'll tell him in my own good time."

"Yes, quite."

"Will you accept me as a client, Mr Marlowe?"

"With pleasure, Mrs Nicholson."

"May I leave the drawin' up of the contract of partnership to you then?" Kirsty said.

"Absolutely," said Mr Marlowe. "Do you wish me to look out for suitable premises too?"

"No, I'll manage that myself."

"Do you have any inkling of what a rental will cost you per annum to rent a decent shop?"

"According to my brother-in-law, I should be able to find a suitable place at about thirty-five pounds a year. Since I'm not after buyin' an existin' business, I'll have nothin' to put out on goodwill, fittin's an' the like."

"That's true," said Mr Marlowe. "On the other hand, you'll have no indication of trade and potential turnover. And you will have to purchase all your fittings from scratch. Do you have a location in mind?"

"Greenfield."

"Are you sure that's the best place?"

"It's where my customers will come from."

"Hardly a centre for the carriage trade, however."

"It's not far from Dowanhill."

"Local custom is the mainstay of any business, Mrs Nicholson."

"There's more money about in the Greenfield than you might imagine, Mr Marlowe," Kirsty said. "Most of the men are in work an' wages are on the rise; at least, so I've been told."

"Do you not fear competition from the new department stores?"

"There are none in our burgh."

"I hope you don't object to my questions," Mr Marlowe said. "Not at all."

"Now," the lawyer said, "what about staff?"

"I have somebody in mind."

"Somebody experienced?"

"Yes, they've done a lot of sellin'."

"And reliable?" Mr Marlowe asked.

"Highly reliable."

"May I ask this person's name?"

"Taylor," Kirsty said. "Her name is Greta Taylor."

Six

White Elephant

It was still the custom for young women of marriageable age to be governed by strict principles of propriety. Many a soulful little debutante gazed with longing from a brougham window at the free-and-easy midinettes and factory girls who paraded of an evening on the Kelvin Way or, having snared their beau, clung possessively to the gamecock's arm as they were led round the bandstand and up the garden path.

In spring Nature seemed so profligate in flinging the sexes together, in providing a lad for every lass, that it was hard cheese on maidens with a price on their heads.

They could not shake off the shackles of their breeding, neglect their worth, run wild in search of a man. They were held in thrall by a generation to whom courtship was a game as strategic as a colonial war, by mothers, grandmothers and conventicles of aunts who had forgotten what it was like to have blood in your veins.

The daughters of The Knowe, however, were prisoners not of convention but of Oedipus. Nursemaids and nannies might have brought them up decent but mother was never far away and Dolphus's little pitchers had learned a lot by flapping their ears in all the wrong places. They had long since acquired the basic facts of life. They knew perfectly well what it meant when voices were raised in the master bedroom, and shouts turned to screams. Quite naturally there was a bit of apprehension among the cadets but Amanda's precocity turned anxiety into gossip and brought about a clandestine agreement that, come what may, they would always be on mother's side.

Dolphus was too stupid to appreciate the dangers of a nursery revolution, to realise that his daughters knew exactly what was going on and thought it all incredibly romantic, not tawdry or tragic at all.

Olive, on the other hand, was well aware that she had her

daughters' uncritical support. She encouraged it by giving them more time and attention than Nanny considered healthy, by trotting them off on picnics and excursions into town, and by filling their heads with stories of her flirtations and adventures in society.

It wasn't right. It wasn't Christian. It certainly did the children more harm than good in the long run. When you studied the portrait of Grandfather Carruth, however, beetle-browed, black-bearded and about as lovable as Artaxerxes, and compared it with the shining vivacity of Grandmother Morrison, a famed Edinburgh beauty painted, and seduced, by Kelso Hollander, then the wilful sexuality that marked the female line became explicable if not excusable.

Even so, if it hadn't been for the pernicious influence of her male cousins, Amanda might have grown straight in spite of all and been redeemed by that cheerful, honest upstart Gordon Nicholson.

Why Amanda had fallen for Gordon was one of life's little mysteries. She had been attracted to him from the moment she saw him in Uncle Albert's house. True, she had found the other brother, Craig, more magnetic at first but as soon as he'd opened his mouth and betrayed his rude disposition she'd rapidly got over that brief infatuation.

Gordon was quite different from his tall and handsome brother. Gordon was courteous, candid and jolly; and he had none of the cynicism of the other young men who had thrown their hats into the ring and indicated that they would not be averse to a courtship, an engagement and a marriage as soon as she came of age.

"Oh, Mother, what shall I do?"

"Encourage him."

"But how?"

"Discreetly, dearest. Discreetly."

There lay the difference between mother and daughter; the factor of experience. Olive had forgotten what it was like to be without it, and Amanda did not know that she lacked it.

She did not see Gordon often enough and he did not seem willing or able to make the running. Foolishly, she enlisted the aid of her cousins, Eric and John.

"She's mad about the little beggar," Johnnie said to Eric.

"Beyond me what she sees in him," Eric responded.

"Oh, you know what females are like at that age," Johnnie said. "Perpetually on heat."

"Some of 'em never grow out of it."

"Fortunately for us, what!"

"She wants us to help make the match, I gather," Eric said.

"And so we shall, so we shall," said Johnnie. "Bring them together and let nature take its course."

"I thought you wanted Mandy for yourself."

"Indeed, I do."

Eric grinned. "It's the money you're after, you old devil, ain't it?"

"Among other things," said Johnnie.

"How will we do it? Bring them together, I mean."

"Throw a little party," Johnnie said.

"Just the four of us?"

"Far too intense," said Johnnie. "What do you say to a theatre evenin', just like the old days, hm?"

"I'd say that would fill the bill admirably."

"Shall we fire ahead then?" said Johnnie.

"Without delay," said Eric.

* * *

"I've been invited to a theatre party," Gordon said.

"That'll be nice," said Kirsty. "When?"

"Saturday."

"At the Gem?"

"Good God, no. This lot wouldn't be seen dead in the Gem."

"Lah-de-dah to you then, Mr Nicholson," Kirsty said. "Who sent the invitation?"

"Johnnie Whiteside. It's a family affair, for the younger generation, apparently. I can't say I fancy it much."

"Won't Amanda be there?"

"Expect so."

"You'll have a hard time keepin' your eyes on the stage."

"Knowin' my luck, Amanda'll be in one box an' I'll be in another," Gordon said.

"Boxes, indeed! Who's payin' for this soirée?"

"Johnnie, I suppose. It was his idea."

"Is it his birthday, or what?"

"God knows!" Gordon shrugged.

In fact he knew more about the 'evening' than he pretended

103

to. There would be a dozen in the party, second generation Adairs, Beadles and Whitesides too. He would be the only one there who was not blood kin. He was nervous about meeting those other cousins, of seeming inferior to them, of being patronised.

He hoped that he might receive some sympathy and encouragement from Kirsty but he saw now that she was too caught up in her own affairs, too eager to see the shop that he had found for her, through Breezy's good offices. He couldn't blame her, really, and tried to keep in step with his sister-in-law as she hurried along Dumbarton Road at a great lick.

Breezy had certainly moved with alacrity. The man they were to meet, Mr Farley, was one of Breezy's factors, and the shop had been found and the appointment made within twenty-four hours of Gordon's mentioning the matter to his stepfather.

"Goin' into business, is she?" Breezy had said. "Good for her. I like a bit of initiative in a woman. What's she after? A shop, is it? No problem there, son."

"Craig doesn't know about it yet."

"I suppose she'll want to make a start before she tells him," Breezy had said.

"She's asked me to be her partner," Gordon had said. "What do you think of that idea?"

"Splendid."

"You're takin' this very casually, if you don't mind me sayin' so," Gordon had said.

"It's nothin' to get worked up about," Breezy had told him. "Kirsty isn't the first woman to look for a measure of independence; and she won't be the last. Is it the money she inherited from the Frew woman that she intends to use as capital?"

"Yes." Gordon had tactfully made no mention of the bet he'd made on Camberwell Beauty, of Kirsty's big win. "Look, are you sure you don't mind me havin' a wee sideline of my own? Bein' a partner in a retail shop?"

"It'll be beneficial. Broaden your outlook," Breezy had said. "For a start it'll teach you how much retail differs from the wholesale trade."

"When it comes to stockin' the shop . . ."

"One step at a time, Gordon, hm?"

"You're right, Breezy. You're right."

"I usually am," Breezy had said.

The following forenoon a letter had been delivered to the warehouse informing Gordon that an appointment had been made to view a shop property in Dumbarton Road the next day. Because of the speed with which Breezy had acted it crossed Gordon's mind that perhaps the property had been lying vacant and that old Breezy was personally going to find it beneficial to have a stepson in Retail.

"Is that it," Kirsty said, "on the corner?"

"Could be," Gordon said.

Unsettled by the situation and by changes he had detected in Kirsty, he was not in the best of moods. However sympathetic, however 'modern' he might believe himself to be, there was something unnerving about a woman with money and the determination to use it strictly for her own ends.

Perhaps he should have told Craig what was in the wind, would have if there had been harmony in the family. As it was, he was already too deeply involved to risk his brother's wrath.

The shop's entrance was not on Dumbarton Road, but three steps around the corner in Gascoigne Street, a narrow passage that ran diagonally into Kingdom Road and carried a fair bit of horse traffic to a blacksmith's yard tucked behind the tenements.

The window, set hard against the corner and facing into Dumbarton Road, was protected by padlocked shutters. Paint and varnish surrounds were cracked and peeling and the door came off a worn pavement hardly wide enough to accommodate one person let alone a crowd of shoppers.

The gas-lamp above the entrance hung drunkenly from a rusted bracket and cast a shadow over the lettering above the door, lettering so ancient and faded that Gordon could barely read it.

Hands on hips, he craned his neck and squinted.

"Oh, my God!" he exclaimed.

"What is it?" Kirsty asked. "What does it say?"

"It says *Wines*."

"So?"

"It says *Vokes*," Gordon told her. "By God, I'll have Breezy's ears for this."

"For what?" said Kirsty. "The place isn't that bad."

Gordon turned. "Haven't you heard of Vokes?"

"No, I can't say I have."

"Harold Vokes?"

Kirsty shook her head.

"The murderer," Gordon said, "the poisoner, Harold Vosper Vokes?"

"Oh, no!"

"Oh, yes," said Gordon. "It seems my miserable, money-grubbin' stepfather has tried to sell us a pup, a bloody white elephant. Did he reckon that because we're country folk we'd never have heard of 'Orrible 'Arold?"

"But what did he do? Who did he murder?"

"Women, young women. Six or seven of them," Gordon said. "He poisoned them – in there."

"But why?"

"Don't ask," said Gordon just as young Mr Farley, the factor's agent, came jauntily round the corner with the keys in one hand and the lease agreement in the other.

"*You!*" Gordon shouted.

The toothy professional smile faded into Mr Farley's face and he stopped dead in his tracks.

"*You connivin' bastard!*"

"What? I ain't done nothin'."

Young Mr Farley wore a little round trilby on his curly head and a cheap half-length coat with a catsfur collar, a garment of which he was inordinately proud. Its loose front provided Gordon with a two-fisted grip as he hoisted the factor's agent on to the tips of his neat button boots and hissed, "Harold Vosper Vokes."

"Wh . . . wh . . . who?"

Gordon yanked the factor's agent close against his chest and glared up his nose.

"Don't patter me, sonny. You know bloody well who Vokes was. What's more there'll be another murder done on these premises if you don't start talkin' straight."

"I . . . I thought you knew."

"Codswallop!"

"It was years ago; nine, ten years," Mr Farley got out. "Jeeze, nobody remembers Vokes now."

"No? Then how come the damned place is still lyin' empty?" Gordon snapped.

"It's a mystery to me." Mr Farley struggled a little.

"Just how long has it been vacant?" Kirsty asked.

"All right," Mr Farley conceded. "I admit that it's not had a tenant since the polis took the bod . . ."

"Breezy put you up to it, didn't he?" Gordon demanded. "He

saw his chance to be rid of a white elephant. Come on, out with it. Breezy Adair owns this property, doesn't he?"

"No," said young Mr Farley. "No, he doesn't."

"Who does then?"

"You do," said the factor's boy. "So there!"

*   *   *

The outer door had been lined with a sheet of iron, though whether this had been done to keep hooligans out or the shade of Harold Vokes in was a moot point.

Kirsty had no qualms about entering the shop. She had never heard of Vokes or his murky deeds. She had not breathed the air of menace and revelation that had given many a Greenfield girl nightmares a decade ago. In fact public imagination since had added so many gruesome details to the original crimes that even 'Orrible 'Arold, if he hadn't been topped, would have been shocked by them.

Gordon had snatched the withered parchment from the agent's hands and scanned it, scowling. The deed of ownership was as ornate as the Burgh Charter and almost as ancient.

"Hell's bells, it's true. Breezy *has* signed over the property to me," Gordon said. "What in God's name am I expected to do with it? Open a peepshow?"

"Do what you like with it." Mr Farley smoothed the ruffled catsfur collar and adjusted his buttons. "It ain't my concern no more."

"Hell's bloody bells!"

"I can't see what you've got to gripe about," Mr Farley said. "I wish some rich relative would present me with a wedge of prime property."

"At least let's look inside," Kirsty said.

"You can't go in *there*," said Gordon.

"Why not?"

"You just can't, Kirsty, that's all."

"Not scared, are you?" young Mr Farley smirked.

" 'Course not," said Gordon. "I just don't think it's proper for a young lady to be subjected to . . . to that sort of experience."

"Nothin' scary inside," said Mr Farley. "I been in an' out more times than you've had hot dinners. There's nothin' left to see."

"Where . . . where exactly did it happen?" Gordon asked.

"They was done in down in the cellar," Mr Farley answered.

"The cellar? There's a cellar?"

"No need to shout," said Mr Farley. "The cellar's been filled in an' blocked up. Cost a pretty penny too, I'm told."

"Why don't we go in, Gordon?" Kirsty said.

"See," said Mr Farley, twirling the keys. "The lady ain't scared."

"All right, all right," said Gordon.

The inner door, antique oak with fine bottle-glass panels, creaked on its hinges as the factor's agent pushed it open.

"After you, Mr Nicholson."

"After you, Mr Farley."

Kirsty stepped into the gloom.

The shop was narrow and ran to an angle beyond which was a pitch-black alcove.

"No gas, of course," said Mr Farley. "Mr Adair had it sealed for safety's sake. Beams are solid and sound. I've seen to it that the vermin are kept down an' that there's no trace of rot, wet or dry."

"We can do without the agent's spiel, thanks," said Gordon.

Mr Farley lit a carbide lamp and led Kirsty and the reluctant owner up the length of the shop. To the left was a long deal-topped counter and on the right shelves towered from floor to ceiling. The floor was gritty with city dust but there was no litter and no droppings from rats or mice, Kirsty noticed.

She did not find the faint odour of wines that had lingered through the years at all unpleasant but when she followed Mr Farley into the back shop and caught sight of two great iron hooks jutting from the ceiling even she quailed a little.

Mr Farley followed her gaze. "Pulleys, that's all. Used to be used for lowerin' casks into the cellar which, as you can see, is definitely a thing of the past."

He tilted the carbide and cast chalky light upon a patch of mortar as even as frozen water. When he tapped it with his heel there was no echo, no hollow ring.

"Filled it stiff," Mr Farley said. "Best thing, really."

Even in the spooky light Kirsty experienced no fear, no sense of the dreadful deeds that had been done here all those years ago. She could not summon up an image of Harold Vosper Vokes and confused him in her mind's eye with Daniel Malone who was a criminal of quite different stamp.

"Will you be good enough to go outside an' open the shutters, Gordon," Kirsty said.

Mr Farley handed Gordon the bunch of keys and minutes later, after much rattling, one shutter was removed, and then the other. For the first time in a decade sunlight poured into the shop's interior and Kirsty's last doubts vanished with the gloom.

She stepped behind the long counter and looked through the glass. Gordon scowled grimly back at her but, to Kirsty's delight, a moment later two women and a young child materialised by Gordon's side and, drawn by curiosity, peered in through the window too.

Suddenly she could see laden shelves, goods racked in the window, a throng of passersby come to gaze at bright and attractive displays of domestic wares that she would have for sale. Electric light, the smell of scented soap and the jingle of a till bell would exorcise the ghost of Harold Vokes once and for all. In future the only entity that would haunt No 1 Gascoigne Street would be her.

She put her hands flat on the counter and, when Gordon returned, said, "I'll take it, Mr Nicholson."

"What?"

"You heard me. I said I'll take it. Now, how much do you require by way of rent?"

"What?"

"Gordon, stop that."

"Fifteen pounds per annum," said Mr Farley. "Three years initial lease, with an option for twelve thereafter."

"Kirsty, wait. You can't just plunge in. For all you know the place could be fallin' apart."

"Structural flaws are usually the owner's responsibility," said Mr Farley. "I can put a special clause into the lease to that effect, Mrs Nicholson."

"Please do," said Kirsty.

"Wait, wait, wait, wait," said Gordon. "*I'm* the bloody owner."

"Sure you are," said Mr Farley. "That's why I suggested it."

"I'm also a partner in the business."

"Got it goin' all ways, ain't you?" said Mr Farley.

"Twenty a year," Gordon said.

"Not worth it," said Mr Farley. "Beat him down, Mrs Nicholson."

"Ten," said Kirsty. "After all, it's a white elephant; you told me so yourself."

"Twenty."

"He's a robber," said Mr Farley. "Stick to your guns."

"Fifteen," said Kirsty. "That's my last word."

"Done," Gordon told her and grinned sheepishly when Kirsty sealed the agreement by kissing his cheek.

"Me too?" said Mr Farley, hopefully.

"Sod off!" said Gordon.

*   *   *

Breezy remained unrepentant when challenged by his stepson. He had, he claimed, signed over the ill-starred property in a spirit of paternal affection. If Gordon managed to make it pay so much the better. From little acorns, and all that, hm? Was he not, after all, just giving the boy a flying start? Madge was not appeased. She saw through Kirsty's scheme immediately and berated her son and her husband for being parties to it.

She had been deeply hurt by Craig's attitude to her marriage and his wilful separation from the family circle. She did not, however, wish to see her firstborn humiliated, his authority as breadwinner swept away.

It was odd that a woman of such strong character should cling to the traditional view of marriage, that a man should be master in his own home and a woman subservient to his will. In any case, what need had Kirsty Barnes of extra cash? She had only one young mouth to feed, twenty-six bob a week coming in and a subsidised house.

As Madge's harangue was delivered across the polished dining-table in the mansion on Great Western Terrace while she was dressed in a gown that cost more than a policeman earned in a year, somehow her protests lacked base.

Gordon and Lorna were wise enough not to argue. Even Breezy, the great placator, just nodded and murmured, "Yes, dear. Of course, dear. Quite right, dear," as if he were as much of a weakling as her first husband had been and had been defeated too.

Meanwhile, down the hill in Canada Road, Kirsty was in the process of breaking her news, piece by piece, to the breadwinner in question.

"What about Bobby?" Craig shouted. "Are you goin' to leave him wi' a stranger every damned day?"

"I'll take him with me."

"To some dank, dirty shop?"

"It's not dank," Kirsty said, "an' when I've finished with it, it won't be dirty either."

"Was it Adair put you up to this? Is that where the money came from?"

"I'd a pound or two left over from the sum Nessie left us," Kirsty said.

"It costs more than a pound or two to rent a shop."

"I won money on a horse."

"Horse? What horse?"

"It was owned by a friend of Gordon's. I backed it an' it won," said Kirsty.

"How much, how bloody much?"

"Thirty pounds, if you must know," Kirsty said.

"Why didn't you tell me this?"

"I didn't think you'd approve."

"This shop, it's Adair's, isn't it?"

"Gordon owns the property," Kirsty said.

"Christ! So it was Gordon put you up to all this bloody nonsense, was it?"

"No, it was all my idea," Kirsty said. "I took the idea to Gordon."

"Why didn't you talk t' me about it first?"

"Because you'd have tried to stop me."

"Too damned right, I would," Craig shouted. "Anyhow, you're not allowed to own property."

"It's not against the law, is it?"

"You're a policeman's wife," Craig said. "You can't."

"Aye, but I can," Kirsty said. "In any case, Craig, to save you embarrassment I've put the business under a partner's name."

"Partner? Who the hell . . ."

"Your brother, Gordon."

"God, that wee bastard'll not be happy until he's in your bed an' all."

"Shut your dirty mouth," Kirsty exploded. "I knew I'd get no help or encouragement from you, so I went to somebody I could depend on, somebody I could trust."

"An' Gordon told you to blow our nest-egg, did he?"

"I didn't 'blow' anythin', Craig. I'm not like you."

"What's that supposed t' mean?"

"It means the next time you decide to cut an' run," Kirsty said, "you can take *all* our money, an' not just forty pounds of it."

Craig's anger drained away instantly. He seemed to be left without fight, without stuffing or resistance.

"Next time you fancy it," Kirsty went on, "you can abandon Bobby an' me without a qualm because we'll be protected."

"There . . . there won't be a next time, Kirsty."

"Aye, well, just in case you *should* change your mind," Kirsty said, "I thought it might comfort you t' know that your wife an' son can look after themselves."

"I wouldn't leave Bobby wi'out a father."

"Changed your tune, I see," Kirsty said. "Well, Craig, you're free now, free of all responsibility."

"Listen, you don't really want me to go, do you, Kirsty?"

"It's up to you," Kirsty said. "I'm only your wife; not even that, come to think of it."

"Don't you care what I do?" Craig said.

And with some satisfaction Kirsty gave him back the answer he had once given her.

"No, Craig," she said. "Not much."

*　　*　　*

Soon after breakfast Kirsty togged her son in his smart little suit and Tam o' Shanter and took him out with her into the dry, brisk morning air.

She walked along Dumbarton Road and down Gascoigne Street just to make sure that nobody had stolen the shop since yesterday; and then she turned west along Kingdom Road and headed, without further delay, for Benedict Street and a second meeting with Greta Taylor.

The child, Jen, was romping about in vest and knickers, a baby blanket thrown over her shoulders to simulate an opera cloak and to keep her warm. Her face was unwashed, hair uncombed, and in one small sticky fist she clutched a roll dripping with treacle.

It was industry not laziness that had caused Greta to neglect her daughter's grooming that morning. Oilskin covered the kitchen floor. Table and chairs were pushed to the wall to make room for a galvanised bath filled with soapy water. Piles of clothes were everywhere, draping chairbacks and bed as well as a wooden horse. An old iron mangle was viced to the side of the sink and two kettles hissed steam from the hob, giving the kitchen the atmosphere of a torture chamber.

Greta was no neater than her daughter. Red-faced, moist,

straggle-haired, her body was covered in an enormous canvas apron, her head in a spotted bandana, and her arms were bare.

"God, what a way t' catch me," Greta said.

"I can come back another time, if you'd prefer it," Kirsty said.

But Jen had caught sight of Bobby, and vice versa, and they had gone simultaneously into a bashful pantomime, with coy peeps and smiles and tiny waves of the hands, while each hid behind mother.

"Is this just . . . just a friendly visit, Mrs Nicholson?"

"No, I can't honestly say it is. I'd like a word with you, if you can spare the time."

"If you've come t' make trouble . . ."

"On the contrary," Kirsty said. "I've come to offer you a job."

Greta's reaction was immediately defensive. "I don't need your damned charity, Mrs Nicholson."

"Six hours a day, six days a week would hardly be charity," Kirsty said.

"Did he put you up to this?"

"I've a mind of my own, Mrs Taylor," said Kirsty, testily. "No, Craig would have a purple fit if he knew I was here."

Greta dried her arms and hands on a towel and regarded Kirsty warily. "What sort o' job is this?"

"I've rented a shop."

"You have, have you? Does he not have a share in it?"

"For the last time, let me assure you that Craig's got nothin' to do with it," said Kirsty. "In fact, he's dead set against it, as you can well imagine."

"I thought you were as hard up as the rest o' the Greenfield," Greta said. "How can you afford t' buy a shop?"

"I didn't buy it; I rent it," said Kirsty. "Just for your information, Mrs Taylor, I inherited a piece of money of my own, an' what I intend to do with it is open a shop."

Greta leaned back against the sink. "Jen," she said, "don't you get that young man wet now, y'hear?"

"Helpin' you, Mammy," Jen answered, and pulled Bobby down on to his knees on the rubber sheet. "Right?"

Bobby eyed his mother, dubious but eager too. The lure of a bathful of suds was irresistible.

"All right, Bobby," Kirsty said. "But roll up your sleeves, an' don't make a mess."

Greta still had not given an answer. She watched the children, head cocked, while Kirsty, in spite of herself, glanced round the kitchen.

It was here that Craig had made love to this woman. Somehow Kirsty could not associate the flushed, untidy person with those acts of betrayal. She seemed too mundane, too forthright and honest to be wicked.

"I'll pay a wage of twelve shillin's for the half week," Kirsty said.

"That's generous for a shop assistant."

"Perhaps, but I'll require the hours to be arranged to suit my convenience; to suit my husband's shifts, in fact."

"Where is the shop?"

"Gascoigne Street."

"Number one?"

"Aye," said Kirsty. "'Orrible 'Arold's lair.'"

Greta laughed. "By God, Mrs Nicholson, you do have brass neck. I suppose the rent costs next to nothin' since the place has been empty for years?"

"My brother-in-law's the new owner."

"Gordon? Did Breezy . . .?" Greta bit off the question.

Kirsty said, "I'm offerin' you the job for three reasons. You've had experience in sellin' across a counter. You're in a situation when you can work hours that might not suit my circumstances."

"And?"

"And I want to teach my husband a lesson."

"Aye, I thought that might be it."

"I need to be sure it's all over between you an' my husband."

"I could tell you lies, y'know."

"Yes, but I don't think you will," Kirsty said.

"I think you should know that I encouraged him," Greta said. "This is Benedict Street, not Park Gardens. Down here you take what you can get. There's no room for finer feelin's, or conscience."

"I don't need your excuses," Kirsty said. "I just want to know if you'll take on employment for me?"

"God, he'll be furious when he finds out."

"Does that bother you?"

Greta hesitated, then shook her head. "Funnily enough, it doesn't."

114

"Would you object to workin' for a woman?"

"Not for twelve bob a week I wouldn't," Greta said. "By the way, what are we sellin' in this shop of yours?"

"Domestic wares."

"Thank God for that," said Greta. "I thought we might be goin' back into the wine business."

It was Kirsty's turn to laugh. "Vintage Vokes, you mean?"

"Hangover guaranteed."

Kirsty pulled a face. "*Yuck.*"

Immediately Bobby caught the expression of disgust and mimicked it. "*Yuck, yuck, yuck,*" he cried, slapping his hands into the floating woollens in the tub, and when Jen also took up the chant the din became too much to bear.

"That's enough, you two," Greta said.

When order had been temporarily restored, Kirsty said, "Do you want time to consider my offer, Mrs Taylor?"

"I think you'd better call me Greta."

"All right – Greta."

"I just need to know one thing."

"What's that?" Kirsty asked.

"When do I start?" said Greta.

*　　*　　*

Kirsty had not felt so cheerful in months. Perhaps it was spring, the occupation of shopkeeping or the knowledge that she had shaken off complete dependence on Craig that revived her spirits. She hardly thought of David Lockhart at all now and when she did it was only to wonder what he would have made of her progress.

Though Kirsty could not have guessed it, Craig was not entirely opposed to having a shopkeeper for a wife. He respected her more than he ever let on, and was secretly proud – at first – of her initiative. He also saw humour in the fact that the property had once been the scene of a series of murders.

He did not keep the news to himself, as Kirsty had assumed he would. At the first opportunity he strolled down Gascoigne Street and inspected the premises with a professional eye. The padlocks would need to be changed for stouter models and she would be advised to insure the glass which, he reckoned, would be at risk from stones thrown up by horses and passing carts. Gordon, or Breezy Adair, would probably keep her right on that score. But once the stock began to arrive, he would ensure that Nicholson's, as the shop was to be called, was recorded in the station log and put into the Beat Book.

Craig adjusted very quickly to Kirsty's move towards independence and discovered that his guilt was relieved by it. He began to look forward to working in the shop now and then, behind the scenes at least.

And then he learned the truth.

Kirsty was seated in an armchair by the fire. She had a book in her lap – *The Wheel of Commerce* – and a pencil in her hand to mark certain passages that might be of use to her. Craig noticed that she did not have to struggle to comprehend the words as he'd done when he studied for his Constable's examinations. He was looking at her with something close to admiration when she glanced up and casually remarked, "By the way, I've taken on a shop assistant; a friend of yours."

"Uh, who's that?"

"Greta Taylor."

"No, Kirsty, no, you can't do that."

"What's to stop me?"

"Kirsty, for God's sake . . ."

"Greta has no objection to workin' for me, why should you?"

He felt as if he had been bound by a chain of circumstance, each link forged and fastened to make him her prisoner: Walbrook Street, Nessie Frew, Lockhart, his mother and Breezy Adair, Gordon, the money, always the money.

Suddenly her complacency sickened him.

He sprang to his feet and slapped her across the face, a stinging, voiceless blow.

Remorse gripped him instantly.

The sensation of her soft flesh shuddering under his hand, the sound of it, dead and flat, filled him with self-loathing.

He waited for her tears, her cry, her anger so that he could kneel before her and take her in his arms and show her that he was sorry, sorry for the slap, for all that he had done, make her realise that she had driven him to it.

But she defied him still, would not weep, would not cry out, though the weals that his fingers had printed on her cheek turned livid white and, even as he watched, to purplish red.

Kirsty uttered no sound at all.

She shook her head, auburn hair flying, blinked, then returned to her reading as if nothing at all had happened.

"Kirsty, I . . . I didn't mean . . ."

The bruise flared hotly on her skin. She did not look up. "She starts on Monday morning, prompt at half-past eight."

Craig turned on his heel and, a minute later, boots in one hand and tunic over his arm, plunged downstairs to seek refuge in the streets of the Greenfield and Glasgow's April gloaming.

*   *   *

Gordon, under the impression that the Robert Cunningham Opera Company was still in residence at the Royal, had braced himself for four hours of Teutonic gloom which, for appearances' sake, he would have to pretend to enjoy. On arrival at the theatre, however, he was gratified to discover that Faust had exited in favour of J. F. Elliston's Company of Selected London & American Artistes who were performing a musical review entitled *In Old Kentucky*.

The Royal was much, much grander than the Gem, all etched glass and marble and glittering chandeliers. Gordon felt no end of a swell as he followed Johnnie, Amanda and the other cousins along the plush-lined corridor to the private boxes.

Theatre evenings had long been part of the Adairs' social calendar and the sons and daughters of the clan felt thoroughly at home with furs and evening gowns, opera glasses and glacé fruits, and with being perched between the proletariat in the gallery and the bourgeoisie in the stalls.

The younger girls were all agog, of course, at being out on the town without their parents or nannies but took their cue from Amanda and from Josephine Adair, Edward's eldest, and behaved with hauteur that only occasionally broke down in fits of giggles.

It seemed to be generally accepted that Nicholson was Amanda's new beau and that she was 'breaking him in' rather well, passing him her fan, her glasses, the big yellow card programme, forth and back, back and forth. Gordon, on the other hand, began to feel like the tiny black boy in *In Old Kentucky* who scampered about the stage at everyone's beck and call and eventually fell asleep under the magnolia tree and dreamed that he had been called to rest, to rest.

In spite of their silks and satins the inhabitants of the boxes were really quite human. They laughed along with everyone else at the antics of eccentric dancers, wept at deep-voiced spirituals, sang along with the chorus and, when the show was over, stood up and applauded the cast with unsophisticated enthusiasm before spilling out into the Glasgow street in search of the supper that Johnnie had promised them.

Lobster bisque and crabmeat sandwiches awaited them around the corner in Findlater's Supper Rooms whence they walked in column-of-route, laughing and singing excitedly, and from whence, about eleven, the younger ones were fetched by trusted servants sent along in cabs and carriages by anxious daddies.

Amanda was billeting with Aunt Heather but it had been arranged that Gordon would escort her home to the Whiteside house alone. After some ribald advice, whispered by Johnnie to Amanda, and some lewd remarks by Eric to Gordon, the couple left the pavement outside Findlater's in a hired hackney and settled for the drive back to Dowanhill.

Gordon was flushed with wine and lobster soup and he did not resist when Amanda nuzzled against him and covered his hands with hers.

All evening long, whether he'd liked it or not – and of course he'd liked it – Gordon had been treated to glimpses of Amanda's breasts raised by the lightest of corsets and exposed by the deep neck of her evening gown.

"Tell the cabby to extinguish the port light," Amanda whispered.

"He can't do that," said Gordon. "It's against the law."

"He'll do it for a florin. Go on."

Embarrassed, Gordon fished a half-crown from his pocket and conveyed the lady's request to the driver, a knotty stalwart of the night-time carriage trade, who, with a wry snort, palmed the coin, clicked open the lamp with the butt of his whip and let the breeze blow out the flame.

Amanda had loosed the clasp of her cape. Her face and hair were framed against the black material. She reached for Gordon and drew him down into the darkened corner of the cab, the leather creaking under the shift in weight.

Gordon barely had time to take off his hat and toss it on to the seat before Amanda kissed him.

She kissed him passionately and, Gordon believed, expertly. Eyes wide open, he had no option but to let her make the running. She kissed him until he was out of breath and had to disengage.

"Amanda, d'you think this is . . . .?"

She touched a finger to his mouth to silence his uncertain protest, and wriggled down until she was practically beneath him. To avoid crushing her, Gordon was obliged to jam one foot against the door of the box and straddle her skirts.

From this unusual position he could see street-lamps flickering past and the odd Glaswegian toddlin' home along the pavement. What in God's name must those casual observers think? Obviously that he was ravishing some helpless maiden. He only wanted to be nice to her, tender and kind and affectionate.

"Amanda, wait . . ."

"Do you love me, Gordon? Oh, say that you love me."

Her vowels were round, her consonants perfectly formed, as if she had rehearsed the words in advance. In contrast his voice sounded as dry and coarse as old straw.

"Please, Amanda . . ."

She took his wrist between her fingers in a gesture so delicate that he could not believe what she did with it. She lifted his hand and put it upon her breast, not beneath but on top, against the soft, bare flesh.

"Say it. Say that you love me, Gordon."

He was not quite man enough to resist entirely. He could not afterwards forget that he had taken advantage of her, had caressed her breasts for several breathless seconds until Amanda moaned, "You see. You see, you do love me."

Immediately Gordon released her and drew back. He seemed to have five legs and four arms and had never in his life felt his body to be such an alien thing.

"What's wrong, darling?"

"It isn't . . ."

"Show me how much you love me. I don't mind, really."

He surprised himself by his authority.

He said gruffly, "No, Amanda. Not here an' not like this."

She elbowed herself into a sitting position.

"What's *wrong* with you, Gordon Nicholson?"

"In a hackney cab? Come on!"

"It's me, isn't it? You find me repulsive."

"Amanda, for God's sake, it isn't you," Gordon told her. "I find you damned attractive, of course I do."

"What's wrong, then?"

How could he explain to her that, though he did want to

119

touch her, even to make love to her, her eagerness had put him off. If he'd only wanted an education, an experience of that sort, then he would have picked a woman off the street and paid for it.

"Nothing's wrong, Amanda," Gordon said. "But I won't take advantage . . ."

"Oh, you are *such* a silly man."

"The driver . . ."

"He's seen much worse than what we were doing," Amanda said.

"How do you know?"

"They all have," said Amanda, then, "I thought you really liked me, Gordon."

He reached for her hand.

She permitted the liberty without enthusiasm.

"I do like you," Gordon said.

"Obviously you don't like me enough."

"Enough for what?"

"I don't arouse you, do I?"

"Amanda," Gordon said, "stop."

Sulking too was an act, as artificial and rehearsed as her passion had been. She said nothing and, when he tried to kiss her cheek, turned quickly away. Suddenly Gordon was determined not to give her what she wanted, what she had demanded. Damned if he would say he loved her when he was still so unsure. In the mirrored sheen of the cab's side window he studied her pose of injured pride and, after a time, released her hand and lit himself a cigarette.

It was a relief to reach the Whiteside house and find Robert Whiteside, who took a dim view of his son's goings-on, waiting on the steps to escort his niece to safety.

Amanda flounced from the cab, with a little toss of her head. Cringing, Gordon realised that Mr Whiteside would be bound to misinterpret that gesture and would assume that he, Gordon Nicholson, had behaved like a cad and not a gentleman.

"Good night, Amanda."

She did not respond to his desperate farewell and all Gordon got in lieu was a savage over-the-shoulder scowl from Mr Whiteside as the man led the poor child indoors.

"Goin' on somewhere, guv'nor?"

The cabby's tone was neutral, his expression blank.

"Great Western Terrace," Gordon snapped and flung himself back into the corner to brood darkly on the inconsistencies of womankind and his own naivety.

*   *   *

Frustration rather than anger prompted Craig to follow Ronnie Norbert's trail. He had chinned Ronnie after the monthly parade at Percy Street but had received no further information about Greta Taylor's past. Ronnie claimed to have run into a blank wall, to be not one step closer to discovering the whereabouts of Lizzie Straun or the elusive Sylvie McNish than he had been a month ago. At the time Craig had been content to let things stand. Now, however, he was eager to spike whatever game Kirsty was playing and shake Greta Taylor from his life for ever.

To this end, Craig, in mufti, ventured down into the rump of the burgh, into the network of cobbled streets and dismal tenements that surrounded that infamous slum, the Madagascar. He did not know what he hoped to find there, what he might unearth that Ronnie had missed, but the Madagascar was a place where almost anything might happen.

In the Madagascar Sammy Reynolds' father had drunk himself to death, from the Madagascar Sammy had been duly rescued. To Craig, in his innocence, it seemed just the sort of place where a trade in unwanted infants might flourish and tiny souls be passed back and forth for cash.

As it happened the drinking-den that Craig first entered was not the one in which Ronnie had cultivated Hog Moscrop's friendship. Slattery's was even lower down the scale, a hole in a wall of ramshackle cottages that overlooked the ashpits and the old graving dock at the bottom of Eel Street.

In spite of a ship's lantern hung over the close and a painted signboard depicting a hairy Irish colleen with a foaming tankard in her hand, the tavern was far from picturesque. Only if you wanted a woman or a skinful of hootch at budget rates would Slattery's seem attractive and even then you ran the risk of being beaten and robbed and tossed into the dirty brown waters of the Clyde for your temerity.

It was a particularly dangerous place for policemen, on duty or off, but danger was part of the attraction for Craig in his present frame of mind. He wanted drink and he wanted information and, damn it, he would go to hell itself if he felt like it. But to Craig's consternation the first person he saw when he ducked through Slattery's doorway was Constable Andy McAlpine and Andy had already put sobriety behind him.

"Hoh!" Andy called out. "Here's a sight for sore eyes."

The villains who frequented Slattery's knew Andy for what he was. They treated him like a pet monkey. They dosed him with liquor, teased him and extracted from him what information they could about happenings at Ottawa Street police station. The arrival of another copper, one who had not been tamed, was unsettling, however, and one by one, like mules in a stall, Slattery's customers turned and glowered at Craig with sullen suspicion.

"B'God, you're well off your beat," Andy shouted. "Got a ren . . . ren . . . rendayvouse wi' another bunty then?"

The door closed behind him. Ten or a dozen men made the cramped parlour seem crowded. Craig was too far into the tavern to retreat.

Beer mugs and tankards littered the barreltop tables. The counter, barely an arm's breadth in length, was buffered by casks and kegs like a redoubt prepared for sudden attack. At one end of the room three bruisers were roasting chops on wire forks over an open fire. Choking smoke from coals and cooking hung in the air like a pall.

Craig swung round. Two large men had stationed themselves by the door. Each puffed furiously on a short clay pipe as if to cloud the intruder's senses and screen from witnesses what might happen next. Craig stood his ground. He was not afraid. In fact, he experienced a curious stimulation from the situation. It was something wholly masculine and comprehensible, unlike the sort of threats that women posed.

Two women occupied a table hard by the street wall. Craig reckoned that they were mother and daughter and, caught between pay-days, were plying a sticky trade that weekday night. He let his gaze linger on the girl for a moment. She poked out her tongue at him and winked both eyes. Her mother, blonde too but raddled, laughed hoarsely and beckoned. "C'mon over here, copper. C'mon an' talk wi' ma Angela. She's real fond o' men in blue."

Craig shook his head.

Andy McAlpine gripped him by the arm, drew him close to the counter and introduced him to the bald, blunt-nosed barman.

"Bennie, I'd like for you t' meet Con . . . *Mister* Nicholson from our close. Right, Craig, what'll it be?"

"Beer," Craig said. "Heavy."

"It's all heavy here, *Constable* Nicholson," Bennie told him.

Andy said, "Ach, gi'e him a taste o' whisky on my slate."

"Your slate's full, Mr McAlpine."

"Well, start a clean one for my pal here," Andy said. "He's rollin' in money. Bloody rollin' in it. Sure ye are, Craig? I mean, his wife's just gone int' business."

"Hear that, ladies," Bennie said. "It seems like ye might be havin' some extra competition."

The women laughed uproariously.

"If he canna afford his wife," said the young thing, "he can still afford me."

"Two for the price o' one, Mr Polisman," the mother offered. "How about that for a bargain?"

Craig put a florin on to the counter and instructed Bennie to give Andy whatever he wanted to drink.

"I'm no' needin' t' scrounge drink from you, Craig," said Andy, even as he signalled to the barman that a glass of whisky would not go amiss.

Craig leaned his elbows on the bar. He ignored the threat of the men behind him, the women's jibes. He watched Andy lift the stubby glass between finger and thumb and throw the hootch over his throat in a single swallow.

"Give him another," Craig said.

Obediently Bennie poured the measure.

Craig wondered if this was how Ronnie Norbert got his information, by pouring alcohol into men whose resistance was already minimal, by trading on weakness. It would be just the sort of method that Ronnie would employ.

Craig sipped and slid another glance towards the women.

"Do you know them by name, Andy?"

"Eh?" Andy swung round, glass poised between finger and thumb. "Who? Them?"

"The older one," Craig said, softly. "She isn't called Lizzie, is she?"

"Nah, her name's Prue," said Andy. "Are you scoutin' for another bunty, eh?"

"Lizzie Straun," Craig said. "I'm lookin' for a woman named Lizzie Straun."

Craig watched Bennie carefully but there was no reaction at all from the barman to the name that he had dropped.

"Lizzie Straun?" Craig repeated.

"Never heard o' her." Andy McAlpine shrugged and raised the little glass to his lips.

"Make it last, Andy," Craig said. "That's the last tonight."

"God, that's a statement t' chill a man's blood," Andy said. "But it'll no' be the last for me, no' by a long chalk."

"You shouldn't be here, Andy."

"Who says?"

"You should go home."

"Home! Jesus, don't you start preachin'. What have I got t' go home for?"

"Joyce'll be worried."

"Nothin' worries Joyce. Christ, I tell ye, if she'd shut her mouth an' open her . . ."

"Andy, keep it down."

"Ach, they all know me here. They're all pals o' mine here." He raised the glass, miraculously empty. "We're all pals here, right, lads?"

"Aye, right, Andy."

"Anyway," Andy said, "it's the pot callin' the bloody kettle black."

"What d'you mean?"

"You an' your bunty in Benedict Street."

"She was only a friend."

"Pull the other one, Craig," Andy said. "If things is so bloody great at home why are *you* no' sittin' at your own fireside? Tell me that."

Craig could not answer. He lifted the beer glass to his mouth but did not drink. He put it down untouched. He had suddenly lost his taste for it. Andy was right; what the hell was he doing here? Why *did* he feel compelled to evade the issues that lay at home? It would be all too easy to slither down into the dream world that Andy McAlpine inhabited, where all men were pals just because they shared drink and a selfish indifference to responsibility.

"You've had enough, Andy."

"I'll tell ye when I've had enough."

"Suit yourself, Andy," Craig said, turning from the bar with the intention of leaving.

The two large men still barred the door. The woman and her

124

daughter had gone quiet. They were watching him slyly, without amusement. Craig hesitated then approached the table in the alcove. Every eye in the place was on him now. He put his fists on the table and leaned close.

The woman was not so old as he had imagined; thirty-four or -five at most. In the girl he could discern the blonde daintiness that had been the mother's hallmark before gin and prostitution had taken their dreadful toll. Now she was gaunt and bony, her eyes without lustre, her hair like tow.

"D'you have a place?" Craig said.

"Aye, but I'm no' goin' there wi' you."

"I thought you fancied men in blue uniforms?"

"I'll go wi' ye," said Angela, without a smile.

"What age are you?" Craig asked.

Except for a crop of pimples at the corner of her mouth Angela was unblemished. Pointed chin and high cheekbones made her seem elfin and innocent. Taking her hard would flatter most men. Why she remained here in the Madagascar Craig could not imagine; to look out for her mother, perhaps, or because she hadn't the wit to realise her own worth.

"She's old enough," the woman said.

"Fourteen, fifteen," Craig said. "Nah, I like more experience than she's got."

"Craig, for God's sake, man. Think what you're . . ."

Andy McAlpine had come shuffling to his elbow, disgusted at such a candid display of sexual barter. Craig pushed him away with the back of his arm, holding him off. The silence in the tavern was like stone.

"How much?" he said.

"No' wi' you," the woman said. "Take Angela. I'm old enough t' be your grannie."

"No," Craig said. "No, you're not. How much for the whole night?"

"Aw, God! Craig!"

"Go back to your whisky, Andy," Craig said and reached to take the woman's arm. "Come on now, Prue."

She recoiled, shrank back against her daughter who, knowing no better, assumed that her mother was playing coy to raise the price and giggled nervously. One shriek, one audible signal from Prue, however, and the men in the bar would be upon him. He wouldn't have an earthly, not him and not Andy.

Craig said, "Fifty shillin's, how's that?"

"Oh, Mam!" Angela was astounded.

"At least go for the youngster," Andy said. "No' yon old baggage."

Craig spun round and, in a flash, caught Andy McAlpine by the back of the neck. The men with toasting-forks up by the fire rose as one, knocking over stools and beer mugs, and Bennie dived beneath the counter and whipped out the mahogany chair leg that he used as a pacifier.

Pinned by Craig's fist on the nape of his neck Andy McAlpine was drawn forward to the table and his face thrust close to the woman's.

"Apologise," Craig shouted. "Apologise to the lady right here an' now."

"For what?" Andy cried.

"Insultin' her," Craig shouted.

"Insultin'! She's only an old . . ."

Craig pumped down his arm and banged Andy's forehead against the table, making gin glasses rattle and hop.

"Say you're sorry, Andy, or I'll break your bloody nose next time."

"I'm . . . I'm . . . sorry."

"Louder," Craig said. "An' sweeter too."

"I'M SORRY, PRUE. REALLY I AM."

There was movement by the door. Craig sensed rather than saw it but he heard the crack of Bennie's pacifier on the bar top and knew that his boldness was paying off. He had disconcerted them, all of them. He had been gallant, and he had been violent too, and he had cooked up on the spur of the moment a motive that none of them could quite evaluate.

"She's a lady, Andy," Craig said, "an' don't you forget it."

He released Constable McAlpine who, utterly bewildered, slumped into a chair and rubbed his forehead with the back of his hand. Angela was gawping at Craig, her mouth open and her blue eyes as round as saucers.

Craig gave a bow, offered the woman his arm.

"Shall we go now?" he said, softly.

"I . . ."

"Perhaps Mister McAlpine would be good enough to escort Angela home in an hour or two. Andy?"

"What? Aye, right, yes."

126

Craig put his hand on to the bar and lifted it and left a florin there. "Give them what they want, Bennie."

"I'll do that," Bennie said. "Sir."

Guiltily Bennie slid the chair leg out of sight and, having done so, came out from behind the bar, brushed aside the two large men and personally opened the door for the constable and his lady.

"Good night, all," Craig said.

But nobody in Slattery's had voice enough to answer and Craig, the woman leaning heavily on his arm, ducked through the doorway and swaggered out into the street as if he had rescued a princess and not just bought himself a whore.

*   *   *

"Did y'mean it?" Prue Alston asked. "I mean, d'you really think I'm a lady?"

How much gin had it taken to preserve such vanity, such self-delusion?

Craig said, "'Course you're a lady, Prue. You might be a bit down on your luck, but there's somethin' swell about you, an' I could see it right away."

She laughed and hugged him to her. "Ach, awa' wi' your blethers, sonnie. Your pal was right. I am an old baggage an' you should've gone wi' Angela instead."

"Are you complainin'?" Craig said.

"Was it fifty shillin's you said?"

"It was."

"You'll not regret it," Prue promised. "I'm no spring chick now but I've learned a trick or two that'll make your eyes roll, I'll bet."

"Where do you live?"

"In the Madagascar."

They had emerged from Eel Street, arms linked, and had come along the broad expanse of what had at one time been the carriage road to the gigantic trading house of the Africa Import Company, a merchant group whose fortunes had foundered when slavery had gone out of favour thirty-five or forty years ago. It stood stark against the April sky, a ghetto for Lascar seamen and Irish labourers. Beyond it Craig could see the decaying façade of the building that gave the Madagascar its name, another monument to a trading house that had failed.

He did not know when to tell her, how to tell her that he did not want her arms about him or her body joined with his.

They went on across the waste ground, through the shadow of the African house, on to the ridge of ash that gave a view of the bulbous little docks where once the sailing ships had moored and poured out their exotic cargoes; disused now, choked with oily silt, piles and piers rotting like bones, gnawed to the marrow by stealthy brown tides, year by passing year.

"You'll not have been in the Madagascar before?" Prue Alston said.

"Aye, but I have," Craig told her. "I was here a couple of times, when Reynolds was alive."

"Huh!" she said. "You're the copper that took the boy awa'?"

"You heard about that?"

"He was never a bad boy."

"I know," Craig said.

"Where is he now? The workhouse?"

"Nah, Sammy has a job, a caretaker's assistant," Craig told her. "An' he bides in the Claremont."

"Does he now," Prue said. "You see him?"

"Sometimes."

"Tell him Auntie Prue sends her love."

"I will," Craig promised, doubting if Sammy would remember the woman or any small kindnesses that she might have bestowed on him in those grey years when he was only half an orphan and his father's victim. "I'll tell him."

It was a strange, strange evening, the light peculiar, not bright, not dark. He could see Partick in profile and Govan across the water, the University tower and the heights around it, and craft on the river hung, it seemed, on the current, and still too, resting.

He didn't want to fight with her. He regretted the deception, the cunning, even the hurt he had inflicted on Andy McAlpine, and the swagger had been all show.

She walked unsteadily over the rough ground, looking down, hanging on to his arm for balance and support. He could have coped with this better if he'd been in uniform, but as it was he felt as embarrassed as if he were going to do what she thought he was going to do.

The Madagascar was a weird old tenement, dead as a tomb. No wifies leaned on the window ledges, no lads raced about the broken pavements or hollered in the middens, no menfolk slouched by the close mouths; yet the reek of life was evident, a charred unwholesomeness, and all the sounds associated with bustling burgh streets were muffled here by the reticence of poverty, by shame.

Prue Alston led him in by the end close. Twisted and burned out, the gas-lamps gave no light. The water closet on the first landing was cracked and leaked a slimy flood down the stairs. The smell was dense, the atmosphere foetid, and the last of the evening light prettily reflected in the broken panes of the stair window seemed like a mockery, a jibe.

"Here we are then," Prue said.

For the first time since they had left Slattery's she released Craig's arm. She took a key from her pocket and unlocked the door, pushed it open with her elbow and, catching him by the hand, drew him inside.

To Craig's surprise the hall smelled of pipe tobacco, a ripe but not unpleasant aroma, overlaid by perfume and then by coffee. He would never have associated such scents with the Madagascar, nor with Prue Alston.

He said, "Do you have a man here, livin' here?"

"It's my auld faither," she told him, as she unbuttoned her overcoat and unwound a feathery thing from about her throat. "He stays up above. Comes down every day for his feed."

"Does he know what . . . what you do?"

"Keeps him in baccy, doesn't it?" the woman said.

"Does your daughter stay here too?"

"She's no' my daughter," Prue Alston said.

With a gesture that reminded Craig of Greta, the woman smoothed down her dress and gave her hair a primp.

The kitchen was slatted with the last of the sunlight and dark, leathery shadows. The windows were uncurtained and a tiny fire burned in an iron grate that seemed to be in process of detaching itself from the wall. Old, old wallpaper, tanned by pipe smoke, showed a dim pattern of acanthus leaves.

Prue lit a lamp and placed it on the table. The kitchen was similar to Greta's, except that the bed recess was draped with a heavy velveteen curtain, tied with a gilded sash. On a low-slung rope over the sink hung two pairs of corsets, three pairs of black stockings and a diaphanous chemise.

"Do y'want a cup o' real coffee? I can make it in a minute," Prue said. "I don't keep whisky in the house."

Craig shook his head. He did not know what to do now, how to ask the question that had brought him here. He had a queer feeling that she knew his purpose and had hinted that she would give him value for his money.

He said, "Is she your sister then? Angela, I mean?"

Here in her own kitchen, in the glow of the oil-lamp, she looked younger, softer, almost desirable.

"She was my investment," Prue Alston said.

"Aye," Craig said. "Where did you get her?"

"I paid ten pounds for her, twelve years ago."

"You bought her from Lizzie Straun, didn't you?"

Prue said, "You don't want me at all, Mr Polisman, do you?"

Craig said, "It's got nothing to do wi' the police, Prue. I need to find Lizzie Straun for personal reasons."

"She's out the market now. Both her an' her boss."

"Her boss?"

"McNish."

"Out the market? How do y'mean?" Craig said.

"I'm for makin' coffee."

"I'll take some," Craig said, and watched her open a cupboard in a tall pinewood dresser. "Ten pounds? Was that the goin' rate?"

"Angela was special. I had t' wait a while for her an' she cost me an' m'dad all we had in the world, near enough."

"Couldn't you have a bairn o' your own?"

"I was doctored once too often," Prue Alston said.

Craig listened to tap-water dribble into the tin coffee-maker and watched the woman light not a gas ring but a spirit stove. She set the percolator on the butterfly-blue flame and, from a caddy, poured in ground coffee beans.

It was hard to believe that he was inside the Madagascar; the ritual seemed so refined, the aroma so luxurious. In Slattery's the woman and the girl had appeared slovenly and unfeminine, strident and calculating and hard. Small things, coffee, a chemise, a spirit stove, the knowledge that she had a father just upstairs, gave Prue Alston definition and veracity.

Craig felt a terrible wave of pity for her and his tone, when he spoke again, was as quiet and sympathetic as if he were speaking to a child. The irony of it was that, in this milieu, he was the child.

"Anyhow," the woman said, "I could never have done it wi' a bairn o' my own. It wouldn't have been nat'ral, or right."

"Done what?"

"Put her out."

"I see," Craig said, though he saw only imperfectly what Prue Alston meant, and what her past implied.

"I'd t' wait for her for a long while. I wanted one that looked like me, see. Had my colour. An' Dad wanted one that had a pedigree."

"A pedigree?"

"Good breedin'. Dad always said the breedin' would tell. I think he was right, don't you? I mean, can y'not tell her father was a baronet?"

"Who told you her father was a baronet?"

"Lizzie Straun."

"An' you believed her?" Craig said.

"She was a bonny, dear wee thing. I knew as soon as I saw her she'd be just right for Dad an' me. For when I got old."

"An investment."

The lid of the coffee-maker chugged. Both Craig and the woman glanced at it. It chugged again and let out a fragrant wisp of steam.

"Doesn't tak' long, see," Prue Alston said.

"When did you put her out?"

"Last year."

"How did she . . . Did she not complain?"

"She knew what would be expectit," Prue said. "She just wanted t' be like her mam, like me."

Craig said, "Why are you tellin' me all this?"

"For fifty shillin's."

"For fifty bob you'd shop the woman who got you Angela?"

"Ach, there's no' much the law can do t' Lizzie now. An' Sylvie McNish is gone."

"Dead?"

"Nah, just departed."

"Departed where?"

"I canna tell ye that," said Prue.

"Why not?"

"Because I don't know."

"Would Lizzie Straun know?"

"She might." From the tin spout came a stream of black liquid, filling two china cups without saucers. "There's no cream, only milk if y'want some."

131

"Just sugar," Craig said. "What did this McNish woman do?"

"Are you goin' t' pay me?"

He had already crushed the banknotes in his trouser pocket. He brought them out now, flattened them, added four half-crowns, and put the payment on the table by the side of the sugar jar.

"I need it for a dress for Angela, y'see," the woman told him. "I'll need t' get her out o' this place an' up the town. She'll do well for us up the town when she's fitted right."

Craig said, "Aye, I'm sure she will."

"Sylvie McNish, is she the one ye want t' know about?"

"Yes," Craig said. "An' Lizzie Straun too."

"Lizzie was just a runner for Sylvie. Sylvie did the business," the woman said. "She bought an' sold bairns."

"Where did she buy them?"

"From servant lassies, from country girls, now an' then from fancy-dans who were against doctorin'. Believe it or not, some men do have a conscience o' sorts."

"Did Sylvie arrange the doctorin' too?"

"When it suited her. She cost too much for me, though."

"Who did she sell them to?"

"Folk who needed labour."

"Your sort?"

"Often enough, I suppose."

"Greta Taylor?"

"Who's she?" said Prue Alston.

Craig judged that her puzzlement was genuine. He did not press that particular point.

He said, "Let me get this clear; we're talkin' here about a trade in babies, in infants, right?"

"Aye, you buy them straight off the shelf, like, when they're new."

"Jesus!" Craig said. "I suppose they're put t' work at the age o' five or six?"

"In the sweatshops, aye," said Prue, "usually. Other times somebody just wants a bairn, wi'out awkward questions from the parish or the law."

"Men?"

Prue shrugged. "Sometimes."

"Christ, that's horrible," Craig said. "The poor wee bastards have no chance."

132

"Better than bein' dead," said Prue. "Better, I think, than ten years in one o' the institutions."

Craig said, "Was it in Greenfield that Sylvie McNish carried on her business?"

Prue laughed. "God, son, but you've an awfy lot t' learn. Nah, nah, it was up in Glasgow. Sylvie McNish fancied hersel' for posh. She lived in a big apartment in Mandeville Crescent, latterly, an' let folk like Lizzie do the runnin' for her."

Craig said, "An' you've no idea where the McNish woman is now?"

Prue shook her head. "No idea at all."

"An' Lizzie Straun?"

"I know where she lives," said Prue.

"So tell me," Craig said.

"Potiphar Street," said Prue. "Number three, Potiphar Street."

"Where's that?"

"In Kelvinhaugh."

*   *   *

Monday morning was dry, though hardly warm. Kirsty was up at six o'clock but with none of that dragging weariness that indicated reluctance to start the day. She was bursting with energy and had lighted the fire and made her bed and had a cooked breakfast ready to serve to Craig the moment he stepped in from the night-shift.

For the past few days she had been unsure of his mood and their relationship, glazed by her excitement at having acquired the shop, had been remarkably unruffled by sarcasm or argument. Now and then she would catch him looking at her, not glowering but with a strange wee frown on his brow as if he'd found a fresh puzzle in her and was trying to figure out an answer to it.

He made no comment at all about the new tin bucket, the new mop and broom that were propped by the coal bunker in the hall and did not seem to notice that she was already dressed in her overcoat and outdoor shoes.

He ate breakfast in silence while Kirsty whisked through her routine chores; then, as soon as Craig had gone to bed, she wakened Bobby, washed, dressed and fed him, cajoled away his grumpiness and, prompt at ten to eight, left the house with her son and a clanking armoury of cleaning utensils.

Gordon was not best pleased to have been dragged down to Greenfield at such an hour but, as requested, there he was on the pavement outside McGivern's dairy, pacing up and down and puffing on a cigarette.

He did not share Kirsty's excitement as he handed her the keys to No. 1 Gascoigne Street and received in return a plain manila envelope containing three crisp five-pound notes.

"What are we meetin' here for?" Gordon said.

"I thought it would be more convenient for you," Kirsty told him.

"Are you tryin' to keep me away from the shop?"

"Of course not, Gordon."

"In that case, I'll walk round there with you."

"Oh, you don't have to put yourself out."

"I'm the owner, damn it. I have to be on hand to make a list of anythin' that might need urgent repair."

"Well," said Kirsty, "if you insist."

"I do."

"In that case," Kirsty said, "perhaps you could carry Bobby for a bit."

"Oh, God!"

Gordon forced a crooked smile and hoisted his nephew up on to his shoulders, fell in behind the warrior wife and tried to keep up with her as she charged off towards Gascoigne Street, her mop and broom at the ready.

Greta and her daughter waited at the awkward corner where Gascoigne Street joined Dumbarton Road. The little girl was neatly dressed and had a rag doll to keep her amused. Greta wore a canvas apron and a shawl and, in spite of her small stature, looked solid and ready for business.

Rounding the corner and catching sight of Greta, Gordon stopped dead. Bobby swayed dangerously on his shoulders and gripped his uncle's collar with both fists.

"What the hell is *she* doin' here?" Gordon demanded.

"Oh, I forgot to tell you," Kirsty said. "Mrs Taylor is my new assistant."

"Your new what!" Gordon swung Bobby to the ground. He angled himself so that his back was to Greta, and hissed, "What the hell're you playin' at, Kirsty? Don't you know who that is?"

"Aye, she's my new assistant."

"Damn you, Kirsty, you've gone a bit too far this time," Gordon said.

"I don't know what you mean."

"Does Craig know about this?"

"Of course."

"How did he react?"

"It's not his shop, nor his capital," Kirsty said. "He can't tell me who or who not to employ."

"This is spite, Kirsty, an' it's not like you," Gordon said.

"Shall I open up, Mrs Nicholson?" Greta called.

"Please do," Kirsty said, and lobbed her the keys.

Gordon said, "You don't know anythin' about this woman, Kirsty. You don't know what she's really like."

"Craig seemed to find her pleasant enough."

"Nah, nah, Kirsty. I'm not gettin' drawn into his battle," Gordon said. "This is a whole lot more than I bargained for when I let you sweet-talk me into takin' a share in the shop."

Kirsty sniffed. "If you wish to raise objection t' my choice o' staff then you'd better have good grounds for the complaint. What's more, you'd better put it in writin' in a letter to my legal adviser, Mr Marlowe."

"Hey, now, just hold your horses," Gordon said. "I'm not tellin' you to sack her or anythin'. I just think you might have told me in advance what you were plannin'."

"I didn't plan anythin'."

"Balderdash!" said Gordon. "You've had this manoeuvre in mind for weeks. In fact, it's probably the sole reason you decided to go into retail an' open a shop."

"I'm sorry you think that."

"What else am I t' think?" Gordon said. "It's a clear case o' revenge."

"I've nothin' against you, Gordon."

"I should bloody well hope not," Gordon said. "But Craig *is* my brother, in case you've forgotten."

"I'm not tryin' to test your loyalty."

"Then why employ her? Why choose Greta Taylor?"

"Craig won't come here now. He daren't."

"I see," Gordon said, disgustedly. "You've finally managed to shut him out."

"No, Gordon. *He* shut *me* out. When he took me away from Dalnavert that day I thought I'd belong to him an' he'd belong to me. But I was wrong." Kirsty paused. "I've learned some hard lessons since we came t' Glasgow, an' that's one of them. If you want somethin' of your own then you've got to earn it for yourself."

135

"I wish that bloody horse had come in last."

"The race had nothin' to do with it. Winnin' money on Camberwell Beauty just speeded things up," Kirsty said. "If it hadn't happened as it did, I'd have been patient an' found another way to get free of him."

"You could leave him," Gordon said. "That simple."

"Nah, but it's not that simple," Kirsty said. "I wish to heaven it was."

Gordon tutted and shook his head. "Breezy isn't goin' to like this either."

"Breezy! What's he got to do with it?"

Gordon did not answer.

He said, "I'll have to go. I've got work t' do."

"Aren't you comin' inside?"

"No."

"Does Greta embarrass you?"

"Yes, if you must know."

Kirsty said, "When will I see you again?"

"When you need somethin' from me, I suppose," Gordon said.

He gave his sister-in-law a curt nod of farewell, swung on his heel and hurried off around the corner into Dumbarton Road.

Kirsty was not as stung by Gordon's remark as she might have been. Perhaps a certain callousness had crept into her character these past months, though it had not been her intention to confront him with Greta, to embarrass him. It was just one of those pieces of ill-timing for which nobody was really to blame. Then too she had become wary of the power that even kindhearted young men like Gordon Nicholson could wield.

"Mammy?"

Two little faces, one above the other, peeped from the shop doorway.

"I'm here, son."

"Are y'comin' inside now?" Bobby asked.

"I certainly am," said Kirsty.

Seven

The Garden Party

Astonishment, envy and admiration in about equal measure greeted the news that Kirsty Nicholson had opened a shop of her own. Among the wives of No. 154 Canada Road, however, what really set the cat among the pigeons was the rumour, soon substantiated, that Kirsty had actually employed that woman from Benedict Street to be her assistant.

Even Joyce McAlpine, who had troubles enough of her own, God knows, was aflame with curiosity and would sidle into the wash-house to pass a half-hour with the ladies, to join them in speculation and assessment of a situation that had become too complicated for simple minds to grasp.

The general consensus of opinion was that the original rumour, that Craig had been having it off with the woman from Benedict Street, had been nowt but hot air and that Kirsty Nicholson had known more about it than she had ever let on.

Charitable souls like Mrs Piper wished Kirsty luck and wasted no time in trotting round to Gascoigne Street to make a token purchase; a wee tartan box for collar studs that cost her sevenpence and yielded a bonus of new-minted conversation.

"Did you see her there? The other one, I mean?"

"What does she look like?"

"Dark, that's all I know."

"Aye, she was there. She wrapped the studbox up for me. She seemed nice enough."

"Well, it *must* be above board. One thing about Kirsty Nicholson, she's no' daft."

"Maybe it was him. Maybe he insisted."

"Insisted? For why would he do that?"

"'T' put all his eggs in one basket, so he can have one or the other whenever he feels the urge."

"That's terrible!"

"Maybe, but I wouldn't put anythin' past him."

"Well, I heard it wasn't her shop at all. I heard that Breezy Adair put up the money because he's hoppin' mad at Craig for cuttin' off wi' the family."

"I've always said that pride was Craig's failin'."

"I heard there'd been questions asked in Percy Street but they couldn't find anythin' illegal about the shop since it wasn't in his name or hers."

"The brother, Gordon; it'll be him that signed the documents."

"If y'ask me Kirsty's done the right thing. At least wi' a shop they'll no' starve. It's somethin' t' fall back on in case he blots his copybook again an' gets dismissed."

"Dismissed for what?"

"I shudder t' think."

"Well, whatever the story, I think it's a lovely wee shop," Mrs Piper concluded. "She's got a lot of nice things for sale. Even American tongs."

"American tongs! How much?"

"Six an' six."

"My God, they're a guinea at the Colosseum."

"I fair fancy a pair o' American tongs."

"Aye, but can y'afford them?"

"I think it might be arranged," said Jess Walker with a wink that drove her neighbours wild.

*   *   *

Before she plunged into making the shop ready for opening Kirsty made a promise to herself. She vowed that the master of the house, her husband, would suffer not one moment's inconvenience because of it.

Shopping, cooking, washing and mending were duties that she would not neglect and her days were still patterned according to Craig's shifts. Oddly, though, she seemed able to perform her domestic chores in half the time, as if time had magically expanded to accommodate the demands she put upon it. She was never tired now, never bored, and willingly chopped an hour or two off her night's sleep to meet the requirements of G. A. Nicholson's Domestic Emporium as well as caring for Craig.

She could not have managed at all if it hadn't been for Greta Taylor's unstinting co-operation. Together the women scrubbed the shop from floor to ceiling, scraped the dirt of ages from the exterior woodwork and, daring to take on the roles of tradesmen, stained, painted and varnished without assistance, even laid the tiled linoleum and lengths of hardwearing carpet that Gordon had had sent down from Adair's.

Calloused hands and broken fingernails worried Greta not one whit. She enjoyed tackling jobs which men made much of and had a patience that Kirsty lacked. On the other hand, Greta was not comfortable with pen and ink and left all the paperwork to Kirsty. The attempted installation of a stone sink and drain in the backshop put an end to self-reliance, however, for Greta, keen to try her hand at plumbing, almost drove a pickaxe through a gas pipe and, at Kirsty's insistence, thereafter relinquished the task to an expert.

The relationship between Kirsty and her assistant was forged in those weeks of hustle and hard labour. Craig was mentioned only out of necessity and reduced from person to pronoun.

"Is *he* on the back-shift?" Greta would ask.

"Aye," Kirsty would answer. "I'll need to go home soon to cook *his* dinner."

Eventually every trace of Harold Vosper Vokes was eradicated and any nosy parker who peeped into the doorway expecting a thrill was doomed to disappointment. For the women of Greenfield, Partick and Dowanhill, though, thrills of less gruesome aspect lay in store as the first boxes of stock began to arrive on handcarts and barrows from the inner recesses of Adair's warehouse.

Though Gordon steered clear, he did not withdraw his promised support. On the contrary; he took it upon himself to predict Kirsty's requirements and communicated advice by means of detailed, typewritten notes delivered with each consignment.

"Herewith," he would write, "7 Imitation Bamboo Triple Folding Mirrors, 10×10 size, Invoiced at 4/10d per Item. We'd suggest selling at 12/6d each. Retail catalogue prices run 18/3d to 23/9d for similar. We'd bear 13/3d each item, at y'r discretion.

"Enclosed also, 6 Red Japanned Coal Hods at 1/1d per Item, to sell at 2/6d each. Also 6 Half-Covered Copper-Oxydised Wellington Coal Hods at 2/10d per Item. Suggest selling latter at 7/6d each, against standard retail price of one guinea.

"Terms – 90 days, sale or return."

Boxes would be opened, items checked against invoices, costs entered in the Purchase Book, price labels tied to each article;

exciting stuff for Greta and the children. As the shop filled up with valuable goods, however, Kirsty became increasingly apprehensive. Fears of fire, flood and theft filled her mind and in the days before G. A. Nicholson's finally opened its doors to the public she fretted horribly and had to be calmed by frequent cups of tea and Greta's reassurances.

"Who's goin' to buy a copper coal hod," Kirsty would girn, "when their children are starvin'?"

"You'd be surprised what folk'll spend their money on," Greta would say. "Anyway, there aren't as many starvin' bairns about here as you might imagine."

"Would you buy a coal hod at that price?"

"Not me," Greta would answer.

"See, there you are."

"But I'd have one o' those triple mirrors in a flash."

"Why?"

"Because there's such a pretty face in them."

A couple of days later, at Kirsty's instigation, one of the triple mirrors was prominently displayed in the centre of the window with a professionally-lettered card beneath it: *Such a Pretty Face for 12/6d.*

Kirsty could not have guessed at the energy that her brother-in-law was expending to scoop up so many Small Stock items or how busily he buzzed around manufacturers to collect bargain wares to fill the shop's shelves.

"What the devil's this, Gordon?" Johnnie Whiteside would complain. "A measly half-dozen mirrors delivered from that rogue Wattle. And look at the terms! Good God, we pay Wattle cash then grant ninety days Sale or Return to your dear sister-in-law!"

"Buildin' up a customer, Johnnie, just buildin' up a customer."

"Damned nepotism!"

"Aye, I reckoned the Greeks would have a word for it," Gordon would say. "Look, just stamp the bloody invoice an' stop your moanin'."

"Does Breezy know what's going on?"

"Of course he does," Gordon would say.

"And he approves?"

"He'd better. It was his idea."

Brass trivets, toasting-forks, lightweight seamless washing-tubs, Kafe Kannes, unbreakable tumblers, candlesticks in sundry shapes, clothes-peg holders, surgical hot-water bottles, egg cups, cruet stands and butter shells, fancy boxes, dinner pails and Keep-Hot flasks poured into Nicholson's via Adair's in the course of the week.

Now that the word was out, troupes of salesmen from other warehouses arrived in Gascoigne Street by the hour eager to offer treasures from their sample cases; all sorts of silly things from carbolic tooth powder to chuck drills, at extravagant rates of discount.

"Gordon sent me," some would claim. "He's an old pal o' mine."

"I've come at great personal inconvenience to demonstrate the value of our new line in rawhide hammers."

"Embroidered pillowcases, Mrs Nicholson. I can just see your lovely head at repose on one of these."

Though she was friendly to the salesmen and not brusque Kirsty did not trust them and bought very little from that source.

On Friday, just before opening day, Gordon's best buy arrived: twenty-two sets of curling-tongs each with a patented soft muffled edge and with a picture of a golden-haired maiden preening under the legend *Miss Boston's Authentic American Curling-Irons* on the stiff pink cardboard lid.

"By God, I'd sell my soul for a pair o' those," said Greta, "especially at that price."

"You don't need tongs," said Kirsty. "Your hair's lovely."

"But straight," said Greta. "Ooo, curls! I'd love curls. I'd love to go bob-bob-bob along the road for once."

"Curled hair's just panderin' to vanity."

"'Course it is," said Greta. "It's all right for you, Kirsty; you've a natural wave. Me – I look like somebody's done a quick job wi' a blacklead brush. As soon as I can afford it, I'll buy a set o' those."

"Do you really think they'll be popular?"

"They'll be sold out by Saturday week, mark my words."

"Well, I hope you're right," said Kirsty.

"I'll put a box in the window, shall I?"

"Please do," said Kirsty.

* * *

Late that afternoon Kirsty ran home to Canada Road and, cheating just a little on her vow, left Craig a plate of cold meat cuts and

141

a salad and, to appease him, two chocolate eclairs from O'Dell's most expensive tray. She had expected Craig to be at home but was not unduly surprised to find that he had gone out. His uniform was still on its hanger and his boots, awaiting polish, on a newspaper by the hearth. He would have to return before his shift began and, if she was not kept too late, she would see him before he went out for the night.

She had no curiosity as to where her husband might be. She assumed that he had gone to the swimming-baths or to play billiards with another off-duty constable. She polished his boots to a high gloss and, still in her overcoat and hat, burnished his belt buckle and tunic buttons, brushed his trousers and set the lot out ready by his bed.

After a hasty snack of toasted cheese she left the house again at the gallop and was back in G. A. Nicholson's Domestic Emporium by half-past five, out of breath but glowing with excitement.

The shop looked wonderful, all new and shiny, an Aladdin's cave of copper, brass and silver-plate, softened by sunshades and purses, pillows and cotton towels; three hundred and forty pounds' worth of stock in all. Hands on hips, Kirsty surveyed the shelves and laden counter.

"It really does look like an emporium now, doesn't it?" she said.

"Better than the Colosseum," Greta agreed.

Kirsty had put Greta's weekly wages into a brown envelope and gave them to her now.

"Won't you miss your Saturdays at the Irish Market?"

"God, no," said Greta. "Too much like hard work, that. Gatherin', mendin', washin' clothes for six days, then eight or ten hours shiverin' at a stall for a handful of coppers. I'd far rather be here, believe me."

"Even . . . even under the circumstances?"

"I expect you have your reasons for treatin' me so well," said Greta.

"We've a lot in common."

Greta stiffened, her dark eyes suddenly angry.

"No, I don't mean . . ." Kirsty said hastily. "I meant that we're both orphans, an' we both came up the hard way."

Greta relaxed, nodded. "So long as you're satisfied, Kirsty, I am too."

"I'll be satisfied when we actually manage to sell something."

"Never fear about that," said Greta. "They'll be flockin' in here tomorrow."

"I hope you're right," Kirsty sighed.

She had a wad of unpaid bills in the drawer behind the counter and could not rid herself of fear of failure. If the shop did not succeed then she would have lost her nest-egg and would be back in Craig's pocket, at his mercy worse than ever.

"What you need's another cup of tea," Greta said. "I'll put the kettle on right now."

A gas ring in the backshop provided a cooking facility but, before Greta could pass through the curtain, the front door opened and Gordon staggered in.

He carried a heavy plyboard crate in his arms. His knees were buckling, his cheeks red and his hat was tipped so far over that it seemed to hang from one ear.

"Jeeze!" he gasped, as he slid the crate carefully on to the counter and slumped over to recover his breath. "I was never cut out t' be Samson, that's for sure."

"What do you think of it, Gordon?" Kirsty asked, gesturing towards the shelves.

"Not bad, is it?" Greta said.

Gordon rolled on his elbows and took a long look at the interior of the shop.

"For a hole in the wall," he said, "it's all right, I suppose." He grinned. "Pretty magnificent, actually."

"Do you really think so?"

"Aye, it'll knock a lot of eyes out on Dumbarton Road. Give some o' those lazy devils that call themselves shopkeepers somethin' to think about." He poked a finger into one of the plump feather pillows that hung in a net from a hook behind him. "I see Bruno got here?"

"He said you sent him," Kirsty said. "Did you?"

"'Course I did," Gordon answered. "Hell, Adair's warehouse is practically empty, since everythin's down here on Sale or Return." He turned deliberately to Greta. "Good evenin', Mrs Taylor. I trust you're well?"

"I'm very well, thank you, Mr Nicholson."

"I'm glad t' hear it," Gordon said and, having begun to make his peace, continued the process by prising open the lid of the crate and scooping out handfuls of straw packing.

"What have you got there?" Greta asked.

143

"You'll see," said Gordon.

Bobby and Jen, who had been dabbling at the sink in the backshop, emerged now, dripping wet, to watch Uncle Gordon climb on to the counter and slip his hands into the crate. Slowly he lifted out a gleaming metal check-till and lowered it gingerly to the counter.

He hopped to the floor and brushed a fragment of straw from the till with his cuff. "Handsome, ain't it?"

"Oh, Gordon, it's gorgeous," said Kirsty.

"The mechanical cashier," Gordon reeled off the facts, "is simple to operate, easy to maintain and prevents deception on the part of the customer and error on the part of the staff. It provides a printed record of all purchases and a total of the day's takin's."

"How does it work?" Greta asked.

"Easy-peasy." Gordon prodded one of the machine's red keys and a drawer sprang open with a *ping*. "It's all in the book of instructions. First one of these in the country; not even Sir Thomas Lipton has one yet."

"But how much does it cost?" asked Kirsty.

"It's my treat," said Gordon. "A peace offerin'."

"Oh, Gordon, there's no need . . ."

"Aye, but there is," he said and offered his cheek to Kirsty who, laughing, kissed it.

He bent down so that Bobby and Jen in turn could plant a smacker on his cheek but he was startled when Greta touched his arm, held him steady and kissed him too.

"You don't mind, do you?" Greta said.

"On the contrary," said Gordon, blushing, while behind him, for no apparent reason, the mechanical cashier went *ping*.

*   *   *

It was a warm, dry, dusty evening in the heights of the Kelvinhaugh. A scouring breeze off the river brought the chatter of rolling stock over the Stobcross engine sheds and the undulating whine of saws from the nearby moulding mills which, with work on hand, were digging in with night shifts over the weekend.

The tenement in Potiphar Street was respectably nondescript, not too posh, not too much of a slum. Faced with grey stone, not red, it sank into the long shadows cast by the buildings opposite and its gas-lights seemed niggardly and self-effacing even in thickening gloom.

Craig had walked from the Greenfield. He wore his uniform. Tonight he needed its authority, its assurance. He had a conscience about what he was going to do, and gut nervousness about confronting the woman, Lizzie Straun.

He walked faster than copper's pace, found the close and climbed the stairs. He paused on each landing to peer at the brass name-plates, to listen, without cause, at the deeply recessed glass doors or the wooden ones that protected them.

It was a silent building, empty, not in the way the Madagascar seemed empty but with a strange sepulchral hollowness, as if each of the large apartments were occupied by some one person who, sensing his youth, felt threatened by it and lay quite still, listening too as he passed on.

He reached the top landing, did not find her name there either and thinking, not without relief, that Prue Alston had lied to him or had lost touch with the woman, Straun, he was about to turn and descend again when he caught sight of a narrow stone staircase going up, up into the roof, it seemed.

Lizzie Straun lived up there in the garret flat.

The door too was narrow, with a peculiar arch over it, and no glass, only a brass plate and a brass knob for a bell-pull. He jerked the knob with his fingers, brought it out on its rod and heard the response inside, a fragile tinkling sound as if the bell were made of glass.

He wanted a cigarette. He wanted a drink.

"Who's there?"

"Police."

"Who's there?"

"Police. Constable Nicholson."

"Who?"

"Open the door, please, Mrs Straun."

"I'm alone."

"I just want a word with you, that's all."

Her voice sounded strong, with a rough defensive edge to it, something he had grown used to hearing in his years on the streets. He was prepared for a type, for a rawboned, scowling woman who would greet him with hands on hips, to whom the law would be a natural enemy.

Lizzie Straun, however, was withered with age. A little lace

145

cap clung to her wispy grey hair. A lace bib was pinned to the bosom of her dress with a cameo brooch. The dress itself was of rich stuff but even Craig could see that the cut was quaint, all stiff frilled, with the remains of a bustle that hung from her hips like a deformity, so shrunken was the woman now.

She held the door in one hand, and advanced the other, palm out, as if to ward him off. She was not small in stature but crouched dwarfishly in the half-open doorway and squinted up at him.

Craig bent, as if to converse with a child.

"There's nothin' to be frightened of, Mrs Straun. I just want a wee word wi' you, that's all."

"Miss, I'm Miss, Miss Straun."

"Well, Miss Straun . . ."

"They're all gone away."

"Pardon?" Craig said.

"None o' them here now."

"Who's gone away?"

"You should see Jamie, no' me."

"Jamie?"

"Jamie'll pay ye."

"I'm not here for pay," said Craig.

He glanced down the steep staircase into the grey stone emptiness below.

She caught his sleeve, and he flinched.

She said, "What day is this?"

"Saturday."

"Is it Christmas yet?"

"No, it's April," Craig said. "A while yet t' Christmas, Miss Straun."

"You're dark. Are you him? Are you come for me?"

"No, I haven't come for you at all," Craig said. "I just want a wee talk with you, Miss Straun; half an hour of your time."

She nodded jerkily, the cap bobbing loose as if her skull had diminished in size even in the last few minutes.

"Come in then," she said, "for what it's worth."

She shuffled away into the interior of the big square hall and left Craig to close the door and follow.

He had not anticipated that a garret flat in the Kelvinhaugh would be so spacious. Confronted by three doors, all opening on to unlighted rooms, he loitered uncertainly. "Where are you, Miss Straun?"

"In here. Sittin' down."

Hesitantly he entered a drawing-room to the front of the house. The dormer window was screened by a fine mesh curtain that let in a wash of light, hardly light at all but only that late-evening memory of light that the riverside wards seemed to retain in this season. There was coal in the iron grate but hardly enough of it to give smoke, never mind flame.

If, at that moment, the woman had not struck a match and held it to the wick of an oil-lamp, Craig would have tripped over the cradle that stood just inside the door. It was a little swinging thing of wicker and carved pine. It was neatly made up, pillowed, shrouded in muslin and faded lace and he could not help but peep into it.

"Nah, nah," said Lizzie Straun. "I told ye. They're all gone."

She was seated in an old smoking chair. She held the lamp in both hands, its base on her knees, its glow defining every crease and wrinkle of her face. Suddenly she elevated the lamp, raised it high.

"See for yourself," she told him. "None o' them left for auld Lizzie to look after now."

"No babies, is that what you mean?"

"I'll be greetin' my dear wee ones in heaven all too soon," the woman said. "I'll no' be denied that, will I?"

"I'm sure you won't," said Craig.

"Who are you?"

"I'm Constable Nicholson."

She gestured to him to come closer. Craig picked his way to the chair. She gave him the lamp and he placed it, as instructed, on top of a miniature harmonium.

The room was cluttered with many small pieces of furniture; a sewing-table, a workbox, footstools, chests and coffers, and a number of ornamental clocks, none of which seemed to be working.

Sepia portraits, framed in fretwork or stamped tin, hung on the walls and were propped on every available surface, including the fender. Suspended here and there from eyelets and rails were tiny petticoats and frocks in *broderie anglaise*, shawls and satin pelerines. White satin hoods, trimmed with silk braid, were capped on wooden stands and by them, row by row, a dozen pairs of boots, small as snailshells, gaitered in cloth or cashmere and tassel-trimmed.

Craig shivered. He folded his arms to hide his distaste.

Lizzie Straun said, "Is it Glasgow you're from?"

"Greenfield."

"Did Hugh Affleck send you?"

"No, I came off my own bat."

"But Hughie told you where I lived?"

"Greta Taylor told me where to find you."

"Too late," said Lizzie Straun. "It's all done, the last o' them seen off."

"You mean you've gone out o' business?"

"Aye," she admitted. "Hugh Affleck never got us caught, though it wasn't from want o' tryin'. Him an' Sergeant Payne."

"How long ago was this?"

"Years ago. Years an' years ago."

"Is this where you kept the infants while you found homes for them?"

"Here," said Lizzie Straun, "an' elsewhere."

"At Sylvie's house?"

"Sylvie! That – "

She spat out an obscenity, one that Craig had never heard a woman use before.

"Is Sylvie out o' business too?" he said.

"Fine for her, och, aye. She's swannin' it up wi' her man, swankin' it in down by the sea."

Craig said, "Greta said you could help me."

"Greta?"

"Greta Taylor," Craig said.

He had shifted his position, come closer to the hearth. On the floor by the side of the smoking chair hidden from view until now, were bowls and basins, a stained towel and a fluted green bottle that, if his guess was right, contained an opiate.

"I don't know any Greta Taylor."

"How about Prue Alston?" Craig said. "Do you know her?"

"Look," the woman said, pointing. "See that one, the one in the maplewood frame? Bring me that one."

The frame was greasy with dirt; in daylight, Craig thought, the whole room would show its neglect. He carried the photograph to her. It was, in fact, a collage. Eight or ten tiny faces, sickly as seraphim, stared out through the greasy glass; not photographs at all, he realised, but coloured scraps, blurred like reality and faded by the passage of time.

The woman patted the broad arm of the chair. Craig hunkered down by her side. He could smell syrupy opiate on her breath, and her desiccated flesh beneath unwashed clothes. He was glad that he had chosen to wear his uniform. He had squared up to worse things in uniform.

She angled the glass, stroking it, as if she could caress the skin of the babies that the scraps represented in her mind. He might have supposed that she had loved them all, cared more for them than for the profits they had made for her, except that he could not put from his head the foulness of the word she had used against McNish.

He steadied himself, said softly, "Are these all yours?"

"All mine," the woman answered.

"Until you sold them?"

"Got them good homes."

"How much a head?"

She rubbed the glass, spat on it, dry spit, and rubbed again, making it squeak. Heavy paper, impressed with gaudy colour, soulful expressions, ringlets, curled lashes; Craig stared in revulsion and saw among the faces a likeness to Greta and to Kirsty too. He felt sick suddenly. He shot to his feet and stepped back, stepped away from the old woman.

None of the scraps bore the slightest resemblance to Greta or to Kirsty. Illusions, sentimental lies; the bairns that Lizzie Straun had handled had been nothing like this. They had been poor and ailing and unloved. They had been abandoned, sold off for a few shillings, deserted, flung aside.

If he had not been in uniform he might have wept.

Sammy was like that and, he realised, Kirsty. He had wanted her too much to take account of her past, to see into the time before the time he had known her. She had always just been Clegg's lassie, the girl from Hawkhead. She had never talked of her childhood, when she had belonged to nobody at all, when she was just another brat in the Baird Home, shorn and numbered and destined to be got rid of as soon as she was grown.

He had a sudden flashing image of nights at Dalnavert with his mother and father. However bad the bickering had seemed it had been nothing to the emptiness of being alone, alone without end. He thought of Sammy Reynolds and the old whistle, how the boy blew and blew upon it until his cheeks turned red, and knew now, there in the baby-room, what desperate sound Sammy heard that he could not.

He reached forward, took the frame from the woman's hands and flung it aside.

"Now listen t' me, you old bitch . . ."

"Leave me alone."

"You do know Greta Taylor. You sold her the child, Jen."

"Aw, naw, naw."

"You took her to Benedict Street, settled her there."

"I'm . . . I'm dyin', y'know."

"Maybe you are, maybe you're not," Craig said. "That's none o' my business. I need to know about the child you sold t' Greta Taylor."

"It wasn't sold. *She* was paid."

"Who paid her?"

"Sylvie McNish."

"An' who paid Sylvie?"

"How would I know?"

"Because you *do* know," Craig said. "Do you want me to send for Hughie Affleck an' Sergeant Payne? They'll wring it out you fast enough."

"Payne's dead," she told him, smugly.

Craig placed a hand on her shoulder and pushed her gently back against the scuffed leather upholstery.

"Whose bairn is she?"

"Ask Sylvie."

"I'm askin' you."

"I do not know. That's the God's truth. I do not know. Sylvie attended that one herself. All I did was keep the bairn here for a while an' then see to it that she was took to Greta at the new house in Benedict Street."

"Who paid for the house?"

"I heard, only heard, that it was Breezy Adair," the woman said. "D'you know who Breezy Adair is?"

"Oh, aye," said Craig quietly. "I know him all right."

"He owned the property. He paid the fee, an' support."

"Support?"

"Bread money."

"Was that usual?"

Lizzie Straun laughed. She was not afraid of him. She had tried to gull him with sentimentality and had failed but her gutter origins were bred in the bone and would rescue her now, at the last, as they had rescued her time and again in the past.

"Never," she said. "It was an important man fathered that bairn, I'll tell ye."

"Breezy Adair?"

She shook her head. "I doubt it. Nah, it was somebody else."

"Who?"

"Only Sylvie could tell ye that."

"Doesn't Greta Taylor know?"

"Probably not. Just Sylvie."

"An' where's Sylvie McNish now?"

"Doon the watter."

Craig had been in Glasgow quite long enough to understand the popular jargon. Sylvie McNish had retired, down river, to one of the Clyde's coastal resorts.

"Which town?"

"Dunoon," Lizzie Straun said, and told him the address without further prompting.

He straightened and stepped away from her again, still queasy in that atmosphere of sickness and decay.

She said, "I am dyin', you know."

Craig said, "How many o' *them* died, Lizzie?"

"Precious few," she said. "I took good care o' them, whatever else you might think."

"Assets, eh?"

"Poor wee bastards," she said. "For some I was their only chance."

"What about those that didn't survive? What happened to them?"

"Tam McNish took care o' them."

"Sylvie's husband?"

"Aye," said Lizzie. "He'd come an' take them away."

"The bodies, you mean?"

"Aye."

"What did he do with them?"

She shook her head.

"What else did Tam McNish do?" Craig asked.

"He ran the girls for a while," said Lizzie, "until he discovered there was more money in babies."

"An' Hugh Affleck tried to nail him, didn't he?"

"For ten years, give or take," said Lizzie Straun. "But Tam an' Sylvie were too clever by half for the Inspector."

"An' now they've retired."

"Aye, an' left me t' die," said Lizzie.

She swore again, the same filthy word, and struggled to get to her feet.

Craig did not offer to help. He might have got more from her yet, details of how the trade had functioned, how the children had been acquired and to whom they had been sold. But he had no stomach for more questions, more answers.

He had been shaken by recognition of his neglect of Kirsty. Until that night he had assumed that he had given her all that she was entitled to, that he had provided for her needs, and that her needs had been compatible with his own.

He watched the woman stoop and lift the framed collage from the floor. She rubbed it tenderly with her thumb and stared at the vacuous little faces, pressed out of paper.

"Have you got a wife, copper?" she asked.

"Yes," Craig said.

"An' bairns?"

"One son."

"Lucky them, eh!" said Lizzie Straun then prodded him ungraciously with the picture frame, steered him out of the drawing-room, out of the garret and back down the steep stone steps to the street.

*   *   *

By mid-summer it was apparent that Nicholson's Domestic Emporium was on the road to success. American curling-tongs and triple mirrors at bargain prices had lured customers into No. 1 Gascoigne Street and even thrifty ladies from the other side of Dumbarton Road were not above dropping in to survey the ever-changing stock. Gordon remained on the alert for small lots of domestic goods, the sort of thing that Kirsty could retail at a profit and the shop's high monthly turnover was due largely to Gordon's diligence and flair. Bills were paid on time, lines of credit established with warehouses other than Adair's, and a regular clientele, as well as a passing trade, established rather more quickly than had at first seemed possible.

Mr John Whiteside and Mr Eric Adair were sufficiently intrigued by the new retail phenomenon to stroll along Dumbarton Road one Saturday afternoon to see for themselves just how busy and bustling Nicholson's had become.

They stood across the road from the shop and watched the

window-shoppers and the steady traffic in and out of the door of No. 1 Gascoigne Street with their usual supercilious indifference.

"Seems our Gordon is doin' rather well for himself," Eric said. "Two or three years of reapin' the benefit of that wee gold mine and he'll be buying us out."

"Oh, I would doubt that, old chum," said Johnnie.

"Shall we put a spoke in his little wheel?"

"Not yet," Johnnie said. "In time, perhaps."

Eric said, "Is her highness there? Can you see her?"

"Indeed she is, lookin' frightfully decent and respectable."

"But we know better, don't we, John?"

"She can't hide *her* little secrets behind a clean frock and frilly cuffs, not from us, she can't."

"I wonder if Mrs Nicholson knows just what she's taken on?"

"I doubt it. Mrs Nicholson is just an innocent country lass," John Whiteside said, "even if she does fancy herself as a lady of business."

"I could do a little business there myself, if you know what I mean?"

"Kirsty Nicholson? She'd never wear it," said Johnnie. "She'd have the law on yer quick as a flash."

"She's already got the law on her; that's the trouble," Eric said. "Seen enough?"

"Quite enough," said Johnnie Whiteside.

The cousins were not the only ones interested in what was happening in Gascoigne Street. In spite of her reluctance to make the first move Madge had been too curious to stay away for long. She had turned up, one moist May afternoon, in a landau fit for a queen, complete with her new lady's maid in tow.

Kirsty, however, was not behind the counter but had popped off home to prepare an early-evening meal for Craig who was, inconveniently, on the day-shift that fortnight.

"Yes, madam," said Greta. "May I help you?"

The shop contained no other customers which was just as well, for Madge had assumed her loudest and most proprietorial air. "Will you inform Mrs Nicholson that Mrs Adair wishes t' speak with her."

"Mrs Nicholson isn't here," said Greta.

"Why is she not?"

"She's at home makin' her man's dinner."

"An' who, may I ask, are you?"

"I'm Mrs Nicholson's assistant."

"My son owns this property, y'know."

"Aye, madam. I know," said Greta. "Gordon's told me all about you."

"Gordon? Do you think it's proper for you t' refer to your employer wi' such familiarity?"

Greta could hardly keep her face straight.

Not only had she been to bed with this pompous woman's elder son, she had once been hired to give young Mr Nicholson his first lesson in the art of love.

Prudently Greta said nothing. She watched Madge poke about the shelves in desultory fashion for a minute or two, relieved that Jen and Bobby had gone off with Kirsty and were not present to be patronised by this snooty cow.

Madge purchased nothing and soon wafted off, calling her poor servant to heel as if she were a collie dog.

"She'll be back," Kirsty said, when she was informed of the visit. "She's too nosy to stay away. In any case, she hasn't seen Bobby for months and it's a good way to play at bein' a grandma wi'out havin' to climb down an' call at Canada Road."

"How did you put up with her for all those months?"

"With difficulty," Kirsty said.

Madge, however, did not return to Gascoigne Street.

Instead it was Lorna Nicholson who became a regular visitor to the shop.

With a term at commercial college behind her and some experience of the world, Lorna had lost her sullen shyness. She had always liked Kirsty and had regretted the rift that had separated her from her sister-in-law. Two or three times a week she would make the long walk down from Great Western Terrace for she was fascinated by what Kirsty had achieved and was eager to put her recently acquired commercial skills into practice.

After a certain amount of cat-dancing, Lorna had blurted out a request to see the account books and, in the same breath, swore that she would tell nobody what secrets they contained. Kirsty had no objection for she liked and trusted the girl. So, on many a summer evening, Lorna would be found perched on a stool in the backshop in Gascoigne Street, inkcuffs over her sleeves and pen in hand forging ahead with paperwork that Kirsty had laid out for her attention or compiling columnar tables of stock-in-hand

and profit analyses, all of which impressed Gordon no end when he was shown the results of his sister's labours.

Though he had made his peace with Kirsty, Gordon was not a frequent caller at the shop that bore his name. It was too much of a woman's world for him. He confined his visits to the last hour of business, between seven and eight in the evening, when Greta was sometimes alone. He would help her put up the shutters, count the cash and lock the door, would walk her to the corner of Kingdom Road and would even carry Jen in his arms if the day had been warm and the child was sleepy.

Craig was the only member of the family who appeared to have no interest at all in Kirsty's bold venture. He betrayed not the slightest curiosity about the shop and, for obvious reasons, did not deign to call there. He even managed to ignore most of Bobby's innocent prattle about Jen Taylor and the adventures of the day. At home Craig was more civil than he had been for months, however. On the two or three occasions when Kirsty tripped over her schedule and was not there to make his evening meal, he did not berate her, but simply shrugged off her neglect as if it were unimportant.

Everything seemed to be settling for all of them and Craig fell into habits that pleased Kirsty. He would go swimming with the newly-formed Greenfield Aquatic Club or would play bowls with Archie or Peter Stewart on the public green at Marlborough instead of mooching about the house when he was off-duty.

Kirsty's only fear was that she would become pregnant. At this time pregnancy would be very inconvenient. Craig still made love to her, but not demandingly. The almost wordless love-making satisfied her, for Craig's vigour had not been affected by the shift in the basis of their relationship, though he no longer took her for granted. It was at those times, however, that she would recall David to mind and realise, with a faint sense of loss, how seldom she thought of him now and how her romantic notion that they would remain united in spirit had not lived up to itself.

The letter arrived by first post on a balmy morning in mid-June. Craig had been fed and had gone to bed after a night-shift and Bobby was crouched on the floor contentedly mutilating a newspaper with a pair of safety scissors.

The envelope bore the markings of strange foreign ports and currencies and seemed so out of place among the toast crumbs and porridge plates that she could not quite believe that it contained a letter from a man she had loved.

Outside it was a warm weekday morning in Greenfield Burgh. China, and David, seemed so incredibly far away. For a moment she was tempted not to open the letter at all but to put it, unread, on the fire. She was shocked, made ashamed, by her lack of interest and concern about David Lockhart now. When she thought of it, all she wanted was to be told that he still loved her, to be assured that his passion had proved more enduring than her own.

She opened it at last.

The handwriting was tiny, controlled, run so close to each margin that the letter resembled a tract or scholarly essay. It had been written at the American Mission in Shanghai five weeks ago.

She read:

Dear Kirsty,

This is mail day and I only have time to write you the shortest of letters if I want to catch the steamer, the Peking. I came over on this same ship, in fact. She has been to Hong Kong and is now on her way back to England, back home. I find it strange to set down that word – home, I mean – for I have finally lost all sense of true direction and I can truly say that I am not sure whether I am coming or going.

Having travelled so far from good old, grey old Glasgow, and having been 'holed up' – as my American friends would say – in Shanghai for many days now, I confess that I am anxious to press forward.

All my thoughts are of my family, of finding a train that will take me to Weimein and another that will transport me to Kuang where Jack will meet me. From there we will ride on horseback up to Fanshi, some six days into the hills. I would not have tarried so long in this city but I have been informed by Mr Abbott, o/c the American Mission, that charging off on any old puffer that is heading north is not a sound idea at the moment as the political climate is far from stable.

Kirsty felt her heart go cold. She could not conceive of railway journeys that took weeks to complete, of destinations so far removed from their starting points in time as well as distance.

On the second page of the letter David had used the phrase again: "All my thoughts are with my family now."

She began to realise that his residence in Glasgow, and perhaps his love for her, had been nothing but a disruption to the true and undeviating purpose of his life, that China, his father and brother and the mission had never lost their hold on him after all.

He asked after Bobby, Lorna, Craig, even enquired about Sammy Reynolds, of all people, in a single short polite paragraph, as if each now had an equal measure in the mixture of memories of home.

Kirsty read on:

Sometimes I think that I would like to drop in on you unexpectedly, just to see what you are doing and to surprise you. Here in Shanghai it is four o'clock in the afternoon so I suppose that it will be the middle of the night in Greenfield and that you will be fast asleep. But there is precious little chance of a return to Glasgow for a long, long time so perhaps it is better if I give up dwelling on it and continue to look forward to reaching Fanshi instead.

Kirsty began to cry. She hid her thin, sipping sobs from Bobby as best she could and dabbed her eyes with the corner of a handkerchief.

If the doorbell rang now and she opened it, found David on the step, what would she do? How would she react? She no longer knew, and, in that moment, recognised that her love for him had been selfish and immature.

Bobby was staring at her, scissors poised over a strip of newspaper. He was all ready for the day, face washed, hair combed, waiting to be taken to the shop.

Kirsty dried her eyes, tucked the handkerchief away and got to her feet. She folded the letter, put it into its envelope and hid it beneath a loose board in the bottom of the pot cupboard.

She did not know why she kept it, however, for she did not intend to reply.

*   *   *

In July the Whitesides, Beadles and Adairs would separate the tenuous bonds that held them together and each family would go off in a different direction to spend the summer in residence by the sea or in the mountains. Before the parting of the ways, however, there fell one of those odd clan rituals that had somehow sneaked on to the calendar unbidden and, since it could not be removed, had to be endured.

Invitations to James Randolph Adair's Garden Party were received with shudders and groans.

Vivid memories of previous garden parties at The Knowe gave rise to pessimism and a desperate search for excuses to be elsewhere on that day of days. Death might have got you decently out of it; anything less definite would be regarded as an insult to Dolphus and his indelicate spouse.

The trouble with Dolphus's garden party was that it was done on the cheap. The long buffet would consist of garden salads, wrinkled sandwiches and cheeses that had narrowly escaped the soapworks. The wine would be Belgian and only the beer, Carruth's, of course, would be drinkable. One marquee, all brown and tattered, would have been rolled out and erected to give shelter from sun or rain, and admission to the house was emphatically not encouraged. The dearth of sanitary facilities meant queuing for hours in the hall or a nervous and undignified expedition into the brambles and ferns beyond the garden wall.

Gordon's invitation, on a cheaply printed card, came second post to the warehouse.

"What the hell is this?" he asked, holding it up.

"Dolphus Day," said Johnnie, bleakly.

"Oh, God, not another one." Eric held his invitation as gingerly as an unsprung mousetrap. "I've barely recovered from last year's fiasco."

"What's wrong with a garden party?" Gordon asked.

"Nothing," said Johnnie. "But this isn't an ordinary garden party. Our dear Uncle Dolphus has yet to realise that you can't buy style on the cheap, you see."

Gordon turned the card over.

Penned on the back in violet ink was a personal message: *I forgive you, dearest. Please do come. A.*

Flustered, he tucked the card hastily into his pocket.

He had no idea what sin required Amanda's forgiveness. It was he who had been embarrassed by her forwardness, not the other way about. Nonetheless he felt a stab of guilt, along with relief that Amanda thought enough of him to offer absolution and a second chance.

"Aw, wook, the widdle man's blushin'," said Eric.

"A *billet-doux*, by God, from his light o' love," said Johnnie. "What else could it be?"

"Has he been forgiven then?" said Eric.

"Of course he's been forgiven," said Johnnie.

In unison the cousins chanted, "But what's he been forgiven *for*, that's what we'd like to know."

"Nothin' happened," Gordon mumbled.

"Perhaps he touched her . . . sensibilities," said Eric.

"Or penetrated her . . . defences," said Johnnie.

"Oh, bloody put a sock in it," said Gordon. "She's only a young girl and deserves more respect."

The cousins laughed uproariously at such a display of naivety as Gordon grabbed his hat and stalked out of the office.

When the subject of James Randolph's garden party came up again that evening at dinner, Breezy was more stoical.

"It's a bit of a bore, really, I suppose. But we can salvage the evenin' by havin' dinner at the Crabtree Inn. It's not far from The Knowe and they set a damned good table there. What do you say?"

"Us?" Lorna glanced at her brother, who shrugged.

"It won't kill the pair of you to dine out with your mother and me."

"I've . . . I've made other plans," said Lorna.

"Plans to hang round some cheap shop in the Greenfield, like as not," said Madge.

Lorna poked her spoon at the sponge pudding on her plate and did not answer.

Gordon said, "I'm still not clear what this garden party's in aid of."

Breezy said, "I reckon Dolphus just likes to give us all an annual reminder that he's got more money than any of the rest of us."

"From what I hear," said Gordon, "he's hardly lavish with it."

"He means well," said Breezy.

"That," said Gordon, "is a phrase that covers a multitude o' sins."

Lorna said, "It's all right for you, Gordon, your 'friend' will be there."

"There'll be lots of young folk there, sweetheart," said Breezy. "You'll enjoy yourself. Why, I'll bet you're the belle of the ball."

"Is there a ball afterwards?" said Madge, perking up. "What can I possibly wear for a . . . ?"

"No ball, chookie," said Breezy patiently. "A buffet lunch, of sorts, a few daft games on the grass, a band . . ."

"Don't tell me," said Gordon. "The Boys' Brigade?"

"How did you guess?" said Breezy.

"I'm otherwise engaged," said Lorna.

"Oh, no, you're not, milady," said Madge. "You're goin'. You're both goin', like it or lump it."

"The best thing about it is that it's all over by six o'clock," Breezy said. "So – I'll order us a proper carriage an' we'll show Dolphus what real style looks like, right?"

"All right," Gordon agreed.

Madge smiled. "It'll do us all good to enjoy a breath o' country air an' get a touch o' the sun on our faces, won't it, Albert?"

"Yes, dear," said Breezy.

*   *   *

Rain came in from the west about twenty past twelve. It had been lying all morning like a wet cloth draped over the hills and, just as Albert Adair's hired carriage ground up the road from Milngavie, cloud closed in and enveloped The Knowe in a cold, heavy drizzle.

Madge had ignored her husband's advice and had dressed for the occasion and not the climate. She wore a creamy white satin creation, trimmed with net frills and baby ribbon and complete with trailing hemline. Satin slippers, a huge hat composed of flittering ribbons and a muslin parasol suggested that she was bound for Monte Carlo and not Milngavie.

Sensibly, Breezy had changed his cream flannels and striped jacket for a tweed suit, shoes for boots and his best boater for a deerstalker with earflaps.

Lorna too had used her noddle and had buttoned herself inside a machine-stitched day dress whose heavy folds hid several layers of underwear. Gordon seemed to be clad for mountaineering not socialising and as the carriage ran into the barrage of raindrops that swept horizontally over the driveway and lawns he was damned glad that he had not given in to vanity after all.

"On a day like this," said Madge, "lunch is bound to be served indoors."

"I wouldn't bank on it," said Breezy.

"Why ever not?" said Madge.

"Because the passage of all those feet would wear out the carpets," said Gordon.

"You can't be serious," said Lorna.

"Oh yes he can," said Breezy.

The gravel of the drive had already begun to turn to mush and the coaches of sundry Adairs stood like abandoned river-craft under flexing pines. The house itself presented a façade as dour and impenetrable as the temple of a Nilotic rain god. In the mouth of the marquee guests huddled like the sheep in a dog trial. Already the tent had begun to list a bit and Sinclair Smith, looking less than debonair, sheltered under a ragged scallop on the lee side and, from a distance, appeared to be making a book on the survival rate of certain ladies in the company.

Since no other refuge offered itself, Lorna and Gordon scuttled for the camp in the middle of the lawn while Breezy helped Madge pick her way across the puddled grass and held her silly parasol over her silly hat.

The marquee was crowded. Camp stools had been unearthed for some of the less youthful guests but most folk were standing. Gordon recognised Edward and wife Lizzie, Donnie and Nuala and son Phillip. Sister Polly was making the best of it but Robert and Heather Whiteside were sulking while Aunt Evelyn Mungall, ignored as usual, was consoling herself with a tankard of German beer.

The younger generation had shaken itself into the sagging corner of the tent. They were, for the most part, animated and sarcastic to the tight-lipped chagrin of the two maid-servants who were ferrying bowls of salad from a handcart by the door. Cigarette smoke mingled with the odours of pickled onions, boiled beetroot, crushed grass and sodden canvas.

"Penance," Johnnie Whiteside was saying to an audience of girl cousins. "Penance, that's what this is; a religious rite to which we are all subjected to remind us how fortunate we are not to be farm labourers or field hands."

Patricia, Polly's middle daughter, giggled.

"If you are very wicked in this life," said Johnnie, "perhaps you'll be sent back as a peasant in the next."

"May I remind you," said Josephine, Walter's eldest and a bit of an unknown quantity, "that our grandfather is a so-called peasant. And I for one do not believe that we should poke fun at the lower orders."

161

"I offer sympathy, dear child," said Johnnie. "I'd never poke fun at our noble ancestor."

"Even if he is, let's be honest, something of a piggywig, really," said Eric.

"Have you ever met him?" said Josephine.

"Actually, no," said Eric, who was not pleased at being challenged by the tall and angular cousin.

"Well, I have," said Josephine.

"Did you hoe a few rows of turnips while you were out at Garscadden?" said Johnnie. "To justify your peasant origins, sort of thing."

"Grandfather's a dairy farmer."

"A piggywig, from what I hear," said Eric.

"No, Eric," Josephine said, "*you're* the piggywig," and she turned on her heel and walked pointedly away.

Eric, without contrition, tapped a finger to his brow to indicate that he thought his cousin crazy to hold such radical opinions and Johnnie laughed his suave laugh to cover the moment.

Lorna tugged Gordon's sleeve. "Is *she* here?"

"Who?"

"Your sweetheart."

"No," said Gordon. "And she ain't my sweetheart."

"Then you're not tryin' hard enough," said Lorna and slipped away to find her stepfather at whose side she felt comparatively safe.

There were no signs of Dolphus, Olive or any of the daughters and some guests were beginning to mutter mutinously.

"Beggar'll be snug indoors scoffin' his lunch."

"Pea soup an' steak pie, no doubt."

"For two pins I'd storm the bastions, an' forget my manners."

"Why don't we just leave, dear?"

"What, and forgo this wonderful hospitality?"

"I'll give him a piece of my mind when he does show up."

"No, you won't. You never do."

"Ah-hah! Here's his majesty now."

There was a general movement towards the door to witness Dolphus's arrival.

He wore a frock coat, black button boots, gaiters and, of all things, a top hat. A rusty mackinaw draped his shoulders and a wizened little man hopped behind him vainly trying to keep a brolly raised over the master's head.

Behind James Randolph came Olive, Nanny and the four daughters, all as bedraggled as pullets and squabbling volubly among themselves.

"Oh, my Goad!" exclaimed Aunt Evelyn Mungall loudly. "Will ye look at that now!"

It was not just the pomposity of Dolphus's arrival that tickled the collective funny bone but the fact that he had obviously rehearsed it. The instant that Dolphus set foot upon the lawn the band of the local Boys' Brigade squelched from a hiding-place in the shrubbery and bravely tootled *Chieftain's Welcome* with shivering lips and frozen fingers.

Breezy did his best to choke his laughter but he could not restrain it. Out it came in a hoot as the poor band boys slithered to a halt by the marquee. Sinclair Smith was next to lose control; then Polly, shrill and cackling. Brother Donnie's booming laugh, so rarely heard, started others off and soon even cool-mannered youngsters and timid children were falling about, some so overwhelmed that they had to be supported or supplied with stools.

Dolphus stared down his nose at his relatives.

He adjusted his topper, waved back the lackey with the brolly and strode through the company to the buffet table, followed by his ruffled, rain-speckled brood, while the band thumped and tootled and guessed at notes that the rain had washed into an inky blur.

Dolphus howked an orange box from under the trestle. He climbed on to it, amid gales of laughter, and held up his arms for silence.

Nobody bothered.

"Gie's a song then, Randy," yelled Aunt Evelyn Mungall, and waved her tankard to encourage him.

"Yes, yes. Song, song."

Gordon glanced at Amanda. She had buried her face in her hands and leaned on Nanny as if the woman could rescue her from humiliation. Olive, on the other hand, seemed quite unperturbed. Indeed, the little smirk on her lips suggested that she might even be enjoying this turn of events.

"Come along, Dolphus, old chap," called out brother Walter. "Don't disappoint us."

"Aye, give us *Wearie Wullie*," shouted Sinclair Smith. "By God, man, you used to warble that a treat."

Dolphus did his best to ignore his cousin, and all the other rebels too.

"I am glad . . ." he began. "I AM GLAD . . ."

"Glad, glad, glad," cheered Heather and Polly together, clapping their hands in patacake fashion.

". . . GLAD TO SEE THAT THE WEATHER HAS NOT DAMPED THE ADAIR SPIRITS."

"Spirits! Make mine a double whisky, thanks."

"As your host . . ."

The bandmaster, thoroughly lost, led his lads suddenly into a Scotch medley, conducting them at a frantic tempo so that they might possibly finish the piece before the rain wiped out the music once again.

Dolphus closed his eyes and swayed.

Olive prompted him, "We welcome you to our humble home."

"Yes. WE WELCOME YOU TO OUR HUMBLE . . ."

"TENT," the brothers bawled together.

"What's wrong with you?" Dolphus called out. "Have you forgotten your manners? Have you forgotten how to behave like ladies and gentlemen?"

"We're pissed on an' pissed off, son," Aunt Evelyn told him, "in case you hadn't noticed."

"OH, SHUT UP," Dolphus commanded.

The bandmaster, not being an Adair, obeyed instantly and left a blank silence through which raindrops spattered and pine trees moaned.

Dolphus massaged his brow with his fingertips. "Where . . . where was I, hah?"

"You were saying," Olive told him sweetly, "that we welcome all these good people to our bloody home."

"Yes, welcome to our bloody home," said Dolphus.

Laughter enveloped him again, shaking the tent. Adairs, Whitesides, Beadles and Smiths; they were all just tykes from a basement in Glasgow where Breezy had taken them to escape their peasant inheritance. They were vulgarians at heart, streaked with a deprecating lack of respect for each other, though not for the family. They had been through too much in those early years to tolerate that which Dolphus had become.

"Do you mean it, Randy?" Breezy cried.

"Of course I mean it," said Dolphus.

"Then what are we doing here?" said Edward.

"Hah?"

"What's wrong with the house?"

"It's a damned *garden* party," said Dolphus.

"It's pourin' wet an' freezin' cold, old man," said Walter.

"He means," said Olive, "why don't we go indoors."

"No," said Dolphus desperately. "No, you can't. The food's here, the beer's here . . ."

"You're not feedin' the five thousand, Dolphus."

"It's a moveable feast, old man."

"It's *dry* inside, ain't it?"

"You are," said Dolphus, "ungracious *swine*."

"House, house, house," chanted Heather and Polly, clapping hands together again, like children.

"Surrender, old son," Breezy advised.

"It's the last time I'll give a garden party," Dolphus threatened.

Cheers rang out in the wet tent which, caught at that moment by a gust of strong wind off the moor, listed worse than ever, with a creaking of poles and a twanging of guy ropes.

Dolphus raised his eyes and scanned the sagging roof as if his dominion were being challenged not by his brethren but by a divine force.

"BUGGER YOU THEN," he cried. "DO AS YOU DAMNED WELL PLEASE."

"Does that mean Yes?" Breezy asked.

"That means Yes," said Olive as the tent leaned further towards the ground.

"Man the boats," shouted Donnie.

"An' don't forget the beer."

*   *   *

By mid-afternoon the fragility of gentility had been proved once again and Dolphus's guests had taken complete possession of The Knowe. Fuel buckets had been raided, logs piled in fireplaces that had burned nothing but twigs for years. Kegs of Carruth's best bitter were brought in from the marquee, along with the buffet tables and, when that source ran out, Dolphus's cellars were plundered for more.

Prowling the library Donnie, Edward and Walter discovered a couple of bottles of French brandy and a box of smokable cigars hidden behind the tomes and settled down to make an afternoon of it. Quantities of tea and bread-and-butter were ordered from the kitchen to warm up the ladies and gradually The Knowe became a lively haven against foul weather, with hen parties in drawing-room and parlour, a bull session in the library and children playing leaps and chases up and down the staircase.

The brass band remained in the marquee until a quarter past three at which time, to a great cheer from guests at windows, the tent finally collapsed like a whale's lung and the lads were dragged out and marched into the kitchens to dry out over hot chocolate and buttered toast.

Gordon missed this last entertaining incident entirely for he had found Amanda or, to be precise, Amanda had found him and had led him away to admire the greenhouses that lay beyond the walls of the kitchen garden.

Glass domes, warmed by kerosene, were filled with the salty odours of the tropical plants that Dolphus had inherited with purchase of the house. Here Gordon strolled with Amanda or rested on wooden benches that a previous owner, of more romantic bent than James Randolph Adair, had screened with trellises and Venus bowers.

There were even statues, marbled nymphs and doe-eyed female slaves chained to Greek pillars, modestly coated in moss and sparrow droppings now, and a fountain of sorts and a pond in which hardy little goldfish flittered under a scum of old leaves.

The greenhouses had been playground and sanctuary for Amanda and her sisters for many years. Here they would come with Mother on wet afternoons. Here they would hide when Nanny wanted them and turn the bowers into Prospero's Island or the Garden of Eden, or would pretend that they were sisters of the chained Greek slave girls or nymphs awaiting the arrival of unwary shepherds.

Gordon had very little notion of what Amanda was talking about but he didn't care any more. She wore a thin dress of pale-peach silk, boned only at the seams, and he could feel the softness of her body through it and the slither of the material against her warm flesh.

Amanda knew what sort of young man she was dealing with now and, following her mother's sage advice, went about bewitching him with a spell that seemed to suit. She kissed him tenderly, not passionately, murmured inconsequential endearments with her chin tucked in and eyes averted from his serious face. She did not cling to him when he cuddled her but let him support her and when, eventually, he put a hand lightly upon her breast she drew herself modestly away, saying softly, "No, Gordon, no."

They sat awhile in the most effusive bower, his arms about her, and her thigh touching his and he didn't even blink when she said, "Shall we be married some day soon?"

"Yes, I think so, darling," Gordon said, "if you will have me when I ask."

"I'm seventeen in November. I should like to be betrothed by then."

"I'd like that too," said Gordon. "But I've no prospects, Amanda. I couldn't keep a wife just yet."

"Daddy will see to it that you have prospects."

"How long will that take?" Gordon asked, stroking her throat with his fingertips and trying not to drown in the sight of her breasts.

"Not long," she whispered.

"Your father doesn't like me, though."

"He does. He thinks somethin' can be made of you," Amanda said.

Gordon said, "Where would we live?"

"Here, of course."

"Here, in the greenhouse?"

"No." She slapped him lightly on the hand. "With Daddy in The Knowe."

"I'm not sure I'd . . ."

"Until you were settled," Amanda said, quickly, "and we could afford to live in town, in our own house. Just us. Together."

Gordon sighed.

The conversation had no root in reality. Only his sexual stirring was real, too real to be encouraged for more than minutes at a time. What he would recall of that remarkable afternoon, however, was not his longing or the half-promises he had made but the sight of Amanda framed against vines in the strange sea-green light of evening-under-glass.

By the time Lorna came looking for him to tell him that the family were ready to leave for dinner at the Crabtree Inn, Gordon was already a goose plucked and ready to carve.

"Gordon," Lorna called. "We're waaay-ting."

"I'll be with you shortly."

"The carriage is reeeaaad-dy."

"What can I say, darlin'," Gordon whispered to Amanda.

"Say nothing, dearest. Your eyes say it all."

"Walk with me to the carriage."

"No, leave me here. I prefer to be alone for a little while," Amanda whispered.

Lorna leaned against the doorpost, her arms folded, grinning. Gordon took Amanda's hand, drew her into the greenery, embraced her, kissed her lips.

"Shake a leg, Gordon," Lorna called. "I want my dinner."

"We'll meet again soon, darlin'," Gordon said.

"Very, very soon," Amanda said. "Say that you love me, Gordon."

"I do. I do."

With a sense of melancholy he felt her fingers slip from his grasp and left her there in the green gloaming still holding his heart in her hand.

"About time too, you greedy devil," Lorna said as he pushed past her into the damp evening light.

They walked rapidly along the flagged path that skirted the kitchen garden, Lorna skipping to keep in step.

"Well, big brother," she asked when he stopped to unlatch a gate, "did you?"

"Did I what?"

"Try harder."

"None of your damned business, Lorna."

"Ooo!" Lorna chirped. "He's in love. Our Gordie's fell in love."

"What if I have!" said Gordon crossly.

"How bad?"

"Pretty bad," he snapped and strode out ahead of her along the garden path.

Eight

A Day by the Sea

It took Kirsty and Greta a little longer than one might have expected to become exponents of the noble art of acquiring discount. So raw were the girls in the retail trade that it did not occur to either of them that they might, without risk, turn the Nicholson account to personal advantage.

Warehousemen were only too eager to sell anybody anything. Travellers who dropped in at the Emporium carried in their cases or displayed in their catalogues lots of stuff that was not quite suitable for Kirsty's shelves but which any housewife would die to possess.

Kirsty, of course, could afford to purchase goods outright but old habits of thrift faded slowly. It was not until she found herself staring at an illustration of a Constant Hot Water Heater in the pages of young Mr Tubbs' stock list that the light went on in her head.

Greta and Kirsty were leaning on the counter, the stock list open between them. Mr Tubbs, tall, gawky and sporting a linen suit that made him look like a colonial tea-planter, hovered behind them, ready to plunge into a sales pitch at the first sign of interest or even hesitation.

"Now that," he said, "is a really first-class piece of domestic equipment."

"Safe?" said Greta.

"As houses, madam."

"Who'd fit it in?"

"Any registered gasman. It's been specially designed for ease of erection, believe me."

"Is that the price?" said Kirsty.

"That's the price to you, Mrs N.," said Tubbs. "'Course, if we're talkin' bulk purchase – say three or four of that model – I could knock off a bob or two more."

"Is it in stock?"

"Always in stock."

"I'll take two," Kirsty said suddenly, without any strain. "Now, what about stoves?"

"Just turn the page," said Mr Tubbs, licking his pencil.

"There's a cupboard model stove here," Kirsty said, pointing, "that would do you nicely, Greta."

"I can't afford it."

"Think of the advantages," said Mr Tubbs. "Boil a kettle in three minutes, cook a casserole in . . ."

"Yes, we'll have two stoves an' all," said Kirsty. "The cupboard model. What colour do you prefer, Greta?"

"I can't let you . . ."

"What colour?"

"Red."

Generosity, like materialism, generated its own kind of power but it was not power over Greta that Kirsty sought. She wanted to share the satisfactions that money could buy with somebody who would appreciate them; who better than another orphan who had been damned to poverty and had risen above it?

"I'll work extra to pay you back, Kirsty," Greta promised.

"If you like," said Kirsty nonchalantly.

"Now, ladies," said Mr Tubbs, "what else catches your fancy? Bathtubs, a lawnmower, a meat safe, perhaps?"

"Get out of here, Tubby," Kirsty said. "You've made quite enough commission for one day."

The new appliances were installed in Kirsty's kitchen one afternoon when Craig was on duty by a man and a boy from Monarch Gas Fitters who, the following day, would do the same sort of thing in Benedict Street.

When Craig returned from shift and saw the shiny thing he did not bat an eyelid and made no comment at all. He used the water heater as casually as if it had been there for years and only glanced at the pots simmering on the new stove.

He seated himself at table and was served within seconds.

"Well," Kirsty said, "what do you think?"

"What am I supposed to think?"

"You might at least say somethin'."

"If this is what you want out o' life . . ."

"It is," said Kirsty, tightly.

"Then I've no objection."

Craig propped his newspaper against the sauce bottle and buried himself in its pages.

Kirsty's neighbours were less reticent. Jess Walker had owned a barrel heater for several years but the capacity and convenience of Kirsty's new acquisitions made her the envy of all. The cost of such labour-saving devices was beyond the means of most families and Kirsty was conscious of the paradox: that those poor women who could have made best use of gadgets were the ones who could not afford them while the class of person who could, had servants to drudge for them anyway.

What was said about her in backcourt enclaves did not concern Kirsty in the slightest, or so she told herself. She understood the changes in attitude towards her, even Jess Walker's 'sniffiness'. She, Kirsty Nicholson, had flouted the traditional values of close society and the other wives no longer knew how to place her. It hardly mattered; the shop at No. 1 Gascoigne Street was where she belonged, where she was happiest.

If Craig had deliberately cut them off from family and had anchored himself to his job why could she not do the same? Marriage was a contract, not a bargain. She made sure that she fulfilled her obligations to him but the manner of fulfilment was of her choosing now.

Sometimes, though, she wondered what she had lost in gaining independence. She could not define the vague feeling of loss or put words to it. But it was undeniably there from time to time. It was at its strongest in the waning twilight of long wet summer evenings when she glimpsed poor, pallid faces through the window of the shop, saw them peering in at things they could not afford to buy; women and girls in ragged shawls, small boys with cropped hair and runny noses. She would turn her back on the strangers on the grey pavement, pretend they did not exist, and yet they seemed to be always there, always watching, in that last late hour of trade.

"Greta," she would say, "attend to the counter, please," and she would go into the backshop to open the ledger or account book or to slip a little mirror from the desk drawer and stare at herself in her blue dress or her brown and speculate on what *they* saw, the outsiders, and what *they* thought of this woman, so clean and neat and mature.

"Time t' go home, Kirsty," Greta would tell her, a hand on her shoulder. "Business is dead for today."

Soon after, she would be back in Canada Road, Bobby half asleep in her arms, perhaps. And she would pop the flame on the new water heater and watch hot water stream forth, smooth and curling and comfortable until her awkward and unsettled mood vanished and self-assurance was restored.

*　　*　　*

One night, towards the end of June, Craig said, "I'm due to take a week's leave. I don't suppose you'd like to go away?"

"Go where?" Kirsty said.

He shrugged. "Doon the watter, to the seaside, just for a day or two."

"I can't leave the shop right now."

"I thought not," Craig said.

"Perhaps next year," Kirsty said.

"Aye, perhaps," said Craig.

*　　*　　*

Craig had never set foot upon a floating vessel, apart from the Clyde ferry, which didn't really count. He boarded the powerful and commodious Royal Mail steamer *Kilbrannan* at its berth by No. 1 Shed at the south end of Jamaica Bridge with some trepidation. It was a clear, calm, sunny morning only days before the start of the annual trades' fair holidays after which, for a month or so, the coastal packets would be crammed to the gunwales with families heading for a day on Arran or Rothesay's golden sands.

Craig's voyage had a purpose, though that purpose was not uppermost in his mind as he picked his way up the sagging gangplank and stepped on to the sloping wooden deck. He had borrowed a small suitcase from Archie Flynn and clutched it nervously to his chest as he found his sea legs and breathed deeply of oil, tar and the coal smoke that belched from the steamer's stately funnel.

In new season's paint, with crests gilded and brasswork gleaming, the *Kilbrannan* looked handsome, though you might have thought her tame if it hadn't been for the weathered decks, taut rigging and that splashy intestinal growl that suggested that she was secretly straining at the leash and keen to clear the river, to dash her bows into big waves off the Tail o' the Bank.

Craig wished now that he had brought Bobby with him, someone with whom he could share the stimulation of his first maritime experience. He had sprung for Cabin Class but could not settle in the saloon. He was all over the steamer, even before she cast off and her huge paddle-wheels churned up the mud and she swung out into the channel and set her course down river for the sea.

Craig was entranced by the novelty of vistas and sensations, the shudder of the engines under his feet, the feeling of speed, the landmarks of Glasgow flowing past in fresh perspective; Anderston, Stobcross, shipyards and docks, Pointhouse, Govan steps, the Kelvin's mouth, and Greenfield, where he lived, with its train tracks and tenements all turned inside out.

Well-to-do families had laid claim to the best seats on the foredeck. Mothers were ensconced on pillows with luggage and children around them while fathers took lordly turns about the deck or escorted favourite sons below to look at the engines. Soldiers drank in the saloon, oblivious to scenery and weather. Weather-beaten old men, alone and used to it, leaned on the rails and studied the rivercraft and the great iron-plated ships that towered in the slips. Brown-skinned farmers and country women travelled home to their flocks and herds in Cowal's green hills.

Craig did not become aware of the women until the steamer was on the last leg of its voyage. The elder was past thirty, the younger only a year or two less. They were pert and saucy and full of gay little mannerisms designed to attract attention. They eyed Craig up and down and whispered together and laughed. The elder's dark brown eyes reminded Craig of Greta. The younger was slim and dimpled and wore a skirt that showed her ankles. They were the kind of women who should have been travelling with a servant. The fact that they were not spoke of their adventurous intentions. Craig knew well enough what to do, knew how to return their smiles, touch his hat, swagger close enough to introduce himself. The women had made it clear that they would welcome such an approach but Craig deliberately turned his back on them.

He leaned on the rail and looked out across the Firth to the farmlands and forested slopes of the hills above Kirn. He heard the women laughing behind him and suddenly felt quite lonely. What, anyway, could possibly come of it? Kisses in the aisles between the decks, a stroll along the shore, a brief, insincere promise of a rendezvous back in Glasgow? He did not want them. Besides, he had a job to do in Dunoon, even if he had no stomach for that either now.

Hugging the little suitcase he drifted away and hid himself

173

behind the hot wall of the funnel where smoke fell like black pepper and the predatory ladies would not follow him.

Twenty minutes later the *Kilbrannan*'s gangplank grated on to Dunoon pier and Craig, looking neither left nor right, hurried down it and into the arms of the town.

*   *   *

Gordon had seen his mother at dinner the previous evening but to run into her, almost literally, on Dumbarton Road at half-past ten o'clock on a weekday morning was definitely disconcerting. Out of doors, separated from Breezy, she seemed like a perfect stranger for a second or two; and what he saw was the broad, tyrannical vulgarity of a farmer's wife done up to look like a lady, quite different from the mother he had known in Dalnavert before times had changed and changed them all.

"So this is what you do for a livin', is it?" she said.

Madge had on an unsuitably heavy outfit and was perspiring slightly on brow and upper lip. She carried no accoutrement today except a floral purse and she had clearly just begun a shopping trawl along Dumbarton Road, heading, no doubt, for Byres Road.

The clock above the tearoom door told him it was thirty-eight minutes past ten. The morning was already hot and the street smelled strongly since there had been a drove of cattle from the docks to the market in the early hours and the burgh watercarts had not been by yet.

Gordon did not put down his wickerwork cases, though they were heavy with samples of a new hardwearing carpet material that he hoped to sell in quantity to the Convener of the Baptist Church Hall with whom he had an appointment of sorts.

"An' where are you off to at such a lick?"

"Purdon Street," Gordon said.

"I've been meanin' to have a quiet word wi' you, Gordon," Madge said. "An' this is an ideal opportunity."

"Mam, I'm workin'."

"Nonsense. We'll go an' have a cup of tea."

"Mother, I . . ."

"Purdon Street won't run away."

Gordon sighed.

In fact he was too early for the Baptist Convener and had been hurrying more out of habit than necessity. He also felt sorry for his mother, which was daft, really, since she had been in clover ever since they'd come to Glasgow. But neither he nor Lorna gave her much of their time these days and when Breezy wasn't about she seemed, to Gordon at least, quite lost sometimes.

"Just one quick cuppa, then," said Gordon.

Hoisting a case under his arm to free a hand, he took his mother by the wrist as if he were very young or she very old, and led her across Dumbarton Road into Dorrit's Tearoom.

As soon as they were seated at a table by the window and had been served with tea, Madge said, "Have you seen anythin' of our Craig lately?"

"I haven't seen him for months," Gordon answered, adding, "but I saw Kirsty on Monday, as it happens."

Madge sniffed and glanced down into the road below to indicate that she was not interested in her daughter-in-law but only in her prodigal son.

"He should be doin' better for himself," she said.

"Nah, bein' a copper suits him just fine."

"If you ask me," said Madge, "it's her that's split up the family, her that's keepin' him away."

"Do you mean because of the shop?"

"You shouldn't be encouragin' her, Gordon."

Gordon felt his stomach muscles tighten. He should have been more alert to the signs that indicated that his mother was about to interfere in her children's lives, and not for the first time.

Madge said, "An' you could do better for yourself too, young man."

"I'm doin' fine, Mother," he said, feigning an airiness he did not feel. "Property owner, an' all that."

"Property!" She snorted. "Some tuppenny-ha'penny shop."

"I have to start some place."

"Don't think I don't know what you've been up to."

So far Gordon had done nothing sinful. Nevertheless he felt a pang of guilt at his mother's accusation.

"I . . . I . . . I haven't been up to nothin', Mam."

"With that girl."

He blushed scarlet; the curse of his light colouring.

"What girl?"

"The Adair girl."

"If you mean Amanda . . ."

"Oh, is that her name?"

175

"Come off it, Mother," Gordon said. "You know bloody well
. . . perfectly well what her name is."

"Albert thinks it time he had a word with you."

His mother never called her husband by his familiar nickname
and this somehow seemed to give Breezy two separate identities,
one solid and uxorious and the other raffish.

"About what?"

"Your opportunities in that direction."

"Opportunities?"

Gordon realised now that his mother's attitude was not one of
condemnation but of wheedling. She had never had much talent
in that direction. Though he could read her now like a pamphlet,
knowledge and maturity had not changed his response to her and
he could not bring himself to laugh off her ridiculous machinations.
Perhaps that was the real reason that Craig had broken with her,
just to give himself room to breathe.

"It seems you've given the girl a hint that your intentions are
honourable." Madge held the teacup in both hands and watched
him over its rim. "Have you, Gordon?"

"Jeeze! I've got no intentions towards Amanda, honourable or
otherwise."

"Apparently the poor girl thinks differently."

"Who told you that?"

"She thinks you're as good as engaged."

"What!"

"A wee bird told me," said Madge with a blood-chilling simper,
"just what went on at that garden party while I was lookin' the
other way."

"Lorna."

"No, not our Lorna," Madge said. "As a matter of fact it was
Mr Adair."

"You mean . . . Dolphus?"

"He wants you to go an' work for him. He's spoken to Albert
about it. He thinks you'd go far in the brewery trade."

"What do I know about brewin' beer? I don't even drink the
damned stuff," said Gordon. "Anyway, I'm happy workin' for
Adair's warehouse."

Madge said, "I want you to accept."

"Accept what exactly?"

"Whatever's offered." Madge covered his hand with her own.
"Albert's a generous man but he can't offer you an opportunity

like this one, Gordon. An' he won't stand in your way. I'll see to that."

"I'd prefer to make up my own mind, Mother."

"You like the girl, though, don't you?"

He could not resist the confidential tone of the conversation. "Aye, I like her a lot."

"So it wouldn't be a hardship havin' her for a wife."

"Hoy, hold your horses," said Gordon, with a grin. "I'm only a boy, Mother. I'm not ready for marriage yet."

"It's different wi' toffs," said Madge. "They don't just plunge into marriages. It's not like Bankhead. You don't just turn up on a lassie's doorstep wi' nothin' to your name but a blanket an' a steady wage. You need to have prospects."

"Yes, Mother."

"Look at what happened t' Craig when he dived into wedlock wi' the wrong girl."

"Kirsty wasn't the wrong girl."

"I want you t' have the best out o' life, Gordon," Madge went on, ignoring his defence of Kirsty Barnes. "I don't want you t' have to wait until you're my age before you get your due."

"What does Breezy think about all this?"

"Albert thinks you should take it seriously," Madge said. "The Carruth breweries are worth hundreds o' thousands o' pounds. You could learn about business properly."

"Brewin's not like sellin' carpets," Gordon said. "It's highly specialised. You have to be born into it to understand it at all."

"Randolph Adair wasn't born into it."

"That's true," Gordon admitted.

"An' look where he is today."

What his mother had framed in words had been floating in his mind since the day of the garden party.

Questions as to his suitability, as to why a pompous snob like Dolphus Adair would select an upstart for a son-in-law, seemed to have been brushed aside by his mother's interventions. However, he could not quite be rid of the niggling suspicion that it would be no bed of roses being Dolphus's apprentice and living in The Knowe, even with Amanda as his bride, or that he would be able to live up to everyone's expectations.

"You're right, Mother," Gordon said.

" 'Course I am."

"What do I do now, Mam?"

"Leave it to Albert," said Madge.

* * *

Dunoon exhibited a charming indifference to regularity. Its villas, cottages and kirks, surrounded by gardens and trees, nestled between the old sea margin and the sleepy blue heights of Cowal. Steam navigation had brought summer prosperity and bunting fluttered on the towers of baronial piles and painted awnings protected the shop fronts from the sun. Grim Dalriadic chieftains who had once ruled the roost on this stretch of coast and the Scandinavian rovers who had routed them would hardly have recognised the scenes of their triumphs and defeats which lay buried beneath the terraces of hydropathic hotels and the steps of the burgh buildings.

Craig, though, had very little time to sample the rambling pleasures of the town. In four and a half hours the *Kilbrannan* would return to take him back to Glasgow. Before then he had to find Lorne Cottage and coax some home truths from its occupants.

The softness of the June day, the town's nodding atmosphere, made him feel mean and malicious. If he'd had company of any sort he would, perhaps, have abandoned his quest and given up the whole notion of revenge there and then. He had come too far to change his mind now, however, and asked directions in a tobacconist's shop and was steered towards the West Bay, a mile or so along the shore.

Lorne Cottage stood off the Innellan Road, at the end of a long well-tended garden. Bent pines guarded the wicket gate but the prospect was otherwise wide open to the sea. There were rose bushes, herbaceous borders, a trainer of sweetpeas and glimpses, to the rear, of flourishing rows of vegetables. The cottage itself seemed dwarfed by such abundance. On the roof ridge two huge herring gulls perched like sentinels and on the carpet of green lawn three Scotch terriers dozed in a shaggy bundle of ears and paws.

On a bench by a grey drystone wall an elderly woman was seated. She wore a fisher skirt and flannel shirt and a sunwheel straw hat; and she was watching him long before he put a hand to the latch of the gate, more alert, it seemed, than the little dogs.

Craig opened the gate and stepped through it.

The gulls squawked, spread their wings and swooped lazily

down from the roof across the back gardens and the dogs wakened, rose, shook themselves, and growled.

The woman continued to watch him from under the brim of the round straw hat, head on one side. She was as tiny as a goblin, white-haired, black-eyed. Her hands, like shrew claws, were folded in her lap. She offered no greeting and did not stir a muscle as Craig came down the path and stepped carefully over the border.

The terriers growled and bristled. A man appeared silently at a corner of the house. He was big, broad-shouldered, with a heavy gut. He wore a spotted red bandana knotted over his bald head and a cotton shirt with sleeves rolled tight against the thick flesh of his upper arms. A broad leather belt was clasped over his belly and his corduroy trousers were hitched up with string. His feet were bare and loamy and his hands had dirt upon them too.

Craig was sweating now, conscious of the dogs behind him and the man off to his right.

"Mrs McNish?" he said. "Sylvie McNish?"

"Who wants tae know?"

"I do," said Craig.

"You're a copper, ain't ye?"

"That's right," Craig said.

"Who sent ye?"

"I came of my own free will."

"Who else knows we're here?"

"Nobody," Craig said. "Not yet."

She stiffened slightly. There was more resignation than menace about her, Craig thought.

"Tam," she called out. "Tam, come bye."

Sun-tanned skin and earthy hands could not disguise the sort of man that Tam McNish had been. Craig recognised the type immediately; a bully boy, a professional hooligan. There was a hulking threat to him still, even if he was well past sixty.

The terriers, tails wagging, gathered behind the man as he lumbered, barefoot, across the pebble path.

The woman said, "Here's a young blue-boy cam' tae visit us, Tam."

"Is that a fact," said Tam McNish.

"It's hardly what you'd call a visit," Craig said. "Not an official visit. I just thought I'd drop in for a quick word while I was passin'."

"An' what would that word be?" the man asked.

"The word would be a name," Craig said, "an' the name would be Greta Taylor."

The woman released a strange hiss that left a smile of sorts upon her face. "Aye, so it's Greta, is it? Was it Greta sent ye here?"

"Greta doesn't know me," Craig lied, "though I know somethin' of her. What I need to know is who fathered the child, Greta Taylor's child?"

"How would we know a thing like that?" said Tam McNish.

"Because it was you did the deal," said Craig. "It was you sold the bairn . . ."

"Is that an accusation? 'Cause if it is . . ."

"Aye, sure, it's an accusation," Craig said. "It's goin' to save us all a lot o' time if we stop beatin' about the bush. Hugh Affleck would still like t' get his hands on you an' maybe I'll just help him do that."

Craig sensed the movement. He stuck out his right hand and caught the man's wrist before the fingers could close on his, Craig's, neck.

"Nah, nah," Craig said. "Your day's done, McNish."

"Leave him alone, Tam," said Sylvie, as if her man had the upper hand. "It's too nice an afternoon for fightin'."

Craig said, "I'm not interested in you. I'm only interested in Greta Taylor an' her child. Tell me what I want t' know an' that'll be an end of it."

McNish, released, lowered himself stiffly to the grass and gathered the eager little dogs about him, clapping and petting them. "What's Greta done?"

"She's done nothin'," Craig said. "Who sold you the child?"

"Is this for the court?" said Sylvie.

"No, you'll not be dragged into a witness box, I promise."

"Huh, what's a copper's promise worth!"

"It better be worth somethin'," Craig said, "or Hugh Affleck will be steppin' off the *Kilbrannan* tomorrow with a warrant for your arrest."

"Hughie Affleck has nothin' on us," the woman said.

"No, but I do," said Craig.

Both the woman and her husband stared out to sea, at a scut of sails that had appeared from the direction of Hunter's Quay.

"I'll make it simple," Craig said. "Either you tell me what I need to know about Greta Taylor's bairn or I tell Superintendent Affleck everythin' that Lizzie Straun told me."

"So it was Lizzie, was it?" Sylvie hissed.

"I should have done for that bitch when I had the chance," said the man.

"Too late now," Craig said. "She's in a bad way. She'll be dead before the year's out; as if you cared."

"How did you find her?"

"It wasn't difficult," Craig said. "By the way, I'm from Greenfield Burgh, not Glasgow, so what's past is past as far as I'm personally concerned. Everythin' that Lizzie told me, an' the documents she gave me, will be forgotten if you just . . ."

"What documents?" said Sylvie.

"Lizzie never had no documents," said McNish.

"That's what you think," Craig said.

"Where are these . . . these documents now?"

"Safe in my keepin'," Craig said.

"This is blackmail, ain't it?"

"'Course it is," said Craig.

"Bastard!"

"How much do y'want?" said the woman.

"Keep your money," Craig said. "It's information I want, that's all."

"I never knew the name o' the father." Sylvie McNish capitulated suddenly. "Discretion was our hallmark, ye see. I never needed to know who fathered the bairn."

"Who paid you?" Craig said.

"Adair."

"Which Adair?"

"Albert," said the woman. "Breezy."

"Heard of him, have ye?" the man asked.

"I've heard of him," Craig said. "Go on."

"Breezy sent his boy . . ."

"Johnnie Whiteside, would that be?" Craig asked.

Sylvie and Tam McNish exchanged a glance.

Craig said, "Was it Whiteside?"

"Aye, it was. He did all the dirty work," Sylvie went on. "He even brought the infant, after it was born."

"An' it wasn't Breezy's child, you're sure o' that?"

"Nah, it came from the brother's house."

Craig paused, then said, "Who found Greta Taylor?"

"I did," said Sylvie McNish.

To Tam McNish, Craig said, "Was she one o' your fancy girls? Was she on your string?"

McNish shook his head. "She was a friend o' Isa Thomas. Isa . . . she worked for us when she was younger."

"But Breezy did know Greta?"

"He'd met her, aye."

Craig said, "How much did Breezy pay you to farm the child?"

"Five hundred pounds."

"Christ! Was that the goin' rate?"

Tam McNish laughed hoarsely. "By God, copper, you've a lot t' learn."

"It was a hundred times the goin' rate," said Sylvie McNish. "That sort o' money was what the nobs paid if they wanted it done right."

"Meanin'?"

"If they required the bairn t' thrive."

"You mean survive?"

Sylvie McNish shrugged her thin shoulders.

The little dogs had fallen asleep again upon the grass and Tam McNish stroked them soothingly, fondly.

"How much did Greta Taylor get out of that?" Craig asked.

"One hundred," Sylvie said. "She got other things too; the house in Benedict Street an' some money now an' then from Breezy. We had nothin' t' do wi' that arrangement, though."

"Greta was trustworthy," the man said. "She wanted the bairn, wanted one o' her own. She couldn't have one natural."

"Had Greta been . . . doctored?"

"Not that I know of," said Sylvie. "She was clean, clean enough for Breezy Adair, anyway. Last I heard the girl child was thrivin'."

"Did Greta know where the child came from?"

"Don't be bloody daft, son."

"All right," Craig said. "Tell me the name o' the brother, the Adair who farmed out the child."

"Randolph."

"Aye," said Craig. "I see."

"It was brought t' me when it was new-born. I took it t' Lizzie who had a wet nurse laid on. It was with Lizzie for five months, an' then it went t' Greta. He came t' see it several times when it was new."

"Who? Randolph?"

"Breezy."

McNish said, "It was t' save a stain on the family name that the bairn was removed. If you've got the money you can do anythin', even buy your way out o' scandal."

"So it wasn't Randolph's child?"

"Father unknown," said Sylvie.

"Mother known, though," said Tam McNish. "Is that what you want from us, copper? The mother's name?"

"I think I can guess," said Craig.

"Guess then, copper."

"Olive Adair, was it?"

"Olive Carruth Adair," said Sylvie.

"The lovely wife," McNish added.

"Right," Craig said. "Yes, right."

"It fits, does it?"

"Fits perfectly," said Craig.

*   *   *

He undressed at the bottom of the sea wall and struggled awkwardly into his bathing costume under cover of a towel. Though there were few folk about and none close by, he felt uncomfortably exposed as he picked his way over the shingle to the water's edge. He took a deep breath and, before his nerve could fail him, waded straight in.

It was cold, very cold, but not like the water in Cranstounhill baths, not licking and tingling cold. The sea seemed to encase him and the cold was like stone, solid not liquid.

Craig shivered then swooped forward and embraced the green surface with wide arms. He gasped, tasted salt, coughed and surfaced and, kicking his feet, drove himself away from the shore.

Twenty yards out he rolled on to his back and squinted at the line of the town and at the sky. He let himself float. In the sea he felt better; cleansed, he supposed, was the word for it. There was no triumph in what he had discovered about the lives of the Adairs, their petty scandals. He thought of the wee one, Jen, pretty and inquisitive, and of Greta who loved the child just as if she'd been her own. How could he possibly use the knowledge he had gained for revenge? No matter how she'd hurt him, he could not hurt Greta in return. He could not expose her to a criminal charge, could not risk having the child taken from her.

Pursuit of the truth had been a waste of time. He had added

nothing to himself. In fact he had lost something. He could not fathom what it was, however, though its absence made him feel calm, calm and empty and sad, out there alone in the stone-cold sea.

* * *

Gordon came late to the shop, though, with summer nearing its height, it seemed that it might not grow dark at all.

The streets were rowdy. The weather had been simmering hot for a fortnight. The men had been paid for the trades' holiday that very afternoon and a great deal of drinking was being done. Brewers, Dolphus among them, were making a fortune. Served straight off ice, new light German lagers were having a say at last in all but the most traditional public houses.

The officers of the burgh constabulary were run ragged breaking up fights and sweeping insensible bodies off pavements and out of closes, and Billy King's gang, quiet of late, had gone on the rampage again along the riverside and several arrests had been made.

Greta had insisted that the shutters be put up soon after the pubs opened and Kirsty soon saw what a wise move it had been, for drunkards were careless and bumped and crashed against the boards and apprentices, some tasting liquor for the first time, went mad, ranted and raved and flung stones until they were lugged off in the Black Maria to be charged with disorderly behaviour and spend a night in the cells.

Gordon was relieved to reach Gascoigne Street and Kirsty was glad to see him. There was something in the air on the eve of the holiday that made her uneasy.

Gordon was less perky than usual. He carried his jacket across his arm and had loosened his necktie and seemed rumpled, hot and ill-at-ease too.

"Everythin' all right?" he asked at once.

"Trade hasn't been too good these past few days," said Kirsty. "We've sold very little."

"That's normal for this time of year," Gordon told her. "It'll pick up again in a month or so."

"You look tired."

"I am," Gordon admitted.

"Why don't you go home? Greta and I can take care of things here."

"I've brought you some news, Kirsty."

"Oh! Good news or bad?"

"Good. Good for me, that is."

Greta came through from the backshop, Jen in her arms. The child was flushed and sleepy. Bobby was drowsing in an old tub chair that Kirsty had bought and even the sound of his uncle's voice did not rouse him.

Gordon said, "I'll be leavin' Adair's at the end o' the month."

"But why? Have you fallen out with Breezy?"

"No, nothin' like that," said Gordon. "I'm startin' another job elsewhere."

"I thought you liked workin' at the warehouse?"

"I do." Gordon shrugged. "But I have to look t' the future, to advance my prospects."

"Does Breezy know?"

"Yes, of course. He encouraged me to make the change."

"Where are you goin'?" said Greta.

"To work in Carruth's brewery."

"You," said Kirsty, "in a brewery! What do you know about brewin'?"

"Not a sausage," said Gordon. "I'm bein' employed to learn, though. For the first six months or a year I'll be Carruth's representative on the road."

"Sellin'?"

"More or less."

"When was all this decided?" said Kirsty.

"We had a meetin', Breezy an' me, with Dolphus Adair and thrashed it all out then."

"It's the girl, isn't it?" Kirsty asked.

"Amanda is a consideration," Gordon admitted.

"Did she talk you into it?" said Kirsty.

Greta was walking her child, short, soft steps, back and forth between the shelves in the cool interior part of the shop. She seemed to be uninterested in the conversation but Kirsty knew that she would be taking in every word.

"If things work out," Gordon said, "I suppose that in due course, in the fullness of time, Amanda an' me *might* wind up gettin' married, perhaps."

"Have you asked her?"

"Not yet," said Gordon. "It's sort of agreed, though. Things are done different in that branch o' society, Kirst. Cut to a pattern, y'might say."

"I wish you luck," Kirsty said, curtly.

"You sound annoyed."

"Why should I be annoyed? It's got nothin' to do with me," Kirsty said. "I just wish you luck, Gordon, that's all."

"It's not as if you really need me any longer," said Gordon. "I mean, I'm not lettin' you down or anythin'. The pair o' you have the warehouse agents wrapped round your fingers from what I hear. You won't go short o' quality stock, Kirsty. The shop can run fine wi'out my aid."

"Oddly enough," said Kirsty, "I wasn't even thinkin' about the shop."

"Workin' for Dolphus instead of Breezy won't interfere with our partnership," Gordon said. "Nothin' will change there."

"We'll see," said Kirsty. "Meanwhile, I think we'll just close up. It's been dead all afternoon, anyway."

"I'll help," said Gordon.

"No, I can manage here. Why don't you see Greta safe back to Benedict Street?"

"He doesn't have to bother," Greta said.

"It's no bother," Gordon said. "Here, give Jen to me."

He took the sleeping child into his arms and rested her body against his shoulder, brushed her damp curls with his fingertips to soothe and reassure her. She settled trustingly against him, thumb in her mouth. Gordon kissed his sister-in-law on the cheek and led the dark-haired woman out into dusty Gascoigne Street.

From the doorway Kirsty watched them go.

If she hadn't known better she might have supposed them to be a couple, both small in stature, well matched. The sins of the past would always stand between them, however, and Gordon's life was charted to a different course.

Gordon was drifting away from her too now. She hadn't driven him off, of course, but nonetheless she'd lost him to another. She had no right to feel jealous of Amanda Adair and yet she did, and couldn't help it.

For the first time in weeks she thought of David Lockhart and how much he had meant to her; yet she had managed to cope perfectly well without him when it had been forced upon her.

She glanced up at the strip of coppery sky that showed above the tenements. It would break soon, this fine spell. It always rained on Glasgow Fair Monday, so folks said. She wouldn't mind the rain, the approach of autumn, the coming of the long nights, not this year.

With a wistful sigh, Kirsty stepped back into the shop to count her meagre takings, collect her son and go home to Craig.

*   *   *

In Banff Street, away from the clamour, the evening was soft and downy and the farther shore of the Clyde was visible above the dockland's cranes and masts.

"Is she not too heavy for you?" Greta said.

"Nah, she's no heavier than my sample case."

"I'll take a shot, if y'like."

"An' ruin your posture. You're wee enough as it is," Gordon said.

"I'm not wee," said Greta. "I'm *petite*. That's what the Frenchies would call me."

"Have you ever known a Frenchie?"

"Can't say I have," Greta answered. "I knew a Norwegian once. Couldn't make out a word he was sayin'."

"I don't suppose that mattered," Gordon said.

Her step faltered. They had not been walking at any great pace and the hesitation was obvious.

"In spite of what happened wi' your brother," Greta said, "I was never what you think I was."

"It's all water under the bridge anyway."

"I think I can guess what Johnnie Whiteside says about me," Greta said.

"I never listen to Whiteside," Gordon said. "I know only too well what he's like."

"I can't think why you'd want to marry into that family," Greta said.

"I'm in that family already, Greta, like it or not."

"Too many skeletons in too many closets."

"Cut it out, Greta. I've had enough o' that nonsense from my brother. It's just jealousy."

"I'm not jealous o' the Adairs."

"No, but Craig is."

"Craig's right to be wary of gettin' too close to that lot."

"What do you know about it?" Gordon said.

"I've heard stories."

"Listen," Gordon said, "what's Whiteside got on you?"

"Whiteside's a pig."

"Agreed," said Gordon. "I haven't forgotten how he pimped . . ."

"That's a rotten word to use."

"You'd have gone to bed wi' me that night, though, wouldn't you, Greta, just because Johnnie Whiteside told you to?"

"I might have."

"You would have, until you discovered Craig was my brother."

"Do you want t' go to bed with me now?"

"No," Gordon said quickly.

"But you don't mind carryin' my bairn down a public street," said Greta. "There's not many men in this town would do that."

"It's no skin off my nose," said Gordon, hugging the sleeping child to him.

She had, however, made him aware of the women who hung from the open windows, taking a last breath of air, and the knots of men who lounged by the close mouths and by the hot-pie van at the corner of Banff Street, and how weak he must appear to them, weak and strange.

He said, "Why did you let Craig . . ."

"There's somethin' about Nicholsons I just can't resist," said Greta.

"Never mind the jokes," said Gordon. "Tell me the real reason, Greta."

"I needed him."

"Surely you could have had your pick o' men."

"I needed Craig's protection," Greta said. "Besides, I liked him a lot."

"Didn't it matter that he was married?"

"It mattered a great deal," Greta said. "In the end it mattered too much."

He looked at her, saw hardness as well as vulnerability in her dark eyes.

"Kirsty understands," Greta said.

"Kirsty only took you on so she could have revenge on him, you know."

"Aye, but she understands now."

"Understands what?"

Greta did not answer that question.

She said, "If I was as rich as this Adair girl, would you marry me instead?"

188

Gordon hesitated, then shook his head. "It's a daft question, Greta."

"I wouldn't expect you to change, not your job, not anythin'."

"I . . ." Gordon stammered. "I . . . don't know what to say."

"Is it because I'm older than you? I'm not that much older than you."

"Greta, I'm not on offer."

"Och, I know."

"Are you teasin' me?"

"Aye, 'course I am."

"In any case," said Gordon, "I'm not marryin' anyone for a while yet."

"When you do, I hope they make you happy."

"They?"

"The Adairs, the Carruths."

"Hell, I'm not marryin' all o' them, you know."

"Good prospects, Gordon."

"Take what's offered," Gordon said. "I thought that was your philosophy too?"

"I'm envious, that's all."

"What? Envious of me?"

"Of her, if you must know," Greta said. "God, I've made you blush."

"Nothin' of the kind."

"Here, I'll take Jen now."

"Yes," Gordon said. "I think you'd better."

They had reached the head of Benedict Street, only a hundred yards from Greta's close. He glanced towards it and thought of the nights when he had gone out of his way to pass by her window and the desire that had been in him, how he had wanted to touch her, look at her, go to bed with her. He still did – in a way.

What he felt for Greta Taylor was quite different from his attraction towards Amanda. He wasn't so afraid of Greta as he was of Dolphus Adair's daughter. She challenged him in a different manner, on another level of reality altogether. He understood now why Craig had been unable to resist, the magnetism that had drawn his brother into adultery, that had made it so easy for Kirsty to forgive the woman who had almost ruined her marriage.

"Do you want to come in, Gordon?" she asked.

"I . . ."

"I know you won't," Greta said. "I'm just askin' if you want to?"

"No, I think this is far enough."

"Aye," Greta said. "I think so too."

Without knowing why he did it, Gordon kissed Greta on the mouth, then kissed the sleeping child.

"Good night, wee lamb," he said, turned on his heel and set off quickly for Great Western Terrace before he could change his mind.

Nine

Drink and the Devil

Deauville was not for Dolphus Adair, nor Nice, Rome or Baden-Baden, nor even Hastings or Torquay. The plaintive cries of his daughters, which rang out from the beginning of March and continued, against all reason, until the train chuffed out of Glasgow on the first Saturday in August, fell on deaf ears. The Golfers' Hotel in Seawalls, Fife, had always been the site of the annual vacation and Dolphus, who hated holidays anyway, saw no reason to make a change.

There were no temptations to be found in Seawalls, unless you were scoundrel enough to nudge your golf ball out of the rough or neglect to record on your score card the three extra swipes you'd had in the bunker behind the eleventh. Dolphus didn't much care for golf but strictly for the benefit of his wife and children he would embark on a daily round with voluble enthusiasm.

When the girls had been young they had enjoyed their month at Seawalls well enough, romping on the sands, dabbling in rock pools, riding the beach donkeys through the east coast mists. Such simple pleasures paled, however, when compared with the tales that their schoolfellows brought back from the Continent, and Seawalls had come to seem boring in the extreme. Even Nanny, this past year or two, had admitted that she'd had enough of The Golfers' and, given choice, would prefer a month in a cell in Greenock jail.

Only Olive did not complain. She professed to enjoy the break and the relaxing atmosphere of the stuffy hotel on the edge of the links, the pleasure of being *en famille* with her girls for the second half of the month, after Daddy had returned to work.

Amanda was fourteen before she learned the reason why her mother was so willing to endure the stultifying monotony of four

191

weeks in Fife, learned of the rustic cottage a mile inland from grey, God-wrought St Andrews where Olive would spend a few stolen hours in her lover's arms.

The August rendezvous were not the only times that the lovers met, far from it. For five years now there had been secret assignations in Glasgow, Edinburgh and out at Bree, most often at Bree. Stolen afternoons at Clover Cottage were, however, desperately romantic and conducive to passion and it was there, so Olive confessed to her eldest, that she had once more conceived.

Dolphus knew nothing of the cottage or he'd have had the family off to Deauville in a flash. He did know about Bree Lodge and the love-child, of course, but he had swallowed his wife's repentant tale of a touch-and-go liaison with a groom, a brief infatuation that had ended when the rogue fled back to Derry in disgrace, leaving Olive pregnant and Dolphus to cover up the scandal as best he could.

Amanda had asked, "How did Daddy know that the child wasn't his?"

"Daddy has not been a husband to me these past seven years," Olive had explained, with more tact than usual. "It's not that he does not . . . try. It's just that he cannot."

"Cannot what?"

"Do what is necessary to be a proper husband," Olive said. "The word, dearest, that describes Daddy's condition is 'impotent'."

"Is it Daddy's fault?"

"Not exactly," Olive had said.

"I remember how glum Daddy was when he came to the nursery to tell us that we were going to have another little sister or brother, though we all thought it was a lovely idea," Amanda had said. "Then you went away to Edinburgh and came back without it. When Daddy told us that it had died we *were* disappointed."

"Fortunately you were a little too young to understand," Olive had said. "But you understand now, don't you?"

"It didn't die, did it?"

"No, it – she – is alive and well."

"Where is she? What's her name?"

"That doesn't concern you."

"Why are you tellin' me all this?" Amanda had asked.

"So that you will not think too badly of me if ever the day comes when I decide to leave Daddy."

"Leave Daddy? Will you take us with you?"

"No, Amanda, you will be old enough to look after yourself by then, I promise."

"Will you run away with him?"

"Who?"

"The father of your child?"

"If he will have me, yes."

Measured in exact ratio to Amanda's capacity to comprehend and sympathise, over the next three years more information about her affair had been imparted by Olive to her eldest.

Amanda took a vicarious delight in Olive's romantic entanglement. She was sure that love would triumph in the end and that she would play a major role in bringing that victory about.

Now they were all back in Seawalls, in the chilly hotel where no orchestra played and there were no tea dances or evening soirées and menfolk and their wives were content to golf and play bridge. Olive endured it patiently for the sake of the afternoons to come. Amanda, and Phoebe too now, shared their mother's forbearance, aware of the thrilling pleasures that were in store for Olive after Daddy had gone home and she could be with a man who loved her more than life itself.

Phoebe was not unlike her older sister. She had not yet shed her puppyfat, however, and had about her an air of guiltless precocity and would, within a year, become what her cousins termed 'fair game'.

"Perhaps Gordon will come on a visit and you can borrow the cottage for an afternoon," Phoebe suggested.

"Gordon is far too busy to trail up here to Fife," Amanda said.

"Can't see the advantage," said Phoebe, "of havin' a sweetheart who works for Daddy if he's too busy to court you."

"There will be time for that when Gordon is established."

"I do envy you so," said Phoebe, sighing.

"Oh, do you?" Amanda's note of irony would have been picked up by anyone less innocent than her sister. "At least you'll be free to marry who you like, when you like."

"I thought you were in love with Gordon?"

Nanny was down on the beach vainly trying to interest the youngest in collecting shells. Phoebe and Amanda were seated on the old sea wall that ran out to black tarpaper shacks where haddock were smoked and shellfish washed and handsome fisher lads flapped about in ragged woollens and gigantic, thigh-hugging boots.

Amanda broke the bubble of a strand of weed between finger and thumb, sniffed the salty essence and said, "I am, I suppose. But I wish . . ."

Phoebe said, "You wish he was more like Captain Wells, don't you?"

"No, Gordon will be a good husband."

"He isn't a real gentleman though, is he?"

"Phoebe . . ."

"If I could find a man like Captain Wells I wouldn't bother about marriage either. I'd *fling* myself into his arms and let him sweep me away. I'd rather be loved passionately than married just for the sake of it, wouldn't you?"

"No," said Amanda, firmly.

After a pause, Phoebe said, "I wonder what she's like."

"Who?"

"Our sister," said Phoebe.

"I expect she looks like us."

"She may not, you know. She may look like Captain Wells," said Phoebe. "I think I'd rather like to meet her one fine day."

"We don't know where she is."

"Put out to a good family, I expect," said Phoebe. "It must be strange not to know who your real mother is."

"We may all be together some day," said Amanda. "Eventually."

"What makes you say that?"

"Mother told me."

"Do you mean that Mother wants her back?"

"Of course she does, silly."

"But why, for heaven's sake?" said Phoebe.

"Because she's a child of love," said Amanda.

"And what," said Phoebe, sharply, "does that make us?"

"Heirs," said Amanda.

She swung herself down from the wall on to the old stone promenade.

"Is that what we are?" Phoebe called after her. "Is that *all* we are, Amanda?"

Her sister did not answer but went sauntering off to watch

the fisher lads unload their catch on the steps by the tarpaper shacks.

*   *   *

August was humid and overcast and Kirsty felt sluggish, headachy and out of sorts. After the trades' holidays there was no money to spare and custom in the shop remained slack.

Only the tray of penny favours seemed to turn over cash without remission. Shop hands, factory lassies and pig-tailed girls from school were irresistibly drawn to the trays of little trinkets that Mr Tubbs delivered by the one-pound bag.

Two hundred items were sold at a wholesale price of nine shillings. Kirsty wondered who could possibly turn a profit from the manufacture of such trivial goods; wire rings with glass stones, bangles that stained your wrist viridian, brooches stamped out of tin and hairclips with roses embossed in blood red resin.

"Birmingham," said Mr Tubbs. "Manufacturers down in Brum make fortunes out of stuff like this. It's imported at great expense to our firm an' sold at a loss to valued customers like yourself, of course."

"Of course," said Kirsty.

"Two pound bags next week, Mrs N., is it?"

"One will be quite enough, thank you kindly, Mr Tubbs."

Greta was impatient with the youngsters' tight, giggling cliques as they browsed noisily among the jewellery in the penny trays. She was strict with them, almost snappish, for she suspected them all of being thieves.

"Come on, make up your mind," Greta would say. "I haven't got all day."

"Do you think it suits me, missus?" a girl would ask, anxiously holding a clip to her hair or a brooch to her budding bosom. "Ga'n, tell me the truth."

Greta would relent. "Aye, it makes you look a treat."

"Honest?"

"See for yourself."

Greta would flash a fan-tailed mirror kept for the purpose. The girl would pout, sigh, eventually pay the price of vanity and depart.

Now and again, though, Greta would skip round the counter, catch some unfortunate miss by the wrist and force open a guilty palm.

"An' what's this?" Greta would shout.

Kirsty would hurry from the backshop, Bobby and Jen too, and watch rings and ear ornaments patter to the floor.

If she was the brazen sort the girl would cry, "I was just goin' t' pay for them, so I was," or might burst into crocodile tears that turned real enough when Greta uttered the dread phrase, "Send for the polis, Mrs Nicholson. I think we've caught a thief."

The constable would not be summoned, of course. Compromises would be negotiated and the culprit seen off the premises by Nicholson's holy terror while other young customers reached quickly for their pennies or slipped hidden favours back into the tray.

Small stock at least put something in the cash register on days when there was no other turnover at all.

Pay Within Twenty-Eight Days: invoices bristled on the spike or fattened the file that Lorna had opened for them. Kirsty would wring her hands and fret. She could not accept the fact that credit was not the same as debt and that the wheel of commerce was lubricated by it. She blamed Gordon for the summer slump, for abandoning the business, for leaving her to flounder.

Lorna brought news of her brother. Apparently he was spending fifteen hours a day at the brewery in Bishop Street in smoky St Rollox, learning how to tell good brew from bad. He came home at night, Lorna said, so dead beat that he often fell asleep at dinner. Kirsty was not appeased. She was convinced that all sorts of saleable items were escaping her attention, channelled elsewhere, and that somehow Gordon's presence would have kept things buoyant.

Mr Tubbs assured her that it was not so. But Kirsty had lost confidence and, in spite of Greta's advice, bought less and less as August progressed.

"What rubbish are you offerin' me now?"

"Blanket warmers, Mrs N."

"In this weather!"

"First nip o' autumn, Mrs Nicholson, an' you won't be able to stock enough o' them, believe me."

"I'll buy them when the time comes."

"Might not be able to. Might not be able to find any. Besides, the cost price will have soared."

"Take a half-dozen at least," Greta would say.

"Run up more credit?" Kirsty would shake her head.

"Toastin'-forks, best brass. Ninepence farthin' cost. Special ten per cent extra discount on orders of twenty-four."

"No."

"You must buy before you can sell, Kirsty," Lorna would remind her.

"But we're not *sellin'* anythin'," Kirsty would retort. "So what's the point in *buyin'* more?"

"It's just the seasonal slump," Greta would say.

"No, it's gone. The novelty's worn off. Bills, invoices, demands, that's all I've got on my desk. I'll be out o' business by Christmas."

Mr Tubbs would sigh, Greta would growl, Lorna would throw up her hands and all three would wonder why optimism and the spirit of adventure had gone out of Kirsty and whether her uncertainty would indeed close Nicholson's before the winter came.

*   *   *

Sunlight shaded the haze that lay over Fife and brought the great tides of barley that flooded the fields closer still to ripening. The heavy, fecund odour of grain hung over Clover Cottage. Bumble bees, brown as candy, dithered among the blooms that clung to the cottage wall and droned by the wide open window. Thunder, though, was not far away, for the sky to the west was the colour of crumbled earth and the sea was like fish-skin stretched taut against the shore of old St Andrews bay.

Perspiration glistened on Olive Adair's cheekbones and dripped from the brow of Captain Tom Wells. It made the couple's limbs sleek and slippery and Olive's hair felt dense as seaweed when Tom twined his hands into it and jerked her upper body from the bed. He pulled against her and straddled her hips. His thighs, downed with dark hair, were horseman hard. She, in contrast, was as soft fleshed as a peach for she'd borne five children and her breasts were no longer firm nor her belly taut. But none of that mattered in the long climaxes of late afternoon love-making. For hours they had billed and cooed, naked on the panelled bed beneath the open window, with nobody to hear his gasps and her cries, except Tom's mastiff tethered by the wicket gate, ready to bark at intruders.

She made love with both eyes open. She could see the tip of the juniper bush beneath which the dog lay, watch it nod and shake when the animal stirred but there was no motion in the birches that screened the garden, no movement in the sky. She felt as if she had been painted with a dry brush into the centre of a huge, moist, swirling landscape. When she cried out the drone of the bees seemed to stop and the hot faint sigh of the barley fields cease. For minutes on end there seemed to be no sound at all except the thudding of her heart and Tom's panting; then he cried out too, fell forward and buried his face in the pillow by her head. The ringlets of grey hair that rode on his ears were wet with sweat and droplets of sweat beaded his brows and then, with a throaty groan, he rolled from her, satisfied and exhausted.

For a half-hour they lay side by side saying nothing at all. Knee touching flank, forearm about her waist, Tom's fingertips traced the bruised and wrinkled cup of her nipple in endless, ineffectual circles. At length, he rose, fetched a bottle of French wine from the stone cupboard beneath the water tub and uncorked it. Olive watched. The bow to his legs and that flatfooted, swaggering walk made him, unclothed, seem more of a man not less. He sat by her on the narrow bed and offered her the fluted glass.

She struggled to sit up. Solicitously he put an arm about her shoulders, as if she had been invalided by his vigour. He held the glass while she sipped from it and then he let her drink it all. He poured more, spots of wine dripping on the tangled sheets. His hand shook. They looked at his trembling fingers and laughed ruefully together.

Tom said, "Oh, to hell with it."

He drank from the bottle then sank back against the foot of the bed, facing her, to catch whatever breeze came through the open window.

"I must go soon," Olive said.

"God, I'm so weary of deceits and partings."

"In a few months we'll be together," Olive said. "As soon as Amanda marries, in fact."

"Why must we wait?"

Olive lifted his feet and placed them comfortably into her lap. "For Amanda's sake."

"I think it's really for Dolphus's sake," Tom Wells said.

"I haven't been the wife he expected me to be."

"You brought him a fortune, gave him children. What more did he expect from you, Olive?"

"I think he expected me to love him."

"Love *him*! How could you ever love a man as dull, as dismal as Randolph Adair?"

"He wasn't always dull and dismal."

"Do you not love me?"

"Of course I do."

"More than you love Dolphus?"

"Yes, of course, dearest."

"Why then do you torment me by making me wait?"

Olive leaned from the bed and placed the glass on the floor. "I didn't expect to fall in love with you, Tom."

"No, nor I with you. But I did – and now I cannot stand to share you with another man, even if he is your husband."

"Amanda will be engaged by Christmas and will marry in May or June."

"Why, in God's name, if she's so set on him, can't she marry this young fellow immediately?"

"He isn't ready for marriage just yet."

"I know. I've met him," said Tom Wells.

"He may talk with a coarse accent, Tom, but he's not vulgar. He's decent and responsible."

"Not virtues I'd choose for an epitaph."

"I'd rather Amanda married Gordon Nicholson than John Whiteside or any of the so-called gentlemen who run with his fast crowd. They'd pick Dolphus clean in no time at all."

"What does it matter?" said Captain Wells.

Olive stiffened. "It matters a great deal to me."

"All I wish for is to be with you. And with our child."

"We'll be a family soon, Tom, I promise."

"Is our daughter as beautiful as you, Olive?"

"I haven't seen her," Olive said. "I'm not even supposed to know that it was Breezy who found parents for her. Dolphus assumes that I've put her entirely out of my heart."

Tom could not bear to see the tears in her eyes. He leaned towards her, took her into his arms. Olive clung to him, as if to a lifeline.

"The moment you're free of him," said Captain Wells, "we'll have our daughter back to be our very own."

"Yes, oh yes. I want her so much."

She leaned against him, let his arms protect her against the pain while thunder, distant still, rumbled faintly in the glens of the Grampians.

*   *   *

Hog Moscrop, more dead than alive, was brought in by John Boyle after a fight in Benedict Street.

While he waited for the surgeon to come and attend his wounds Mr Moscrop shouted the odds something terrible. His rasping voice, pungent with rum, filled Ottawa Street police station like the trumpet of God. No amount of pleading or patient explanation could make him understand that he had not been arrested and had been lifted from the gutter only for his own protection.

"AH WAAANT THE YOUNG 'UN."

"Who's he talkin' about?"

"Some bunty, I expect."

"GE'MME THE YOUNG 'UN."

"Who attacked you, Mr Moscrop?"

"AH NEVER DONE NOTHIN'. WHERE'S THE YOUNG 'UN? THE YOUNG 'UN KNOWS AH DONE NOTHIN'."

"Hold still, Hog. You'll bleed yourself dry if you thrash about like that."

"'S MA BLOOD, IS IT NO'? AH CAN DAE WHAT I LIKE WI' IT."

"Where's the blessed surgeon? Has he been sent for?"

"Moscrop, sit still."

"GET YER BLOODY HAUNS AFF ME."

In the cell next door Mr Andover, a gentle wee body who had drunk himself out of the teaching profession and even now, ragged and permanently incapacitated, had no regrets about it, smiled, nodded and called out, "Delirium tremens, that's what it is."

"What?" said Peter Stewart, on duty by the door.

"Pink elephants," said Mr Andover. *"Pink elephants is it, Hog, or white rats?"*

"AH'LL GI'E YE PINK BLOODY ELEPHANTS, ANDOVER. WHERE'S THE YOUNG 'UN? AH WANT T' TALK TAE THE YOUNG 'UN."

"Jesus!" said Constable Norbert, who had come through the door to sign off duty only minutes before. "I think he means me."

The desk was temporarily deserted. Both Sergeant Byrne and Sergeant Hector Drummond had vanished downstairs to endeavour to placate Mr Moscrop. It would have been much easier if he had been uninjured, had been an item for the charge sheet instead of the incident book. A bucket of cold water would have settled his hash and a certain amount of physical restraint, like Constable Boyle sitting on his chest, would not have been out of order. But Hog Moscrop had done nothing except lie bleeding in the gutter at the corner of Benedict Street and Riverside while an unidentified man, who had made off when challenged, booted him relentlessly about the head and body.

Craig, waiting too to go off duty, shrugged.

"Better get down there, Ronnie, before the wee man drops your name."

"He's one o' my 'contacts'," Ronnie whispered. "You know what I mean?"

"I'll come with you," Craig said.

"WHA'S 'AT? AH'M NO' DRINKIN' 'AT."

"It's only tea, Hog."

"POUZIN. IT'S POUZIN. AAAHHH!"

"It's not bloody poison. Get it down your neck, man," cried Sergeant Byrne, beard and temper bristling, "or I'll pour it down the tube. Uh, how about that? Do you want a taste o' the tube, Mr Moscrop?"

"AH WANT THE YOUNG 'UN."

"I think he means me, Sergeant," Ronnie Norbert said from the cell door.

"THAT'S HIM. THAT'S THE WAN."

"Do you know this gentleman, Constable Norbert?" asked Sergeant Drummond.

"I have his acquaintance, Sergeant, aye."

"Not a relative, Norbert, is he?" Sergeant Byrne asked, wiping Hog's blood from his fingers.

"No, Sergeant, just somebody I met in the street."

"AH'LL TALK T' HIM AN' NAEBODY ELSE."

"No need to shout, Hog. I'm right here," said Ronnie from the cell doorway. "By gum, you've had a right stramash wi' somebody. Who done that to your face?"

"Who's he?" said Hog, squinting suspiciously at Craig.

"Friend o' mine," said Ronnie affably. "His name's Nicholson."

"'Nother bloody copper."

"What do you expect in a police station, Hog," said Ronnie, "fishmongers?"

Hog Moscrop seated himself on the slab-like cot. He was unsteady not just with drink but as a result of the beating he had taken. Contusions swelled his cheeks and brow, his ear was torn and his nostrils were sticky with bright red blood. He held his left elbow with his right hand and winced when Ronnie, stooping, touched him.

The two sergeants and John Boyle had backed out in favour of the young constable, and the narrow corridor was crowded.

In the cell next door Mr Andover sang to himself, something tuneless and lugubrious from *The Gypsy Bride*. He had a daughter round in Kingdom Road but she would no longer take responsibility for him or pay his fine and Mr Andover would appear alone before the baillie tomorrow morning and would, most like, spend the next thirty days cooling his heels in jail.

"What the devil are you doin' down here, Nicholson?" Sergeant Byrne growled.

"Hog Moscrop may not know me, Sergeant," Craig said quietly, "but I know him."

Hector Drummond said, "You can go home now, Constable Boyle. And you, Mr Byrne, I'd be putting some cold water on those blood stains before they dry, if I were you."

The bearded sergeant, junior to Drummond, hesitated.

"No need for you to be lingerin'," Hector Drummond said. "I will take care of it now."

Byrne's hands were stained with blood, his tunic was smeared with it. He glanced down, grunted, nodded and let John Boyle precede him upstairs.

Hector Drummond drew Craig to one side of the cell door. "Now, son, what's in the wind?"

"I don't know yet, Mr Drummond."

"Why did Moscrop ask for Ronnie?"

"I can't say."

"Aye, but you can say," Sergeant Drummond told him. "Is it because Ronnie drinks down in the Madagascar?"

"I don't know what Ronnie does, Mr Drummond."

"He buys information, that is what he does," said Hector Drummond. "And that is a dangerous habit for a young constable to acquire."

"Moscrop will tell Ronnie who done him," Craig said. "He'd die before he'd tell you, or Sergeant Byrne for that matter."

"What would be your interest in Mr Moscrop?"

"None, Sergeant."

"Go home then."

"I'd rather wait, if it's all the same to you."

"Uh-huh," said the sergeant. "You *are* up to something, you and Norbert."

From the cell came the mutter of Hog Moscrop's voice, an unbroken monologue accompanied by Mr Andover's gentle chanting from next door.

Through the gap in the door Craig could see Ronnie as he squatted by the bed. He looked big and angular, competent in spite of his youth. He blotted out the figure of the little drunkard who was talking still, his gravel voice, disembodied, angry and confiding.

"All right then, Hog," Ronnie said. "We'll see what we can do."

"You, you dae it."

"It'll take more than me to bring him in." Ronnie got to his feet. "I'll take my pal Craig with me, right?"

"Ah never said a word against him, mind."

"Mum's the word," Ronnie promised. "Look, you drink your tea. Mr Penman will be along in a minute t' stitch you up."

"STITCH ME!"

"He's a doctor, Hog, not a copper. He'll attend to your wounds."

"How much'll it cost me?"

"No charge," said Ronnie. "After that's done, you'll be free to go home, or you can sleep here if you like."

"HERE! IN THE JILE!"

"Somebody will see you home."

"AH'M NO' A BLOODY BAIRN."

"*I'll see you home, Hog.*" Mr Andover interrupted his serenade. "*'Specially if you've a bottle hid in your stove.*"

Craig watched Hog Moscrop slump suddenly against the wall, mouth open, eyes screwed shut. Whatever fuel had fired his boiler for the last half-hour had finally burned out. Pain gripped him and he retched, gagging.

"He shouldnae have done it," Hog groaned. "No tae the likes o' me."

Blood filled his mouth and trickled stickily down his stubbled chin. He wiped it impatiently with the back of his hand and stared at the substance as if he could not quite believe his eyes.

"What's 'at?" he asked.

Ronnie picked up the mug of lukewarm tea and, carrying it carefully in both hands, stepped out of the cell and kicked the door closed with his heel.

"I think he has an internal injury, Sergeant," Ronnie said, handing the tea mug to Drummond. "Whatever you do don't give him anythin' to drink until Mr Penman's seen him."

"What did Moscrop tell you, son?" said Sergeant Drummond. "Who gave him the kicking?"

"King Billy," Ronnie said.

"Aye, I thought it might be," Drummond said. "Did Moscrop tell you the reason for the fight?"

"An argument over some bunty," Ronnie said.

"He's sure it was Billy?"

"Certain."

"In that case I think we'd be justified in bringing Mr King round here for questioning," the sergeant said.

"We'll fetch him," Ronnie said.

"Are you not off-duty?"

"No, we haven't signed off yet," Ronnie said.

Craig said, "Go on, Sergeant, give us the chance."

Drummond hesitated then said, "Right, lads. Find King Billy and bring him here to me."

*　　　*　　　*

Silver soup-spoon poised over her plate, Madge sniffed, and sniffed again.

"What *is* that smell?" she asked. "Gordon, is that you?"

"It's beer, Mother," Lorna said.

"Beer?" Madge sniffed once more. "Gordon, have you been at the pub?"

"Work, Mother, he's been at work."

"Well, he might have had a bath before he sat down to eat wi' decent folk."

"Aye, you are a bit niffy, son," Breezy said. "Bathin' isn't against the law, you know."

"Oh, leave him alone." Lorna reached across the dining-table and tucked Gordon's napkin into the vee of his waistcoat. "He didn't have time to wash an' change. Did you, Gordie?"

"Nuh."

"He should have made time," said Madge.

"Look at him," said Lorna. "The poor lamb's absolutely knackered."

"Language, Lorna, please," Madge chided.

"You do look a wee bit the worse for wear," said Breezy. "Eat your dinner, son, an' away to your bed."

"Uh-huh."

Listlessly Gordon dabbled a spoon in his soup while Madge held a tiny lace hanky to her nose and reared away from her son as if he had a contagion.

"What have they got you doin' up there?" she asked. "I thought you were supposed t' be workin' in an office, not swimmin' in the vats."

"Laboratory."

Breezy nodded. "Ah, yes. Bein' taught the constitution of beer on scientific principles, are you?"

"Uh-huh."

"God, you must be tired," said Lorna. "You sound just like Bobby."

"Who's doin' the teachin'?" said Breezy.

"Herr Winkler."

"A foreigner?" said Madge.

"German," said Gordon.

"One of the best, so I hear," said Breezy. "God knows, it cost Dolphus a fortune to lure him over here. He was in charge of brewin' at Hausers', in Bavaria."

"Where's your brother then?" said Madge. "I thought he was supposed to be teachin' Gordon the trade, not some foreign mannie."

"Come on, Madge," said Breezy. "Gordon's got a lot to learn an' this Winkler chap's an expert. Besides, Dolphus is on holiday."

"No, he's back," said Gordon.

"When did he come home?" said Breezy.

"I saw him on Monday," said Gordon. "He put his nose round the door, grunted and went away again."

"I still say it's not right," Madge put in.

"What's not right, dear?"

"Leavin' our Gordon's trainin' to a German."

"It's only for a month," Gordon muttered. "Thank God."

"Don't you like it?" said Madge.

"'S all right," said Gordon, defensively.

"If this German's workin' you too hard," said Madge, "Albert'll have a word . . ."

"Oh no, I won't, Madge."

"It was all your idea," Madge said. "Now he comes in here stinkin' to high heaven, too done in even to be civil to his mother. Gordon, eat that soup."

Gordon took a mouthful of broth then pushed his plate away.

Madge said, "What are you supposed t' be learnin' in this lavoratory, anyway?"

"Laboratory, Mother," Lorna said.

Gordon gathered himself. He realised that he was being churlish and unfair. He had gone willingly to Carruth's. It wasn't Breezy's fault that Herr Winkler was a martinet or that he was suffering physically from the oppressive indoor atmosphere with its reek of coal-gas burners and fermenting cereals. He understood the necessity of it, the need to learn how to tell one beer from another, to recognise by sampling when a brew had been adulterated, ill-stored or otherwise diminished in quality. The language of the trade was totally unfamiliar, however, the mathematics and liquid calculations too. He hated the smell of the little beakers of ale and lager that Herr Winkler thrust at him, the whole messy business of tasting, swilling, spitting and making a stab at a judgement.

"Laboratory then," said Madge. "Just what do you do there all day long?"

"There are four kinds of malt," Gordon intoned, "each regulated in the process of maltin' by duration and control of temperature."

Breezy smiled. "Pale?"

"Below one hundred and forty degrees."

"Patent?"

"No higher than one seventy-five."

"How long does that take?"

"About ninety hours," said Gordon. "Longer for black firin'."

"Have you been through the brewhouse yet?"

"Once," said Gordon. "Herr Winkler has a model to scale. He teaches me off that."

"I thought you were sellin' the stuff, not makin' it." Madge was nonplussed by her son's knowledge of trade jargon and the fact that Breezy had such information at his fingertips too. "All this just for a glass o' wallop. Huh!"

"Best barley?" said Breezy.

"Carruth's buys mainly from Angus, pays the extra charge," said Gordon. "We never take purchase on grain cut after the end o' August."

"That's enough." Madge waved the little hanky as if in surrender.

He had satisfied Breezy and deflected his mother from her harangue but it was all rote learning. He understood about barley, had seen it at various stages of growth and could relate easily enough to the raw material. For the rest, however, the intricacies of the malting process had been crammed up without real understanding.

"A month won't be long in passin', Gordon." Lorna patted his arm sympathetically. "You'll soon be out on the road again."

"Suppose so," Gordon said.

"Not if he doesn't eat his dinner, he won't," Madge said. "He'll be in a hospital bed, that's where he'll be."

"Jeeze!" Gordon lost patience, pushed himself away from the table and hurried out of the room.

"Gordon, come back here this instant," Madge cried.

"Leave him be, Madge," Breezy advised.

"What's got into that boy?" Madge tutted and shook her head. "I just don't understand him."

"Obviously!" Lorna snapped.

She threw down her table napkin and also left the dining-room, an act of rebellion that, for a moment, left Madge speechless.

"Done it now, chookie, haven't you?" said Breezy mildly.

"Have a word with them," Madge said. "Tell them I didn't mean it. Get them back here."

Breezy shook his head. "Not now, Madge. After I've eaten. What's the entrée?"

"Braised steak."

"Ring the bell then, if you please," Breezy said and watched from under hooded lids as his wife, without argument, rose to obey.

* * *

Lorna found her brother in his bedroom. He had thrown off his jacket, kicked off his shoes and lay on top of the single bed with his hands behind his head. Through undrawn curtains the slate roof of the kitchen extension was visible below a patch of dusky sky.

"It's me." Lorna seated herself on the end of the bed. "Are you feelin' all right?"

"I'm fine. Just tired."

"You shouldn't let her talk t' you that way, Gordon."

"It's just her manner."

"If she's not careful she'll drive us off like she did Craig an' Kirsty," Lorna said.

Gordon opened his eyes. "What have you got buzzin' in your head?"

"Oh, this an' that," Lorna said. "Never mind me, though. Tell me, do you really hate it at Carruth's?"

"'Course I bloody do," Gordon said. "It's a nightmare, that place. But," he sighed, "it's only for another week or two an' then it'll get better."

"Will it?"

"Aye, aye, it's bound to."

"Is this what you really want, Gordon?"

"What?"

"To become an Adair?"

"There's worse things to become."

"Kirsty misses you," Lorna said. "Greta Taylor too."

"Huh," said Gordon, not harshly. "If it's any consolation, I miss them an' all. But don't tell them I said so."

"Kirsty's worried about the shop."

"She shouldn't be."

"I've told her so, but she won't listen to me."

"Two or three weeks an' sales'll pick up again."

"Can't you come down, just show your face?"

"I . . . Nah, not right now, Lorna."

"It's all for her sake, isn't it?" said Lorna. "For Mandy? You really have it bad, don't you?"

Gordon pushed himself up on the pillow, frowning.

"Lorna, you're too young to understand."

"I'm old enough to realise that sometimes you have to stand up for yourself."

"What's that supposed t' mean?"

"You'll see," Lorna said.

She kissed him on the nose before he could protect himself,

and got to her feet. "It's braised steak. Are you sure you can't be tempted?"

"Get out of here."

"Nightie-night."

"Bugger off," said Gordon, smiling.

*　　*　　*

Heroes were not supposed to age as other men aged or legends to fray and wrinkle like old socks. None of Greenfield's hooligans could understand what had become of their idol, Billy King.

Billy's refusal to become involved in break-ins, in street wars against the McMahons, even to continue to earn his daily bread by bullying and extortion, worried rival hard men almost as much as it worried disciples. What if this inclination to meekness was catching? No more punch-ups, no more riots, no more bravado, no more exhibitions of bigotry and brutality. What if, by some horrifying process, they were all doomed to turn into law-abiding citizens? Dear God, man, life would hardly be worth living. None of them wanted to admit that the great William King had become a hopeless drunkard.

Billy's father was deeply ashamed of his son's descent into alcoholism. He too pretended that he didn't know what had come over Billy. Mary Shotten, Billy's light o' love, and eyewitness to his degeneration, had been around too long to breathe the truth to anyone, though it was fear not fealty that sustained her silence now.

Mary Shotten did not think in high-flown terms. To her, Billy was sulking, sulking all over her kitchen, while he salved his wounded pride and wrecked his liver with quantities of shebeen whisky. She didn't much care what Billy did to himself. Attempting to commit suicide by alcoholic poisoning was an expensive business, though, and it was her money he was using to do it. He lolled about her kitchen in a haze of cheap whisky while she struggled to earn an honest bob by entertaining sailors and dockers out in the bleedin' rain. Now and then she'd lose her Irish temper and scream at him and he would punch her face, and that, for a while, would be enough for both of them.

If Billy had gone decently down into a drunken stupor Mary might have been able to put up with it until the end. Trouble was that Billy was too strong for his own good. Though small in stature, paunchy and with a dreadful dead-pork pallor, he had the constitution of a damned pit-pony. Sullen patience, which had once been his best defence against police harassment, kept alive a spark of intelligence and an awareness that he needed money not to live but to drink.

Billy tried sending Mary round to make his collections. But he had been gone too long and the wee shopkeepers and small businessmen whom he had milked for years simply apologised politely and hung on to their pennies. Nobody needed protection from a man who was never seen. No Billy, no big bad Billy, no cash. It was out of sheer necessity then, when credit ran out with local shebeen owners, that Billy stirred himself and decided to try his hand at pimping.

Billy knew nothing at all about a business which had little enough status in Glasgow's criminal circles and none at all in the Greenfield, that sad unmanly trade where women made themselves mere commodities and strangers paid for sex without love. Local hooligans were black affronted when they learned what Billy was up to. Bantam hard men hid their eyes when their hero came slouching up the street with Beth Simpson or Connie McLaren. It was embarrassing to see the mighty King Billy tapping prostitutes for beer money and badgering them to share their earnings.

Report of the degeneration of William King should have made its way back to Ottawa Street. But John Boyle, whose beat it was, was a good, God-fearing Christian and embarrassed by sexual matters. He preferred to pretend that prostitution did not exist. Seldom would he book one of the gay ladies for a court appearance, admonishment and a modest fine. In consequence Constables Norbert and Nicholson first learned of Billy's new profession from Hog Moscrop and went striding down to Benedict Street still trying to put the pieces together and make sense of the story.

"Let me get this straight," Craig said. "Prue Alston and Angela are in a pub in the Madagascar. Prue Alston takes on too much drink and passes out. Hog offers to escort Angela home."

"He probably had her price."

"Right," Craig said. "The only thing is that Angela lives in the Madagascar. So what were they doin' in Benedict Street?"

"Goin' back to Hog's place, obviously," Ronnie said.

"King Billy appears, tells Hog the girl belongs to him, an' that Hog better stump up brass before he receives her favours."

"Pay Billy, in other words," Ronnie said.

"Angela's precious," Craig said. "I still can't understand why she'd go off wi' the likes o' Moscrop."

"Come on, Craig, don't be bloody stupid. Women like that take what they can get," Ronnie said. "Aye, an' get what they deserve."

"She didn't deserve Billy, that's for sure."

Ronnie said, "Angela tells King Billy what he can do with himself. Billy grabs her by the hair and Moscrop goes wild."

"He'd be full of rum, of course," Craig said.

"I doubt if Hog would have attacked Billy if he'd been sober," Ronnie said. "But you never know, do you? Chances are they were all pickled. Billy drags Angela into the close and upstairs, throws her into his bunty's house an' bolts the door."

"Hog won't give up. He goes after them."

"To hear Hog tell it you'd think he was a knight in shinin' armour, not just a dirty wee old man," Ronnie said. "Anyway, Hog's out there on the landin' yellin' how he's goin' to fetch the polis, an' Angela's inside screamin' blue murder."

"Was she taken there an' held against her will?" Craig asked.

" 'Course she was."

"Abduction," Craig said. "We can charge the bastard with abduction."

"We didn't draw a warrant," Ronnie said.

"Don't worry about that," Craig said. "I know Billy of old. He won't come quietly. We'll get our chance."

The constables rounded the corner into Riverside. The long arid highway stretched before them, flanked by docks and quays on one hand and by ugly four-storey tenements on the other. It was here that Gordon Nicholson had been beaten and robbed by Billy King, an act of opportunism that Billy had lived to regret.

Craig's excitement was mingled with apprehension, a fear of what this squalid farce might lead to. He was concerned for the safety of Angela Alston and, oddly and irrationally, he feared for Greta too.

"The minute Hog mentioned polis out comes Billy, foamin' at the mouth," Ronnie said. "Hog decides that gallantry has its limits an' scarpers. Billy pursues, catches him at the close an' starts knockin' hell out of him. If John Boyle hadn't heard the commotion an' interrupted it we might have been chargin' Billy with murder."

"Where's the girl, where's Angela Alston now?"

"As far as I can tell," Ronnie said, "she's still up there in Mary Shotten's house."

"With Billy?"

"What d'you think?"

"I think we should get a move on," Craig said.

"I think you're right," said Ronnie.

*　　*　　*

As soon as he entered Benedict Street Craig knew that his fears were justified. The street was deserted. Only two of its five gas-lamps had been lit and the lamplighter's pole, still spluttering, lay abandoned on the pavement. A late-night sour-milk cart stood unattended, three or four broken jugs scattered on the cobbles about it. The horse in the shafts snorted, puzzled and forlorn. Pigeons, Craig noted, were high on the rooftops and not one cocky youngster was to be seen, not even a nose in a close or a face at a window. It was as if a big wind had roared through Benedict Street and swept away its citizens like leaves.

Even as he led Ronnie upstairs to Mary Shotten's house Craig knew that Billy would not be there and had a sickening premonition of what they would find within. The landings' gas-mantles were unlighted. Glaze from the windows turned the stairs mouse grey. No light showed through the open door of Mary Shotten's apartment. That same grey glaze, not hazy but polished, defined the hallway and kitchen within. The kitchen door, torn half off its hinges, sagged on its screws and tangled clothing, bottles and one small worn shoe were strewn outwards, like splashes, from the dim interior.

Craig stopped on the landing. He drew his stick from its holster and gripped tightly. Ronnie piled against him, crouched, armed too with a weighted baton. They had sprinted the best part of a quarter of a mile, had climbed the stairs three at a time, yet they were hardly winded, and conversed in whispers.

"Is he in there? Is he waitin' for us?"

"Nah," Craig hissed. "I think he's gone."

"Go in then. I'll cover."

"Oh, Christ!" Craig said, then raising his voice called out, "*Billy? Billy King?*"

No answer came from within, no sound except a faint puppy-like whimper. Craig gripped the baton in both hands and darted into the kitchen.

She was crouched by the back of the door. Craig almost fell over her. In his tense state he might have swung at her if she had not screamed. He had no idea who she was. In poor light and in her changed condition, he did not recognise her at first.

"*Craig, is he there?*"

"No. Come on in."

He did not go at once to the girl's assistance. He yanked open the larder door then, clinking among bottles, stepped to the hole-in-the-wall and tore aside the ragged curtain. Bedclothing was heaped up in a mound. The bolster had been tossed against the wall. A second woman, fully clothed, lay face down upon the mattress. A bottle rolled from the bed, clanked to the floor, gurgled.

"Ronnie, light the gas."

The creature behind the kitchen door was silent now. She had uttered only one sharp scream then doubled over, brow pressed to her knees, arms folded over her head. Craig heard the scratch of a match, the puffy roar of the room's solitary gas jet. He blinked in the yellow light and then, steeling himself, leaned towards the girl and touched her on the bare shoulder. Her light, cotton dress had been ripped from her body, bodice and half-stays cut away too. Her back was drenched with blood, her neck a mass of small tick-like lacerations where a razor had shorn off her pretty blonde curls. Twists of hair were scattered by the chair, fine strands adhered to the blood on her shoulders and forearms. He must have held her, Craig thought, knuckled in his elbow like a ewe, her face against his hip.

"Angela, is it you?"

"Jesus!" Ronnie hissed. "What's he done to her?"

"Angela?" Craig touched her again, gently.

This time she responded. She scrambled away on her knees, burrowing at the crack in the broken door with her fingernails as if she could escape through it.

Craig straightened. He felt sick, sick with pity, not rage. He moved from the girl to the bed recess and looked down at the woman there.

"Another one?" said Ronnie in awe.

Craig reached out both hands and turned the woman over. Slipping a finger into the neck of her dress, he felt for the pulse on the side of her throat.

"Well, Ronnie," he said, "I think you've got your murder at last."

"Dead, she's dead?"

"Look."

The blow had been heavy and severe enough to kill instantly. The dark-green lead-glass bottle had shattered into her skull. Blood and hair had congealed into something unnaturally ornamental, like an embroidered rose.

Ronnie swallowed. "Who is she?"

"Mary Shotten."

"The other one's Angela?"

"Yes."

"What're we goin' t' do, Craig?"

"The girl's in shock. We need assistance, Ronnie, medical assistance."

"What about King Billy?" Ronnie said. "He's out there, Craig, runnin' amok."

"I doubt it." Craig shook his head. "I doubt if he's runnin' at all."

"If I'd raped an' killed . . ."

"He didn't rape them," Craig said. "He was afraid of them. He did the only thing he knew how to do."

Bottles were everywhere in the kitchen, in the sink, on the draining-board, in the ash bucket, even on the cold iron hob, the dark-green and plain-glass pint bottles that were favoured by back-street distillers.

"I want him," Ronnie said. "I just want to get my hands on that bastard."

"You're not the only one," said Craig. "First things first, though. Go an' find the beat constable an' send him round to Ottawa Street to report this mess."

"What about her?" Ronnie said. "You can't just leave her here."

"I know," Craig said.

The girl had squeezed herself against the broken door, hands cupped over her head. She was weeping at last. That, Craig reckoned, was a good sign. He peeled a blanket from the bed, detaching it from under the dead woman's legs. Kneeling, he draped it over Angela Alston's shoulders.

"It's all right, love. It's all right. You're safe now," he murmured.

214

He lifted her into his arms. To his surprise she did not resist.
Her hands fell slack. Her face had been cut too by Billy's untidy
blade. Her pink scalp showed in ugly patches like the head of a
china doll in need of paint. Stays and bodice flapped about her
waist and Craig gathered them under the blanket and modestly
covered her up.

"Where are you takin' her?" Ronnie asked.

"Across the road to Greta's house," Craig said.

She was as light as a child. Her eyes were fixed on his face
as he carried her out of the kitchen; blue eyes, all that remained
of her impudent prettiness. The facial cuts would not heal without scarring, Craig thought; the ten-pound orphan bought for
her looks all those years ago had turned out no bargain after
all.

*   *   *

Bad dreams had wakened Jen. Greta had lifted her and walked
with her to soothe away the night fears.

Concern for the child robbed her of her usual caution. She'd
heard nothing of the commotion across the way or, if she had,
she'd put it down to boyish horseplay. Perhaps she supposed it
was just Isa Thomas who had come knocking quietly on her door
at that late evening hour. Whatever the reason and cause Greta
was not alarmed and, still with Jen in her arms, unhooked the
chain, pushed back the bolt and opened the door to Billy.

For two or three seconds she did not recognise him. The king of
Riverside, the boss of Benedict Street, had changed. He was clad
only in a collarless shirt and a pair of old trousers, open at the fly,
garments, hands and arms all streaked with blood. In one fist he
brandished a pint bottle, in the other an open razor. Curiously
his feet were bare.

For an instant that fact made him seem less dangerous than
comical. It was a bare foot that he stuck in the door, though,
and a bare foot that pushed her back against the wall, while
Greta, numb with astonishment, quailed before the sight of the
bloodstained razor and drew Jen away.

She asked him what he wanted.

He said nothing. He did not grin or snarl or groan. He uttered
not one word to explain his intention. His expression was as blank
and glassy as the bottle in his fist. Greta could tell by his eyes,
though, that King Billy had gone mad.

215

He pushed her again with his naked foot. The white flesh was soiled with black dirt. He had walked, she thought, down the backs, through mud puddles that, even after a dry month, were sticky still, through strews of ashes, the dust of drying-greens, picking his way into her close from the rear.

The razor's bone handle had been splintered and bound with brown twine. She saw that he had cut himself with the blade. Knuckles and palm dripped little blackish spots of blood as he pushed her into the kitchen.

She crabbed away from him. Wide awake and hypnotised by the sight of the man, Jen clung heavily to her. Because of the child she could neither attack nor defend herself. For a second time she asked him what he wanted.

He shook his head. He seemed bewildered by his motives for coming here at all. He drank from the pint bottle. He swung it up and down in his left hand, spilling the colourless whisky down his chin and chest.

"You should sit down, Mr King," Greta said.

If she struck him with a cooking-pot could she stun him or would his head be too thick for the blow to have effect? She'd had truck with drunkards in the lost years when she'd first been sent to Glasgow to be a servant to Mr Lynch, the rope manufacturer. She had not known enough to fight off his attentions. She'd been too young, too lacking in experience to do other than submit. She would lie on the bed, burning with shame, while he swigged brandy from a crystal glass and told her what he would do to her, taking more pleasure, it seemed, from that obscene preliminary than from the sudden, probing little act itself.

Confronted with Billy King, Greta remembered how Mr Lynch would do it, not with a perverse passion but as a kind of interruption to his drinking. His sister, who knew all along why a servant girl had been bought, crept up and down the corridor outside, sipping sherry and listening to every word, every creak and cry and groan, as if the performance were for her benefit too. Mr Lynch had dropped dead one Sunday afternoon, decanter in hand, and she, Greta, had walked off into the gardens of Pollok while the sister was still crying out for her to fetch the doctor.

King Billy would not die, though. No such luck. He had his razor, his bottle to keep him alive. The dull patina of unpredictable brutality still clung to him and he, or his kin, would go on for ever, diehard and well-beloved, feared and respected. She hated men like Billy, all men, for forcing her to share their impotent reasonless rage against the world.

The men she might have loved and with whom she might have found redemption would not have her. She hadn't been favoured by fortune, like Kirsty Nicholson. Now here was another manifestation of frightened manhood, the king, the daddy of them all, with his weapon and his bottle and his brave assumptions that she would cower before him and make his smallness seem big.

He kicked out a wooden chair, seated himself upon it, back to the door. He swigged again from the bottle. His body was bloated, his brain decayed, yet she could not free herself from him because she was afraid of what he might do to Jen.

"I want t' put her down," Greta said.

"Uh?"

"I want to put her in the bed."

"Ah?"

"Then y'can have what y'want."

"I'm not . . . " He rolled his head like a tethered bullock. "I'm not . . . not . . ."

There had been a man before Mr Lynch, one of her mother's acquaintances. He had taken her into bed one night when her older sisters had been struck down with an illness. His body smelled like seaweed drying on a shore and his legs were bristly with hair. But he had held her tenderly and she had fallen asleep against him in spite of herself. Sometimes she felt that she had never wakened from that night.

Once Jen was safe she would do something, though she didn't know what. He was strong still and mad with dirty whisky. Even so she would not let him take her, not without a fight. She moved towards the bed recess and lowered Jen from her shoulder.

He was on his feet at once. Greta glimpsed the glint of the razor and dipped her head, put her face between the child's and the edge of the blade. But it was not his intention to cut her. He grabbed at Jen, plucked her from Greta's arms, held her at arm's length and peered at her suspiciously, as if she were some small creature that might prove to have teeth and claws.

"I'm gonna cut her hair off," he said.

And Greta shouted, "NO."

* * *

The denizens of Benedict Street had come out of hiding by the time Craig emerged from the close. The lamplighter had retrieved his pole, the sour-milk seller was gentling his horse and a woman was picking up pieces of a broken jug. Boys, young and not so young, were hanging about the corner, aimless and furtive and keeping their distance. The police might be despised and detested but it was soothing to know that they were on the spot when trouble was in the air. The sight of Constable Nicholson with a young girl in his arms reawakened interest. Windows were cautiously opened and heads poked out. Constable Norbert was cheered and jeered as he sprinted down Riverside, pealing away on his whistle.

Craig crossed the street. He had covered Angela's head with a corner of the blanket and carried her without effort. She was twitching now. Shock, of course, would take its toll. He hoped that he had made the right decision, landing an injured girl on Greta. Perhaps he should have stayed put, guarded the girl and the dead woman in that bloody kitchen. But he could save ten precious minutes by making sure that Angela was safe and cared for. Ten minutes might be enough time to track down Billy King.

As he passed the lamplighter Craig called out, "What did you see, Leerie? Did you see a man runnin' away?"

"Aye, it was King Billy, drookit in blood," the lamplighter answered. "Is she deid?"

"Carved up but not dead. Which way did King go?"

"Up there." The lamplighter pointed towards Dumbarton Road. "He wasnae runnin', though. He never had his boots on."

"Up a close, officer," the milk seller called out. "He jooked up a close, so he did."

"Where?"

"Far end o' the street."

"Right," Craig said.

"You goin' tae catch him?" a plump woman called from a first-storey window.

"If I can."

"Ye'll be needin' a gun then."

"Why?"

" 'Cause the bugger's ravin'.' "

Craig stepped into the close of No. 13 with Angela in his arms. He had no compunction about using Greta Taylor in this way. He made a professional separation between his own feelings and the necessity of tracking King without delay.

Angela was whimpering now and he had to hold her tightly as he approached the door.

And then he stopped.

The door stood ajar, unlocked and unbolted.

With the girl in his arms he was vulnerable. For a moment he didn't know what to do. He had a sudden hideous fear that Greta might be lying in there, her dark hair shaved away, her throat cut.

A voice said, "Aye, I think he's in there too."

Isa Thomas pressed against the inner wall of the stairs, two older children cowering behind her.

Craig said, "Did you see him?"

"Naw," the woman said. "But Greta'd never leave her door wide open, not at this time o' the night."

"The water closet?"

Isa Thomas shook her head. "Empty. I looked. Is the lassie hurtit bad?"

"Cuts mainly," Craig said, "an' shock."

They spoke in whispers. The gaunt, raw-boned woman had descended a few more steps to the corner. Behind her the children, both girls, were ready to flee at the first sign of the monster. For an instant Craig wondered if these two specimens had been born to Isa or had been bought through the offices of Sylvie McNish. Curiously the knowledge gave him an affinity with the docker's wife.

He said, "Can you take her? She's not heavy."

Isa Thomas hesitated. "Aye, give her here."

Angela cried out softly as he transferred her into the woman's care. Isa Thomas seated herself on the stairs and cradled the girl in her arms like a baby, rocking her soothingly, while her own children, if that's what they were, looked on impassively.

"Where's your husband?" Craig said.

"The pub."

"Right, I'm goin' in for a look around."

He unsheathed the heavy baton, took it in both hands and

stood by the side of the door. Did he imagine that he could smell King Billy?

And Greta shouted, "NO."

The Thomas children were gone like minnows. Protecting the girl, Isa Thomas scrambled back upstairs. Apparently other neighbours had been listening too. Craig heard doors slamming, startled voices.

Again Greta shouted, "NO."

Craig went in.

Billy King held Jen pinned under his arm. The razor was poised behind her neck. She was weeping but hung passive against the man's hip. The man had no hand to hold her for he had not relinquished his grip on the whisky bottle.

Greta, face scarlet, was screaming, "NO, NO, NO, NO, NO." She seemed oblivious to Craig's arrival.

Craig watched the razor blade, saw how Billy cocked his forefinger around the edged steel, squeezed on it as if it were the trigger of a gun. He seemed to feel no pain at all as the blade bit to the bone and blood ran wet and heavy from the wound.

"Put her down, Billy," Craig said quietly.

"I thought it was you," Billy King said. "I'm gonna cut this yin's hair aff an' all."

Greta was blind and deaf to reason. She leapt, screaming, straight on to the table top and, like a cat, on to Billy's back. Her fingers clawed at his face. Craig swung the baton across Billy King's wrist, saw the cut-throat whirr upward, bright as a dragonfly.

Billy King grunted. He dropped Jen, reached over his shoulder with his broken hand and pulled Greta from his back as if she weighed no more than the child. She fell heavily against the edge of the table, then to the floor. Grovelling out her arms to the child, she dragged Jen towards her and hid beneath the table.

The movements were sluggish yet took no time at all to complete. Craig stepped forward and raised the baton. When he looked into King Billy's face he knew that the man was blown. Nothing at all registered in the eyes, not pain or fear or hatred. Billy had been burned out by alcohol. All that was left was the hard vulcanised core of violence that had nurtured him for thirty years or more.

The baton remained poised. Craig could not bring himself to hit a dead man. Hesitation almost cost him his life. He did not even see the bottle. He had no idea what it was that struck his helmet, driving the rim into his cheekbone. He was suddenly surrounded by a swarm of red-winged insects, robbed for a second of all strength. The baton dropped from his fingers. He blundered into the table and Billy hit him again, then, with a grunt, turned and sauntered out of the kitchen as casually as a journeyman whose day's work is done.

*   *   *

Craig dragged himself up from his knees. The helmet had saved him. It had been torn from its strap by the force of the blow, and tilted over one eye. In his brief period of confusion he wondered if he had been blinded. He leaned on the table and groped with both hands, found and removed the familiar shape.

"Craig, are you hurt?"

Greta was on her feet, Jen cuddled to her breast. Though tears coursed down her cheeks the child uttered not one audible sound of distress, not even a sob.

"No, I'm all right." Craig's head buzzed like a beehive and there was pounding in his ears. "You?"

"Fine," Greta said. "Thank God you came when you did. I think he'd have killed the pair o' us."

"Aye, he might," Craig said.

"Where's he gone?"

"God knows!" Craig said. "I think I'd better nail him before he does any more harm, though."

"Aye," Greta said. "You'd better."

Craig shook his head to clear it, then went out into the close. He had not forgotten about Angela; he had no choice but to leave her with Isa Thomas. One of the Ottawa Street sergeants would arrive with the constables and a whole mob of high-rankers would pour out of headquarters as soon as it became known that there had been a murder. They would clear up the debris that Billy had left behind. His job was to track down the lunatic and secure him without delay. He had been involved in a similar incident before. He had fought in the rain on the railway tracks with Daniel Malone. But King Billy was no Malone. His cruelty had no point to it. Billy had looked for release in a whisky bottle and had found not oblivion but the devil.

Craig glanced along Benedict Street. Not a sign of Ronnie Norbert or Archie Flynn was to be seen. He looked towards Riverside. The citizens had not scattered. Billy had gone past them and, being visible, posed no personal threat. Besides, there was a copper on the scene now. The copper would protect them.

Craig tightened his grip on the baton and set off after the murderer.

Billy had made no attempt to hide. He occupied the middle of the street, shambling and isolated against the soft night sky. Craig did not charge after him. He had no wish to tangle with the madman again. His only fear was that Billy would vanish like a wraith into the distant horizon. Craig jogged for a hundred yards or so then slowed to walking pace, keeping Billy always in sight.

Behind Craig a curious crowd had gathered. They stepped out in single file and did not overtake the constable. They were men mostly, young and old, with only one or two women among them. Some had thrown coats over night attire, others had hurried from their firesides in trousers and shirts, one or two, like Billy, were barefoot. Craig knew what they wanted – to be in at the death.

When he reached the corner of Riverside and Banff Street Billy swung to the right. He kept to the middle of the cobbled road, ignoring the men who clustered about the pub doors like small fish at a feeding station. He did not acknowledge his disciples or his enemies or appear to notice that McMahons mingled with the family Ross, Sheddons with Fitzgeralds, Protestants and Catholics united for his last rites. None of them understood what Billy had done or why and the silence was watchful, bewildered and weird. Far off, the bell of a police van clanged, its urgency diminished by distance. Craig held his pace, eyes fixed on Billy King, his back to the throng that pushed along behind him.

Billy had gone three hundred yards west along Riverside before he broke into a trot. He still held the pint bottle in his hand. It glistened now and then in the street-lamps' light as he raised and sucked from it. He swung suddenly to his left, off the cobbles, over broken paving, down the narrow lane that separated the old tannery from the red-brick wall of the new slaughterhouse. Craig ran too. The crowd followed, massing at last, surging forward into the lane.

Recent ordinances had demanded light along this route to the river. Four electrical globes, cowled in blue metal, kept Billy visible. He lumbered on, rolling from side to side, the gait as eccentric and comical as that of a trained bear.

Shouts from the crowd: "*Billy, Billy, Gi'e yousel' up, man.*"

It was clear at last where Billy was headed.

Craig increased his pace.

Lights on the far side of the Clyde gave definition to the river. The Govan shore floated like a rust-red raft moored by the mouth of Fairfield basin. Beneath the flocculent ground around Linthouse's smoke stacks, scaffolds and cranes seemed to tip and tilt on the tide. Jutting from the little ash quay at the alley's end were two stone bollards and four horseposts of pitted iron. They delayed Billy's progress just long enough for Craig and a dozen or so men to emerge from the lane and to see him leap out in the dark gap.

Craig was first to the edge. He knew that the treacle black waters of the Clyde had taken Billy in and would not, without reluctance, give up such a sterling son. Besides, the whisky bottle, not quite empty, lay abandoned on the dirt.

"Jesus! He jumped!"

"Billy, och Billy, what've ye done?"

A cartwheel of ripples showed where Billy had gone down and the river in its length and breadth seemed suddenly as infinite as the sea.

"His faither's here. See, let him through."

Craig, dropped to one knee, was tearing the laces from his boots. He glanced up. Forty or fifty men and boys crowded the edge of the quay, come to wonder at King Billy's dramatic exit.

Billy's father had his hands in pockets. His shoulders were hunched, cloth cap tugged over his brow as if he preferred anonymity to the notoriety that bereavement would bring. He scowled down at Craig.

"Here, what d'ye think you're doin'?"

"Goin' in for him," Craig answered.

"Naw, naw," the old man said. "Let him go, son. Let him be."

"Sorry, I can't." Craig kicked off his boots, flung aside his tunic jacket, and somebody – stupidly – cheered when he pushed himself from the quay and dropped down into the water twenty feet below.

Craig was surprised at the power of the river. He had braced himself for cold but not for the strong-running current that dragged him away from the quay before he could surface. He was fifteen or twenty yards out before he shook water from his eyes and got his bearings. He tried to tread water, could not hold position, was forced to trust himself to the eddies along the piles where timber, bottles, skeins of old rope slapped against the quayside in a welter of soapy brown foam.

He shouted, *"Can you see him?"*

"Naw."

He filled his lungs, rolled over, and dived downward.

The Clyde was not brown but black, black as molasses. Craig had no fear of its tidal rips but only of what he might find there, what he might touch, rotting things, dead things dredged up from the mud. He swept his arms this way and that, groping blindly while the current thrust against him and threatened to carry him away. Gasping, he surfaced once more. His trousers were lead heavy and the Govan shore seemed miles away. He fanned himself round and round with movements of his arms, kicking hard to hold himself steady.

"There, there. There he is." The head bobbed below him, down river, past the butt of the quay and its slimy wooden ladder. From the corner of his eye Craig saw the crowd shift and sway as he struck out towards the object. Billy King, chin tilted, stared patiently up at the sky but just as Craig reached out to catch him he sank below the surface once more.

Craig almost had him. He touched an ear, hair, a shoulder. Billy was quite motionless, upright, his arms by his side. He did nothing at all to help himself, did not struggle or flail. He simply sank, dead weight, out of Craig's reach.

The crowd on the quay had thinned. Sergeant Byrne, Archie Flynn and Ronnie Norbert had arrived, old Drummond too. They waved and shouted at Craig to surrender to the inevitable. Shoulders and thighs ached. His neck hurt. Cold and effort had sapped him and the river was stronger than ever, hauling him back from the ladder. A shout, the splash of a cork lifebelt; Craig snatched at it and willing hands pulled on the rope and drew him in. Byrne was clinging to the rungs, helmet off, hair and beard bristling. Craig grabbed the sergeant's arm, was hoisted from the water and led upwards step by step.

Ronnie and Archie pulled him over the edge and on to the quay where, to his acute embarrassment, he flopped on all fours and retched up river water while Sergeant Byrne held his head and Hector Drummond draped a blanket over his back. At last, shivering and empty, Craig got to his feet.

Disenchanted, the crowd had melted away. The lads could not

stand the company of coppers and knew the river too well to suppose that Billy's corpse would be retrieved before morning. Only Billy's father remained, hands in pockets, cap tipped down.

Craig shook his head. "I lost him. I'm . . . I'm sorry."

The old man snorted. Without a word, he turned on his heel and trudged off down the lane, the bottle that his son had thrown away protruding from his pocket, corked with a rag to protect the last precious inch of whisky that King Billy had left behind.

Ten

Wheel of Fortune

Full report was required by the Fiscal, of course. Sheaves of hand-written statements were extracted from Hog Moscrop and similar recalcitrant witnesses. Angela Alston, patched and turbanned, was returned to her mother's house in the Madagascar. Even with strong doses of sedative inside her, however, the girl was too shocked to surrender her prime eyewitness information without floods of hysterical tears. When, in due course, Billy's body was washed up on a shoal of mud by the mouth of the Yoker burn, though, it seemed that the police case was open and shut.

Though he sustained no physical harm from his ducking, for a time afterwards Craig was indrawn and depressed. Perhaps, Kirsty thought, he felt persecuted by the endless interrogations of Percy Street high brass or perhaps, like Greta, he just found them burdensome. He took no pride in the fact that he had once again found temporary fame, that the *Glasgow Herald* as well as the *Partick Star* praised him for his courage and devotion to duty and that even the lawless elements in Greenfield Burgh considered that he had acted democratically by jumping into the Clyde to save a raving lunatic who had just done in a prostitute. Behind the lurid press accounts lurked many little mysteries and personal complications and Kirsty's concern for the welfare of Greta Taylor and her daughter was mixed with a fear that their meeting, however bizarre, would revive Craig's interest in the woman from Benedict Street.

Canada Road neighbours were unimpressed by Craig's latest adventure. Kirsty's refusal to conform had already separated her from the other wives. Besides, she had become disenchanted with their gossiping ways. She was well aware that they were privy to all the malicious rumours that circulated in Ottawa Street and that they suspected there was more to Craig's discovery of Mary Shotten's body than met the eye. She ignored their sly, suggestive remarks and busied herself instead with keeping shop.

Even in the comparative sanctuary of Gascoigne Street, though, there was for a time no escape from celebrity.

"Here, Mrs Nicholson, was that your man got his name in the papers?"

"Yes," Kirsty would stiffly reply.

"An' was it you the bad man knockit doon?"

"Naw," Greta would answer in her gruffest manner.

"But Ah thought it said . . ."

"*I* knocked *him* down," Greta would explain, small fists clenched threateningly on the counter. "Are you for buyin' that bobbin box or do y'just like seein' your face in it?"

Some of the youngsters, egged on by their peers, were even more direct and insulting: "Ma mam says old Billy fancied you rotten an' put his haun up your skirt."

"I'll put *my* hand up *your* nose if you don't buy that brooch."

"How much?"

"Tuppence."

"Here then."

The precocious adolescent would clap coins on to the counter and, head cocked, would insolently pursue her questioning as if she were entitled to intimacies as makeweight on her purchase.

"Were you no' scared when he took his troosers doon?"

Greta's reply to this ridiculous question, and the fabrications that lay behind it, was too graphic even for the most hardened youngster. The girl – it was always a girl – would blanch or blush scarlet and creep away to confide the latest revelation in awed whispers to her very best friend in the dark shelter of a nearby close.

The lingering effect of King Billy's attack on Jen Taylor was less easily dealt with. For a week or more the little girl had to be pampered and coddled in a manner that made Bobby quite cross with jealousy. He was too young, of course, to understand the reason for his pal's bouts of tears and pettedness and too much the little man to offer her much sympathy.

"Jen cryin' again," he would announce with a sigh, nodding to her hiding-place under the counter.

He would observe the fuss that was made with bewildered scorn or, hands stuck in pockets and underlip thrust out, would declare,

"I'm no' cryin', see," until Greta or Kirsty took him on to her lap and gave him attention too.

It was the last week in August, a Tuesday, when, to Kirsty's surprise, Mr Albert Adair breezed through the door of No. 1 Gascoigne Street lugging a big canvas suitcase under each arm.

He dumped the cases down on the counter, whipped out a spotted silk handkerchief, mopped his brow and titivated his moustache as if to suggest that he had personally toted the samples the whole length of Dumbarton Road.

"Ladies," he said, "Adair's warehouse is at your service."

"An' who might you be?" Kirsty asked.

"It's young Mr Nicholson's replacement," said Greta.

"Not up to much, is he?" said Kirsty.

"I am, alas," said Breezy, "the best the firm could do at short notice."

In spite of his jocular manner Kirsty noticed that the man's eyes contained no humour, were alert and hard, almost scheming. He studied Greta covertly while he wagged the handkerchief about and, as he tucked the cloth away, scanned the shop's shelves critically.

"Did Gordon send you?" Kirsty said. "Or was it Madge?"

"I came off my own bat, as a matter of fact," said Breezy. "First, to see how you're farin' after that nasty episode with the late an' unlamented King. Second, to press upon you a selection of choice autumn lines from Adair's stock." He looked at Greta directly. "No harm?"

Greta shook her head. "No harm."

"And the bairn?"

"Jen's fine."

"Good." Breezy covered his real concerns by unbuckling the straps that bound the sample cases. "Will you have to appear before the Procurator, do y'think?"

"I've made several statements," Greta said. "In fact, I'm sick o' makin' statements to coppers."

"But the Fiscal will want to ask you questions?"

"Aye," said Greta. "I expect he might."

"About the events of that dreadful evenin'?"

Kirsty watched the man's nimble fingers fumble with the light brass buckles. It was all too clear that Breezy Adair was nervous and she could not quite imagine why. Surely he'd had no connections with William King or the murdered woman?

Greta said, "It's not a court case. Nothin' will get into the papers, don't worry."

"Why should I be worried?" Breezy glanced over his shoulder and twitched his brows. "You'll just tell the Procurator Fiscal the truth, an' that'll be that. Won't it?"

"Yes," Greta said. "That'll be that."

"And the child isn't damaged?"

"Damaged?" Greta said. "No, Jen isn't 'damaged'. Do you want to see her?"

"Is she here?"

"Havin' a nap in the backshop."

"No." Breezy hesitated. "No, don't disturb her on my account. Let her sleep."

"That's considerate," Greta said. "But then you've always been very considerate, Mr Adair, haven't you?"

"I like to think so," Breezy murmured. With his forefingers he flipped open the lids of the sample cases. He swung round, flashed a broad and hearty smile and said, "*Voilá!*"

"Goods for sale?" said Greta.

"Best prices, best quality."

Kirsty could detect in Breezy now the same sort of charm as Gordon displayed but it did not sit naturally on the elder man. The ring on his finger was genuine gold, his patterned suit had been personally tailored. He might imitate the brash manner of the commercial traveller but his arrogance lacked desperate edge and his garishness was too studied to be honest.

He brought out a white cardboard box and held it out to Kirsty. "One pierced silver string box, with scissors."

"How much?"

"Listed in the Army and Navy catalogue – same item – at twenty-five an' six. To you, cost on a dozen, three bob," said Breezy.

"I can't use them," Kirsty said curtly.

"Look at it, at least."

She opened the cardboard box, took out the silver box, examined it, extracted the scissors, snipped air with them, reassembled the package and handed it back to Breezy. "No thanks. Not for me."

"Why not?" said Breezy.

"Not the sort o' thing my customers would buy."

"Very well," said Breezy. "How about these?"

He unfolded a velvet cloth and displayed a selection of watches for ladies as well as gentlemen.

"Swiss-made, oxydised steel Repeaters at eight shillings cost." Breezy held up samples between finger and thumb. "Keyless lever strap watch with ten jewels, at eleven and fourpence. Beautiful corsage watch with matchin' pearl brooch; nine an' nine to you. All guaranteed."

Kirsty hardly glanced at the goods. "I think not."

The watches vanished into the velvet, the velvet into the case. Out came other items; electro-plated pie servers, cake knives and forks, an oval sole dish with stand, trays and various dishes, cruets and custard glasses, then Cherub scent bottles, hatpin holders and baby brushes with mock-silver backs. Breezy rhymed off the prices. Though the goods were attractive and ridiculously cheap Kirsty would have none of them. She made one excuse after another until at last even Breezy ran out of steam.

"You're not goin' to buy anythin', are you, Kirsty?"

"Not today, no."

"What is it? Do you have another wholesaler?"

"Nobody *needs* these things."

"Absolutely true an' undeniable," Breezy agreed. "But it's damned high-hat of you to tell people what they can have. If you're concerned about providin' necessities then you should go into the bread an' water business, Kirsty, get out of the retail trade right now."

"Did Gordon send you?"

"I told you – no. Lorna, however, was kind enough to inform me that you were sufferin' from shopkeeper's nerves, an all too familiar condition that eventually causes total paralysis and leads to financial ruin," Breezy said. "God, girl, look at your shelves; half empty."

"Nothin' seems to sell," Kirsty protested.

"You won't last long on the profits from trinkets." Breezy scooped his hand through the penny tray. "But I'm not goin' to *beg* you to buy stock."

"It's my shop," said Kirsty, flushing. "I'll do what I like with it."

"Too much capital, that's your trouble. If you'd started out on ten shillings an' not several hundred pounds then you'd be a real shopkeeper. You're only playin' at it. Candidly, I can't be bothered with dabblers." He began to buckle up the cases then turned and pointed at Greta. "Ask her. Your friend knows I'm right."

Greta said nothing, caught, Kirsty supposed, between loyalty and truth.

"Do you know what I think, Kirsty?" Breezy Adair continued in a quiet furry sort of voice. "I think you're spoiled."

"Spoiled! How can *you* say that? You hardly know me for one thing," Kirsty retaliated. "An' for another you've got more money than you know what t' do with."

"Money I earned," said Breezy. "Aye, the hard way. You weren't the only one who had to slave on winter morns, lass, who had frost blisters on her feet an' an empty belly rumblin' under her skirts. Ever look out that window?" He pointed. "Ever see the poor specimens out there, the ones who can't afford the pie never mind a dish to eat it off?"

"Yes, I've seen them," Kirsty said. "Too often."

"Some of those unfortunates never had a chance," Breezy said. "But others, plenty of others, were too meek, too scared, too spoiled to grab the chances offered them. By God, Kirsty, I tell you, you only make your way in this world by takin' chances."

"That's a fine sermon, Mr Adair," said Greta, not without sarcasm, "for a man come sellin' tin plate an' cheap watches."

Breezy visibly restrained himself. His vehemence had been genuine and, Kirsty realised, her anxieties and uncertainties had triggered in the man some of the old fire, the passion that had brought him wealth and power and the respect of the family. She began to understand what it was that had attracted Madge, to respond in spite of herself to Breezy Adair's authority.

"Cheap watches!" Breezy said, equilibrium restored. "Inexpensive, perhaps, but cheap – never!"

Kirsty paused. "Show me that pearl corsage again. How much was that?"

"Nine and nine, cost."

"An' the fish dish?"

"Three and tenpence."

"How long on credit?"

"Twenty-eight days."

"But . . ."

"Twenty-eight days," Breezy repeated.

"Returns?"

"Nope, no returns."

"Greta, what do you think?" Kirsty asked.

"It's your money," Greta answered.

"All right, Mr Adair," said Kirsty. "Open the cases, if you please."

*   *   *

Greta would not admit how much the episode with Billy King had affected her. She was not oblivious to the fact that it was only good luck that had brought Craig to her rescue in the nick of time. It was the thought of what King might have done to Jen that distressed her most of all. She could not shake off the image of Billy's victims – she had seen Angela Alston, bleeding and shaven-headed, being led out of the close to the police van – and would weep secretly when she was alone at night, hugging her pillow and hating herself for giving in to weak emotion. She had been made aware that her lines of defence against the brutal world were precarious at best and had never felt as unprotected as she did now.

In the years before she'd been paid to take care of the child, she'd had nothing much to lose. How different things were now. Everything she did was done for Jen, out of love of Jen. Even her rash affair with Craig Nicholson had been entered into because he was good to Jen, good for Jen. None of the men she'd known in the past, and there had been plenty of them, had cared a jot for her feelings. Some, like Johnnie Whiteside, had treated her as if they owned her body and soul. Even Breezy Adair, in the brief period of their association, had had a selfish motive for being kind to her. Only the Nicholsons had really seemed to care for her and the Nicholsons would never be for her.

The new items of stock that Kirsty had ordered had been delivered to the shop within twenty-four hours. Brought down by handcart from the warehouse they had been unpacked, recorded and displayed on the shelves by Friday. Greta was only too well aware that Kirsty had been given a sharp lesson by Breezy Adair. But buying was one thing and selling another and she was almost as relieved as Kirsty when the volume of trade increased and the mechanical cashier began to chime once more.

Saturday had been their best day for months and with each sale Kirsty became more cheerful and assured. Toffs were back from their sojourns by the sea, it seemed. There was money about and a need to prepare for winter, and the ladies came to Gascoigne Street prepared to spend on whatever took their fancy. For an hour in mid-afternoon, in fact, the shop had been quite crowded, shawled women from the tenements rubbing shoulders with starchy wives from the mansions on the hill.

Even Jen and Bobby had sensed the excitement and had stood on boxes behind the counter watching their mothers wrap up goods and make change, as well behaved as two wee angels. Later, when things had quietened, they were rewarded with icecream sponges and allowed to make castles out of discarded cardboard boxes.

Gascoigne Street had become as much a haven for Greta as it was for Kirsty. The hours spent in the shop were comparatively free from gloom and anxiety. It was going home that put the blight on Greta's spirits. She had become unreasoningly fearful of Benedict Street and its citizens and even Isa, a chum for many years, seemed tainted by the violence that King Billy had unleashed. In the midst of all this were interviews – five in all – with policemen, no friendly familiar coppers either but grim and disapproving strangers from Percy Street who challenged her every word and seemed tacitly to accuse her of having led Billy on. She was, of course, afraid of what they might discover. She waited for the one question that would lead to another that would lead in turn to Lizzie Straun and how she, a street woman, had suddenly acquired a child.

Craig might have reassured her, might have told her that the officers were not in the slightest concerned with her past but only with clearing up the mess that Billy King had left behind him as quickly and efficiently as possible. But Craig was not her confidant now and she did not know how to go about asking Kirsty for advice.

At last August drifted away. School bells rang in the mornings and the humidity dropped bringing a not unwelcome coolness and, along with the first of the falling leaves, rain. She returned through the rain after another busy Saturday at the shop. There was no pleasure to look forward to tonight and none save rest tomorrow. She had Jen securely by the hand, the wee girl scuffing and tired, and moved down towards the hot-pie stall at Banff Street corner to buy two hot pudding suppers. Later she would wash her hair, mend Jen's coat, bed early.

The night seemed to have drawn in early and the pie stall's lighted lamps stood out in the hazy gloom, bright and translucent as stained glass. She could smell the hot fat in the coal-fed fryer, coffee roasting in its conical urn, a wintry cosiness about the odours, the promise of cheap consolation for the inhospitable months ahead. There was a little knot of people at the shelved counter, boys and young girls mostly, clutching the precious pennies their mams had given them, lips moving as they repeated their orders over and over like silent prayers: "*Five hot pies, three black puddin', fourpence worth o' chips. Five hot pies, three black puddin', fourpence worth o' chips, an' a haddock. Five hot pies, fourpence worth o' chips, three haddock an' one black puddin'.*"

"Salt'n'vinegar?"

"What?" Greta said.

"On the suppers?"

"Aye."

"Tenpence then," said Mr Skinner, offering the dumpy brown paper parcels, one in each fat hand.

"Allow me," said a voice behind her and somebody put the exact sum down upon the counter.

"Gordon!" Greta said.

Jen pressed into her skirts. She had lost her trust in strangers; King Billy had left that legacy if no other.

The rain had diminished his nattiness, had taken the curl out of his hair, slicked the nap of his trilby and beaded his chequered overcoat. His shoes, she noticed, were muddy, and his jovial, juvenile grin seemed somehow muddy too.

"Gordon, what are you doin' here?"

"Just passin'," Gordon said.

"Don't lie."

"All right, Greta," he said. "I came to see you."

"Me? But why?"

He had a leather satchel slung across his shoulder like a newspaperboy's sack and he stuffed the pudding suppers into it to keep them warm. She glimpsed books and papers within the bag but he did not seem to care what damage the greasy parcels might do to them.

"I came t' take a look at the Greenfield," Gordon said as they stepped away from the stall, "just to make sure it hadn't run away."

"Have you been at the bottle?"

"Beer," Gordon said. "God, you can smell beer, right? I'm sorry."

234

"It isn't too bad," Greta said, "to windward."

"Listen, can I walk you home?"

"It's not that far."

"Bloody miserable night, though."

"Aye," Greta agreed.

They walked, not touching, along the pavement and round into Benedict Street. The lamplighter had completed his tour and closes and street-lamps were all neatly lighted. The rain made soft circular rainbows about the globes and you could taste the gas in the soft moist air. Greta noticed that Gordon did not turn his head towards the darkened window that marked Mary Shotten's house, unallocated as yet. He was looking at nothing in particular. He had the dazed appearance of a man who did not quite know what he was doing or why.

"Breezy told me he came to see you," Gordon said.

"He brought down some stock for Kirsty."

"She bought it, I believe," Gordon said.

"Aye, thank God."

"Is it sellin'?"

"It's sellin' pretty well," said Greta.

"Good."

"We turned over twelve pounds today."

"God, that's very good."

"Did you hear about our trouble?" she said.

"I did. I did," said Gordon. "Is it all over now, Greta? I mean, how's you-know-who?"

"Oh, she's fine, I suppose."

"Nightmares?"

"A few. She'll soon forget."

"Terrible," said Gordon, shaking his head. "But I can't pretend I'm not glad he's gone."

They were both so small, she realised, that if Jen had not been with them then they might have passed for two children. They reached the close. He hesitated. He unslung the satchel and fished out the suppers, offered them to her.

"Well, there you are, Greta," he said.

"Your brother used to leave them on the mat."

"Did he?" Gordon said.

"Do you want to come in?"

"Yes."

She went ahead of him, the suppers cuddled to her breast, Jen hanging on to her skirt. She fished out her door key under the gas-lamp, then she stopped, head raised, listening.

"What the hell's that?" Gordon murmured.

"Fairies," Jen informed him, matter-of-factly.

Greta laughed. "It's just music."

"It's fairies," said Jen again.

"No, it isn't," Greta said. "Mr Mulvanney bought a gramophone. Second-hand, of course. He repaired it an' now he gives recitals every blessed night."

Gordon smiled. "What's the tune? Italian?"

"Spanish Love Song," Greta said.

"I like it," Gordon said.

"You would," Greta said, pushing the door open with her knee. "Come on. You can hear it better inside."

"Fairies," said Jen again, and giggled.

"I think you're probably right, lass," Gordon said and, picking her up, quickly followed Greta indoors.

*   *   *

David Lockhart's second letter arrived on a clear September morning.

It was long, so long that it came in a small package secured with brown paper tapes. It had been written, Kirsty realised, all in one sitting; David said as much. He apologised for his handwriting, the small, neat, essay-writer's hand enlarged by passions at which Kirsty could only guess. She opened the letter without hesitation this time. She felt secure, confident of herself now and hoped to find only an avowal of a love that she had already sentimentalised and, to a degree, trivialised.

At first she was disappointed at what David had written, then mesmerised and finally shocked at the contrast between his life and her own petty expectations.

For the first time she understood what it was that had drawn David back to China, not some childish debt to his family but an intuitive sense of danger and the knowledge that to be elsewhere would be to be nowhere at all. There was nothing in Glasgow, nothing in St Anne's or Walbrook Street or Greenfield to approach it. In China, in the Fanshi Mission, Kirsty realised, was a whole other existence, a desperate upheaval of suffering that would involve a man as caring as David and absorb him completely.

She felt diminished by his letter, not betrayed by the fact that he mentioned his fondness for her only once, that he did not retell, for her pleasure, the little story of his Scottish romance, did not, it seemed, pine for her at all. And yet he had written, written at length. He had chosen her of all people to share his worry, his excitement and his strength.

Judgements from Heaven [David wrote] are about to come upon us. We are under threat not only from the I Ho Ch'uan, the Righteous People, but from the calamitous circumstances of drought and famine and the natural hatred of the Chinese for foreigners. It is no time to be an evangelist and many poor native Christians in the province have already been slaughtered. Meanwhile Father sits at his harmonium in the Mission hut hammering out Psalms while the tumult of the rain-processions pass and repass the gate of our compound, with all the banging and jangling that is supposed to be a call to the gods to bring water out of the skies and with it fire to strike down and consume the foreigners.

Father's simplicity is both infuriating and touching. Neither Jack nor I can be angry with him for long, nor can we argue against the Rock of his belief. He is a soldier for Christ, certainly, but he is a soldier who will not draw blood. He denies that 'we' are to blame for much of China's corruption, that it was the white man who brought the sin of opium-eating to this country, the white man who sends engineers to invent ways of stealing iron and coal out of China's earth, that many of the church missions are riddled with political intrigue and a lust for temporal power.

What wounds my father is that the Gospel of Christ has been branded a heresy, his life's work officially condemned as 'reckless and oppressive to the masses'. He cannot comprehend that to the Buddhists, Confucians and Taoists we are blasphemers as well as persecutors, and always have been. But the Celestials are moved by a spirit no less fervent than our own. Their manifestos are like extracts from our own Old Testament. Jack and I imagine that we understand our present predicament but how can we possibly explain to Father that it is not the Gospel of Jesus' love that is at fault but how badly the Gospel has been taught? Father will not compromise. He will not budge. He regards the present tribulation and coming storm as the appointed portion of all who have chosen to live with Christ and who hope to enter His Kingdom. To Father everything is a part of God's will, the Cause behind all causes, even the present horrors and upheavals.

There is a strange harmony in all that has happened, Kirsty. As you know, I returned to China against my will. Now I am no longer dissatisfied. Every day seems centred and real. Even the ordinary meetings of the station, doctoring, teaching, the daily round, are given significance by the threat of persecution and by the need to make myself ready to follow the Lamb, to be tried in the fire to see if I am wanting or if, please God, I am strong.

I am sorry to have gone on at such wearying length, Kirsty. But when I think of peace I think of you at home in Greenfield, of little Bobby, of Craig too. I want to bring it all closer, which this letter-writing business helps me to do. It is not – and I am sure you will understand what I mean – that I would have it back as it was before but that, when I have done what is required of me, it will still be there within, a memory and not a dream.

Years ago in the bleak Baird Home and in the cold bothy on Hawkhead she had dreamed of meeting a man who would adore her unquestioningly, would put her above all else. Now she had grown up, grown wise, and that weak little fantasy of girlhood had been snuffed out. Now she was ashamed of how she had tried to possess David and her tears that morning were tears of remorse for her selfishness.

That afternoon at her desk in the quiet backshop in Gascoigne Street she wrote a reply, composing the letter carefully but with a faint disquieting feeling that it would never reach its destination, that somehow it was destined to remain unread.

*   *   *

The brothers dined on beefsteak and black porter in the cellar of Proudfoot's restaurant. It was one of those establishments that the commercial gentlemen of Glasgow had recently taken over from honest working men by a process of infiltration.

Trappings of brass and sawdust and barreltop tables remained and the top-hatters felt quite virile and hairy-chested as they supped on plain meat and potatoes and drank draught beer from thick glasses. Dolphus didn't much care for the atmosphere but as Breezy was footing the bill he uttered no word of complaint and ate heartily enough.

It was a rare event for Breezy to be on the town after dark without his wife on his arm. He had chosen Proudfoot's for the meeting because there would be no women there to offer temptation and because he could tuck himself away with his brother in one of the cave-like alcoves and get down to business without distractions.

"When," Dolphus said, after the usual fraternal exchanges had been made, "is your lad going to pop the question, hah? That's what I want to know."

"Patience, old chap, patience," Breezy said. "It's not as if Amanda is growin' long in the tooth."

"I'm not forcin' it upon her, you know," Dolphus said. "The girl herself is eager to be wed."

"All girls of that age are eager to be wed," Breezy said, "which is why responsible fathers have to apply the rein, isn't it, otherwise the daft wee things would be runnin' off with postmen or carters or pledgin' their troth with apprentice brickies."

"I've done what you asked, Albert," Dolphus said. "I've taken the boy into Carruth's and will pay him a good wage while he receives his trainin'. Now I expect you to keep your end of the bargain."

"Push, push, rush, rush," Breezy said. "You must be very damned anxious to lay hands on those public houses of mine."

"When will they marry?"

"Next year; June, probably."

"Can't you encourage him to elope with her?"

"Dolphus, for God's sake!"

"It would be cheaper too."

"An' what would Olive have to say to that?"

"It's none of Olive's business."

"Can't agree, old chap," said Breezy. "It's very much Olive's business. Besides, my own dear wife would have a purple fit if there was an elopement. She's not too sure about this marriage as it is."

"Doesn't like Amanda?" Dolphus's voice rose. "Hah?"

"Smells fish," said Breezy.

"Placate her. She's your wife."

Breezy said, "Look, there will be no elopement. There will be an engagement, formally celebrated, and a midsummer marriage; then you'll be at liberty to do whatever it is you intend to do."

"What the devil d'you mean by that?"

"The public houses that you're buyin' from me won't be registered as Carruth's, will they?" Breezy said.

Dolphus drank a mouthful of porter, swallowed and dabbed his mouth with his wrist. "They'll be tied houses, of course they will, tied to sell Carruth's products and nobody else's."

"I know what a tied house is, Dolphus," Breezy said. "I'm also very well aware that the competition to sell beers on the domestic market is becoming ever more fierce. I understand perfectly why Carruth's want to add to their property list."

"Fine, well – "

"Makin' purchase through a subsidiary company of which you are sole director, that's your game, isn't it?"

"Preposterous suggestion. Nothin' of the kind."

"Dolphus, I've known you since you were ten minutes old," said Breezy. "I can read you like a book."

"I didn't ask for any of this, didn't invite it," Dolphus said. "Damn it all, Breezy, I married the bitch in all good faith. I didn't expect her to betray me with every Tom, Dick and Harry."

"Why *did* you marry her, Dolphus?"

"Because you told me to."

"Oh, come now!" said Breezy. "All I did was point out the advantages."

"You knew her. God, you actually introduced us. Could you not have warned me, hah?"

"Warned you of what?"

"That she was . . . was . . ."

"That she couldn't resist other men, do you mean?"

"My, but you have an uncultured tongue on you sometimes, Breezy," Dolphus said. "Other men is one thing, but a groom, a common groom . . ."

"How much have you managed to salt away?"

"Hah?"

"You heard," said Breezy. "How much have you separated from the Carruth fortune; money you can legally an' morally call your own?"

"How did you . . .?"

Breezy sighed. "All this niggardliness, this tight-fisted, penny-pinching behaviour, Dolphus, is somewhat against character. Polly and Heather assume you've become a miser in your old age. I think otherwise. I think you've feathered a nest of your own an' that buyin' a clutch of public houses from me to lease out to Carruth's is just personal investment. Are you goin' to leave her, leave Olive, is that it?"

"No!" Dolphus shouted, then, more quietly, "No, I'm not goin' to leave her. Not yet. Not at once. In fact, I'm not goin' to leave her at all in spite of all the humiliation and shame that she's heaped upon me."

"Does she still share your bed?"

"Good God, Breezy! How dare you ask me that."

"She doesn't, does she?"

"I'm not like you. I can live perfectly well without *that* indulgence. I do not regard *that* as essential to my happiness and welfare."

"So there isn't another woman waitin' in the wings?"

"Of course there isn't," Dolphus said. "What could I possibly want with another woman?"

"What would you do if Olive left you?"

"Sue for divorcement," Dolphus answered, without a second's hesitation.

"Aye, an' collect in consequence a settlement from her private funds, the fortune you can't otherwise get your hands on," Breezy said.

"Don't take that holier-than-thou tone with me, Breezy. It's exactly how you would do it."

"'Course it is," Breezy agreed, "*if* I'd been daft enough to marry a famous beauty strictly for her money."

"You're a bloody hypocrite, Breezy. You *encouraged* me to marry Olive Carruth. You practically *insisted* on it."

"How was I to know you couldn't take care of her?"

"I've taken perfectly good care of her. Given her a fine house, four children, a comfortable existence all round," Dolphus protested. "*And* I have remained faithful. What else can she expect of me, hah?"

Breezy said, "More, apparently."

"Damn them, they all want more," Dolphus said. "Well, I have no more to give to Olive. I've done more, a great deal more, than most husbands would have done under the circumstances."

"Dolphus, what do you really want from me?"

"Business, it's just business," Dolphus said, flushing.

"My pubs an' my shares?"

"I've laboured long and hard for Carruth's," Dolphus said.

"I've not only preserved the company that her father left, I've built upon it. I might even say that I've saved it from ruin."

"Yes," Breezy agreed. "You've kept that side of the bargain, no doubt about it."

"I won't risk losin' it."

"It's all to do with Amanda, isn't it?" Breezy said. "She inherits a portion of her mother's shares when she reaches twenty-one."

"Twenty-five," Dolphus put in.

"Or on her marriage?" said Breezy.

"All right, all right," said Dolphus. "We didn't come here to discuss my private affairs."

"I'm your brother, Dolphus. You can't keep secrets from me," Breezy said, "particularly when you need my help so badly."

"And you'll lose out of it, hah?" said Dolphus.

" 'Course I won't," said Breezy. "I never lose."

"You're not *giving* me the public houses; I'm payin' sweetly for them," Dolphus said. "You'll get full market value for your shares too."

"And you'll be independent at last," said Breezy. "Olive will no longer have the upper hand."

"I could have divorced her four years ago, you know," said Dolphus. "Any court in the land would have upheld my claim for redress at that time, considerin' the evidence. But I didn't. Now – when Amanda marries – Olive will need *me*."

"I wouldn't be too sure about that, old son."

"Hah?"

"There's one flaw in your logic, one wee fly in the ointment."

"What?"

"Amanda's little parcel of stock will belong to her, not to you. She may decide not to put it at your disposal after all."

Dolphus smiled. "Community property, Albert. You've forgotten the law of community property. What belongs to Amanda will, under the terms of the new marriage contract, be at her husband's disposal."

"I hadn't forgotten," Breezy said.

"And Mr Nicholson will be on my side."

"Will he?"

"He'll soon see who butters his bread for him, where his future lies."

"Uh-huh," said Breezy, nodding. "He'll be dependent on you, just as you were dependent on Olive."

"Hardly the same sort of thing at all."

"Ain't it?"

"He'll have a beautiful young wife, a home, a career, and a share of Carruth's prosperity. Now even you must admit that isn't bad for a lad from the hayfields."

"He isn't a lad from the hayfields," said Breezy. "He's my stepson."

"Absolutely," said Dolphus. "And you've steered him on the right course, Albert."

Breezy frowned.

"Just as you did me," Dolphus continued. "Difference is that this time it's all in the family, our family. In twenty or twenty-five years' time, when you and I are old and Nicholson is in his prime and owns Carruth's lock, stock and barrel, he'll thank us from the bottom of his heart."

"Unless . . ."

"Unless what, hah?"

Breezy shrugged.

Encouraged by his brother's apparent acquiescence, Dolphus rubbed his hands and, smiling, said, "Now, what about it, brother o' mine?"

"What about what?"

"Namin' the day," said Dolphus.

"I can't," said Breezy. "First nature has to take its course an' Gordon has to pop the question."

"Tell him to get on with it then."

"How can he?" said Breezy, still frowning slightly. "He hasn't time to breathe right now let alone court your daughter."

"Ah, so that's what's lackin', is it?" Dolphus said.

"Opportunity," Breezy said. "Yes."

"I'll give him a little rope, shall I?"

"It might be no bad idea," said Breezy.

*　　　*　　　*

It was one of Craig's rare spells without duty; sixty hours between change shifts. He had put his tunic and boots away and had spent the whole afternoon on the bowling-green at Marlborough with his sleeves rolled up and his collar undone, enjoying the autumn sunlight to the full. He had partnered Peter Stewart against two wily old men whose gnarled fingers seemed able to direct the bowls exactly into the right position and who took winning for granted. It was impossible to grudge them their victories, however, for, in the dog-days of a full life of labour in the shipyards, the exercise of skill with wood and jack was all they had left to live for, that and a quiet pint of beer in the Northern Lights two or three evenings a week. What they did in the long winter months, how they survived, was one of the ineffable mysteries to which young men like Craig and Peter gave no thought at all, for they seemed, those old men, to have been there for ever, snug and safe and eternal like the swing of the seasons.

It was well after five o'clock before Peter and Craig left the green. Peter had to scurry away to reach the police barracks in time for supper for, unlike Craig, he had only his copper's wage to live on and could not afford to miss a meal he had paid for in advance. With his jacket slung over his shoulder, hand in his pocket and a cigarette in his mouth Craig strolled down Dumbarton Road at a leisurely pace. It was too early to go home and too early, really, to slip into a pub for a half and half pint. In any case, he had lost his taste for liquor. He could not put from mind its part in the downfall of Billy King or the havoc it was playing with Andy McAlpine.

He did not consciously head for Gascoigne Street and had no intention of going into the shop. He was merely taking the air, passing the time, at ease with himself and the world at large. He stopped for a moment, looking across the thoroughfare to watch the horses turn out of Dumbarton Road and head down the narrow little street past the shop's front door; a string of four led by a young boy. The boy was much like he'd been just a year or two ago, trousers tied in at the knees, an old sack about his shoulders, a cap stuck jauntily on his tousled head. Fine horses they were too, Clydesdales in matched pairs, probably being taken from the coal yards at Partick West to the blacksmith's in the Kingdom Road. They were docile, used to traffic and to the boy, who controlled them with a rope and a little whisk.

The sight of them there in the September sunlight gave Craig a tingle of nostalgia for Dalnavert, for Bankhead's harvest carts and clean-shorn fields and the golden-brown days of autumn down in the Carrick. And then the horses passed out of sight and he was looking instead at the window of his wife's shop, at a vignette of his sister, his wife, his son and Greta gathered there as if posed. They were laughing together in that way that women have. He thought it queer that he could see them so clearly, and that they could not see him at all. He had no notion what they were laughing at.

It was not Greta that he stared at through the glass but Kirsty, freckled and fine-looking in her gingham dress. He felt towards her as he had done ten years since, as if the disappointments and disillusionments of their common-law marriage had not intervened. He wanted her, yet he was afraid of wanting her too much, of the ebb and flow that carried desire into love and love into caring.

Craig watched for two or three minutes. He saw them change positions, saw a fourth woman whom he did not know – a customer, perhaps – and a young man, also a stranger, all of them capering and laughing together at the long counter. He felt suddenly old, old and rather lost. What in God's name had happened to him? Why could he not, on this calm September evening, simply cross the road, go in and be with them, his sister, wife and son? What was to stop him?

He knew the answer to that question only too well.

* * *

At first Kirsty was irked to find Craig at home. She had been in a particularly good mood.

They'd had a right good laugh in the shop that afternoon, with Mrs Russell come in to buy a clock for a wedding gift and Mr Tubbs, dropped by for no apparent reason, telling her how to feed the beetle that pedalled the crank and assuring her that beetle-replacements were not expensive to buy. Lorna had taken it up, inventing a whole trade in clock beetles. Black, Deathwatch & Cockroach Ltd., she'd said, had warehouses full of them, travellers who did nothing else but sell beetles in assorted sizes to manufacturing jewellers.

"Awa' ye go, the pair o' ye," Mrs Russell had wheezed, wiping tears from her eyes. "Beetle travellers! Who ever heard the like."

"It's true, honest," Lorna had said. "Go on, Tubby, show her your samples."

"Nah, I mustn't. General public ain't supposed to know about this."

"Oh, go on. Mrs Russell isn't goin' to tell."

"Well – all right."

The sample case had been put on the counter and Mr Tubbs had gone through a performance of reluctance and caution with such conviction that Jen and Bobby were thoroughly taken in, Mrs

Russell half convinced and even Kirsty had begun to wonder just what the case contained.

When the lid was half open Mr Tubbs had cried out, "Get back, y'brute. Get down," and had closed it again with a snap. "Can't risk it," he'd explained. "It's Bertram. He's needin' fed. An' there's nothin' more bad-tempered than a hungry beetle, believe me."

Jen had hugged Kirsty's skirts, her lips trembling. But not for worlds would any of them have stopped Mr Tubbs in full flow. He'd put his mouth down close to the lid, had said sternly, "You'll get your steak pie later, Bertram. Now, behave yourself." He had slipped his hand inside. He'd let out a gasp of pain, had struggled to free his fingers. Bobby had darted behind Kirsty, Jen clung more tightly to her leg and even Greta had taken a half-step back. "Leggo, Bertram. Leggo," Mr Tubbs had cried, then, grinning, had brought out his hand and opened it.

Balanced on his palm was a little black indiarubber creature about the size of a tangerine. It had pop eyes, a straw hat, feelers, six rubbery legs and painted on its face a wide, toothy grin. "Bertram Beetle," Mr Tubbs had said, "meet the folks."

Mrs Russell had bought the clock, of course, and three rubber beetles too. Kirsty had ordered five dozen to sell and Jen and Bobby, soon over their fright, had been given one each.

It had been a daft afternoon but great fun. Then she'd come home to find Craig slumped in a chair by the hearth, a cigarette in his mouth and a newspaper in front of his face and her good mood had wavered, soured by the sight of him.

"Daddy, see what I've got."

Apprehensively she watched Bobby scuttle to his father's side, the new toy held by one rubbery leg. On occasions she had seen Craig treat his son with an indifference that was almost cruel. Tonight, however, Craig tossed aside his newspaper and lifted Bobby on to his knee with a welcoming smile.

"What's this then, son?"

"Be'tram. Be'tram's a beetle."

"So he is now. Where did you get him?"

"At the shop. Be'tram eats steak pies."

"What else does he eat, I wonder?"

The question gave Bobby pause and while he considered the question of the beetle's diet Craig glanced up at Kirsty and said, "I didn't know you sold novelties."

"I'll sell anythin' that turns a penny."

"What does this thing cost?"

"I charge tuppence."

"What does it cost you?" Craig asked.

"One penny, farthin'."

"You'll not get fat on that, love."

"Every little helps."

"Well," Craig said to Bobby, "have you got an answer for me yet?"

"Cu'tard," Bobby said. "An' . . . an' toffees."

"Isn't that funny?" Craig said. "I just happen to have a bag o' toffees right here in my pocket."

"Oooooo!"

"Not before tea," Kirsty said.

"Be'tram likes toffees."

"Aye, well, if he eats up all his fish, he can have one afterwards," Kirsty said.

She stooped to light the oven gas.

Later, after Bobby and Bertram, fed and fattened, had been tucked up in bed in the front room, Kirsty washed the dishes, rinsed the sink and settled down in her chair to see if a torn sleeve on Bobby's shirt could be mended.

The pleasure of the day had been sustained. Craig was seated opposite her. She was aware that he was watching her, but not with malice or suspicion. She sensed that he wanted to talk and that later he would come to her, kiss her, put his hands on her breasts and hope to be invited to share her bed. Strange that he should have relinquished to her that prerogative, that male province. She supposed that, perversely, she had Greta Taylor to thank for that. Guilt not loyalty had made Craig a more considerate husband.

"Managin' a shop agrees with you, Kirsty," he said.

"Does it?"

"You look real well on it, nicer than ever."

"Thank you very much, Mr Nicholson."

"I mean it," Craig said. "Listen, do you mind if I ask you how much the shop pulls in?"

Her immediate response was to tell him to mind his own damned business. She checked her refusal, however. She had resented his studied lack of interest in her business before and could not deny him an answer now, not without hypocrisy.

"I haven't really worked it out," she said.

"After everythin's paid – rent, gas bill, stock in hand, Greta's wage – how much profit is left on average?"

"For the first tradin' quarter I cleared almost seventy pounds."

"Good God!"

She was gratified by his reaction. She smiled modestly. "Not bad, is it? I'm told it'll get even better when winter comes in, especially at Christmas an' New Year time."

"Seventy pounds a quarter," Craig said. "Jeeze, that's about six quid a week."

"I suppose it is."

"It makes my contribution o' twenty-six bob look paltry."

"I hope you're not thinkin' o' takin' an early retirement an' becomin' an idler."

"Hell, no," Craig said. "I'll bet the Chief Constable doesn't take home much more than that on a Friday night, though."

"I think you might say we're doin' quite well," Kirsty said.

"Quite well!" said Craig. "In my book we're very nearly rich."

"Yes," Kirsty agreed, "by some standards, I suppose we are."

"Aye, if we're just careful for a year or two we could be set for life, could we not?"

"Careful?"

"With the money, I mean."

She felt again a twinge of resentment. She was inclined to inform him that it was her money not his and that she had taken risks to gain financial security only because she had been so unsure of him.

Craig said, "I know what you're thinkin', Kirsty."

"Oh, what am I thinkin'?"

"That I haven't done much to help," Craig said. "I'm only too well aware o' that fact, Kirsty. It's all been your doin'."

She softened. "You took me away from Hawkhead, Craig. It was you brought me to Glasgow, gave up your family."

"That wasn't much of a sacrifice, as it turned out."

"Would you do it again?"

The question seemed to come to her lips of its own accord. The needle, thread and half-mended garment lay neglected on her lap as she awaited his answer.

"Aye, I would," Craig said. "But I'd make sure we were married legal next time."

"Is that it? You want me to marry you?"

"Nah, nah." Craig had guessed what was on her mind. "If

248

you're happy wi' things as they are, I am too. I'm not pressin' you, Kirsty. I'm no bloody Adair. I'm not after control o' your finances."

She was pleased by his sincerity.

She said, "What are you bletherin' about, Craig?"

"Don't you know?"

"No, I don't."

He got out of his chair and went down on his knees before her. Carefully he put aside her mending.

"I married you because I fancied you, Kirsty Barnes," he said. "An' I still do."

His hands were brown, his neck too. His dark hair was almost long enough to have a curl to it. He'd need to have it trimmed soon or Sergeant Drummond would dock him marks for untidiness. He gripped her lightly on the soft flesh of her thighs just above her knees, drew himself forward, kissed her lips.

Kirsty tried to pretend that she was unmoved by his desire for her, amused by it. She tried to tighten the thread of cynicism by which their relationship had been suspended this past year or so, but could not.

"What are you doin'?" she murmured.

"Helpin' you get ready for bed."

"Oh!"

"You don't mind a helpin' hand, do you?"

"You're awful big for a lady's maid," Kirsty said.

"I'll need to practise then," Craig said thickly. "Lift up a bit."

"What for?" she asked.

"So that I can find the buttons."

"Those buttons?"

"Aye, them's the ones," said Craig.

*   *   *

It was late now, very late. She lay on her side facing the window. Craig sprawled against her. Never before had they made love for so long or with such startling variety. She wondered just how much of that had been learned from Greta too. She was satisfied, however, more than satisfied. Soggy with sexual exhaustion, she was willing to allow him his smugness. He had earned it.

He had been ready for her in more ways than one, however. She could not quite be rid of the suspicion that he had exerted himself not just to demonstrate his love but also his prowess, his value. Why should she condemn him for that? It was, after all, what men were all about.

She looked now at the vertical rail of light that showed faintly between the paper blind and the curtain. She could see the shape of the water heater, its tiny pinprick of pure blue flame and the flicker of soft warmth that the fire made on the knobs of the new brass fender. Too comfortable now to struggle into her nightgown, too stimulated to find sleep, yet too tired to stir, Kirsty's thoughts whirled and whirred.

She had done everything that Craig had asked of her. She had given him pleasure. She too enjoyed a little enfolding feeling of complacency. It snuggled within her as she imagined Greta – Greta alone in her bed in Benedict Street while she was here with Craig. She felt no pity for Greta Taylor at that moment. She had Craig here with her and would keep him, somehow. He had even settled himself on the inside of the bed because it was her bed and he was the guest in it. Strange how daft wee things like that became important, how sensitivities too small, too intimate to be put into words heaped up like castor sugar or grains of salt and eventually filled you like a bowl.

The things she had done with Craig tonight, for instance: was that her mother's legacy? She had lost, or had never had, any clear memory of her mother. When she thought of her mother these days she seemed to see only Greta Taylor, mingled with images of other street women glimpsed briefly in the passing. But there was no more than a faint, fleeting regret in that, of less weight and moment than Bobby's cough, the sale of a clock, hot water running freshly from a tap, Craig's arms about her waist in a bed in a room in a town that was never dark.

Lazily she turned, opened her arms and put them about Craig's body, holding him as he held her, belly to belly and face to face. She kissed him gently, let her tongue linger on his upper lip.

"D'you miss it, love?" he asked sleepily.

"What?"

"My moustache," Craig murmured. "I'll grow another if you like."

"I like it better the way it is," Kirsty said.

"Yes, so do I," said Craig.

Eleven

The Wise Child

First frosts had finally taken the fire out of autumn. On that early October day, without a breath of wind to stir the beech hedges, the countryside about Bree Lodge was calm, serene and beautiful.

Gordon had come up by the first train on Saturday morning in response to a command from his employer, James Randolph Adair. It was not the first such command that Dolphus had delivered in the past few weeks. On two occasions Gordon had dined with Dolphus and his daughter in the city and, a fortnight back, had been a weekend guest at The Knowe when he had been warned that, however inconvenient, he would be expected to spend more time with Amanda in future. Gordon was not at all reluctant to spend time with Amanda, particularly as it meant that he was released from work to enable him to keep the engagements. Still under training, his days were split between travelling about the Glasgow pubs with Mr McDade, a dour and disapproving salesman of the old school, and learning accountancy under the eagle eye of the ill-named Mr Friendship who was the master of Carruth's main office.

The flat-racing season was winding down. Hunters and hurdlers were preparing for the excitements of the weeks ahead and conscientious trainers, including Russell Smith, had gone off to Dublin for the annual bloodstock sales. Gordon was met at the station not by Uncle Sinclair but by Captain Tom Wells who, driving a little pony-cart, whisked him back to Bree in no time at all.

Captain Wells was as brisk and friendly as ever, the sort of no-nonsense chap that Gordon liked.

"Did you bring the gear, Gordon?"

"I did, sir."

"Expensive, was it?"

"It didn't come cheap," said Gordon.

"Boots and comfortable breeks are really rather essential. No sense in startin' off on the wrong cheek, what?"

Gordon laughed. He had shelled out thirty-five bob for the cord breeches and a couple of quid for the riding boots and had dug out an old tweed jacket which he felt would do nicely for the lessons that he was about to receive and would render him comparatively inconspicuous. In fact he was full of enthusiasm for the venture and did not grudge the cost.

It had been Amanda's bright idea that Gordon learned to ride properly. It was, she said, an attribute of a true gentleman, one that her father had never managed to master. There were plenty of hands at Bree to teach him and she, though a mere female, could also give him a pointer or two if it came to it. Would it not be nice, she'd said, to ride out together and enjoy nature? Gordon had agreed that it would. Would it not be nice, she'd said, to have an interest in common and perhaps, when he was a bit more expert, they might apply to join one of the hunting societies? To all of which Gordon had nodded approval.

It was not the bounties that might accrue that fired his enthusiasm for Amanda's suggestion, however, but the fact that he would be out of the damned office and off the streets. Besides, he had always been fairly fond of horses and had even ridden – bareback, of course – one of Dalnavert's massive stallions on the way home from the harvest field. In fact, he knew more than he let dab about horses but he listened with solemn attention and without interruption while Captain Wells went over the basic points of horsemanship on the drive to Bree.

When the Lodge came into sight Gordon found his gaze wandering to the neat pathways and spaced paddocks until Tom Wells broke off his dissertation on the necessity of developing sympathetic hands and the principle of give and take on the reins and, smiling, said, "Amanda isn't here yet."

"Ah!"

"She'll be along, never fear. About dinner time."

"Dolphus too?"

"No," said Tom Wells. "No, I believe Dolphus is in Edinburgh this weekend. So I heard. Indeed, I was hopin' you might be able to . . ."

"I'm not on the board of Carruth's, sir," Gordon said. "To be honest, I'm somewhat lower in rank than the brush boy just at present."

"Sure," Tom Wells said. "I understand."

Though 'the boss' was absent there was no slacking of activity in Bree's paddocks and stable yards. Gordon was dropped off at the door of a room behind the room where saddles and bridles were stored. He glimpsed the array of tackle hung on pegs from the walls like exhibits in a museum and two craftsmen bent over a saddle on a frame, making some sort of repair. He changed in the locker room and waited, not daring to smoke, until Captain Wells, already accoutred, returned for him.

Hobbling a little in his brand new boots Gordon followed the man out into a gravelled lane behind the long stem of the stables where a small boy in a large cap – mandatory headgear for Bree's youngsters, apparently – handed over charge of a small, docile cob to the great man and gave Gordon the once-over before he dived off to other duties. Captain Wells, it seemed, did not believe in wasting time.

Ten minutes later Gordon was seated, comfortably enough, on the saddled animal with the reins resting lightly in his fingers and the ball of each foot balanced and steady across the stirrup iron. The training field was tucked away on low ground below the house, protected by a stoop of blackthorn and alders and ringed by heavy pinewood fencing, a safe place to learn. Gordon was not at all nervous. He felt quite secure on the animal's back. He was, he realised, extremely privileged to be receiving instruction from such a famous jockey as Captain Wells. The captain's manner was casual and relaxed and he seemed not to have forgotten what it was like to be a novice even though he had himself been practically born to the saddle. The cob, name of Dandy, was well used to novice riders. He could have done the whole thing by himself, just about, especially as the chap on his back this morning weighed hardly more than a girl.

For an hour and more horse and rider went round and round the little field, up the slope and back across it, with Tom Wells walking beside them, talking in that quiet, disciplined, manly voice of his.

Gordon's senses were heightened by exercise and concentration. He felt good, very good. He was conscious of the colours of the morning, the bracken's faded gilt, the dun-green grass, sunlight on the hunch of the high hills, the motionless patience of the trees behind the fence as, bobbing in the saddle, he passed them again and again. Drawn into a temporary rapport with Captain Wells, he remembered how his father, a small man too, could not reach to his waist on Dalnavert's stallions but held him by the calf; the touch of that paternal hand came back to him now across the years, reassuring and strong.

"You certainly have the knack, old son," Captain Wells told him. "Natural, very natural indeed."

Gordon grinned. "I've ridden before, a bit."

"Thought you had, yes," said the captain. "Ponies?"

"Draught horses," Gordon said.

"Big fellows?"

"Shires an' Clydesdales."

"Handsome but not much cop in the huntin' field," the captain said. "You may take the cob out on the loch road this afternoon if you like."

"Will you be with me?"

"No. Amanda."

"Am I ready for it?"

"If you're cautious and promise to behave," said Captain Wells. "No heroics."

"Not me. I'm a born coward," said Gordon.

He glanced down, grinning, to wink at the man by his side but had lost the captain's attention to the ladies who had appeared on the hill.

*　　　*　　　*

It was more of an amble than a walk, pleasant but fairly unexciting. Dandy, Amanda had informed him in the course of midday dinner at the lodge, could find his way to the loch and back blindfold and had never been known to be 'sparky'. He really was an amiable beast and he, Gordon, must not be afraid of him.

Gordon had tried to exchange a glance with Captain Wells, to receive a discreet gesture of reassurance from his mentor. The captain, however, had been engaged in conversation with Amanda's mother and had paid his star pupil no compliment, no attention at all in fact.

Soon after dinner, about half-past one o'clock, Gordon and Amanda had taken the horses out and along the broad unpaved road between pastures and the jumping-field. Olive Adair had come to see them off, had stood by the white-painted fence at the top of the rise and waved her handkerchief while behind her, two or three steps back, the captain waited, arms folded across his chest.

"Why don't they come with us?" Gordon asked.

"Mother isn't keen on horses."

"It's nothin' but horses round here," Gordon said. "Won't she be bored?"

"I expect she'll find something to do," said Amanda.

She wore again the handsome riding outfit whose severity of cut and hue set off her beauty and she rode a tall, black stallion that her father had bought for her three or four years ago. The stallion was more fiery than the cob and now and then would grow weary of the clopping pace and would shy and whinny and frisk until Amanda controlled him, speaking first softly and then sharply but never, Gordon noticed, sawing at the rein to cause him pain.

Down into lanes of privet and thorn and through them on to the Duke's land, to the path by the river, over the wooden bridge, on to a walk sheltered by birch trees and grey old firs. They passed estate workers, fence-menders, a girl in charge of milk cows, two fishermen with tall rods, a ploughman and his lad sizing up a hilly field for Monday's first furrows, some late straw being raked from stubble. To Gordon it all seemed curiously quaint, unlike the wide, dyked pastures of Bankhead and Dalnavert. The agriculture here was not hard, not businesslike, but dawdling and picturesque as if survival were assured and profit unimportant.

"Is your father in Edinburgh?" he asked.

"Who told you that?" said Amanda. "Somebody at Carruth's, I suppose."

"Tom Wells mentioned it, as a matter of fact."

Amanda resettled herself on the saddle, leaned forward and stroked the stallion's long black ear.

"I would prefer it, Gordon, if you didn't tell him we were here today."

"What?"

"Father, I mean," the girl said.

"What'll I tell him then?"

"Don't tell him anything."

"What if he asks?"

"Tell him what you like, except that we were here today at Bree."

"I thought he encouraged your interest in ridin'?"

"Oh, he does. It's just . . . just something you don't understand."

"He doesn't like you comin' alone?"

"That's it," said Amanda. "You won't say a word about it, will you, Gordon? Mother and I would be awfully grateful."

Gordon shrugged. "Right."

She repaid him with a smile then laughter. "You must think we're a rum lot, Gordon. But we're not so bad, really. All families have secrets, little secrets."

"My lips're sealed," Gordon promised.

"And you're to come back with us for dinner tonight, at The Knowe," Amanda went on. "Mother feels she doesn't know you well enough yet, quite."

"The last train leaves Milngavie at ten past nine."

"Stay over."

"Well – " Gordon hesitated.

"You're not seeing someone else, are you?"

"What?"

"Another string to your bow, another young lady?"

"God, no."

"Is it arranged?"

"Yes," Gordon said, with more enthusiasm than he felt. "Of course, I'd love to come."

*   *   *

How it was that Mr Tubbs got himself behind the counter that Saturday afternoon, Kirsty could never fathom. It wasn't done slyly but, rather, by a process of honest infiltration.

Lorna had arrived about noon and there had been such a lull in trade in early afternoon that Kirsty had sent Greta off to the park with the children. It was about half-past two when Mr Tubbs popped in. He wore his usual rather florid business suit but carried no sample cases and declared that he was 'just passing'. He'd had the forethought to buy a box of macaroon cakes, however, and with Kirsty's permission, went into the backshop, made tea, brought out cups on a tin tray, macaroons on a plate and joined the two young women for a bit of the old *al fresco* behind the long counter.

It was difficult to be annoyed at Mr Tubbs. He had a different sort of charm from Gordon's, not boyish, more cavalier, yet always polite and courteous, not seeming to impose. Lorna liked the chap;

the feeling, Kirsty felt sure, was very mutual. She did not dare tease her young sister-in-law about it, though, for Lorna was at that prickly stage and would have denied it volubly.

Long, generalised debates with Greta on the subject of life and female liberty had become a feature of Lorna's sojourns in Gascoigne Street. Stuck, at Breezy's insistence, with an additional half-year at Prosser's Commercial College, Lorna had decided that once she had graduated from that midden she would spend the rest of her days avoiding serfdom, would take charge of her own destiny and eschew dependence on males for ever.

Kirsty was Lorna's heroine, her ideal. In spite of the fact that Kirsty was married to Craig and had voluntarily entered motherhood, a state that Lorna regarded as one down from slavery, Lorna saw strength and an enviable sense of purpose at work in her sister-in-law. No amount of reasoning by Greta Taylor could shake the young girl's unrealistic zeal for a career of self-dedicated solitude and Mr Tubbs, though he knew what was in the wind, was far too downy a bird to try. But macaroons, sweet tea and badinage with the commercial gentleman took Lorna's mind off her pilgrimage for a while.

Kirsty, in the backshop, listened to the girl's cries of outrage as Mr Tubbs scored off her in their long-running exchange of insults, her squeals of triumph when she chalked up a point against Tubby and, smiling, kept herself discreetly out of their way for a time.

Kirsty was polishing one of the triple mirrors which had been in stock long enough to acquire a coat of Greenfield grime when she heard the shop doorbell jingle and the couple fall, quite properly, silent.

After a moment, Mr Tubbs said, "Good afternoon, sir, may I be of assistance to you this fine afternoon?"

Kirsty skinned off her polishing gloves, touched aside the curtain and peeped down the length of the shop.

The sun had wandered round to the west and slotted its rays down through the girders of the railway bridge. In a haze of dust motes by the door stood the most elegant man she had ever seen. He looked, she thought, as if he might be a courtier to a foreign king, or even a prince himself. He wore an immaculately-cut, silk-faced morning suit, and carried in one hand a silver-topped cane, a topper and a pair of snow-white kidskin gloves. He was in his late thirties, she guessed, or early forties. His hair was jet black, sleek as sealskin, and his moustache hugged the line of his upper lip like a nap. A single-pearl tie pin glistened on his cravat and a pale pink rosebud was held against his lapel by a filigree silver chain.

The man bowed slightly, flashed a smile that was both cold and charming at one and the same time. Kirsty realised that he had detected her presence there in the gloom of the interior. She smoothed her skirts and went out.

"Good afternoon, sir," she said.

Mr Tubbs was behind the counter, close to the mechanical cashier. Hands spread wide, head cocked, he exuded unctuous affability towards the customer but when he addressed Kirsty his tone was curt and imperious.

"Thank you, Kirsty. I'll serve the gentleman personally," Mr Tubbs told her. "Return to your polishin', please."

Kirsty opened her mouth in amazement and Lorna was on the verge of shouting out aloud when Mr Tubbs slipped one hand from the counter top and, under the ledge, made frantic and threatening signals with his closed fist.

"Now, sir, G. A. Nicholson is entirely at your disposal," Mr Tubbs said to the stranger. "What may I show you from our commodious stock?"

Kirsty, though obviously puzzled, was moved by Mr Tubbs' frantic and hidden gestures to obey his order. She retired to the backshop again, not, of course, to polish anything but to crouch by the curtain, listening and watching.

"Allow me to introduce myself," said the stranger in the sort of quacking English voice guaranteed to raise any good Scotsman's hackles. "I am Austin Whiting: my card, sir." Smoothly Mr Whiting slipped a leather wallet from his vest pocket, smoothly extracted a printed card, smoothly passed it to Mr Tubbs who hardly did more than glance at it. Austin Whiting went on, "I have but recently returned from abroad and have taken lease of apartments in Marlborough Street. I wish to purchase certain items of a personal and generally domestic nature."

"Certainly, sir," said Tubbs. "What, for instance?"

"Silver," said Austin Whiting. "Servers, cruets, that sort of thing."

"Anythin' else?"

"Clocks."

"Uh-huh!"

"A watch."

"Can do."

"Only your very best quality."

"Of course, Mr Whitin', that goes without sayin'." Mr Tubbs snapped his fingers in Lorna's direction. "Don't stand there gawpin', girl. Fetch out our very best for Mr Whitin' to inspect. An' bring the man a chair, quick, quick."

The only chair was in the backshop, a fact of which Mr Tubbs was well aware. Lorna, playing her part to perfection, scuttled off like a frightened mouse and scurried through the curtain.

"What's goin' on? What's Tubby playin' at?" Kirsty hissed.

"Not sure," Lorna whispered. "But seems t' me our Mr Tubbs has spotted a fancy-dan."

"What?"

"A trickster, a dud," said Lorna. "Here, give me that chair; then dig out the best stuff you have back here, Kirsty."

Minutes later, relieved of his topper, gloves and cane, Austin Whiting was seated sedately in the centre of the shop while Lorna and Kirsty fetched and carried and Mr Tubbs went through an act of complete, and calculated, subservience to the gentleman's wishes.

The Englishman's act was polished to perfection. He showed no great eagerness for the higher-priced items at first, displayed rather the studied indifference of a man to whom the whole business of shopping was no more than a chore. When Tubby asked him a question, he had an answer on the tip of his tongue, nor did he trip himself up by inconsistencies. He was, he explained, á bachelor, transferred from the Calcutta branch of the Colonial & Commercial Insurance Company to direct the founding of new Scottish offices in Royal Exchange Place.

Behind the curtain again, Kirsty whispered, "Are you certain this mannie's a fraud, Lorna? What if he's not? He's got twenty pounds worth o' stuff picked out already."

"Aye, but how's he goin' to pay for it?" said Lorna.

"A wise choice, sir," Kirsty heard Tubbs say from the shop. "It's quite the best timepiece we have on the premises. I can see you're a gentleman who truly appreciates quality."

"What's he bought now?" Kirsty whispered.

"The eight-day regulator you told Gordon you'd never sell," said Lorna.

"Forty-six shillin's," said Kirsty. "It only cost me twelve. That's . . ."

"Girl." Tubby interrupted her calculations. "Girl, fetch down the Royal Crown coffee service, the one with the tray."

"Yes, Mr Nicholson," Lorna shouted and grimaced at Kirsty before she hurried away to the ladder.

Though he appeared not to hurry, it did not take long at all for Austin Whiting to select some fifteen items from Nicholson's stock. The boxes, large and small, were piled upon the counter and Mr Tubbs rang each sale into the register with a flourish until the red flag in the glass showed a total of £44/10s/6d.

Kirsty's willingness to trust Mr Tubbs' judgement of the customer's character dwindled with each *ping* of the cash register. Forty-four pounds was a fortune by any standards and she had detected nothing in Mr Whiting's behaviour to hint that he was other than he seemed. When Mr Whiting got to his feet and reached for his hat and cane, Kirsty emerged, bustling, from the backshop. "Mr Tu . . . Mr Nicholson, a word with you, if you please."

"One moment, Kirsty." Mr Tubbs held up a warning finger. "Now, sir, will it be a monetary transaction or will you be payin' by cheque?"

Kirsty's intrusion had startled the customer. He hesitated, hand on heart. "Is something wrong with your young lady, Mr Nicholson?"

"Nothin' at all, sir." Mr Tubbs scowled at Kirsty and did not return at once to the question of payment. "Do you wish us to have the goods delivered, Mr Whitin', sir?"

"Ah – yes," said Austin Whiting. "Why not?"

"Your private address then, sir, if I might make so bold?"

"On my card, Mr Nicholson."

"So it is. How daft of me. My apologies, Mr Whitin'," said Mr Tubbs. "Well, we'll have them round first thing on Monday – unless, that is, you require them tonight."

Kirsty stood tense and angry by the counter's end. Lorna had taken position close to the door and was making all kinds of weird faces at her from behind the Englishman's back. When Austin Whiting glanced at her, however, Kirsty could not meet his eye. He gave a tiny smirk, produced his wallet and drew from it not some doctored cheque or banker's warranty but a wad of five-pound notes, all white and crisp.

"Cash, I think," Austin Whiting said. "I think you'd prefer cash, would you not, Mr Nicholson?"

"Well, aye," said Tubby, nonplussed. "I mean, yes, if it's convenient."

Austin Whiting's smirk broadened and he raised his brows. "Admit it, Mr Nicholson, you would not quite trust a cheque signed by a total stranger. I know I wouldn't."

Tubby laughed too, allowing his embarrassment to show. He shrugged. "You read me like a book, Mr Whitin'."

Kirsty let out her breath and sagged against the shelving. Lorna, still by the door, pulled yet another face and expressed not relief but total bewilderment while the Englishman separated nine large Bank of England notes from the wad, snapped each one lightly with finger and thumb and passed it over to Mr Tubbs. The mechanical register sang out again as change was made in silver and copper and a receipt delivered, duly initialled by Mr Tubbs and carefully pocketed by Mr Whiting.

Kirsty watched the stranger put on his gloves and topper and hoist the silver-topped cane up under his arm. She saw him shake Mr Tubbs' hand and turn towards the door. The pile of goods that he had purchased still stood on the counter. He had not managed to spirit them away and had, besides, paid hard cash for them. Nothing could possibly go wrong now.

Mr Austin Whiting paused.

"I suppose," he said, casually buttoning a glove, "I *could* take the articles with me, Mr Nicholson. I have a carriage waiting at the rank. If one of your charming assistants would be kind enough to help me with the boxes, which are not inordinately weighty, I *could* fit them into the hansom and have them home with me this very evening."

"So you could, sir," said Mr Tubbs.

"I take it then that you have no objection?"

"No," Kirsty heard herself say, "that's fine."

And Mr Tubbs, stepping out from behind the counter, said, "I take it, Mr Austin Whitin', that you have no objection to stayin' here while my young lady runs for the polis?"

"Tubby! Good God!" Kirsty exclaimed.

"I think I do have an objection," Mr Whiting said.

At that moment Greta returned from the park with the children. They trailed into the doorway and made the shop bell chime and Mr Austin Whiting made a dive for the half-open door and Lorna flung herself upon him, her arms about his elegant waist, and Mr Tubbs shouted, "*Stop him! Stop that man!*" Bobby was under

261

Whiting's feet, Jen whisked back by her mother. Kirsty was shouting at Mr Tubbs to stop his damned nonsense and Mr Tubbs, in turn, was holding fast to the Englishman's arms and yelling at Greta to run out and find a constable.

"What is it? What's wrong?" Kirsty cried as Lorna and Mr Tubbs threw themselves on top of the unfortunate Englishman and all three fell in a heap on the floor. "What's he done, Tubbs?"

"Forgery," cried Mr Tubbs, waving a fistful of pure white fivers.

And Greta said, "The bugger," and, with Jen on one hand and Bobby on the other, headed out into Gascoigne Street to summon the might of the law.

*　　*　　*

Never before had Gordon been the focus of so much female attention. He was the lone male in The Knowe that evening and, with Dolphus gone, the whole atmosphere of the house seemed changed. The sisters had been released from their bondage. Nanny Pearson had not only brought them down for an early dinner but had been invited to the table too and all the ladies had done themselves up like dishes of fish just for his sake. He could not be other than flattered, though he felt self-consciously shabby in plain suit and clumsy boots and wished that he'd had some warning of what the Adair ladies had had in store for him.

He had driven home from Bree with Olive and Amanda. Captain Tom had come part of the way with them, riding a small dainty mare, and saying very little, though he'd kept the animal close to the side of the gig, close to Olive who was at the reins.

At first Gordon had supposed that Tom Wells was merely being a gentleman but when they had parted company at the old Endrick Bridge he'd noticed how the captain lingered and how Olive Adair had turned, and he had seen, almost in spite of himself, that look in her eye, and had begun to have an inkling of what might be what.

It had been a strange, dreamlike ride. The sun had gone down behind the glass-smooth hills as if it might never rise again, leaving a starry shimmer in the clear, cold, cloudless sky and a rim of red on the very edge of the fells. Olive had urged the shaft-horse hard along the high road, singing a sweet, urgent song to herself, and Amanda had clung to him in the cosy curved seat, purring and swaying and somehow proud.

Back at The Knowe they had put him into the library, had

served him hot wine to warm him and had sent down the little sisters to keep him amused. They were beautiful girls, all three, ringleted and ribboned, in their not-quite-grown-up frocks. He recalled Johnnie Whiteside's disparaging remarks about Phoebe but found nothing 'feeble' about her. On the contrary, she seemed mature and assured and was quick to put her sisters in their places when they became too outspoken. Next came Nanny, her dress too heavy for fashion, her hair still pinned, but with a dab of rouge on her lips and powder on her gaunt cheeks. Olive Adair, when she appeared, was opulent in a rich black satin which fitted smoothly over her hips. Her hair was arranged high in the back, showing three small curls at the nape of her graceful neck. Amanda, in deliberate contrast, was in creamy white, with a frilled, trailing hemline to her dress and dainty curls on her brow.

Gordon got to his feet. He was no longer awed by the girl or her mother, but he knew that no spur of the moment invitation had brought him here and that he would be lucky to escape now that they had him all to themselves. He gave Olive Adair his arm and escorted her into a dining-room ablaze with light from candles and electrical bulbs.

The whole show was for his benefit. Without Dolphus to lay down his miser's law the ladies had gone daft with largesse. They meant to impress but also to pamper him and Olive had gone to infinite pains to select the courses and the wines. She seemed to be telling him, Gordon thought, that there was style behind money and that she had more in her little finger than all the Adairs put together.

If he had not spent the day in the fresh air, if he had not been stimulated by riding, Gordon might have resisted the Adair ladies.

Half-way through dinner, however, he gave a sigh, less of contentment than of resignation, and allowed himself to drift towards that moment, which would surely come, when he would be left alone with Amanda and would go down on one knee and beg for her hand in marriage while Olive and the sisters would cluster not far off awaiting Amanda's happy cry of "*Yes*."

*   *   *

Craig heard nothing of the affray at Nicholson's shop until he returned to Ottawa Street at the end of his day's shift. The station was buzzing with news of the arrest of Charles Jackson, alias Austin Whiting. Ronnie, who, by sheer chance, had made the collar, was strutting in front of the sergeants' room or nipping down below to the cells to make sure that 'his prisoner' had not miraculously escaped. Detectives had converged from Percy Street, also from Glasgow, and bigwigs, in and out of uniform, were standing about looking pompous or following Constable Norbert downstairs to stare through the bars at Charles Jackson as if he were a specimen rare in captivity, which indeed he was.

Sergeants Drummond and Stevens, and a young constable from Headquarters who had shorthand writing at his fingertips, were locked away with Mrs Kirsty Nicholson, Miss Lorna Nicholson and Mr Tubbs, to take their separate statements. Quantities of goods, in and out of pasteboard boxes, were lined on a table in the muster room where Peter Stewart and John Boyle, working in tandem, were checking each item off against a long receipt. The core evidence, twenty-three brand new Bank of England five-pound notes, removed from the person of Mr Charles Jackson, were being exhibited with the aid of a large magnifying glass to the wondering gaze of all and sundry as prime examples of the counterfeiter's art, the like of which were seldom seen north of the Scottish border and never in backwaters like Greenfield Burgh.

Charles Jackson was a much-wanted man. Apparently he had been spreading dud fivers all over England, south and north, and had only moved the seat of his operations to Central Scotland within the past month. He had passed notes in Edinburgh, Aberdeen and Dundee in exchange for goods that could easily be converted into cash. No downtrodden fly-by-night, Jackson was a clever criminal from the middle classes and English to boot. Radical journalists would find no stick in this arrest with which to beat the police. Fame, clean as a whistle, had come to Ottawa Street and everybody wanted a share.

"Done us proud this time, your missus," Ronnie said. "Want to take a look at him 'fore he's swept away to Percy Street?"

"Not particularly," Craig said. "Where's my wife?"

"Makin' her statement." Ronnie nodded towards the pebble-glass door of the sergeants' room. "Not to be disturbed on any account. Her an' your sister – nice-lookin' girl, by the way – an' the traveller chap have to be grilled slow an' careful."

"From what I hear they've got Jackson dead to rights."

"Red-handed," said Ronnie. "Tubbs, the traveller chap, had heard about Jackson from others of his ilk; the commercial boys' grapevine. Recognised him straight off. Now it's all go to find out where the counterfeiters hole out. London, I expect. Lieutenant Strang thinks Jackson'll turn Queen's."

"How did you get there?"

"She came for me. Your wee . . . the woman from Benedict Street."

"Isn't she a material witness too?"

"No, she arrived just in time to gallop for help."

"An' she got you?"

"I just happened to be passin' along the Kingdom Road." Ronnie winked. "Lucky for me, eh?"

"Was there a struggle?"

"Nah, Jackson came quiet as a lamb. I think he was puffed, what wi' your sister an' the traveller chap sittin' on him. Anyway, he's not the violent sort. Kid-glove criminal. He's only the utterer, as far as we know, not the forger, but Lieutenant Strang's been on the telephone to Scotland Yard an' the detectives there know. all about our Mr Jackson."

"So they'll get him on more than a misdemeanour?"

"You bet your socks they will."

"Where's Greta now?"

"Left in charge o' the shop," said Ronnie, "and the bairns."

Craig left the young constable to his glory. He reported to Sergeant Byrne at the desk, signed off and slipped away from Ottawa Street. Ten minutes later he arrived at the shop in Gascoigne Street where, curiously, he found Greta alone with the children.

"Daddy, we caught a bad man," Bobby cried and ran at once to his father.

Craig picked the boy up, sat him on the counter and put an arm about him, while Jen, who had not grasped the connection between Bobby and Craig before, hugged her mother's waist and, petted, pouted.

"Mr Tubbs satted on him."

"Aye, so I heard," Craig said.

"Auntie Lorna satted on him too."

"I wouldn't want Auntie Lorna sittin' on me," Craig said and was gratified when Bobby laughed.

Greta said, "I thought you'd be with Kirsty?"

"She could be hours yet," Craig said. "I'm off-duty an' not involved, so I came round for Bobby. I'll take him home."

"Not goin' home," Bobby said. "Shutters no' up."

"I'll put the shutters up, darlin'," Greta told him.

"When do you usually close?" Craig asked.

He was surprised that he did not feel more awkward with her. He had done things with Greta that would not bear telling, yet he felt no shame in retrospect and no embarrassment now. It was the first time that they had really spoken since she had turned him down. He did not count the episode in her house with Billy King, that had been a rescue, a desperate rescue, nothing more.

"Half-past seven or eight o'clock."

Craig said, "I doubt if Kirsty'll mind if you lock up before that. Unless I miss my guess you'll have a crowd o' gogglers hangin' round as soon as the word gets out."

Greta nodded.

"How are you, Greta?"

"All right. You?"

"Fine."

Jen was still staring at him, frowning. Bobby, sensitive to the little girl's incomprehension, snuggled possessively closer and slung a comradely arm over his father's shoulder.

Greta said, "The man we caught, will he plead guilty?"

The question surprised Craig. "Dunno. He might turn Queen's evidence against the forgers. If he was willin' to do that, to reveal all, then it would go lighter with him, though not much."

"Will I have to appear in court?"

"You might," Craig said. "If he tries to brazen it out, you might well be called as a prosecution witness."

"I don't want that," Greta said. "I've had enough o' police questions to last me a lifetime. Can you not do somethin', Craig?"

Craig shook his head. "Nothin' I *can* do. It's in the lap o' the gods. Kirsty's bound to have to appear, Lorna too, but perhaps you'll be lucky, Greta, an' the lawyers won't need you."

"I can't do it. I just can't face it."

"It's not so bad in court," Craig said, to calm her. "I mean, you'd just have to say what you saw an' . . .'"

"Not more questions, God!"

Craig said, "You're afraid they'll find out about you, is that it?"

"What d'you mean?"

"They won't," Craig said. "There'd be no reason for them to pry into your past. Take my word for it, Greta."

"My past?"

"You know what I mean," said Craig.

"Damned if I know what you mean."

"You're frightened they'll discover the truth about her," Craig said. "About Lizzie Straun, Sylvie McNish, all that stuff. You're scared you'll lose her."

"You bastard, Craig," Greta said.

"Bad man," said Bobby, fortunately adrift in the conversation. "Auntie Lorna satted on his tummy."

"You've nothin' to fear, Greta, not from the lawyers or the detectives. It's Jackson they're after, not you."

"It's not the lawyers an' detectives I'm worried about."

"Me?" said Craig, surprised. "I thought you knew me better than that, Greta."

"How much *do* you know?"

"Pretty well the lot."

"You bastard!"

Craig said, "Watch your tongue, Greta. I don't want his lordship pickin' up bad language. You know how quick he can be."

"Who told you about Lizzie Straun?"

"The information just came my way," Craig said.

"Breezy Adair told you, didn't he? You asked him 'cause you wanted to get somethin' on me."

"Ach, Greta!" Craig said. "Adair didn't say a bloody word about you. I don't talk to Adair. I'm not interested in that lot, not in the slightest."

"I suppose if I don't . . ."

He raised his hand, finger stiff, and his voice had gravel in it. "Cut it bloody out, Greta. Do you think I'm the kind o' man who would do that?" He snorted. "Christ, do you think Kirsty would let me?"

"I don't know what kind of man you are, Craig Nicholson."

"Nah, well, I don't know myself most o' the time," Craig said. He lifted Bobby on to his shoulder, gripping him snugly with his left arm. "But I know what kind o' man I'm not."

"*Will* I have t' appear in court?"

"I can't get to him, to Jackson or Whitin' or whatever his name is. If I could get to him I'd put the fear o' God in him," Craig said.

"Aye, you're good at that."

"But I can't. So you'll just have to sweat it out, Greta, until he pleads."

"I wish . . ."

"I know what you're goin' to say," Craig told her. "But it's not our fault; not mine, not Kirsty's. It was bad business an' you shouldn't have got mixed up in it all those years ago."

She gave a toss of the head, not defiant. Her eyes were sullen and scared. He understood her fear of him, the dread that somehow the law would discover her secret and she would have Jen wrested from her. He did not know how to comfort her, though, because anything he might say or do in that direction would be construed as seduction, as male and selfish.

"Do you know who her father was?" he asked.

"No."

"Her mother?"

"They didn't want her," Greta said. "They couldn't wait to be rid of her. If they hadn't been well-off she'd have wound up in the river. Think of that, Craig. How'd you like to find *her* in the river some cold mornin'?"

"*Wheesht*, Greta," Craig said. "You shouldn't say things like that. She knows we're talkin' about her."

The little girl was pressed against Greta's skirts, hugging her thigh. The pout had gone. Her eyes were huge, filled with frightful uncertainty as she stared up, not at him but at the woman she thought of as her mother.

Perhaps Kirsty had once looked like that, had the same hollow uncomprehending fear in her heart and had never quite been rid of it. He had come too close these past months to the edge of hopelessness to dismiss Greta's fears as groundless. He was so damned glad that he had fathered a son not a daughter, for then he would have been touched by fear for her future that was in itself as close as any man can come to understanding the nature of female waywardness and female love.

Greta slid her hand down and cupped Jen's fair head. The child rubbed against her, secure in her closeness, nurtured by her warmth. Adults' words were, after all, meaningless and without threat.

Greta said, "She doesn't know. She'll never know. I'll make damned sure o' that."

"What happens when she starts t' ask questions?"

"I'll tell her somethin' nice."

"Not the truth, though?"

"No, not the truth," Greta said.

"Because she'd be hurt by it?"

"Because I would," said Greta.

* * *

He did not put Bobby down. He walked with rapid, big-booted strides away from Gascoigne Street, hugging the boy to him.

Head up, he side-stepped pedestrians and skirted the intermittent horse traffic that clacked along the Kingdom Road. He could smell the river very distinctly for some reason, the sour odour of pubs, smoke and cooking-fat held in it like oils in suspension.

He felt unusually tall with Bobby in his arms. It was as if the boy's small size had adjusted him to scale. He took a wry pleasure in his son's delight at the fast rate of progress as they weaved along the pavements and across the cobbles. Just as he turned into Ottawa Street the police van from Percy Street came rumbling past.

Black-painted, windowless and cramped, the van was pulled by the constabulary's best matched pair. Two uniformed officers stood on the board at the back and leaned their weight against the bolted door. The forger, Jackson, would be inside, handcuffed to burly Sergeant Byrne, or to Frank Walker, perhaps.

"See, son," he said, stopping at the kerb.

"Hosses."

"The bad man's inside that van."

"Wi' Auntie Lorna?"

Craig chuckled. "Nah, nah. He's bein' taken to prison."

One of the guarding officers was, of course, Ronnie Norbert. He gave no sign of recognition as the vehicle rounded the corner. He stood as straight as he dared, hands behind his back to grip the brass safety handle, and stared straight ahead, noble and proud. Craig would have given a month's wages to be inside the black van, to be alone with the forger for just ten minutes. Confession and a guilty plea would be assured, by God it would. By the time he'd finished with the said Charles Jackson, Greta's wish would have come true.

Bobby waved to the van as it disappeared behind the tenements and Craig moved across the street and headed towards the station. He arrived just as Kirsty and Lorna were ushered out of the main door by Sergeant Drummond.

"Och, just in time, Constable Nicholson," he said. "I think we have tired out your good lady wife with all our questions."

Kirsty did indeed look pale and solemn and Craig, on impulse, gave her his arm.

"Was it too much for you, dearest?" he asked.

"It had to be done, I suppose," Kirsty answered, brushing Bobby's unruly hair and giving the chanting boy attention.

Lorna grinned and, without being asked, relieved Craig of Bobby's weight and hoisted the child into her arms.

"That's what I call a good day's work," Lorna said. "I loved every minute of it."

"You satted on the bad man's tummy."

"Would you like me to sit on your tummy?" Lorna asked.

Bobby answered, "Noooooo."

"Well, I'm going to wait for old Tubby," Lorna said. "Unless they've thrown him in clink, he shouldn't be long now."

"I just want to go home," Kirsty said. "Craig, will you take me home?"

" 'Course I will," Craig said and a moment later, with Bobby hand-in-hand between them, Constable Nicholson and his wife set off for Canada Road.

*   *   *

It was raining heavily on Monday morning. Smoke from the St Rollox engine works hung under a bleak grey lid of cloud and the reek of barley-wash and maltings that pervaded Carruth's brewery was so strong that Gordon almost gagged on it. He kept a handkerchief to his mouth as he walked the length of the building and across the yard behind the bottling shed towards the narrow, two-storey red-brick 'house' which contained the board room, the company secretary's office and, on the upper floor, Mr James Randolph Adair's private suite.

Intricate systems of communication, to do with status and precedent, had been set in motion by Gordon's request for an interview with Mr Adair. It had taken twenty minutes for the request to be conveyed from the accounting office to the house and another twenty for word to come back that, at a quarter past eleven o'clock, Mr Adair would grant Nicholson a few minutes of his precious time.

"Not a complaint, is it?" the deputy assistant clerk had asked Gordon, scowling.

"No, Mr Holinsworth; a personal matter."

"Somethin' on your mind I should know about, Nicholson?" Head of Accounting had sibilantly enquired.

"No, Mr Green, it's a personal matter."

Everybody knew that Nicholson had been placed in the firm simply to rise and, naturally, they resented him for it. They were also wary lest he turn out to be a spy for the managing director. Gordon found the position invidious and as he slunk along between the brewery's walls that wet autumn morning he longed to be back in the warehouse on Dumbarton Road. Even so, he had chosen his path and would follow it without, as yet, enthusiasm but also without complaint.

He should, of course, have invited Dolphus to dinner in Glasgow outside working hours. But his betrothal to Amanda seemed somehow linked to Carruth's and it was therefore more fitting that father and prospective son-in-law met face to face within the brewery's walls. He had put on his best suit, a discreet green tweed, and had polished his brown brogues until, even with rain upon them, they shone like mirrors.

He had been in the house only once before but he climbed the staircase, past portraits of the firm's founders and murky old photographs of the original brewery in Edinburgh, without curiosity. He knocked on the carved oak door on the carpeted landing and waited, heart thumping.

"Come."

Dolphus was seated behind a huge desk, his back to the window. A fire burned in an ornamental grate. There were three or four potted plants in corners, and a couple of horsehair-stuffed chairs and an Indian rug, faded enough to be genuine.

"Ah, Nicholson," Dolphus said, not rising. "What can I do for you?"

"Did Amanda not . . . I mean, did you know that I was out at The Knowe at the weekend?" Gordon stammered.

He'd hoped that the girls, or mother, would have been carried away by their excitement and would have broken the news to Dolphus, at least given him some inkling of what had taken place in the drawing-room on Saturday night after dinner.

Apparently they hadn't. Apparently they were sticklers for protocol and hadn't wished to steal his thunder. Apparently Daddy hadn't a clue what he was talking about.

"Yes?" Dolphus said.

The tweed suit was damp, the room warm enough to bring a little steam from Gordon's shoulders. He looked down at his shoes, at the raindrops pearled on them, breathed in the aroma of brewing beer.

"If . . . if you . . . if you will be kind enough t' accept me, sir, I wish to become engaged to your daughter . . . to your eldest daughter . . . Amanda, I mean."

"I know who my eldest daughter is," Dolphus said.

"I think . . . I think you know what my prospects are, sir, but you have my assurance that . . . young as I am, I'll be . . . diligent an' industrious an' will look after Amanda as best I can."

Dolphus pursed his lips. He had been smoking a small glossy brown cigar and it still burned furtively in a brass ashtray on some unseen ledge of the desk, purling smoke against the light from the window.

Gordon had no notion of what to expect; a hearty arm about the shoulder, pleasure, reluctance, prissy nitpicking over details, dictatorial warnings, a solemn handshake, his signature in blood?

Dolphus said, "I take it you've asked Amanda?"

"Aye," said Gordon. "I mean . . . yes, sir, I have."

"She wouldn't say no."

"She said . . . she said it would be all right with her if it was all right with you."

"All right? Hah?" said Dolphus. "Didn't she shriek and kiss you and rush off to tell Mama?"

"Actually . . . yes, she did."

"Didn't my wife pour champagne and clasp you to her bosom and Amanda's sisters all kiss you on the cheek?"

"Actually . . . yes, they did."

Dolphus spread his hands and hunched his shoulders in resignation. "There you are then."

"What?"

"Done," Dolphus said.

He plucked the small cigar from its ashtray and sucked on it.

"You mean . . . you mean it's all right with you?"

"Perfectly all right by me," said Dolphus.

"Can I tell my family?"

"By all means."

"Congratulations," Gordon heard himself say.

"Hah?"

"I mean . . . I mean, thank you, sir."

"No, thank *you*, Gordon," Dolphus said and, leaning back in the leather chair, puffed lightly on his cigar.

"Will . . . will that be all, sir?"

"Yes, Gordon, that will be all," said James Randolph Adair and, to Gordon's astonishment, laughed aloud.

He was still laughing when Gordon left the room, still laughing when Gordon reached the yard, still audibly laughing when Gordon turned the corner by the bottling-shed and trudged glumly back to Accounting in the rain.

*   *   *

It was, of course, Johnnie to whom the message was entrusted. For the past five years he had been a go-between, Breezy's right-hand man, doing all the things that Breezy, to preserve some respect in his stepson, would never dare ask of Gordon. This time, however, the message came from the lovely Olive. It was hand-delivered by a Post Office courier to the warehouse in Partick East and passed on at once to Great Western Terrace to catch Breezy before he finished his breakfast and set out on his daily rounds.

"So he's done it, has he?" Eric Adair said. "Popped the vital question at last."

Johnnie said, "Yes."

"There will be joy and jubilation in all camps, I expect, a lighting of beacons and a raising of flags," said Eric. "And the nuptials? Soon?"

"It was only a telegraph message, Eric, not a three-volume report," said John Whiteside snappishly.

"Hazard a guess?"

"Spring, summer. May or June."

"So that her bed may be strewn with blossoms fresh and the buds of May observe her hour?"

Johnnie swung his feet to the floor. "I'm sick of that bloody little upstart. What right has he to shoulder us aside?"

"Oh-hoh!" said Eric. "I do believe I detect genuine passion here; a slighted lover, no less."

"Shut up."

"Is it, I ask myself, the loss of the girl or the boodle that makes my chum Johnnie grieve?"

"I told you to shut up about it."

"Perhaps Olive's urgent request for a meetin' with our dear employer has somethin' to do with this," said Eric, tossing down a folded copy of the morning's *Glasgow Herald*. "Have you seen it?"

"Yes, I've seen it," said John Whiteside.

"If it isn't one of the Nicholsons, it's another," Eric Adair said. "Becomin' quite famous all of a sudden, ain't they?"

"Coincidence," said Johnnie. "In any case, it's mostly to do with the policeman's wife and sister, and that grubby little fellow, Tubbs."

"It isn't every day you catch a forger and get your name in print. Greta's mentioned again too," said Eric. "She's becomin' frightfully *visible* is our Greta. For somebody in her delicate situation, that is."

"Exactly what I was thinking," Johnnie said.

"Do you think young Gordon knows what's afoot?"

"I doubt it."

"Perhaps we should tell him," said Eric.

"No," John Whiteside said.

"Do you have somethin' else in mind?"

"Naturally," Johnnie said. "Don't I always have something else in mind?"

"To do with Greta?"

"To do with Amanda," John Whiteside said.

*   *   *

Gentlemen, it seemed, preferred to descend into cavernous depths to partake of a spot of lunch while ladies rose ethereally to meet their friends in wide-windowed tearooms on the third or fourth floors of new departmental stores and daintily nibble on chicken breasts and grilled lemon sole amid flower bowls and fine china.

Breezy had never been in Miss Stoddart's Lunch & Tea Rooms before. While they did not top a department store they were situated high on a Bath Street terrace and had big bow windows through which ladies could see and be seen. He was the only male person on the premises, a fact that did not disconcert him in the slightest.

"Well, Olive," he said, after he had been served with a sweet veal cutlet, "I can see there's goin' to be nothin' clandestine about this meeting. I feel like a fish out of water."

"No, you don't," Olive told him. "You love having all the ladies stare at you."

Breezy touched up the ends of his moustache and raised an

eyebrow. "Are you passin' me off as your sweetheart or your father, hum?"

"He didn't tell you?"

"Oh, this *is* serious."

"Yes, it is. Didn't he tell you? I asked him not to but I thought perhaps he would."

"Olive, dear, I don't know what you're bletherin' about."

"Gordon has asked my daughter Amanda to become his wife. And she has agreed."

Breezy paused. "I see."

"It doesn't come as a surprise?"

"No, no," Breezy said. "No, no, not at all."

"Gordon will be making a formal request for Amanda's hand today, from Dolphus."

"Dolphus won't stand in the way."

"On the contrary. My husband will be only too delighted to have Amanda married off."

"Well, it's every father's wish to see his offspring settled, I suppose."

"Do not pretend, Breezy."

"Pretend?"

"I know that you have an arrangement with Dolphus."

"Really?"

"Are you not helping him to be rid of me?"

"Certainly not," said Breezy.

"To be rid of me while retaining the controlling interest in Carruth's?"

"What put the daft idea into your head?"

"I can scotch it, you know."

Breezy paused. "But you won't, will you?"

"I should never have married your brother."

"He was right for you at the time."

"I thought he would be more like you," Olive said.

"Oh, we're not that far apart, Dolphus an' me, temperamentally speakin'. We just got old, older, that's all."

"Why did you not ask for my hand, Breezy, all those years ago?"

"I didn't think I could make you happy."

"And now you marry this . . . this . . ."

"Have a care, Olive. I happened to have a high regard for my spouse as well as bein' in love with her."

"She's a damned peasant."

"Aye, and so am I."

"All right, yes, I apologise," Olive said. "That was an ill-judged remark under the circumstances."

Breezy leaned forward and, ignoring the fluttering glances of the lady diners, covered Olive's hand with his own. He said, "You were the most beautiful woman I'd ever seen, Olive. You still are, in fact. Too good for me. You made me feel inferior."

"Except when you took me to bed?"

"I couldn't resist you."

"Dolphus can. Dolphus has."

Breezy lifted his hand away and sat back. He diced the portion of veal that remained on his plate, dabbed a cube in sauce and put it into his mouth. The lightness had gone out of him, the charm. He said, "I didn't drive you into the arms of other men, Olive. You managed that all on your own."

"Don't be a hypocrite, Breezy."

"I stood by you when you needed me, didn't I?"

"Where is she?"

"I've no idea."

"Where's my daughter?" Olive said.

"I told you, I've no idea."

"I want her back."

"Don't be bloody daft," Breezy said.

"I'm leaving him," Olive Adair said. "As soon as Amanda marries your stepson, I'm leaving Dolphus. He may have his divorce, his settlement, the lion's share of Carruth's."

"And the rest of your children?"

"They will understand."

"You've indoctrinated them, haven't you? God, you've got them all on your side, turned them against their father."

"For all he cares."

"He cares more than you think, Olive."

"Who has her?"

"She's safe an' well, in Ireland."

"Liar," Olive said. "I think it's the girl in the newspaper. I think my child's being cared for by a street woman."

"Newspaper?"

"Oh, come now, Breezy."

"You mean that business with the forger? Och, aye, Lorna's been goin' on and on about that all weekend. She's like a pup wi' two tails since she got her name in the paper. She did well, the lass."

"I won't be put off."

"The child's four years old. She doesn't know you at all," Breezy said.

"I am her mother. I'll change that. She'll be better off with me. She'll have the best of everything. You can't seriously expect me to believe that she'll have a better life with some tart from the back streets of Greenfield, with one of your little whores."

It was a trap. She intended to anger him, render him incautious. She had deliberately set their meeting in this bourgeois female sanctuary because she knew he was too proud to make a scene here.

Breezy smiled. "I don't know *what* you're talkin' about, Olive."

"I still have your letters," Olive said.

"Letters? What letters?"

"Five letters."

"I never wrote you letters."

"Indeed you did, Albert."

"What . . ." Breezy hesitated. "What did I say in them?"

"Enough to indicate that we were lovers."

"Twenty years ago?"

"It's something that Dolphus did not know," Olive said. "It's something that, even now, would cause him grievous pain and would destroy his faith in you completely."

"Is this blackmail, Olive?"

"Call it what you will."

"Haven't we had enough scandal in this damned family without you stirrin' up more?" said Breezy. "Dear God, what have I ever done to you, Olive, that you'd drive a wedge between my brother an' me?"

"I don't suppose that your wife . . ."

"Aw, that too," said Breezy. "I should've guessed as much."

"Who has my daughter?" It was Olive's turn to touch hands. "Please, Breezy, please tell me."

"The woman who has her loves her very much," Breezy said. "She looks on her now as her own. She won't part with her at any price, believe me."

"Nonsense," Olive Adair said. "She took her for money. I'm sure she'll let her go for money."

"Money? Money won't buy back the bairn, not now."

277

"It *is* the woman from Greenfield, isn't it?" Olive said. "Of course it is. She resides in one of your properties and is employed by one of your relatives."

"No, Olive. You're wrong."

"When the time's ripe I shall offer her more money than she's ever seen in her life. She'll give up my child without a whimper, you'll see. I know the type."

"Jesus!" Breezy said through clenched teeth.

"And if, for some reason, she proves difficult then I'll put the law on her."

"How can you be so . . ."

"I want my baby back."

"If you're so bloody keen to have another bairn, Olive, then why don't you saddle up for bloody Tom Wells again? I'm sure he'd be delighted to oblige."

"Greta Taylor, that's her name, isn't it?"

"Olive, you're a selfish bitch."

"Isn't it?"

"Yes, damn you," Breezy said.

He watched her tension change before his eyes into a kind of sinister arrogance. He had been in love with Olive Carruth once, a fleeting passion that had burned out as quickly as a bracken fire. He had been afraid of her then and he was afraid of her now; he knew that she would let nothing stand in her way.

"By the way," Olive said, "if you have it in mind to warn this woman, if you have more regard for her feelings than for mine, remember, Albert, that I still have the letters. If this Taylor person isn't where I can find her when the time comes I shall use them."

"I don't doubt it."

"Who else knows the truth?"

"Only John Whiteside."

She laughed as if she already had Johnnie in her pocket which, Breezy thought, might very well be the case.

"No one else?"

"Nope," said Breezy.

"In that case," Olive said, "eat your lunch, Albert, and let's talk of more pleasant things."

"What, for instance?" Breezy said.

"The wedding, of course," said Olive Carruth Adair.

Twelve

No Case to Answer

There were those in the police offices of Percy Street who were disappointed when Charles Jackson, alias Austin Whiting, pleaded guilty to all the charges that had been ranked against him and, in the presence of two detectives who had travelled up post-haste from Scotland Yard, sang his little heart out.

In the light of information freely given by said Charles Jackson a gaggle of forgers, confidence tricksters and sundry felons were tracked down and rounded up in Manchester as well as London, and a precious collection of engraved plates, together with the engraver, were finally run to earth in a house in Basingstoke. Though the *Partick Star* as well as the *Glasgow Herald* continued to report on the progress of the sensational coup, and Mr Tubbs remained a bit of a hero to his clients and customers, for the rank and file of the Greenfield constabulary it was soon back to old clothes and porridge.

It was a vast relief to Kirsty and Greta when they learned that they would not be summoned to appear as witnesses against Jackson, that the man's fate had fallen out of the hands of the police and into the hands of lawyers and judges.

Kirsty had been less frightened than embarrassed by the incident. She had no wish to appear in court and undergo another period of public scrutiny. She sympathised with Greta who, through no fault of her own, had been subjected to a blaze of unwelcome attention not once but twice in the past few weeks and had become tense and defensive because of it.

Lorna, on the other hand, regarded the whole thing as an adventure and lined her pouch bag with all the newspaper snippets that mentioned her by name. She would foist them on to anyone who showed even the slightest interest and, by mid-term, had become a notorious bore at Prosser's Commercial College. Indeed it was not until Jackson had been sentenced to twelve years

279

for his crimes, his voluntary witness against criminal colleagues notwithstanding, and committed to Barlinnie prison that Lorna began to comprehend what exactly she had done and to stop boasting about it.

Besides, another matter closer to home had arisen to claim the family's attention and to divide it once more into squabbling factions: Gordon's betrothal to Miss Amanda Adair.

It was Lorna who carried word to Kirsty and Kirsty who passed it on to Greta and then to Craig. None of them was particularly pleased at the prospect of losing Gordon to the Adairs. Only Lorna, however, was outspoken in her criticism of her brother's ambitious marriage. She went on and on and on about it, at home and in the shop, until Madge took her aside one evening, wagged a finger in her face, told her to hold her tongue and make her peace with Gordon or she'd find herself homeless and out on the street.

"That wouldn't worry me at all, Mother," Lorna had retorted. "I'd go an' live with Kirsty an' work in the shop."

"What makes you think Kirsty'd take you in?"

"Oh, I know she would."

"Aye, but it isn't Kirsty's house. It's Craig's, and he might not be so keen to have *you* for a lodger."

"Anyway," Lorna had said, "Breezy would never throw me out."

"Don't try him too far, m'lady," Madge had warned. "Albert's very much in favour o' this marriage."

"God!" Lorna had cried, theatrically. "It's all so damned commercial, so . . . so incestuous."

"What did you say?"

"I can't believe it's really our Gordon that's bein' bartered off like a slave. How can you stand by and let this happen to him?"

"Just you leave him alone. You know nothin' about it."

"About what? Love?"

"Aye, among other things."

"Love! God!" Lorna had made her disgust palpable. "Gordon's not in love with that girl. He just thinks he is."

"Don't you dare tell *him* that."

"Too late, Mother," Lorna had said. "I've told him till I'm blue in the face. He just won't listen."

"Why should he listen to you?" Kirsty had said, later that same evening in the shop in Gascoigne Street after Lorna had recounted at great and indignant length the details of her argument with her mother.

"I'm his sister, for God's sake."

"Reason enough for *not* listenin' to you," Kirsty had said.

"Don't tell me you approve of this marriage?"

"Whether I do or not," Kirsty had said, "is immaterial. Besides, I haven't seen Gordon in weeks."

"Have you seen him, Greta?"

The woman from Benedict Street had been fitting a fresh roll of stiff brown paper on to the rod on the counter's edge. She had looked up, startled at the question. "Why should I have seen him?"

"Dunno," Lorna had said. "I just thought you might've bumped into him in the street."

"Well, I haven't," Greta had said.

"None of us has seen Gordon," Kirsty had said, "since he started in Carruth's full time."

"He's ashamed, that's what it is," Lorna had said.

"He's got nothin' to be ashamed about," Greta had put in. "I don't see what you're goin' on about."

"I'm goin' on about Gordon bein' bartered . . ."

"Nonsense!" Kirsty had interrupted. "Amanda Adair seems like a perfectly nice girl. She'll probably make him a good wife."

"Hah!" Lorna had cried. "What does Craig have to say about all this? I'll bet he doesn't approve."

Kirsty had hesitated. "We haven't discussed it, in fact."

"Well, I think you'd better discuss it," Lorna had said, "'cause our Gordie's got it in mind to have Craig for his best man at the weddin'."

"When is the weddin'?" Greta had asked.

"June, the first Saturday."

"Did Gordon tell you this?" Kirsty had said.

"Hinted at it," Lorna had said. "First, though, there's the engagement party. That's to be held in our house on the second Saturday in November. You'll both be invited; Craig an' you, I mean."

"I don't know if Craig will come."

"I wouldn't blame him if he didn't," Lorna had said.

"'Course we're not goin'," Craig had said when Kirsty had told him the latest news from Great Western Terrace. "It's not for the likes of us, Kirsty."

"Gordon will be disappointed, Craig. Accordin' to Lorna he's got his heart set on havin' you as his best man at the weddin'. Who else can he ask?"

"Whiteside, maybe, or another o' his fancy chums."

"Don't you think it's time you made peace with your mother an' Breezy?" Kirsty had said. "This is a perfect opportunity, dear."

"It's also a perfect opportunity for a partin' o' the ways," Craig had said, without apparent rancour.

"What do you have against them?"

Craig had shrugged.

He had been to the swimming club at Cranstounhill after his shift and his hair was still damp. He always looked so clean, so unstained when he returned from the baths, younger too. He was at table, eating a late supper of pickled herring and cold boiled potatoes. With Bobby in bed asleep the kitchen was quiet and peaceful.

Kirsty said, "It's difficult for me to cut them off. I mean, Gordon's a partner in my shop an' Breezy gives me quite a lot of help. An' there's Lorna too."

"I'm not criticisin' you for seein' them, Kirsty," Craig said. "It's just that I feel we've our own lives to lead an' we're better off without interference."

"Them up on the hill, us down here?"

"If you like," Craig said.

"What if Gordon comes here? I mean, he's bound to come to see you eventually, if what Lorna says is true."

"I'll talk to him," Craig said. "I'll just explain how we feel."

"I'd like to go to the party."

"Nah, nah, Kirsty. They're not our kind at all. They've nothin' I want to share."

"Do you think Gordon's doin' the right thing?"

"It's up to him."

"Craig?"

"Entirely up to him," Craig said and politely but pointedly asked her if she could find another herring lurking in the dish.

*   *   *

It was the beginning of the wet season, the onset of winter with a vengeance. Not for the Scots the clean, dry cold of far northern climes; instead they suffered weeks of drizzling rain, raw and clawing, with nary a glimpse of sunlight through the short

November days. Gloom seemed to enter the soul through the pores of the skin and the only relief was the pub or the fireside, administrations of whisky or hot tea, the clashed pan.

Even on week nights, in the trough between pay days, enough men had scratched up enough money to pack the bar of The Northern Lights and crowd its private parlours to the doors. Shipwrights and cartwrights, coopers and middenmen, lamplighters, bakers, grocers and clerks, old men and young, stole out from home to seek cheery company round the pub's black iron grates, to play dominoes, draughts or argue the toss on subjects as deep and diverse as politics or war or football form.

Drink for some was the magnet, the whole, sole reason for enduring hours of toil under the plates of a ship in the making or crouched on the stool of a grinding-shop. They drank as if taking medicine to mend a wound that would never heal. Work was the wound and drink the cure, wife and weans no more than interference in the spiral down to poverty and illness and an intemperate death.

"You," Craig said, crooking his index finger, "out."

It was not the uniform now that did the talking but the very manner of the man. He wore no blue serge, no helmet or holster or belt, only a dowdy black donkey-jacket and brown corduroys, a knitted scarf tucked round his throat; yet they recognised his authority at once, peered blearily up from their puddles of beer and nips of whisky and, lifting their glasses, vacated the small wooden-walled room to the left of the porch without a murmur of protest or muttered threat.

"Why here?" Gordon said.

"It's handy," Craig said.

"I thought it was sentiment?" Gordon said.

"Uh?"

"First time we ever saw Breezy Adair was here. Not remember? Just through the wall there, in the bar."

"I remember," Craig said. "You set me up."

"Aye, but you wouldn't bite."

"I didn't like him then an' I don't like him now," Craig said. "Do you want a drink?"

"Nope," Gordon said. "But don't let me stop you."

"Breezy owns this place, doesn't he?"

"He's sellin' it, I believe."

"To Carruth's?" Craig asked.

283

"Yep."

"Why?"

"Carruth's will pay sweet for it," Gordon answered. "Anyway, I think Breezy wants to retire, kind of."

"Now he's fulfilled his obligations?"

"What?"

"Now he's got you married into money."

"Is that what you think?" Gordon said.

"Isn't it the truth?" Craig said.

"Nowhere near it," Gordon said.

"How is the brewery business? D'you like it?"

"Aye, it's all right," said Gordon.

He took a cigarette case from his vest pocket, flipped open the lid and offered it to Craig.

"Turkish," Gordon said, "or Virginia?"

"Christ!"

"Just jokin'," Gordon said. "They're plain Gold Flake, both sides."

"Still, I'll smoke my own."

"Take one, for God's sake."

Craig hesitated, picked a cigarette from under the elasticated wire and examined it suspiciously. Gordon groaned, shook his head, struck a match and lit both cigarettes from it.

"I heard," Craig said, "that you wanted to see me."

"Ah, so that's it, is it?"

Gordon sat back in the chair and stretched a hand behind him to warm his fingers at the fire. In spite of the buzz of conversation from beyond the partition, the warmth and friendliness of the atmosphere, he did not care for The Northern Lights much. He had developed a dreadful antipathy to all public houses, dram shops and licensed victuallers, to any place that smelled of the products of the vat and the still.

"Didn't Lorna tell you?" Craig said.

"Only that you wanted to meet me here," Gordon said. "Naturally, I cancelled all other engagements."

"Except the one that counts."

"Lorna's got a big mouth," Gordon said.

"You didn't intend to marry in secret, did you?"

"All right, all right," Gordon said. "I suppose Lorna told Kirsty an' Kirsty told you."

"That's it," Craig said.

"Bloody women!" Gordon said. "Well, will you do it?"

"No," Craig said.

"Lorna said you wouldn't."

"Now you have it from the horse's mouth," Craig said. "So there's no point in Mam comin' round to try to wheedle me into it, or Breezy either."

"She'd like you back; Mam, I mean."

"Back? I haven't been away."

"She'd like you to visit; you, Kirsty an' Bobby."

"What about you?" Craig said.

"I just want you to be there when I get married, that's all," Gordon said. "I really would appreciate it if you'd be my best man."

"Wear my uniform?"

"Eh, no. I doubt if that'd go down very well with my intended."

"Gordon, you can still change your mind."

"What?"

"Don't marry this girl," Craig said.

"Jeeze, you've got a nerve, tellin' me not to marry when you . . ." Gordon paused. "You don't even know her."

"Oh, she's pretty, I don't deny," Craig said. "But it's not the girl; it's the rest of them."

"Don't start that again," Gordon warned. "I suppose you'll be tellin' me that Dolphus Adair is a crook too?"

"Maybe he is, for all I know," Craig said. "But it's not the old man you have to watch out for, Gordon, it's the mother."

"What? Olive?"

"You sound surprised."

"I *am* surprised. What the hell have *you* got against Olive?" Gordon said.

"Take my word for it, Gordon, you're just bein' used."

"Balderdash!"

"I'm not makin' it up," Craig said. "I could tell you things about the Adairs you wouldn't believe."

"Coppers' gossip," Gordon said. "Tittle-tattle, that's all."

"What do you really know about Olive Adair?"

"She's all right is Olive."

"You've heard nothin', have you? Breezy hasn't even had the decency to tell you what's really goin' on."

"For God's sake, Craig," Gordon said. "If you've got wind of the fact that Breezy's sellin' off pubs to his brother as a sort of dowry . . ."

"It isn't that at all."

"What the devil is it then," Gordon said, "or aren't you goin' to tell me?"

Craig said, "Olive had an illegitimate child."

"Is that all?"

"You knew?"

"No, I didn't know. But it's got nothin' to do with Amanda an' me," Gordon said. "Here, wait a minute! You don't mean Amanda's . . ."

"Nah, nah," Craig said. "The child was farmed out soon after it was born."

Gordon, quite grimly, said, "God, you love washin' dirty linen, don't you, Craig? Well, I'm not surprised that Olive had a fling. It can't have been any bloody joke puttin' up with Dolphus for twenty years."

"So you're goin' to put up with him instead?"

"Instead?" Gordon said.

"When you marry, when the daughter's off her hands, she'll be off," Craig said. "She'll be gone. You'll be stuck with the father an' the whole mess."

Gordon laughed. "What a bloody fertile imagination you've got, Craig. If you aren't tryin' to convince me that Breezy's a deep-dyed criminal, which he ain't, then you're blackenin' the name of my intended's mother."

"Don't get in any deeper, Gordon, please."

"Please, is it? That's bloody rich. Did you say please to Kirsty before you jumped into bed wi' Greta?"

"I made a mistake."

"You've made a lot o' mistakes, Craig," Gordon said. "But it seems it's other folk that wind up payin' for them."

"Listen to me . . ."

"Like hell I will."

"Don't fly off the handle."

"Don't fly off the handle, he says," Gordon cried, "after he comes in here wi' a pack o' lies, tryin' to convince me my girl's a bastard . . ."

"I didn't say that."

". . . an' her mother's a tart." Gordon got to his feet. "You don't have to justify yourself to me, Craig. All you have to do is *tell* me to bugger off, tell me you don't want anythin' more to do wi' me. I may be thick as mince to your way o' thinkin' but I can definitely take a hint."

"It's for your own good, Gordon."

"Jesus!" Gordon shouted. "Who do you think you are – my mother? Nah, Craig, this is the end o' the road for you an' me. I've sussed you out at last. You're a wrecker, that's what you are; a bloody wrecker. Because you're miserable you want everybody else to be miserable too. Well, not me, chum. Not me."

"Listen, the bairn, Olive Adair's child . . ."

Hand upon the door, white-faced with anger, Gordon said, "I should've listened to Greta."

"Greta?"

"She warned me about you," Gordon said. "She told me you'd try to bring me down."

"Did she tell you about Jen?"

"That's it, Craig," Gordon said. "Brothers or not, we're finished. Hear me? *Finished.*"

He yanked open the door, stalked out into the crowded bar, veered to his right and was gone through the heavy glass-panelled doors into the street before Craig could gather himself to follow. Craig rose, then slumped back in defeat.

The door of the private room hung open. Through it he could see the drinking men squinting at him, full of suspicion and, here and there, slyly patronising as if they had heard and understood every word. He did not want to be stared at, did not want to be patronised. He had just lost a brother and needed time alone to let the meaning of that separation sink in.

"What the hell're you lookin' at?" he yelled, stabbed out his foot and slammed the door shut on their ignorant faces.

* * *

Kirsty said, "Are you feelin' all right, Craig? You look terrible."

"I'm fine," he answered; then, "No, I'm not fine. I just had a blazin' row wi' Gordon."

"About the weddin'?"

"It wasn't just the weddin'," Craig said. "He wants us back in the fold."

"I suppose he feels a family shouldn't be split," Kirsty said carefully.

He had taken off his donkey-jacket and muffler and had thrown both down upon the carpet by the chair by the fire. He stretched out his legs and kneaded his face with his fingers, covering his eyes. She wondered if he had been crying. No, Craig was not the sort of man who would cry over a quarrel. He thrived on dissent. She was, however, cautious, wary of his mood.

She bit her lip. "Will I make some tea?"

"Aye."

From the shelter of the cupboard where the stove was housed she asked, as casually as possible, "Did Gordon take it bad when you told him you wouldn't be his best man?"

"One thing led t' another." Craig shrugged. "Things were said that shouldn't have been said."

"I'll square it with him next time I see him."

Craig snapped his head up, scowling. "No, Kirsty. Leave it as it is."

"But . . ."

"I'm tellin' you, keep out of it."

"What'll I say when I see him?"

"You'll say nothin' at all," Craig told her. "Anyway, I don't suppose he'll be down our way for a long time."

She brought him the teacup on a saucer and handed it to him. "What did you say to annoy him so much?"

Craig sipped the tea, stooped forward.

"It's what he said to me, Kirsty."

She dipped down and retrieved the jacket and scarf, folded them over her arms and put them down on the table top, still watching her husband, still troubled by his mood. It was beginning to dawn on her that Craig had been hurt and that his simmering anger was not directed at her but at himself.

Risking rebuff, she got down by the chair on her knees and touched his arm.

He said, not gruffly, "I don't want to talk about it, Kirsty."

"I know."

He glanced at her. Some colour had come back to his cheeks and there were milky whiskers on his upper lip which she dabbed away with the edge of her sleeve.

"Do *you* think I'm a wrecker?" Craig asked.

"No, of course I don't."

"Gordon said I was a wrecker," Craig told her. "Maybe he's right. I mean, Christ, I nearly did for our marriage, didn't I?"

288

"That's in the past."

"An' I'd have got myself flung out of a job if I'd tried just a wee bit harder," he said. "I wanted to, y'know. I mean, I wanted to get myself sacked."

"Don't you like bein' what you are?"

"I like bein' a copper," Craig said. "It's the bloody rest of it I'm not too sure about."

"I haven't been entirely fair either, Craig."

"If you mean the shop . . ."

"Takin' on Greta."

"Huh!" Craig said, with a rueful little grunt. "I'm glad you did, Kirsty. Somebody had to take her on an' it was better you than me, eh? Better for her, anyway."

"Do you still . . .?"

He shook his head. "I really don't. It's just gone, that part of it."

"What put it away?"

"You did," he said.

She took the teacup and saucer from him and returned to the sink with them, washed them under the cold tap and dried them with a cotton towel.

Guilt stood thin in her, hard and unpleasant. Now that Craig had softened she felt her own disloyalty all the more keenly. He did not know about David, not even about the letters. Craig would never know what had happened with David or how often she thought of him and of what might have been between them if she had been free of her promises, her debts.

"I don't think Gordon's goin' to speak to me again in a hurry," Craig said. "But I don't want you to fight wi' him. It's my fault not yours that things have got into this mess."

"You could apologise."

"Aw, naw," he said. "I'm not that much in the wrong."

"Won't we be at the wedding?" Kirsty said.

"I doubt it."

"Or at the engagement celebration?"

"No, it's too soon," Craig said.

"You don't hate him, do you?"

"God, no. But he's wrong, you see. This time he's dead wrong, Kirsty, an' I can't make him face it because he doesn't trust me."

"Perhaps he'll realise his mistake in time."

"Aye." Craig sighed. "But by then it'll be too late t' do anythin' about it."

He got to his feet and reached behind the painted vase on the end of the mantelshelf for the matches that were always kept there. He lit a cigarette and, standing, dropped the spent match down on to the breast of the coals that showed through the open lid of the range.

"Do you mind if I sleep in your bed tonight?" he said. "I mean, just to sleep."

Kirsty smiled. "You sound just like Bobby, so you do."

Craig chuckled and scratched his head.

"I suppose I do," he said. "Times are we both need somethin' to hang on to."

"And for better or worse I'm that somethin'," Kirsty said.

"Do you mind?" Craig said.

"I don't mind at all," said Kirsty.

*   *   *

The bill of fare that Breezy selected for the celebratory dinner had come intact from the pages of *Beeton's Book of Household Management* and was chosen without regard for the domestic difficulties it would involve. Dinners *à la russe* required notorious amounts of space, a team of carvers and servers and enough cutlery to arm a battalion of the Highland Light Infantry. A more experienced hostess than Madge would have scotched the whole idea at the outset. Dire warnings from the cook, Miss Rowland, fell on deaf ears, however, and Madge took a stubborn stance that she would later have cause to regret.

In the days before the dinner party a kind of madness descended on the house of Adair, with Cook shouting at Madge and Madge shouting at Breezy and Breezy, in turn, shouting down the newly acquired telephone at fishmongers and poulterers, florists and wine merchants. Three days before the event Breezy chucked in the towel, hired the services of Ralston, Ralston & Dinardo, caterers *extraordinaire*, and let them worry about it.

Within an hour of Breezy having signed the contract, two frock-coated flunkeys arrived in the kitchens of Great Western Terrace to measure the ovens, check the cleanliness and capacity of the larders and the length of the sideboards in the upstairs dining-room. Indifferent to Miss Rowland's yawps of indignation, polite but supercilious in their treatment of Madam Adair, they were gone again before Breezy sailed home and into further storms of protest that raged about his head until Friday dawned and other distractions intervened.

Invitations had been restricted to immediate family and one intimate personal friend. Even so, there would be thirty-six at table, almost all Adairs of one sort or another, and the caterers had spent a morning inserting extensions into the dining-table and lugging chairs from one of their distinctive wine-red vans. About two o'clock more vans arrived in the lane, quite a neat little fleet of them, and men in white aprons began to unload tubs of oysters, cauldrons of oxtail soup, boxes of sweetbreads, game croquettes, par-boiled turkey, chicken cutlets and jars of Italian cream and carry them down the yard and through the kitchen door, like ants storing against a famine.

By then it was clear to everyone, even Miss Rowland, that the two Mr Ralstons and the smooth-skinned, plausible Signor Dinardo knew precisely what they were doing and that disaster had been turned aside.

What the whole thing would finally cost did not bear thinking about but Madge knew her husband too well to carp about extravagance.

Gordon had been given an afternoon off. He did not return home, though. He visited his barber's, then his tailor's and, in the gathering gloom of evening, with a large paper-wrapped box under each arm, caught a tram to Dumbarton Road and stole a quiet twenty minutes in the Greenfield Vaults, not one of Carruth's acquisitions. There he sipped a brandy to give himself Dutch courage for the ordeal ahead.

It was shortly after five o'clock, and a drizzling, sooty-grey rain had begun to fall, when he found himself in Gascoigne Street and popped in to the shop for a brief, and seemingly final, word with his sister-in-law and partner.

The shop was deserted. Gas-lamps did nothing to cheer the atmosphere tonight for the shrouds of rain were too wintry and depressing to be easily dispelled. Kirsty seemed tense, Bobby too, as if, at last, the shade of Harold Vosper Vokes had stirred beneath the mortar in the back basement and you could feel his presence like a draught on the nape of the neck and knew that he had never been the joke that you'd made of him.

Gordon had nothing at all to give his nephew, not even toffees. The little boy did not seem to care. He was listless and petted. He clung to his mother, whimpering and sniffling, and treated Gordon as if he were some sort of stranger and, perhaps, a threat.

"Where's Greta?" Gordon said, after he had exchanged greetings.

"She hasn't been in at all this week," Kirsty said.

"She hasn't quit or anythin', has she?"

"Jen's been unwell," Kirsty explained.

"Nothin' serious, I hope?"

"Oh, no, just a cold an' a touch o' fever. But Greta doesn't like to bring her out an' won't leave her until she's better again."

"By the looks o' his lordship he's got it too."

Kirsty glanced at her son, nodded. "Aye, if he isn't a lot better I'll put up the shutters tomorrow an' stay at home."

"An' lose a Saturday's trade?"

"If you're so worried about the business," Kirsty said testily, "why don't you come down an' look after it for the day?"

"I can't," Gordon said. "I wish I could."

"I'm sorry," Kirsty said. "I shouldn't have snapped at you. It's a big night in your life, Gordon, an' nothin' should spoil it; least of all a grouch like me."

"Ach," Gordon said, "it's just the weather. It's enough to give anyone the pip."

"Is everythin' ready?"

"So far as I know."

"What have you got there?"

"My monkey suit. My *own* monkey suit. Breezy insisted I buy one an' put it on his bill."

"Well, I suppose you'll get wear out of it, hob-nobbin' with the well-to-do."

"Probably," Gordon said.

The shop sounded empty. There was hollowness to it this evening that he had not experienced before. Outside, the Friday evening traffic rumbled and clacked, muffled by falling rain as if sounds were granular like soot and could be washed away too.

For some reason Gordon spoke in a whisper, wistfully. "Craig was right."

"About what?"

"Not to come to the party. Family gatherin's are a bore an' a bind," he said. "Breezy's been the soul o' generosity an' my mother loves showin' off but I wish to God it was all over."

It had been weeks since last he'd seen Kirsty. Greta had kept him informed about the rise and fall of trade, about Craig too, passing on gossip, such as it was. He had missed out on the excitements of the autumn months, on the suicide of William King and the capture of the forger. He had not deliberately kept himself apart. He simply had no time, no time to call his own.

He wondered if that situation would improve as he climbed the ladder of responsibility within Carruth's or if he would be pulled away from Kirsty and his brother, from Greta, from the Greenfield and all that it had meant to him when first he came to Glasgow. He wondered if, in a year or two, he would give a damn about these people or if he would have become a prig like Dolphus or, worse, a calculating snob like Johnnie Whiteside. Amanda and his desire for her now seemed the least part of it.

Kirsty said, "What time will the dinner begin?"

"Seven-thirty for eight o'clock."

"You'd better not loiter here then, Gordon."

"No." He had no reason to stay and yet he was reluctant to go. "No, you're right. I should be on my way, I suppose."

Bobby girned, a strange, unsettled noise, not petulant or demanding but querulous, as if he did not understand what was happening to him and why his mam could not make his discomfort vanish. His nose ran a little and there was a slight flush upon his cheeks and brow.

"So should you," Gordon said. "By the looks of him he should be in bed. I'll help you close up."

"I can manage," Kirsty said. "Really, I can."

At that moment the doorbell jangled on its wire and two elderly women entered. They were feathered all in black, like crows. One gripped the other's arm tightly and peered, blinking and half-blind, about the shop.

"Is it here?" she asked her companion in a dry croak. "Is this the right place?"

"Aye," said the other. "We've found it at last."

Gordon and Kirsty exchanged a glance and Gordon raised his shoulders in a little shrug of resignation. Trade came first, the customer came first, however inconvenient.

"I'll go," Gordon said.

"Yes," Kirsty said.

He turned and passed the women. They seemed to be unaware of his presence and waited with stone-like patience for Kirsty to attend them. They were both, Gordon noticed, short-sighted, perhaps even blind, and their features seemed ill-formed, flattened and distorted by jet-black hats and high black collars.

One hand upon the door handle, Gordon paused.

Still the women waited, unmoving.

He wanted to tell Kirsty what she had meant to him, to take her in his arms, to ask her to tell Greta . . .

"May I help you, ladies?" he heard Kirsty say.

She had Bobby in her arms, her face pale in the gaslight, the summer's freckles gone now. He heard the wee boy whimper and give a tiny cry, disturbed by the dumpy, dark shapes of the sisters, if that's what they were. He felt bad about leaving her, but had no choice. Besides, she was busy now and the women – he thought he knew the type – would claim her attention for some time to come.

"Good night, Kirst," he called out. "Take care."

She did not seem to hear him above the sound of rain falling and growl of the wheels on the cobbles of Gascoigne Street and Gordon went, in the end, without Kirsty's blessing to cheer him as he hurried off into the night.

*   *   *

She had been dressed by her mother's maid, then left to her own devices, to titivate herself listlessly and with the lacklustre feeling that none of it mattered very much since there was nobody she cared to impress. Her pride was too particular to be classed as vanity and she was not at all pleased to be hauled out of her bedroom into her mother's dressing-room, plonked down in front of the huge swanswing mirror and attacked with combs and hairpins.

"What's *wrong* with you, girl?" Madge demanded. "You look like you've been dragged through a hayrick."

Lorna sighed. "It's the style, Mother."

"Style, you call it! I've seen better-groomed scarecrows." She tugged and teased at the back of Lorna's bowed neck, sucked a tiny pearl-headed pin and fastened a wisp of hair tight and smooth to the plait above one ear. "An' it's a lovely dress too, the yellow muslin."

"Frumpy," Lorna said.

"It's nothin' of the kind." Madge worked on as determinedly as if she were shearing a ewe. "You're a grown woman, Lorna, an' it's high time you started actin' like one."

Three or four minutes would undo Madge's inhibitory labours and loose her hair again. Lorna was not quite as diffident about her appearance as she pretended to be. She had copied the hairstyle from an illustration on the cover of a novel entitled *The Adventuress* – what a laugh that would give Mr Tubbs if ever she were daft enough to tell him – and had spent some hours with a frizzer on Sunday afternoon, wafting the niff of scorched hair out of the bedroom window with her mother's ostrich-feather fan. Though the result of the experiment had not been entirely satisfactory, Lorna had convinced herself that she was better in fashion than out of it – and that she didn't really care after all.

"Don't you want the young men to notice you?" Madge spat another pin into her palm and worked it in as if Lorna's scalp were made of cork. "You could so easily be the belle o' the ball."

"Amanda's the belle o' the ball, Mother." Lorna bent her head to contemplate her bosom. "You could scrape me down an' varnish me an' I still wouldn't get a second glance from any man when Mandy's around."

"Amanda Adair's spoken for," Madge said. "An' you're not. That's the difference."

Lorna jerked her head, uttered a little *ouch* as the point of a pin pricked her skin, and demanded, "What do you mean – 'spoken for'?"

"Amanda Adair's only about your age an' already she's engaged to be married."

"Hoy, hold on." Lorna twisted her head. "I'm not on the marriage market. I'm not like poor old Gordon, willin' to be traded off."

"What a terrible thing t' say."

"True, though, Mother. Anyway, there's not goin' to be any prospective grooms at the table tonight."

"I wouldn't be so sure o' that, m'lady."

"Eh?"

"Sit still. I'm nearly finished."

"What've you got in mind now?" Lorna said. "God, you don't expect me to make cow's eyes at any of that lot. Apart from the fact they're all Adairs, there's not one o' them under fifty. An' they're all married."

"Not them all, dear."

"Mother!"

"I've seen the way Mr Whiteside looks at you."

"Good God!" Lorna swayed and, as the dressing-stool tipped to one side, stepped away from it and got to her feet. "Johnnie Whiteside's a . . . a . . ."

"See, you're blushin'."

"I am bloody not!" Lorna exclaimed.

Squeezed by a new corset, Madge's bosom, denying anatomy and monopolising the whole front of the bodice, heaved. She planted her hands on her tightly-skirted hips and declared, "You'll never catch a decent man if you curl your lip at them. For your information, Mr Whiteside'll inherit Albert's warehouse one day."

"Dear God!" said Lorna, more exasperated than angry. "Is that supposed to make me swoon int' his manly arms; a flamin' warehouse in Partick East? Besides, John Whiteside's not interested in marryin' me or anyone. Beddin' them – aye, oh aye, he wouldn't say no to that but havin' a wife would surely cramp his rovin' style."

"How can you say that about such a nice young man?"

"Because it's the truth," said Lorna.

"I still think you should look your best."

"Well, this is the best I *can* look, Mother," Lorna said. "I'm sorry to disappoint you."

"It's hangin' about that shop that's done it."

"Done what?"

"Made you forget who you are an' what you have t' live up to," Madge said. "Look at Gordon; he knows how the land lies."

Lorna's eyes narrowed. For a moment it was on the tip of her tongue to blurt out a few home truths, about Gordon, about Whiteside and his cruel and conniving cronies. She checked herself. She understood how it was with her mother, how Madge still nurtured a grain of guilt about her marriage into the wealthy classes, how she longed to have her sons and daughter support her, not in words but deeds. *Mariage à la mode*, as the books called it, meant, for Madge, not just money and comfort but the kind of iron-clad respectability that would rebuff all harms, hurts and troubles, that would make her not just secure but invulnerable. Young though she was, Lorna knew better but, tonight of all nights, she hadn't the heart to disillusion her mother.

She seated herself again on the stool before the mirror and, to make herself feel better, thought of old Tubby and the account she would give him, later, of the engagement party, how they'd have a jolly good chuckle at the Adairs' expense.

Madge huffed. "What're you smilin' at, girl? I hope you're not laughin' at me?"

"I'm not smilin'," said Lorna. "I'm sittin' here like a damned pin-cushion, waitin' for you to do somethin' with what's left o' my hair."

"Oh!" Mollified only in part, Madge busied herself again with the coiffure. After a moment she said, "If he talks t' you, you won't snap at him. Promise me that much, Lorna."

"Whiteside?" said Lorna.

"Or the other one. Donnie's boy."

"Mother," said Lorna, adopting her sweetest tone, "I'll be as good as gold."

"An' we'll see what comes of it, hm?"

"That we will, Mammy," Lorna said. "By the way, what time is it?"

Madge peered at the watch on the stand on her dressing-table then gave a throaty cry. "God, it's nearly seven o'clock. Here's me bletherin' an' there's a million things t' see to downstairs. I'll have t' fly."

"You fly then," Lorna said.

"But your hair, dear. What about your hair?"

Lorna patted her mother's arm reassuringly.

"I'll fix it," she said. "Don't worry."

"Do it nice then."

"Yes, Mother," Lorna said.

And do it nice she would, not for Johnnie Whiteside or his sly chum, Eric Adair, but for Mr Ernest Tubbs whom she would meet tomorrow, by arrangement, in Kirsty's shop at noon.

* * *

Try though he would, Gordon could not feel other than detached from the proceedings. A strange, false separation from this monumental night had settled on him even before he stepped through the door on Great Western Terrace to be whisked away by Breezy to bathe and robe himself and receive fatherly advice on how to conduct himself through the course of the evening.

No sticklers for exact details of etiquette, and always liable to break into unseemly fits of gaiety, the Adairs nonetheless had risen high enough in the world to pride themselves on their manners and civility. Hand-woven rituals had grown up over the years and the betrothal of Amanda to Gordon was not the first such splicing to occur within the family ranks. This time, however, no outsiders were involved, no new links required to be forged, no expansion of the circle, social and commercial, had to be negotiated and, most relevantly, no genteel in-laws would be on hand to *tut* critically at ruptures in good form.

"Dolphus, you an' me greet the guests in the hall," Breezy had told him, while picking invisible lint from the shiny lapels of his spanking new dinner jacket. "The mothers an' Amanda'll be in the downstairs parlour."

"Dispensing drink?"

"Don't be daft, son. Ralston, Ralston an' what's-his-name will see to all of that. God knows, there's enough of them trottin' about as if they owned the place. No, your mother, your sweetheart and her mother'll mingle an' be nice to everybody until we're all on board, then we'll get the guests upstairs an' round the big table as fast as possible."

"Right," Gordon had said.

"We'll eat, drink an' make merry," Breezy had continued, "until everybody's had enough, then it'll be time for the toast to Her Majesty, followed by the speeches."

"Speeches?"

"Aye, but they're few an' brief."

"I thought speeches were special to weddings."

"Dolphus never passes up the chance to swan it," Breezy'd said. "Apart from which, it's expected. It'll be my brother first on his feet, then me, then you."

"Me! Christ!"

"An' none of that blasphemous language either. Keep it short, pithy an' clean."

"You might've warned me."

"Couldn't risk you doin' a bunk," Breezy'd said, patting his stepson's shoulder. "Just thank them for comin'. Tell them how grateful you are to Dolphus an' Olive for allowin' you to become engaged to their daughter. Lavish a few words of praise on the dear wee lassie and sit down again, pronto."

Gordon had nodded. "Right."

"No need to be nervous."

"I'm not nervous," Gordon had said.

It was the truth too. The prospect of having to get up on his pins and address the discerning multitude caused him no more than passing anxiety.

Nothing seemed to impinge upon his detachment from the events of the evening, except in one glorious moment when he turned and caught a glimpse of Amanda through the parlour's half-open door. He thought – how could he not – how beautiful, how luminous she was and how he would do everything in his power to make her happy, to live up to her expectations, whatever they might be: yet in the very same second he was brooding stupidly about Greta and her youngster and fretting over the last sad image he'd had of Kirsty, pondering, as if it had any importance whatsoever, what the two purblind women could possibly have wanted to purchase from the shelves.

"Good evening, Mr Beadle. How jolly nice to see you."

A handshake, firm and friendly; then a kiss bestowed on sister Polly's powdered cheek, the brush of her sable collar against his ear, the smell of fur dewed lightly with rain.

"Mr Whiteside. I'm so glad you could come."

Severe, disapproving, unforgiving, the solicitor barely touched palms and moved on, stiff and inhibited, to make way for his son, Johnnie. Johnnie grinned and clapped Gordon's shoulder, gave him a wink as if an engagement party was but a lewd preliminary to some other more bawdy event.

Wedged between Breezy and Dolphus, Gordon stood in the hallway, his back to the long table. He watched the front door open and close, open and close, as, in the space of fifteen minutes, the Adairs arrived in their hacks and carriages, and the footman's white gloves became grubby with rain and brass, and his buckled shoes, puzzlingly, rimed with mud.

"All in?" Dolphus wiped his hands on the sides of his trousers. "Everybody aboard, hah?"

"Aye, that's the lot."

Breezy glanced at his pocket watch, signalled to the footman to lock the inner door then ushered Gordon towards the crowded reception room where, amid the buzz, Amanda waited, her eyes shining and her soft lips moist with sparkling wine.

*　　　*　　　*

Panic set in during the course of the afternoon and, by dusk, Greta could no longer contain it. She'd had but little faith in Doctor Kelly to begin with. She'd found him brusque and off-hand, too sure of himself and his diagnosis. He was one of those elderly, white-bearded medical pundits who treated you as if you were a fool; yet, just at first, Greta had found his authority comforting, had been reassured by his assertion that there was nothing wrong with Jen but 'snuffles' and that she would be as right as rain in a day or two.

Indeed it had seemed that Doctor Kelly had been correct to dismiss Jen's illness as minor. His medicine certainly appeared to do the trick. After three or four spoonfuls of the thick brown syrup Jen's temperature had fallen, her mood had improved and, though she complained of a headache and a sore back, her restlessness passed off. Eventually she became drowsy and, to Greta's relief, slept.

Doctor Kelly had not volunteered to return. He had a large successful practice in Hillhead and retained a small, shop-like consulting-room in Greenfield more for show than profit. He liked to be thought of as 'charitable', a man of Christian virtue, but he did not approve of the lower orders, really, and dealt with their trivial ailments not with compassion but with crushing authority and in galloping haste. The fact that Greta had paid him in cash did not alter his attitude one jot and, on Thursday evening, when she sent Isa Thomas's boy to fetch Doctor Kelly round again, he made his annoyance all too clear.

"Madam," he snapped, "what do *you* think the child suffers from?"

"I don't know, Doctor, but she seems so sore, so stiff, I thought . . ."

"It is not your job to think, madam. I told you, she has had a feverish cold. Dampness and wintry weather are the causes. Do you feed her?"

"'Course I feed her."

"Where is her father?"

"He's dead."

"Do you buy fresh milk daily?"

"Yes."

He had peeled away blankets and sheets and yanked up Jen's nightgown as if he were violating and not ministering to her. It had been all Greta could do to stop herself pulling him away. He'd plugged the sounders to his ears and, pinning Jen down with one hand, while she'd screamed and writhed, planted the cup upon her chest.

"She has no congestion," he'd said, rolling up the stethoscope and throwing it into his bag. "Her heart rate is slightly increased but not severely. She's on the mend, madam, I assure you."

Greta had hugged Jen, which made her cry more.

"She says she's got a pain in her back."

Kelly had tutted. "She's been lying on it for a week. Naturally she's stiff and sore. Give her one of these each morning and evening." He'd dispensed a dozen plain, sugar-coated pills, rolled into a paper cone. "Now, if you will excuse me, I have a *very* sick patient to visit and should have been with him an hour ago."

She'd paid him his half-guinea, without thanks, and had let him find his own way out.

During the course of Thursday night the stiffness in Jen's limbs increased. Greta fretted away the dark hours, sleepless and helpless by her daughter's side. It was about dawn before she fell into a doze by the fire in the kitchen, a doze that deepened through sheer exhaustion into deep sleep.

To her horror, it was after eleven o'clock when she wakened, wakened not to street sounds but to Jen's pitiful wailing, muffled by bolsters and sheets. Jen had fallen on to her side and could not find the strength to raise herself again.

Greta gave her two more of Kelly's pills and tried to change her soiled nightgown for a clean one, a process that Jen appeared to resist by stubborn tension and inflexibility. She did, however, drink a cup of milk and then, lying flat, fell quiet again.

It was not until one o'clock, when Isa Thomas appeared, bringing a dish of apple jelly for the patient, that Greta's anxiety began to mount and worry turn to unreasoning fear.

Jen was fully awake. Unblinking, she stared at the two women who bent concernedly over her.

"What did Kelly say?" Isa asked.

"Nothin' wrong with her," Greta answered. "He left pills."

"Wee white pills?"

"Aye."

"That's his usual," Isa said. "I'm sorry t' say this, Greta, but I don't like the look o' her."

"She's had a shake, no doubt," Greta said, trying to be brave and optimistic. "There's no sign o' anythin' in her lungs."

"She's a funny colour, though. I don't like that blue tint on her lips an' cheeks. Jen, Jen, it's Auntie Isa, love. Can y'tell me where it hurts?"

The wee girl did not seem to hear the question. Though her eyes had been fixed undeviatingly on the women's faces her attention was elsewhere, her concentration fastened like a fist on the air about her, as if there were a scarcity of it and she must sip it without spilling. She nibbled at it through pursed and tinted lips, not frightened, not fretful. She had drawn back even from Mammy to deal with the smothering ache that banded her chest.

"Jen, are your legs sore?"

"Nuh."

"Jen, tell Mammy where it hurts now."

"Nuh."

Isa Thomas stepped back from the bed, frowning. She stepped away round the table, her arms crossed loosely, one bony hand covering her mouth.

"I think you should send for another doctor, Greta."

"What is it? Do y'know what it is?"

"No, I do not," said Isa. "But a proper doctor . . ." She shook her head. "Oh, Kelly knows what he's doin', I suppose."

"What doctor?"

"There's Wilson, or Doctor McLeod," said Isa. "Or you could call in a nurse from the Sick Children's Dispensary. I'm sure they'd send somebody to examine her. I'll send our Hughie there on the tram to ask, if y'like."

"Is it a good place, the Dispensary?"

"Oh, aye. It's the best place in the city. I've had three o' mine attended there."

"Where is it?"

"West Graham Street, off the Cowcaddens. Say the word an' I'll pack Hughie off as soon as he's home from school." Isa Thomas hesitated. "But . . . but I don't want him comin' in, Greta. Our Hughie, I mean. I don't want him comin' near Jen. Just in case it's serious."

"Contagious, y'mean?"

"Well, I doubt it. But, well . . . y' never know."

"What could it be? Oh, God, what could it be?"

Still with her hand before her mouth, Isa said, "Och, Kelly's probably right, an' it's nothin' at all. What do y' want to do, Greta? Send for a nurse from the Sick Children's?"

Jen was still now, quiet as a lamb. She lay supine under the neat sheet and blankets, her head on the low, hard pillow, her eyes wide, wide-awake. There was nothing to suggest that she was gravely ill except the pursed mouth and the faint blue tinge to her cheeks and lips.

"No," Greta said. "I'll wait a while. See if she sleeps. She might just need to sleep it off, Isa, don't you think?"

"Aye," said Isa, without much conviction. "She might."

It was after five o'clock before Greta allowed fear to gush forth into panic. For three hours she had contained it, bottled it up, sitting helplessly by her child, aware of dusk coming and the rain drumming on the window and the sudden, small changes in the little body on the bed, the gaspings, the raspings, the twitchings.

One by one they came to torment her, worse than they tormented Jen. Jen was a brave lamb. She did not cry out, did not reach for her mother. She watched darkly as her mother's face crumpled and her mother's tears came, then in a thin, stretched, constricted little voice that seemed to squeeze through leather bands to become audible at all, said, "*Ma Ma Ma Ma Ma Ma*," before the choking began.

*   *   *

The ring was a fine diamond half hoop that Breezy had acquired at a bargain price of £34/12/–, a sum that skinned away almost the last of Gordon's winnings on Camberwell Beauty.

Amanda had been very matter-of-fact and down-to-earth about the giving and receiving of the ring. She was not one to get sentimental over gemstones. She knew perfectly well that her uncle had bought it at considerable discount and that it was worth a great deal more than whatever Gordon had had to fork out, would fetch, in fact, around £70 retail or £50 on the resale market. She did not demand that it be engraved with a commemoration of that day of days, names and a date delicately entwined on the inner shank, and only her sister Phoebe took her to task for putting head over heart in the matter.

Sister Phoebe had been very critical of late, very sniffy about a whole host of matters connected with Amanda's engagement to Gordon Nicholson. The bond between the sisters had slackened considerably over the past weeks, an unfortunate but inevitable outcome of growing up, due in part to jealousy, so Amanda believed, and the fact that Olive had spent so much time alone with her, shopping, chatting and in general preparing her eldest for a not-so-distant marriage.

Dolphus, of course, had no notion that an undercurrent of rivalry, not to say bitterness, had crept into the nursery. He was full of unnatural bonhomie. He demonstrated his ebullience in a manner so loud that even his youngest was embarrassed and usually hid behind her fan rather than watch Father make an ass of himself.

The guests, though, were nearly all Adairs. They knew James Randolph inside out, thought nothing of his raucous behaviour and, indeed, slyly egged him on throughout dinner and plied him with more wine than his poor, fat head could properly take.

By the time Ralston, Ralston and Dinardo's henchmen had got down to serving the punch jelly and *Croûtes Madrées aux Fruits*, old Dolphus was rarin' to make his voice heard and had to be physically restrained from leaping to his feet and blurting out a confession of his happiness and gratitude to everyone who'd had a hand in bringing Amanda to this joyous pass, just one step from the altar.

The engaged couple were seated together at the centre of the long table. They separated the in-laws-to-be, Madge from Breezy, Dolphus from Olive. There was in dinner *à la russe* no great clutter of dishes before the diners, for carving and serving were done at the sideboards, and the table's centre was decorated with flowers and plants in dainty pots and crystal glasses into and out of which wines flowed in profusion.

Opposite to Olive in the seating arrangement was Captain Tom Wells, the only guest who was not kin. He had been invited at Amanda's express wish and nobody, not even Breezy, could deny her request.

In spite of the excellence of the fare, the expertise of the hired servants in delivering food and wine, and the crescendo of jollity that rose about him, Gordon remained oddly detached from the spirit of friendly celebration. He was warm and courteous to Amanda, of course, very aware of her beside him, so beautiful that she seemed almost unreal. And he had enough savvy to exchange badinage with Johnnie or Phoebe or Charlie Beadle when they addressed him. For all that, he could not quite engage with his own engagement party. He felt neither annoyance nor amusement at Dolphus's antics or at Polly and Heather's teasing wit, and had no trace of apprehension about addressing a few words, a few platitudes, to this crowd.

It was Captain Wells that Gordon watched through sprays of

fern and hothouse carnations, inclining his head now and then to catch the glances that passed between the horseman and Olive Carruth Adair. He could not rid himself of the illogical notion that here was prophecy, a foretelling of what might come to pass for him in some future year, daughter like mother, and he, like Dolphus, destined to play the clown.

When Amanda touched him, her knee against his knee below the tablecloth, when she brushed her finger softly upon the back of his hand, he felt mutinous confusion rise within him, a desire to clasp her to him and yet to thrust her away. What he did was to smile, smile, not meet her eye or Olive's, avoid Lorna's small, sour, frowning gaze. Under control, he managed to laugh when Breezy laughed and applaud when, at length, Dolphus was unleashed and got unsteadily to his feet to beg for silence and a hearing.

Amanda's lips touched Gordon's ear. He shivered.

"Your turn soon, my darling," she whispered.

And Gordon murmured, "Yes."

*   *   *

Though Greta had paid the cabby ten shillings cash in advance to make all the speed he could, it took the hired cab that Hughie Thomas fetched from the rank in Peel Street a good half-hour to thread through teatime traffic to West Graham Street. Other hospitals stood closer to hand but Greta had seized on Isa's praise for the nurses and doctors of the Sick Children's Dispensary and their reputation for healing. There, she felt, she would not be brushed aside, palmed off, told to wait. There somebody would understand why she feared for her daughter's life, would take Jen away, cure her and bring her back safe to Mammy. Clinging to that belief as tightly as she clung to life, she petted and consoled the struggling child, crooned to her, pretended that, within the big bundle of blankets and woollen clothes, the little body had not become rigid with pain and that Jen's cries were weakened by sleepiness not by a lack of oxygen.

The cabby was sympathetic. He would have carried Jen into the building for her but Greta would not, of course, release her hold. She went without thanks, hurrying through the door, unintimidated by brass plaques and marble, the half-tiled hall and the smell of stale sweat, sickness and disinfectant. It had not, however, occurred to her until she ran into the entrance hall and

305

saw the crowded benches, nurse and doctor at a waiting table, that this was a charity institution where women put aside their pride, admitted the need for poor relief, for treatment without payment.

For an instant she felt shame that she had come here to steal from the needy. She was needy no more. She was closer to them, however, than to anyone, to the shawled, patched, ragged women who packed the benches, who waited with a patience that defied the fevers of their ailing bairns; three or four dozen of them, not one turned away in spite of the late hour or the long, long day.

Now that she had got here she did not know what to do. Upright and conspicuous among the seated women, she hesitated and glanced helplessly about her. Nursing mothers wrapped their babies to them and infants, some howling, were dandled on broad knees. Heads turned in Greta's direction as she stood, swaying, with Jen wrapped in a cocoon of blankets in her arms.

"Gang for'ard, lass," one woman advised.

"Aye, gang on. No need t' be frightened," urged another, while a third, scooping her toddler behind her as if harm threatened, said, "They have tae book in your name afore they'll let ye jine the queue."

Nurses in puffy milkmaid bonnets were visible in the wide open doorways that flanked the hall. At the table, with its inkstand and pens, a woman in a blue dress and stiff starched cap was writing in a book. She did not look up at the sound of the little commotion that greeted Greta's arrival. But the man at her side did. He wore a stand-up collar, a butterfly bow tie of white piqué and a spotless white linen jacket over a dress shirt. He was not old. His hair was jet black, glossy with brilliantine and parted precisely in the centre. His moustache, black too, was sleek and discreet. He had the observant air of a magpie. His bright beady eye fell quickly upon Greta as she hurried, almost strutting in her haste, towards the table.

The young doctor put down his pen, rose, stepped, long-legged and elegant, from behind the table and, before Greta could utter a word, slid Jen from her grasp.

"I . . . I can pay," Greta told him. "I can pay you t' make her better."

The doctor cradled Jen in her bundled blankets in the crook of one arm. He flicked away the coverings and studied her face.

"How long has she been like this?"

"Today. This afternoon. Doctor Kelly said . . ."

"Kelly!" he exclaimed. "God, that butcher! Nurse Harbin, find Mr Young at once. And Doctor Ness too. Fetch them to the quarantine room immediately."

The nurse got instantly to her feet. "Quarantine, Doctor Anderson? What's wrong with the child?"

"Acute respiratory paralysis," he said.

"Meningitis?"

"Poliomyelitis, I think," he said, then moved away, taking Jen with him.

The women on the benches stirred, their shocked whispers worse than silence.

The doctor barged through a closed swing door, breaking it open with his elbows, shouting as he went, "Emergency, please, emergency. Respiration required. Doctor Ness to quarantine, please. Surgeon on hand at once. Mr Young to quarantine, if you please."

Stunned, Greta stood rooted to the spot as the doctor's urgent summons echoed and diminished in the corridors beyond the door and Jen was lost to her sight.

*   *   *

Gordon had carefully pencilled five headings on the back of a brown envelope that Breezy had produced from his pocket. He held the note in the flat of his hand below the level of the table and studied it while his stepfather raised a final easy laugh from his relations and, with a hand placed fraternally on Dolphus's shoulder, wound up by expressing pleasure that the lovely Amanda would soon be his daughter-in-law as well as his niece.

Leaning far over Gordon, Breezy sought to kiss the girl's blushing cheek but found that she had turned her face to him and offered her lips instead. To cheers from his nephews he kissed her firmly and without hesitation, making an audible smack, and then, grinning, sat down to low whistles and applause.

"What did she do that for?" Breezy hissed.

"'Cause she likes you," Gordon answered, *sotto voce*, and, without prompting, bounced to his feet.

He palmed the envelope discreetly on to the tablecloth where he could see it from the corner of his eye.

"I'll have to watch him, won't I?" Gordon said, for he had already begun to learn what pleased his relatives.

307

"Hear, hear."

"Aye-aye."

"And all the rest, old chum," called Johnnie Whiteside who had drunk too much to be discreet. "Ball an' chain required, what?"

"No ball an' chain for me, John. No padlocks needed to keep my love. I hope – I trust – that I already hold the key to Amanda's . . ."

Gordon hesitated. Eric Adair, imagining that the pause was intentional, sniggered. The sentence was never completed. Signor Dinardo had come through the door of the dining-room and squeezed his way past the backs of the chairs, his sallow cheeks flushed with embarrassment.

"Excuse, excuse," he muttered, then, on reaching the rear of Gordon's chair, bowed and whispered into Gordon's ear; not Breezy's ear, but Gordon's.

"If you'll pardon me," Gordon said to the dinner guests and, without a word of explanation, edged away from the table and rapidly followed the caterer-in-chief from the room.

"Now what was that all about, hah?"

"Search me, Dolphus."

"Rude, damned rude, I call it."

"It's a trick, a joke. You'll see, old Gordie's got somethin' comical up his sleeve."

"That's it; it's a cod."

"Mama," Amanda asked uncertainly, "what's happening?"

"Albert," said Madge, "go an' see what he's up to."

Led by Breezy, the guests abandoned their manners, left the table one by one and drifted curiously out on to the landing that overlooked the hallway below.

Gordon was oblivious to them, careless of his discourtesy. He could see her in the open doorway as he came down the staircase. She was soaked to the skin, head uncovered, hair straggling in rats'-tails about her face, her dress black with rain. She leaned passively against the stone post while the arrogant footman, hands on hips, barred her entrance to the house.

"Let her through," Gordon called out angrily. "Damn you, stand aside an' let her in."

The footman glanced at Signor Dinardo, gave an insolent sort of shrug and stepped to one side.

"Greta?" Gordon said. "Greta, what's wrong?"

She glanced up, saw him, stumbled in a daze over the threshold into the light, her heavy-hemmed skirt trailing mud on to the terrazzo and the polished oak.

She was gaunt and hollow-eyed, her skin the hue and texture of chalk, as dead a white as Gordon had ever seen. He reached her, put an arm about her, felt her fall against him.

"Gordon, is it you?"

"Aye, dear, aye."

"I had nowhere else, y'see, nowhere else t' go."

"I know, I know."

Greta rested her brow against his shirt. He felt wetness seep through to his flesh, smelled the pavement odour of rain from her hair and blouse. He held her close, closer still, took into him, it seemed, the first great, dry sob that escaped her.

Above and behind, along the landing rail, Adairs gathered and looked down. Amanda's lips were pursed in anger, Breezy had a hand pressed to his heart. Olive had begun to tremble as premonition grasped her reason. Afraid that she would somehow forget herself and give the game away, Captain Tom Wells slipped behind her to give her someone to lean on.

"What?" Gordon asked, very quietly. "Greta, what's happened?"

"She's dead. Jen's dead," Greta answered, weeping freely at last. "Oh, God, she's dead. An' I don't know what to do."

High above, distinctly, Olive Adair screamed.

*   *   *

If Bobby had not been so full of the cold and the night so wet Kirsty might have gone round to Benedict Street to enquire in person how Jen was keeping.

It had been Monday since last she'd seen Greta when the woman had popped into the shop, while Isa Thomas sat with the invalid for a half-hour or so. Greta had been worried then, but not unduly, and on Thursday morning Kirsty had received a short letter, sent through the post, which suggested that Jen was on the mend and that, all being well, she, Greta, would be back behind the counter by Wednesday next.

Kirsty hesitated only for a moment at the corner of Gascoigne Street and then, juggling Bobby in her arms, an umbrella in one hand and a shopping bag full of groceries in the other, turned right and headed for home.

Unless his cold was a great deal better, and the weather brighter, she would not bring Bobby out tomorrow but would keep him tucked up in bed at home. In fact, she had already prepared two large hand-printed notices to put in the shop window and on the door announcing the Saturday closure and offering apology to regular customers. Craig was on day-shift. She would give him the keys to Gascoigne Street and ask him to put up the notices. If he could not get away personally she was sure that he would find a willing enough hand in the ranks at Ottawa Street. She would not be sorry to spend a Saturday at home. With Greta off and Lorna fully occupied with her brother's engagement party, as well as her course of studies at Prosser's College, the burden of shopkeeping had fallen heavily upon her.

She no longer cared to ask Jess Walker or any of the other neighbours to look after Bobby; relations had remained strained for months now and she would not risk rebuff. She could not grumble about it, of course. She had chosen to give her time and energy to commercial trade and was not daft enough to imagine that she would get her money for nothing. Even so, circumstances could not have been more irksome and she felt quite guilty at having kept Bobby with her in the gloomy, gas-reeking shop all that long day.

Kirsty could not blame her son for being peevish, for girning and kicking. Obviously he felt miserable. She stopped off at Calder's Pharmacy on the way home to let the chemist have a look at him and dispense a syrup and a course of powders to relieve his snuffles, calm his restlessness and help him sleep.

For a Friday, pay night, the street was uncommonly quiet. Only the most hardened drinkers had ventured out to their favourite pubs, only those hardy sons whose attendance at Boys' Brigade parade was demanded whatever the weather, could be seen scuttling towards the kirk halls. Greenfield seemed a sad place tonight. Gordon's last-minute call, the two half-blind sisters, who'd sought a length of black crepe and were reluctant to accept her word that Nicholson's did not sell such fabrics, had somehow set the seal on a depressing week.

It was a vast relief to Kirsty to enter the close at No. 154 Canada Road, to be out of the rain that lashed up from the river, out of the wind that ruffled the puddles, rattled the slates and made chimney grannies spin like humming tops. Her arms ached and her fingers were numb, and Bobby, poor wee soul, clung to her, to her breast, whimpering like a babby who could not find suck. A hot bottle in the bed, warm milk and one of Mr Calder's powders would, she hoped, see Bobby off into a restoring sleep. It would take her an hour to prepare supper and then, if Craig was home and in the mood, she would ask him to give her a cuddle to cheer her up.

At the door on the top landing she set down her shopping bag and umbrella and fished in her coat pocket for her key. Before she could find it, however, Craig slipped the latch and pulled the door open.

"Ah!" he said. "You're nice an' early."

He had shaved and combed his hair, donned his new maroon-coloured knitted cardigan. He greeted her with a welcoming smile. Three or four months ago such behaviour would have seemed out of character and Kirsty would have wondered what he had been up to, would have felt suspicion instead of gratitude.

"What's that smell?" she said.

"Savoury mince."

"I didn't buy mince."

"No, but I did," Craig said, taking Bobby from her arms. "I'll just turn up the gas a bit an' it'll be ready to serve in ten minutes."

"You cooked savoury mince?" Kirsty said.

" 'Course I did," Craig said. "Best shoulder steak, an' all."

"I didn't know you could cook."

"There's a lot about me you don't know, Kirsty," he said, with a wink. "Includin' how resourceful I can be when I put my mind to it."

"But why, Craig? What's special about tonight?"

"Nothin' special, really," Craig said. "But I just thought to myself – Why the hell should rich folk have all the fun? We should have a wee party of our own, just you an' me, Kirsty."

They had entered the kitchen now and it pleased her too. The table had been set with the best chequered cloth, the best crockery and cutlery. The fire burned bright in the grate and, most pleasing of all, he had even washed up the pan and board he had used to prepare the meal. Potatoes boiled in a big pot, green peas simmered in another. She could not help herself; she lifted the lid on the saucepan and inspected the mince critically.

"It looks all right," she said, surprised.

"What did y'expect; hoofs an' horns?" Craig said.

She smiled at him as she removed her overcoat and hat, slipped

311

out of her shoes. "You've made such a good job, Craig, that you can cook the supper every night, if y'like?"

"Nah, nah," he said. "Don't go gettin' ideas." Bobby had snuggled in against his father, making no sounds of distress or petulance now. Craig looked down at him. "Mince, m'lad, eh? Daddy's mince'll soon put hair on your chest."

"No," Kirsty said. "It's his bed he's needin'."

"Still got that cold hangin' on, has he?"

"Aye," Kirsty said. "I'm keepin' him in bed tomorrow an' if it's not lifted by Monday, I'll get the doctor."

"It is just a cold, isn't it?"

"Yes, yes," said Kirsty. "All the bairns have it. His lordship got it off Jen, I expect."

"Is Greta not back yet?"

"Not yet."

It was no longer strange to hear Greta's name on Craig's lips. It no longer riled her or gave her pain. That he could talk of Greta openly, without furtiveness, showed that whatever fit of passion had possessed him was a thing of the past. Looking back on it now, safe and snug in her kitchen on a dreary wet night, Kirsty could not help but wonder how it was that bitterness and malice had become transformed, how infidelity and deceit, her own as well as Craig's, had brought them to this new beginning.

She could not deny that she felt sure of him now, sure of herself too. And he was right, right to say that there were qualities about him that she had not yet discovered, the tenderness that had lain hidden under his hard Scots shell being just one of them.

Craig stood by the stove watching Kirsty undress Bobby and, using the old baby bath by the fire, gently sponge him down. She dried him with a fluffy towel and put on his clean nightshirt. He girned a little, flinched at her touch but was too worn out by the cold to resist her ministrations.

Obediently he supped the chemist's powder from the tip of a spoon and swallowed warm milk from the cup that she held to his lips. And when Craig carried him through to the front room and Kirsty drew back the covers of the bed, he whimpered to be put down in it as if he had grown weary even of mothering and wanted only to be left alone.

Craig lowered him into the bed. Kirsty drew up the sheet and blankets and Bobby curled his fist to his face and covered his nose with his thumb. He twitched, grizzled for a moment, then his eyes closed and, a second later, he gave a little snuffling snore.

"Gone off?" Craig whispered.

"Hmmm."

"Come on then, love. It's supper time." Craig offered her his arm. "Table for two, all right?"

She let Craig lead her to the door then, on impulse, returned to the bed, leaned and kissed Bobby's cheek and dusted back the little lock of hair that clung damply to his brow.

"He'll be all right, won't he?" Craig asked.

"Oh yes," said Kirsty. "He'll be fine in a day or two, I'm sure."

And then she went through to the kitchen to eat supper and, later, lie snug in Craig's arms in the hole-in-the-wall bed, untroubled by rain on the window or the harsh wintry wind off the Clyde.